THE KOREAN DECISION

Every decision I made in connection with the Korean conflict had this one aim in mind: to prevent a third world war and the terrible destruction it would bring to the civilized world.

—Harry S Truman
President of the United States

. . . It was not only a crucial decision whether or not to meet this aggression; it was no less important how this aggression was to be dealt with.

—Dean G. Acheson
Secretary of State

If we wanted to oppose it, then was our time to oppose it. Not a single one of us did. There were some pointing out of the difficulties . . . and then the President made his decision, which . . . I thought was the right decision.

—Louis A. Johnson
Secretary of Defense

Glenn D. Paige

THE KOREAN DECISION

[JUNE 24-30, 1950]

New York, THE FREE PRESS

London, COLLIER-MACMILLAN LIMITED

TO ALL WHO DIED IN THE KOREAN WAR

AND TO ALL WHO MAKE AND STUDY POLITICAL DECISIONS

ACKNOWLEDGMENTS

The intellectual debts of the scholar, like the components of a major political decision, are many. My indebtedness to my teachers, colleagues, and friends Richard C. Snyder, Harold Guetzkow, and H. H. Wilson is so enormous as to defy articulation. I am grateful to Burton M. Sapin, who first suggested this study to me, and to Henry W. Bruck for initial encouragement. Alexander L. George and James A. Robinson were generous with constructive criticisms of earlier versions of the narrative. Fred W. Riggs and William J. Siffin challenged me to explicate the techniques of proposition building and Edward W. Weidener gave me the opportunity to apply them in this study. Thomas W. Milburn encouraged me to attempt to draw some operational implications in the final chapter but is not to be held responsible for the outcome.

I shall always remember with appreciation the patient cooperation of the decision makers who shared their remembrances of a dramatic moment in American history: former President Harry S. Truman, Secretary of State Dean G. Acheson, Secretary of Defense Louis A. Johnson, Secretary of the Air Force Thomas K. Finletter, Secretary of the Army Frank Pace Jr., Assistant Secretary of State for Far Eastern Affairs Dean Rusk, Deputy United States Ambassador to the United Nations Ernest A. Gross, Ambassador-at-Large

Philip C. Jessup, State Department Counselor George F. Kennan, and other officials. For helpful correspondence I am indebted to the late General of the Army Douglas MacArthur, Assistant Secretary of State for United Nations Affairs John D. Hickerson, Ambassador to Korea John J. Muccio, and Dr. E. Taylor Parks, head of the Historical Division of the Department of State. Former United Press Seoul correspondent Jack E. James, who earned a place in journalism's hall of fame by achieving a "world beat" on the outbreak of the Korean War, was generous in helping me to recapture that experience.

For permission to cite an earlier reconstruction of the Korean decision I am indebted to Beverly Smith, author of "The White House Story: Why We Went to War in Korea," *Saturday Evening Post*, November 10, 1951. The extracted material on pages 223 and 267 is © 1950 by The New York Times Company. It was reprinted by permission.

For financial support at various stages of professional development when this study was taking shape I am especially grateful to the Carnegie Corporation, the National Woodrow Wilson Fellowship Program, the Ford Foundation, the Comparative Administration Group of the American Society for Public Administration, Princeton University, the Institute of Advanced Projects, East-West Center, and the Social Science Research Institute, University of Hawaii.

Appreciation is expressed also to Mrs. Lillian Golan for her editorial and typing contribution to the narrative and to W. Raymond Webster for assistance in compiling the index of names, and to Mrs. Freda Hellinger and the staff of the Social Science Research Institute for helping with the final details of publication. To Harry McConnell, assistant director of The Free Press, and to all his associates is expressed special appreciation for showing how considerate a publisher can be.

Finally I would like to record my debt to my wife Betty and to our children—Gail, Jan, Donn, Sean, Sharon, and Van. They all shared in a difficult task.

Glenn D. Paige

Honolulu
January, 1968

CONTENTS

INTRODUCTION

Richard C. Snyder

Professor Glenn Paige's reconstruction and analysis of the U.S. decision to resist aggression in Korea in 1950 is most welcome. This publication has been long awaited by students of foreign policy and international relations, and by government officials whose first-hand knowledge or personal experiences have endowed it with special interest for them. Fortunately, despite delays in completion, the work is as timely as ever. Our capacity to exploit fruitfully the kind of data his research provides has increased steadily since the project began. And, of course, the Vietnam conflict suggests interesting parallels and historical linkages though there are obvious differences too.

It is to be hoped that this book will not only have a large readership, but that many different types of individuals will bring to it their diverse needs and viewpoints—students of all ages, social and behavioral scientists interested in national behavior, historians both amateur and professional, citizens and policy critics, practitioners of the arts of government and politics, and scholars who specialize in foreign policy and international relations. For we rarely are privileged to partake of so detailed a study of high level decision-making in a situation so fraught with significance. Hopefully, many different and continuing dialogues will be stimulated by Professor Paige who has, wisely and deliberately, left much for readers to do on their own.

I

I should like to pinpoint an important dual contribution to our understanding of how foreign policy is made, of how the international system is affected by decisional responses and outcomes emanating from subsystems we call nations. First, we have before us a fascinating descriptive narrative of the evolution of one of the key U.S. decisions in the post World War II period—the story of seven days of national decision-making, which constitutes a biography of a response to a crisis. Having hinted above that generally we do not know this much so soon about a critical action,[1] it is necessary to underscore the author's candid reminder that, compared to the amount of detail which will be available once the archives are opened to future scholars, even this lengthy recounting will be just the top of the iceberg. However, I, for one, am willing to publicly wager that later detail will not alter fundamentally the structure of events as presented by Professor Paige. Nonetheless, Chapters 4 to 10—Saturday, June 24, 1950 to Friday, June 30, 1950—must be seen as a "round-by-round" rather than a "blow-by-blow" reconstruction.

A second contribution is methodological. Professor Paige has enriched our capacity to explain particular decisions and eventually to construct a more general theory of foreign policy-making. He has accomplished this by testing the fruitfulness of an analytic framework and by attempting explicitly to demonstrate how his

---

1. To my knowledge, this is one of the most detailed reconstruction of a U.S. foreign policy decision available publicly. Elie Abel's *The Missile Crisis* is a richer blow-by-blow analysis of the U.S.-Cuban missile decision. Mr. Abel is a first-rate journalist practicing his own high art. The reader can compare these two cases as a way of highlighting differences in the approach the two authors make.

study might yield new hypotheses and hence guidelines for future research. This is an exercise in the fashioning and use of certain kinds of tools for wringing lessons from experience. In an arena of behavior as complex and murky as foreign policy and international relations, this worthy activity is slow and often risky. Thus to match the biography of a national action response, we have an auto-biography of an intellectual venture: how to create a basis for generalizing from the particular, and how to analyze historical data in such a way as to preserve its integrity yet broaden its meaning— an endeavor clearly full of pitfalls.

It should be emphasized that Professor Paige had to borrow from a very skimpy stockpile of theoretical tools when he began his research. He is in no sense responsible for the deficiencies in the particular scheme he used. On the contrary, his willingness to use the Korean decision as an application led to immediate improve-ments.[2] There were two serious weaknesses among others which bear acknowledgement here: (1) the basic factors (in the technical sense, variables) postulated to exert influence on the process and outcome of decisions were not all spelled out precisely enough to permit the investigator to identify referents in the real world; (2) no hypotheses linking the variables were stated, and therefore no bases for prediction existed and no explanation—even *post hoc*—was possible without further operations implied by the scheme but cer-tainly not explicitly set forth in the initial version. Since 1954, the scheme has been sharpened and extended.[3]

In addition to the detailed nature of the reconstruction and the explicitness of the analysis, the way he has presented the results of his research and the extension of analysis beyond strictly empirical concerns yield additional advantages. For one thing, Professor Paige has made a rigorous attempt to "objectify" the narrative. Each

2. Snyder and Paige, "The United States Decision to Resist Aggression in Korea: The Application of an Analytical Scheme," *Administrative Science Quarterly*, III, 3. (December 1958) pp. 341-378.

3. Developments can be traced in part by a scanning of (a) R. Snyder, et al., *Foreign Policy-Decision-making* (1962), which includes the original framework (pp. 14-186), and the joint article just cited; (b) R. Snyder, "The Korean Decision (1950) and the Analysis of Crisis Decision-making," *Working Group Reports, Military Operations Research Society*, 1963, pp. 242-248; J. A. Robinson and R. Snyder, "Decision-making in International Politics," in H. Kelman, ed., *International Behavior* (1965) pp. 435-458.

sentence contains an observation report, stated at a very low level of generality which can be verified by revisiting his different sources of data.[4] So far as humanly possible he has eliminated those apparently straight forward statements which in fact mask an inference drawn by the writer—an inference neither identified as such or supportable by internal evidence. For some, such a turgid description of what happened makes for dull reading, lacking in the color or style usually characteristic of good writers. Moreover, some critics might say that a case not heavily infused by the personal or professional contribution of the case-writer is either not possible or, if possible, is not a proper "case" at all. A reasonable argument can be made for this conception. To assert the advantages of objectification in the present context is not to deny useful alternatives *or* to impale one's self on the old saw concerning "value free" inquiry. What it does mean is that the "facts," once ascertained, are presented so that the reader can check them if he wishes and so that logical and empirical relationships among facts are not mediated implicitly by the author.

The main events are presented as a chronological story. The *a priori* framework, somewhat visible again in Chapter 11 (derived propositions) is not showing in the narrative. The scaffolding has been taken down. Does this mean a hidden bias undetectable by the reader? All accounts of the past require selection of constituent elements in terms of the investigators' purposes, canons of empirical inquiry, scholarly knowhow, available data, and so on. To minimize the chances that the conceptual scheme might blind him to certain relevancies, Professor Paige went about his task as would a qualified historian or journalist. Given the two-fold purpose of narrative history *and* theoretical insight, primary and secondary data sources had to be searched (a) for the major decisional events of the week of June 24-30, 1950; and (b) for data which could be legitimately treated as indicators of the presence of crucial factors deemed necessary and sufficient to account for what happened. But the chief advantage of objectification is that each reader can be a do-it-yourself analyst, raising his own questions and formulating his own hypotheses.

---

4. For an exposition of what is involved in this "de-contamination" of a reconstruction, see Snyder and Paige, *op. cit.*, pp. 362-366.

I am delighted that Professor Paige has had the courage to extend the context of his study to include two matters normally excluded from systematic inquiry: *evaluation* of processes and outcomes, *and* suggestions of certain *implications for future action.* I shall comment on both later, but suffice it to say here, I use the word courage to celebrate the author's unwillingness to rule out broader concerns purely for the sake of being less vulnerable to criticism. Many readers have little interest in theory and methodology; for them, these two chapters will doubtless be of paramount interest.

II

No dramatic occurrence such as the Korean decision and its aftermath stands by itself in the stream of history. Chapters 2 and 3 provide a sound outline of the main features of the domestic and international environments "on the eve" of the crisis. It is difficult, yet important, to try to understand what long and short term historical relevancies were perceived by the decision-makers and what factors in the immediate pre-June 24th situation exerted strong influence on their deliberations. Given Professor Paige's purposes, the "background" of highest significance is that combination of events *remembered by the decision-makers and interpreted as relevant* to their problem. It's very crucial to note that the reconstruction reveals that decision-makers located the Korean crisis on an historical continuum which began with the Japanese invasion of Manchuria and included the Greek-Turkish crisis of 1947. The subjectively perceived relevancies of the U.S. actors might or might not coincide with an objective analysis of the antecedents as seen by a professional historian. If the latter can "see" more in retrospect, he may also risk identifying as relevant events and conditions which were not so considered by those who actually reacted to the situation.

However, there are two kinds of pertinent background, or "setting" factors to use the author's terminology, which are missing and which would be useful to have. A chronology of events affecting the relationship and international status of North and South Korea would, if it included a record of the actions and reactions of the major powers, provide at least some basis on which to identify sources of misperceptions about the motives of various participants.

Secondly, the study as it stands is ethnocentric in that the Korean crisis is seen from the U.S. outward. It would be valuable to discover whether the viewpoints and reactions of the other major capitols could not be reconstructed. Of course, a very important kind of information used by U.S. decision-makers consisted of reported and observed responses of allies and potential enemies, but what would be interesting is a systematic comparison of the way other major groups of national decision-makers "defined the situation." Moreover, if the data were reliable enough, the perceptions and predictions of the U.S. government could be evaluated for accuracy.

III

Numerous issues arise in an exercise of this kind. Some, but by no means all, have been discussed elsewhere.[5] I shall simply highlight two of the more important ones.

1. The Korean decision was unusual in major respects. The situation was unexpected. A heavy U.S. commitment was made in just seven days. Thus decision-making activities were severely limited: Time was short, the number of decision-makers was relatively small, and the amount of study or intelligence research was restricted accordingly. While Washington, the American public and the rest of the world waited and speculated, the handful of top level policy-makers deliberated in secret. There was no public debate to speak of, and the agencies and leaders normally involved in foreign policy were not agonized by serious conflict and debate.

This episode in foreign policy-making stands in stark contrast, say, to the fourteen month "public process" of argument and voting it took to evolve the North Atlantic Treaty which formally reversed a U.S. position of historic standing on entangling alliances. Or, consider the painstaking legislative and executive history of the Foreign Aid Program beginning with the initial legislation for the Marshall Plan. In a revealing and provocative recent book, (*To Move a Nation: The Politics of Foreign Policy in the Administration of John*

---

5. Snyder and Paige, *op. cit.*; Snyder, et al., *Foreign Policy Decision-making*, especially pp. 186-206.

F. Kennedy, 1967) Professor Roger Hilsman of Columbia University and former Assistant Secretary of State for Far Eastern Affairs in the Kennedy Administration, emphasizes that "the making of policy is politics"—especially in areas of vital national concern. But during the brief period of decision-making in June 1950, there was no time, and no need, for politics in the conventional sense.

In view of all this, is not the Korean decision an entirely unique event? Are not the commonly accepted limitations arising from the single case (which are faced forthrightly by Professor Paige in his first chapter) compounded by special circumstances? My answer sounds like a typical academic dodge: yes and no. Clearly, the decision to commit armed forces in Korea was made under "special circumstances." On the face of it, a quite different activation and functioning of official machinery occurred than was true for other major policies in the postwar period. To the extent that each such instance cannot be repeated exactly as it happened, it is indeed unique.

Now, it is not at all incompatible with this admission to argue first, that legitimate and necessary inductive operations can and should be performed on so-called unique events to enable us to put them in a broader context, and second, having done so, both earlier and later cases may turn out to have *comparable features.* Accordingly it is possible to take the most distinguishing features of the Korean decision and convert them into variables which can then be related to other variables. These relationships can be stated in propositional form—as hypotheses to be tested against similar (not identical) episodes provided the variables are properly defined and the hypotheses are stated at a level of generality which transcends particular cases. An example of an interesting, though familiar hypothesis derived in this manner is:

The shorter the decision time, the fewer the alternatives which will be seriously explored by the decision-makers.

Professor Paige rightly stresses the *crisis* aspect of the Korean decision. Indeed, his research has helped to clarify the problem of conceptualizing crises,[6] as well as adding to our substantive knowl-

---

6. R. Snyder, "The Korean Decision (1950) and the Analysis of Crisis Decision-making," *Working Group Reports, Military Operations Research Society,* 1963, pp. 242-248.

edge about crisis decision-making in international relations. On the basis of recent research and publication, it is possible to relate the Korean decision to the United States response to the Dominican Republic, the Cuban crisis, and the six weeks immediately prior to the outbreak of World War I.[7] These critically important inter-case linkages involve, of course, tricky problems of conceptual precision and data comparability, but they do enable us to transcend the unique.

2. Though the Korean decision occurred more than seventeen years ago, the reader will probably have thought about the "perils of recent history." Most historians wait until the dust settles before tackling outstanding events, partly because "sensitive" information is usually withheld from the scholar and public alike. Once again, the Korean case is, fortunately, different. More than enough was available at the time and in the years immediately following to gain some comprehension of what happened. Newspaper accounts during the week of June 24-30 were surprisingly full and accurate. Beverly Smith[8] captured the outline of decision-making activity remarkably well. Finally, Professor Paige had access to the key decision-makers so that interviews could tap memories, diaries, and informal records before these sources deteriorated or disappeared. Though the Oral History Project at Columbia University (founded by Allan Nevins in 1948) has opened up a new era in historical data collection, normally those engaged in reconstructing the past do not have live respondents.

I have already touched upon the problem of objectification when the researcher entertains aspirations for both rigorous description and explanation. This is a tangled issue to acknowledge adequately, much less explicate constructively.[9] However, a word or two is in order concerning two related matters: (a) the connection between

7. T. Sorensen, *Kennedy* (1965); Hilsman, *op. cit.*; A. Schlesinger, Jr., *A Thousand Days* (1965); R. North, et al., *Perception and Action in the Study of International Relations: The 1914 Crisis* (1964).

8. "The White House Story: Why We Went to War in Korea," *Saturday Evening Post*, November 10, 1951, pp. 22ff.

9. For an overview of the more significant issues, see V. Mehta, "The Flight of Crook-Taloned Birds" I, II, *The New Yorker*, December 8 and 15, 1962, pp. 59ff and 47ff respectively; S. Hughes, *History as Art and as Science* (1964); J. Palmer, "Does the Study of History Promote Behavioral Change?," *Teachers College Record*, 67, No. 2, (Nov. 1965) pp. 81-89.

narration and theory; and (b) the connection between induction and deduction as alternative orientations toward historical materials. Professor Paige takes a stand and it is important to locate his position.

Barbara Tuchman has said: "It is wiser . . . to arrive at theory by way of the evidence rather than the other way around. . . ."[10] Another well-known historian, C. V. Wedgwood, has said: "*Why* has been regarded as a more important question than *How*. It is, of course, a more important question. But it cannot be answered until *How* is established. The careful, thorough, and accurate answer to the question *How* should take the historian a long way towards answering the question *Why*."[11] The former is persuasive if the main point is substantiation of hypotheses and/or the occurrence of hypotheses to an observer contemplating a certain set of facts or events. The latter is persuasive if what is implied is (a) something has to be established before we can account for it, and (b) the transition from the details of *how* to a sufficient basis to determine *why* is a subtle one—often a question of the degree of thoroughness of reconstruction. But the former could be misleading if it is asserted that no prior purpose or conceptualization should precede the gathering of evidence. And the latter could be misleading if the implication is that the boundary line of descriptive analysis between how and why requires no explicit criteria so that the desired answer to why is undergirded by the required knowledge of how. Both Tuchman[12] and Wedgwood[13] stress narrative and style, though Professor Paige omits "corroborative detail" which allegedly makes narrative more convincing, and he is definitely not engaged in narration for its own sake.

Stuart Hughes[14] clearly states the challenge Professor Paige has taken on:

> Hence the historian's supreme technical virtuosity lies in
> fusing the new method of social and psychological analysis with

---

10. "History By The Ounce," *Harper's Magazine* (July 1965); p. 65.
11. *The Sense of the Past,* 1960, Introduction, p. 14.
12. Tuchman, *ibid.,* p. 65; also Tuchman, "The Historian's Opportunity," *Saturday Review,* February 25, 1967, p. 29.
13. Wedgwood, *ibid.,* p. 14.
14. *Op. cit.,* p. 77.

his traditional storytelling function. If he can keep the 'how' and the 'why' moving alongside each other—if he can shift easily back and forth from the multiple doubts and hesitations of the participants to the single certainty of the historian who knows the outcome—then he is a writer who understands his business well.

Hughes is heralding a relatively new convergence of history and social science—in view of the strong opposed opinions perhaps *rapprochement* is a better word. The fact that Professor Paige's study is right in the middle of this young development is more important than whether his effort is completely successful on all counts.

IV

What is involved in analysis—in the probing of why, not just how? What kinds of questions do we want to try to answer in the particular case? What is required in order to create generalizable tools for studying foreign policy decision-making in a variety of situations?

As complex as the consequences of these queries are, the implications boil down to these: why was a decision made at all in this instance, and why this action or policy response rather than some other? What interrelationships among what variables will enable us to say: these are the necessary and sufficient conditions to determine the outcome? Needless to say, other questions are equally legitimate and fruitful, but these are central to Professor Paige's study.

In Chapter 11 he illustrates clearly the operations which are entailed by *a priori and post hoc* analysis, by the connection between *narration and theory*, and by the *search for an empirically based, parsimonious explanation* for the United States response to the invasion of South Korea. These operations would seem to be: (a) identification of variables; (b) weighting of variables; and (c) interrelation of variables. Operation (a) asks what is truly significant in bringing about an outcome. Operation (b) asks what (how much) does variable x contribute to outcome y. Operation (c) asks how the interrelationships of variables v_1 v_2 and v_3 affect their collective impact on outcome O.

All efforts to build theory (really "theories") of foreign policy-making include these basic operations. Different frameworks or approaches can be compared in terms of the categories which shape the reconstruction of decisional events, the questions which are to be answered, the crucial variables and how these are hypothetically linked. The data for the specific case is coded accordingly. The choices which shape the differences among theorist-researchers arise from intellectual purposes (e.g., to explain the general nature of the role of an institutional factor such as public opinion or the presidency),[15] from concern with the range of issues or problems decision makers must handle,[16] from different conceptions of the decisional system or unit,[17] from the requirements of the data or contours of a particular case,[18] and from different conceptions of the decision-making process.[19] The relevant literature of the last dozen years in the United States shows definite progress in narrowing the range of significant variables, greater precision of conceptualization, and explicit formulation of hypotheses stating intervariable relationships.[20] This is particularly true of the study of crisis decision-making.[21]

Professor Paige, following Charles F. Hermann, takes three of the distinguishing empirical characteristics of the Korean decision—*surprise*, the *seriousness* of the event, and *short decision time*—and focuses his analysis on crisis as an independent variable. In a series of propositions, each of which is discussed at some length, crisis is

15. R. Bauer, I. Pool, and L. Dexter, *American Business and Public Policy* (1963).

16. J. Rosenau, "Pre-theories and Theories of Foreign Policy," in R. B. Farrell, ed., *Approaches to Comparative and International Politics* (1966), pp. 27-92.

17. B. Cohen, *The Political Process and Foreign Policy: The Making of the Japanese Peace Settlement* (1957).

18. W. Schilling, "The H-Bomb Decision: How to Decide Without Actually Choosing." *Political Science Quarterly*, 76, (1961) pp. 24-46.

19. Hilsman, *op. cit.*

20. Robinson and Snyder, *op. cit.*

21. C. Hermann, "Some Consequences of Crisis which Limit the Viability of Organizations," *Administrative Science Quarterly*, 8 (1963), pp. 61-82; J. A. Robinson, C. Hermann, and M. Hermann, "Search Under Crisis in Political Gaming and Simulation" (1964).

linked to organizational variables, to information variables, and to the values of the decision-makers. Then decisional units, sub-decisions, alternatives, values, and information are interrelated, and in turn become independent variables for the four stages of crisis decision-making postulated at the beginning of the analysis as dependent variables. In sum, the crisis situation induced a certain pattern of decision-makers, organization, values, flow of information, and sequential choices. That pattern—i.e., the combined effects of these factors—accounts for what happened at the various stages of decision-making and for the overall result.

His conclusion—the answer to the why question—can and should be compared to the one reached in our joint article cited above.[22] The two are not only complementary, but the earlier analysis is more convincing on why a decision at all. Whereas the present one is more specific on why the particular response developed as it did. The reader can, however, decide this for himself.

V

Was the Korean decision a "good" decision? Was it the "right" thing to do under the circumstances? What "ought" the decision-makers to have done? These are the evaluative or normative questions which Professor Paige deals with in Chapter 12. He also makes suggestions concerning appropriate criteria which, of course, are the sticky components of favorable and unfavorable judgements.

I have applauded his inclusion of this topic, not just because it helps to round out the study or because readers, having gone through the reconstruction, will begin wondering about errors and criticism. I do so for these reasons and others: first, the separation of fact and value (one cannot move from *is* to *ought*), paralleled by the separation of empirical and normative theories, have tended to prevent a frontal attack on the problem of evaluation in politics and government; second, the experiential and role distances between official decision-makers and citizens (including nongovernmental foreign policy experts) have thwarted the creation of a widely acceptable, intellectually and politically satisfying way of

---

22. Snyder and Paige, *op. cit.*, p. 377.

engaging in constructive, loyal policy criticism. Those who remember the nagging, frustrating, and unresolvable debate over the Vietnam war should appreciate the meaningful thrust Professor Paige has made toward clarification of the problem of evaluation. The approach embodied in this study assumes an observer-actor (citizen-policy-maker) relationship pertinent to evaluation. A shorthand term for this perspective is "the actor's definition of the situation of action"—something problematical from the observer's point of view, to be inquired into, not assumed or imposed. How important this is analytically can be seen in the Paige study. I suggest the same focus is useful for evaluation. It seems highly likely that the gulf in understanding which seems to underlie many policy disagreements arises from one or more of the following elements:

(1) different facts
(2) different inferences from the same facts
(3) different values
(4) different entailments of the same values
(5) different processes or conclusions when values and facts are joined in a definition of the situation
(6) different roles or different perceptions of the same roles

In the realm of foreign policy, it is not difficult to see how these sources of misunderstanding might compound one another. And it could be naive to suppose that, in certain respects, the policy-maker-citizen gulf can be avoided. Nonetheless, it may be a step forward to establish some ground rules in order to minimize the effects of purely personal preference; closed ideological positions; implicit, arbitrary standards; willful ignoring of differential amounts of information distributed among disputing parties; and competing, but sometimes untestable, theories of how the world operates.

Ground rules should rest on rigorous analysis. Therefore, every step toward tenable theories of foreign policy processes and responses which permits the fitting of a particular case into a general framework strengthens the basis for comparing judgements and for determining the presence or absence of a commonly shared base for comparison. *For the critical objective is a common process of evaluation,* understood and accepted as a norm by both policy-makers and citizens. I will argue that this is not solely a matter of common criteria, but implies an equally necessary agreed methodology for judging performance in a given instance. This kind of judgement, i.e., *that* was a good performance—involves an integration of fact and value, and therefore is an empirical matter at bottom.

The first ground rule might be: no credible or responsible criticism is possible unless and until both parties (policy-maker and citizen) understand how and why the other's position was arrived at. The second ground rule might be: each party is committed to the same criteria of evaluation and to explicit operations for their application. There will still be much room for disagreement and misunderstanding, but the bases of these ought at least to be much clearer and therefore amenable to reason or evidence.

Another aspect of evaluation points in the direction of action implications which Professor Paige treats in Part VI. What can we learn *in general* about the U.S. foreign policy decision-making system? Can any operating rules for decision-makers be derived from the empirical analysis of decisions? An adequate answer to the first question clearly depends on (a) more cases of individual decisions, and (b) rigorous organizational studies accompanied by systems criteria. The pool of useful cases grows and recent organizational analyses are superior to those of a decade ago.[23] The possible lessons drawn by Professor Paige can be checked against this literature. Specifically, it would seem feasible to compare the Korean crisis and the Cuban crisis as possible models of "good" and "bad" responses of our foreign policy-making institutions.

As tested hypotheses accumulate, it should also be possible to pass along to decision-makers conditional statements of regularities sufficiently grounded in empirical evidence to warrant a role in deciding among alternative decisional procedures and organiza-

---

23. A recent educational research experiment at Northwestern University produced some 40 usable cases. Allowing for several new ones since that time, the total is now at least 45. Significant organizational studies are: Burton Sapin, *The Making of United States Foreign Policy* (1966); Henry Jackson, ed., *The Secretary of State and the Ambassador: Jackson Subcommittee Papers on the Conduct of American Foreign Policy*; Don Price, ed., *The Secretary of State* (1960); Brookings Institution, *The Formulation and Administration of United States Foreign Policy* (1960); Charlton Ogburn Jr., "The Flow of Policy-making in the Department of State" in Rosenau, ed., *International Politics and Foreign Policy* (1961); Dean Pruitt, *Problem-solving in the Department of State* (1964); Theodore Sorensen, *Decision-making in the White House* (1963).

tional sub units if such options are available. Here the problem is not deriving ought from is, but rather providing decision-makers with guidelines of the form: "if you would achieve this kind of outcome, then do the following," wherein sound empirical generalizations are converted into reasonably firm predictions of what will happen if organization and procedures are structured in a certain way. Chronic dissatisfaction with the policy-making machinery in the United States may indicate something more than a spasmodic symptom of irritation with the complexities of government or dissatisfaction with policies associated with various philosophies of administration. For over twenty-five years, considerable time and money (about once every five or six years) has been spent on the "organization of national security." Some changes are made—usually not very extensive. But almost daily decisions are made concerning decisional units and processes. I suspect these bear little or no relationship to knowledge gleaned from systematic research.

VI

That this introductory essay has wandered as it has is a tribute to the many facets and uses of Professor Paige's study. While making possible additional independent secondary analyses and provoking fresh thoughts about a number of recurrent issues, he has provided a noteworthy landmark on the road to better understanding of an event in our national history and of what can happen under certain conditions of decision-making. From testing his hypotheses against other published findings, as well as against future research, to further refinements in the identification or interrelating of variables, much remains to be done. But Professor Paige gives us reason to believe we now possess somewhat improved tools and have a sharper sense of what we are about.

THE KOREAN DECISION

PART I

APPROACH

CHAPTER 1

DECISION-MAKING ANALYSIS IN THE SINGLE CASE

It is hoped that this book will interest at least two kinds of readers. The first are those professional students of politics who may have an interest in exploring further the potentialities of decision-making analysis as an approach to political understanding. The second are those persons who are interested in the substance of one of the twentieth century's most important events. For the Korean decision was followed by three years of fighting that brought about the deaths of 33,629 Americans in what became the fourth largest war in American history. It also brought about the largest collective security action yet sanctioned by the United Nations in which fifteen other nations joined the United States in military assistance to the Republic of Korea and incurred an estimated total of 14,000 casualties. For Koreans, who were both the victims and the instrument of Communist military aggression, the war brought about an estimated 843,572 Southern and 520,000 Northern military dead and wounded, at least 1.4 million civilian deaths, and hatreds that have further solidified national partition.

For the Chinese combat allies and the Russian supporters of the North Korean Communists the war also brought bloodshed and bitterness. It is estimated that the Chinese suffered "appalling" casualties of 1.5 to 2 million men.[1] Although the Soviet Union continued throughout the period of fighting to maintain an official posture of noninvolvement, those Russians who were killed while serving in rear area advisory and combat roles must also be counted among the war dead. At times during the conflict as many as 1.2 million Chinese and North Korean soldiers were engaged in battle with 800,000 South Koreans, Americans, and their United Nations allies.

The Korean decision was accompanied by an abrupt reversal of American policy toward Communist China and seems to have initiated a period in which the United States is committed to prevent the extension by violence of Communist rule in Asia. The American decision to fight in Korea, as well as the later decision to fight in Vietnam may well have contributed to the schism within the international Communist movement which is one of the most striking features of world politics at mid-century.

The Korean decision may have other significances that those who have lived close to it are not sufficiently knowledgeable to appreciate. Yet even now it appears to have been an important moment in world history. It was a dramatic, swift, and costly response to a similar initiative.

For students of politics, the Korean decision provides an opportunity for rare insight into crisis decision making in international politics at a high level of government. It provides a fitting example of what Charles F. Hermann has defined as a crisis decision: surprise, short decision time, and high perceived threat to values.[2] It

---

1. Special report of the Unified Command to the United Nations Security Council, U.N. Document S/3079, August 7, 1953.

2. Charles F. Hermann, *Crises in Foreign Policy Making: A Simulation of International Politics* (China Lake, California: Project Michelson Report, U.S. Naval Ordnance Test Station, April 1965), pp. 29ff. A version of this study will be published by Bobbs Merrill.

also offers an opportunity for the scholar to explore the applicability of an analytical framework that has been presented by Richard C. Snyder, H. W. Bruck, and Burton Sapin in *Foreign Policy Decision Making*.[3] Many readers will be familiar with this monograph; for those who are not, it would be very useful background reading for understanding what has been attempted in the present inquiry. For the study of the Korean decision is the first attempt to apply the Snyder, Bruck, and Sapin framework explicitly in empirical research. Thus some explanatory comments are in order about the methodology of application—the features of the decision-making approach that were found most useful, the problems and limitations of the single case in political research, the nature of what has been attempted in the present study, and the sources upon which this inquiry is based.

THE DECISION-MAKING FRAMEWORK

The approach suggested by Richard C. Snyder and his colleagues called upon students of international politics to focus their attention sharply upon organizational decision making as a way of explaining the patterns of action among the political creations of man we call nations. They defined decision making as "*a process which results in the selection from a socially defined, limited number of problematical, alternative projects, of one project intended to bring about the particular state of affairs envisaged by the decision makers.*"[4]

They further stated that their objective was to explain *why* a particular decision was made; why one decision and not another. The underlying assumption, of course, was that if men could only understand why international events occurred as they did, then the events could be placed under greater control. This was not to imply

---

3. *Snyder* et al., *Foreign Policy Decision Making* (New York: The Free Press, 1962). The original statement of this mode of analysis, first published in 1954, guided the present inquiry. Consult Richard C. Snyder, H. W. Bruck, and Burton Sapin, *Decision Making as an Approach to the Study of International Politics* (Princeton University, Foreign Policy Analysis Series No. 3, 1954).

4. *Ibid.*, p. 90.

that decision makers act unconsciously, although preconscious factors may indeed be associated with individual role performance. A widening of conscious application of relevant knowledge by decision makers and other actors was meant. The creators of the framework did not argue that decision-making analysis was the only way to seek such understanding but they did affirm that it was worth serious exploration.

As a basic explanatory hypothesis at a high level of abstraction they suggested that international political decisions were to be understood as the product of the interaction of three major determinants of action. They termed these "spheres of competence," "communication and information," and "motivation." By *spheres of competence* was meant "the totality of those activities of the decision maker relevant and necessary to the achievement of the organizational objective."[5] This concept called attention to the organizational aspects of decision making—to organizational roles and their relationships. The concept of *communication and information* called attention to the kinds of information considered by the decision makers and to the processes by which it was transmitted and received.[6] By *motivation* was meant basically "a psychological state of the actor in which energy is mobilized and directed toward aspects of the setting."[7] Motives were thus taken to be inferences from observed behavior that would help to explain the direction of decision-making activity. In the present study I have found it most useful to conceive of motives as values (desired states of affairs plus desired means for achieving them) and to limit analysis to those explicitly expressed. This is not to deny the anticipated fruitfulness in decision-making analysis of the inferential analysis of implicit patterns that constitutes one of the most powerful contributions of contemporary political psychiatry and political anthropology.

These three basic concepts, sometimes referred to by the authors of the decision-making approach as "variable clusters," were hypothesized to have concrete empirical referents in the activities of real government officials in observer-defined *decisional units*. But

5. *Ibid.*, p. 106.
6. *Ibid.*, pp. 124ff.
7. *Ibid.*, p. 140.

initially no empirical propositions were advanced to link these variables and no systematic attempt was made to offer either a logico-deductive or empirically induced general theory of foreign policy making. The authors presented a set of concepts hypothetically linked in a loose framework and counted upon subsequent confrontations of this framework with actual instances of foreign policy making to provide the elements of a more operational, empirically relevant body of theoretical statements. It was in this sense that they offered their work as a "conceptual scheme" or "frame of reference" and it is in this sense that the present study constitutes an attempt to "apply" their framework in empirical research.

Besides the three basic "variable clusters" and the central notion of the "decisional unit," several other components of the decision-making approach were especially helpful in guiding collection of case materials and in subsequent analytical efforts. A fundamental idea was that the analyst of political decision should attempt to reconstruct decision-making events as far as possible from the point of view of the decision makers themselves. Many critics have argued that *complete accuracy* in such an attempt is impossible and with this criticism the present writer would agree. Nevertheless there is also no doubt but that it is possible to a *considerable extent* since this is one of the bases of social learning and of the subsequent transmission of culture from one generation to another.

Another concept found helpful in reconstructing the decision-making events of the last week of June 1950 was the concept of *successive, overlapping definitions of the situation*.[8] This concept calls attention to the fact that organizational decision making is a temporal process: choices and calculations made at Time 1 are reassessed at least partially in terms of developments that have occurred prior to Time 2 when new decisions are made. The sequence of overlapping assessments plus objectives and associated choices was called the *path of action*. The informational responses to a decision (both anticipated and unanticipated) that were returned to the decision makers were termed *feedback*. The analyst was thus guided to organize the data of Part III around successive,

---

8. *Ibid.*, pp. 77ff.

overlapping definitions of the situation linked by feedback along a path of action.

Aside from motivation, two important concepts of the decision-making frame of reference were found to be especially difficult to define precisely in empirical research. One of these was the concept of the *definition of the situation* (the intellectual process of decision); the other was the closely related concept of decisional *givens* (the pre-existing state of affairs in which an occasion for decision arises.) In an earlier analysis completed shortly after empirical research on the Korean decision began, an attempt was made by Snyder and Paige (1958) to achieve greater precision in specifying the elements of a definition of the situation. Five elements were suggested: "(1) categorization of an event in terms of past experience and existing 'givens'; (2) specification and clarification of generalized values and the bearing of the objective situation upon them; (3) perceived relevancies—factual aspects of the situation 'added to' the objective situation; (4) establishment of a set of goals—a desired state of affairs to be attained; and (5) assessment and selection of one combination of available means and desired ends."[9] Similarly somewhat more precise guides may now be suggested for the analysis of the "givens" that precede an occasion for decision; i.e., (1) specification of major policies in force; (2) understandings about the main features of the internal and external settings; (3) major values evoked and salient; (4) principal constraints upon and pressures for action; (5) outstanding interpretations given to past learning experiences; (6) principal anticipated future states of affairs; and (7) objective capabilities for implementing actual or potential courses of action. The *a priori* analysis of "givens" may thus be accomplished with or without reference to a specific occasion for decision and for a wide range of analytically defined decisional units from individuals to whole governments.

Two more concepts were especially important in guiding the reconstruction of the Korean decision; these were the concepts of the *internal* and *external settings*. They refer respectively to those

---

9. Richard C. Snyder and Glenn D. Paige, "The United States Decision to Resist Aggression in Korea: The Application of an Analytical Scheme," *Administrative Science Quarterly*, III (December 1958), pp. 341-78, reprinted in Snyder, *et al.*, p. 225.

aspects of the domestic and international environments of the decision makers that are relevant for the explanation of the antecedents, processes, or consequences of decision. Elements of the setting may either be defined according to the perceptions of the decision makers or as objectively determined according to the purposes of the analyst. Inquiry into both may often be an enlightening exercise. The main point, however, is that the decision makers are not conceptualized in a vacuum but in at least two decisionally relevant ecological settings.[10]

The major concepts of the decision-making framework that guided the present inquiry have now been briefly reviewed. Since the following study of the Korean decision involves an attempt, guided by this framework, to build empirical theory in a single case, a brief examination of the nature of single-case analysis in political research is in order.

THE SINGLE CASE

First of all, some thought deserves to be given to the question of what constitutes a "case." If the study of the Korean decision is an example of single-case research in political science, what are some of the potentialities and limitations of the political case study?

Conceptions of the nature of a case vary widely from a description of a single instance or example to a factual narrative account rich in detail, and to an essay in which fact and interpretation are combined. One of the most influential definitions of a case in contemporary political science has been contributed by Harold Stein who wrote, "A public administration case is a narrative of the events that constitute or lead to a decision or group of related decisions. Some account is given of the personal, legal, institutional, political, economic, and other factors that surrounded the process of decision, but there is no attempt to assert absolute causal relationships."[11]

---

10. Specification and differentiation of important ecological subsettings (both in the domestic and international environments) will undoubtedly accompany further development of decision-making analysis.

11. Harold Stein, *Public Administration and Policy Development* (New York: Harcourt, Brace and Company, 1952), p. xxvii.

The interests of the behavioral scientist, however, do lead him to attempt to go beyond a narrative of events and the enumeration of relevant factors into a search for explanatory theory that transcends the bounds of the particular case. He seeks, like the poet Stanley Kunitz, "to crack the kernel of the particular in order to liberate the universal,"[12] or like Walt Whitman, "to leap beyond, yet nearer bring."[13] From this point of view the reconstruction and analysis of a single empirical case are instruments by which to advance the building of theory. If there are general laws of human behavior, then even a single case offers an opportunity for potential insight into them.

It thus seems both possible and useful to attempt to formulate a more theoretically relevant concept of the single case to guide political research. A single political case thus might be regarded as a *set of statements at a relatively low level of abstraction which describes something to be explained (the referents of dependent variables) and contains references to those factors and events hypothesized to be potentially relevant for the desired explanation (referents of independent variables).* The case is thus an analytical construct, an artifact created by the observer. Among the possible theoretical uses of single-case research might be included: (1) the assembling of an empirical basis from which theoretical propositions may be induced with or without an explicit *a priori* frame of reference; (2) the provision of an empirical test of pre-existing propositions—possibly a crucial test where propositions of universal validity have been asserted; (3) the demonstration of the empirically possible; (4) the establishment of an empirical basis for creating a conceptual framework or typology; (5) the testing of the empirical relevance of a pre-existing analytical scheme; (6) the provision of sufficient empirical detail to permit the exploration of alternative explanatory hypotheses; and (7) the provision of an empirical data base so rich in detail as to permit the reintegration of fragmented disciplinary insights into a unified body of knowledge. The sustained interdisciplinary study of a developing society on a past, present, or future historical basis would be an example of this.

---

12. Remark made during a reading of his poetry at Northwestern University, May 1, 1959.

13. Walt Whitman, "Song of Myself," XLII, in *Leaves of Grass.*

The single case may have pedagogical as well as theoretical uses. These might be summarized as providing opportunities for the development of five modes of understanding: the apprehension of factual information; vicarious learning through empathic identification with potential models of behavior; the perception of linkages between parts of a cognitive field; the confirmation or disconfirmation of previously held understandings; and the provision of a stimulus for creative problem solving and insight.

In constructing and in interpreting a single case there are several persistent problems which the analyst must solve or at least appreciate. These include questions about (1) the boundaries of the case—what is to be included or excluded; (2) the level of case comparability to be sought—the extent to which the case method employed will permit replication and comparison; (3) the representativeness of the case—the universe of behaviors to which the case findings are hypothesized to apply; and (4) the adequacy of explanation—questions concerning the relative merits of competing explanatory hypotheses, including choices among internally induced and externally introduced explanations.

The decision-making framework employed here permits a somewhat systematic way of proceeding toward solutions of these problems. First, its basic concepts provide an explicit guide for the establishment of case boundaries—although at this stage in the development of decision-making analysis it would be premature to insist upon a compulsive constriction of attention to them. What is needed at this stage is *a semi-structured research design* in which *a priori* concepts and hypotheses are combined with willingness to maintain a receptive mind for the apprehension of significant unforeseen elements. Second, there are no satisfactory scientific solutions to the problem of representativeness aside from examination of all cases in the universe of interest or statistical inference from a sample of cases hypothesized to represent that universe. Yet through the theoretical uses of the single case suggested above and through readiness to be bold in hypothesis but cautious in the affirmation of empirical validity, this problem can be constructively confronted. Third, the decision-making framework provides at least one method for eventually obtaining truly comparative case studies in political research. Systematic gathering of data related to the basic elements of the framework from case to case will permit inter-case comparison. Fourth, the framework provides both a guide for the induction of explanatory theory from within the case and an instrument for the introduction of explanatory theory originating outside the case in the various behavioral science disciplines. Since the framework contains organizational behavior, information theory, and social psychological components it offers built-in opportunities for the interchange of insights with these fields. The more highly validated the external explanatory theory, the greater the confidence in its explanatory power within the single case. Finally, another way of judging among competing explanatory hypotheses is to increase the number of cases considered; for the more numerous the cases, the fewer the explanatory hypotheses that will hold across all cases.

In summary, it would appear that the theoretical contribution of single-case analysis in political research will arise out of a combined process of internal theoretical induction, the application of external theoretical insights, and the progressive expansion of the set of empirical cases subjected to comparative examination.

DECISION-MAKING ANALYSIS IN THE KOREAN CASE

In this book five different modes of inquiry into or uses of the Korean case have been explored. Each can be related to the decision-making framework in one way or another and each has its own objectives, problems, potentialities, and limitations.

In Part II an attempt has been made to recapture the conditions that existed on the eve of the Korean decision. Main emphasis has been placed on the period from 1945 to 1950, although the data of the Korean case has shown that some of the most significant learning experiences relevant for the Korean decision took place in the 1930's. This illustrates the difficulties that arise in capturing the "givens," to which decision-making framework calls attention. Two chapters have been written to present the background of the Korean decision. The first focuses on the three principal decision makers and emphasizes their learning experiences within the domestic political setting. The second chapter traces the general development of American foreign policy after World War II and then seeks to present specific policies in force at the time of the Korean decision. If the reader will imagine that he is faced with the task of reconstructing the most important antecedent conditions of the Korean decision that would provide crucial elements of explanation for that decision—even though he were unaware that the events of June 24, 1950, would occur—then he can appreciate the extent of the challenge posed by a non-self-confirming, theoretically relevant effort to capture the givens in decision-making analysis.[14] The crude effort presented here must certainly be improved upon in subsequent studies of political decision making. More adequate analysis of the nature and implications of organizational learning will no doubt contribute to a more satisfactory solution to the problems of reconstructing the vital antecedent conditions of decision.

Part III presents a day-by-day reconstruction of decision-making events in Washington during the period from June 24 to June 30, 1950. The method employed here may be described as *guided reconstruction*—presentation of a narrative account of events in such a way as to emphasize data related to the categories of an explicit *a priori* frame of reference. Evaluators of the decision-making approach have reacted differently to the method of guided reconstruction followed here. Some have rejected the idea out of hand as an unwarranted distortion of the historical materials, preferring to let the implicit or *ad hoc* notions of relevancies of the researcher guide the collection and interpretation of data. Others have welcomed the analytical framework as a useful intellectual tool since it both focuses attention on admittedly crucial elements and at the same time is so permissively comprehensive that it does not unduly constrain either data or opportunity for imaginative insight. The narrative may also be said to be the product of *semi-structured* inquiry since it includes some materials not necessarily demanded by the decision-making framework.

The concepts of the decision-making framework have not been explicitly introduced into the narrative events but implicitly under-

---

14. Unfortunately, since the author became acutely aware of these problems only after the completion of interviews with the decision makers, it was not possible to pursue them directly with these officials.

lie the reconstruction. Thus in preparatory research and subsequent presentation a sequence of points of decision was identified; a decisional unit was identified with each decisional outcome; special emphasis was given to collecting organizational, informational, and value data about each unit at each point of decision; an attempt was made to describe the intellectual process by which alternatives were identified and evaluated; special attention was given to describing feedback to decisions; and efforts were made to link the decision makers to their internal and external settings before, during and after decision.

One feature of the narrative deserves special mention. An attempt has been made to "decontaminate" it from normative, judgmental, and analytical statements of the case writer. This means that an effort has been made to present the happenings of the period and the views of the various actors involved with as much faithfulness to the original as possible. This is indeed a difficult undertaking and there is no certainty of success. Yet a very determined effort to exclude the analyst's judgments and to include the actor's viewpoints has been made. The result is markedly different from a case study in which the writer's empirical analyses and normative evaluations are interwoven with the narrative of events. Neither empirical nor evaluative analyses have been neglected in this study but they have been separated from the narrative reconstruction of decision-making events. The objective has been to confront the reader with as nearly untreated a body of case materials as possible so that he may have maximum opportunity both to learn from the experience and to exercise independently his own theory-building and evaluative skills. Others may not agree that the "decontamination" of the narrative has been successfully accomplished but it has been seriously attempted.

A note on sources of information utilized in constructing the narrative will be of interest. An initial reconstruction was based upon easily available contemporary journalistic accounts and official public documents. The single most important source of information was an article written by Beverly Smith, Washington correspondent of the *Saturday Evening Post*, who based his account upon interviews and the notes of a historically minded young White House staff member, George M. Elsey.[15] The initial reconstruction was followed by interviews with the decision makers whose assistance is gratefully acknowledged in the preface to this book. Interviews, conducted mainly between 1955 and 1957 were mostly of an open-ended type guided by a sense of the Korean decision's path of action. The officials were first asked to recall their salient impressions of the decision-making events of the last week of June 1950. The decision makers responded to this question with a free narrative of their recollections. Then the interviewer explored points of interest through questions directed toward specific gaps in the data or toward variations in interpretation.[16]

On the basis of these interviews a second reconstruction was prepared and circulated among the decision makers for a review of its accuracy. As a result of the comparison of public materials and information obtained by interviews in this case, the writer agrees with the conclusion of Alexander L. George that "a surprising amount of reliable information about American policy calculations can be obtained from the columns of the better Metropolitan dailies."[17] No classified materials were employed in this study. It will be an exciting event when the archives are opened to the scholar of the future. Compared with the documentation that will be available then, that presented here undoubtedly will be seen as limited indeed. However, one official was kind enough to refer to his notes of the Blair House Conferences as a check on the essential accuracy of the narrative and another generously shared passages from his diary of the period. The Historical Division of the Department of

<hr>

15. Beverly Smith, "The White House Story: Why We Went to War in Korea," *Saturday Evening Post*, November 10, 1951, pp. 22ff. Mr. Smith told me several years later that he had used all the materials available to him in this article and could not remember anything else of significance.

16. The interviewing method employed in this study leaves much to be improved upon and it is hoped that subsequent studies utilizing the decision-making framework will do better. The employment of even simple rating scales to obtain comparative quantitative data on such variables as informational adequacy, value strengths and relationships, and probability calculations assigned to alternative courses of action would have been of enormous analytical usefulness even though some officials might have been expected to object to such techniques as being "too mechanical" to portray adequately the subtleties of foreign policy making.

17. Alexander L. George, "American Policy-making and the North Korean Aggression," *World Politics*, VII (January 1955) p. 210.

State also helpfully answered a written questionnaire on the basis of materials in its archives.

In Part IV an effort has been made to create a set of empirical propositions that will link the variables of the decision-making frame of reference and further contribute to the process of building a body of empirical theory about foreign policy making. The propositions advanced here are to be regarded as a supplement to and continuation of earlier proposition-building efforts of Snyder (1956)[18] and Snyder and Paige (1958).[19] The methodology for building such propositions has been presented elsewhere.[20] Its explication preceded the formulation of most of the propositions advanced in Part IV.

The general method employed for creating propositions in the Korean case might be termed *guided retroduction* in which the decision-making framework performs both organizing and stimulus functions as the observer attempts to build empirical propositions based upon the case materials. This will be appreciated as a second-order usage of the decision-making framework. In first-order usage the framework serves to guide the initial gathering and ordering of data. In the second stage the framework helps to guide and stimulate the induction of empirical propositions of a general theoretical nature linked to that data. Thus the framework serves to guide the perception of patterns, interconnections, and implications of the concrete materials at hand as well as among the analytical concepts themselves. One method of proposition building not employed in this study is the method of analogy in which theoretical propositions from other fields of behavioral science are juxtaposed with the case materials. These points will be discussed further in Chapter 11.

Part V represents an exploration of methods for the normative

---

18. Richard C. Snyder, "Analysis of Case Materials on the United States Decision to Resist Aggression in Korea," Palo Alto, Center for Advanced Study in the Behavioral Sciences, 1956, 87 pp., mimeographed.

19. Richard C. Snyder and Glenn D. Paige, "The United States Decision to Resist Aggression in Korea: The Application of an Analytical Scheme," *Administrative Science Quarterly*, III (December 1958), pp. 341-78.

20. Glenn D. Paige, *Proposition-Building in the Study of Comparative Administration* (Chicago: American Society for Public Administration, 1964), 30 pp.

or evaluative analysis of the Korean case. Here the judgments suspended during the narration of decision-making events are given full expression. Hopefully what has been attempted here will lead to other more satisfactory attempts to provide useful methods for evaluation in the study of political decisions and in other areas of political science. If political man does in fact have the capacity for meaningful choice then it would seem important to illuminate not only those values by which he has chosen but also those values that might have guided his behavior.

Perhaps eventually the decision-making frame of reference and theories generated by it can be used for purposes of the normative analysis of decisional processes; but this has not been attempted here. It remains a task for future exploration. Certainly caution will have to be exercised in distinguishing between the use of the decision-making framework as a tool of scientific inquiry and as a source of evaluative standards. The question of whether a method of scientific inquiry can serve as an adequate framework for ethical judgment will also merit careful study.

In Part VI an attempt has been made to extract from the preceding parts some operational guidelines for coping with crisis situations in international politics. Assuredly this is a primitive initial venture and some colleagues may reject as premature any attempt to be prescriptive at this time. Yet it is believed that the suggestions advanced are not incautious and that it is important for the scholar to take the initiative in calling attention to possible operational implications of his studies where this seems warranted.

This study has an intellectual history and for those readers who are interested in actual versus ideal patterns of the search for understanding, the following path of inquiry is recorded: (1) Study of the decision-making framework; (2) first narrative reconstruction, interviewing, and second narrative construction; (3) exploration of the methodology of the single case; (4) third narrative reconstruction; (5) study of social learning theory; (6) articulation of a strategy of proposition building and the creation of empirical propositions; (7) exploration of the behavioral history of the decision makers and the background of the decision; (8) normative analysis; (9) specification of operational implications; and, finally,

(10) the articulation of an introduction. Although this may appear to have been an erratic intellectual journey almost all of the elements were early perceived as desirable and what remained was to produce the various pieces and then to assemble them. A unity of purpose and intent has thus infused most of the intellectual process: to inquire into a momentous decision and to try to make the inquiry relevant for the development of political science.

But enough has been said by way of introduction. What has been done must now speak for itself.

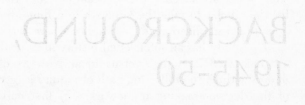

PART II

BACKGROUND,
1945-50

CHAPTER 2

THE INTERNAL SETTING

THREE DECISION MAKERS

The President

Harry S. Truman could have personified the national experience of the United States of America after 1945 when he described his sensations upon assuming the presidency as having been "suddenly catapulted into the midst of world-shaking episodes [where I had] to learn about the past at the same time that I had to act for the present and plan for the future."[1] For Vice-President Truman,

---

1. Harry S. Truman, *Memoirs: Year of Decisions,* Vol. I (Garden City: Doubleday and Company, 1955), p. 481. Hereafter this work and *Memoirs: Years of Trial and Hope,* Vol. II (Garden City: Doubleday and Company, 1956) will be cited as

former county politician and Senator from Missouri, the catapult
had been the death of Franklin D. Roosevelt. For America the
propellant into world political consciousness had been World
War II.

By June 1950, Mr. Truman, then sixty-six years old, had served
as President for more than five years. These years had provided an
important learning experience in which he had been able to test his
ideas about the appropriate role of the President in American
government, to gauge directly his popular appeal in a national election, and to learn about the international environment through a
series of actions and counteractions that had included face-to-face
talks with Stalin at Potsdam. Since there had been three secretaries
of state (James F. Byrnes, George C. Marshall, and Dean G.
Acheson) and two secretaries of defense (James Forrestal and
Louis A. Johnson) in the same period, the President's experience
constituted an important element of continuity at the highest levels
of postwar American policy making.

Mr. Truman's concept of his role included belief in the desirability of a strong presidency, an image of himself as a champion of
the common man with a historical mission, and a confident willingness to accept responsibility for decision. He drew his belief in the
importance of a strong chief executive from his efforts to master the
lessons of American political history. For him American experience
taught that whenever the President weakly deferred to the Congress
or to the Cabinet the public interest suffered. This belief had been
reinforced by a decade of senatorial experience after 1935 during
which he had learned that on occasion powerful special interests
could dominate legislative action. As the highest elected representative of all the people, strength became for him a moral imperative.
Thus Mr. Truman regarded himself as the champion of the common
man in the tradition of the "strong liberal Presidents" whom he
identified as Jefferson, Jackson, Lincoln, Theodore Roosevelt, Wilson, and Franklin Roosevelt.[2] Following their example, he regarded

Memoirs, volume, and page. The following characterization of the President's conception of his role is based primarily upon this source, supplemented by impressions
gained during an interview in 1957 and by comments about him by his associates.

2. Memoirs, II, p. 173.

it as his mission to continue unfalteringly the "historical thread of liberalism" in American politics.

Coupled with these beliefs was a marked readiness to accept responsibility for decisions taken in what he regarded as the public interest. For him, certain decisions that could only be made by the President, such as those pertaining to national defense and foreign affairs, ought to be taken and accepted without partisan considerations.[3] The motto carried by the triangular block on Mr. Truman's desk was both a symbol of the Constitutional imperatives of his office and of his own convictions about presidential responsibility: "THE BUCK STOPS HERE."

By 1950 the President's conceptions of his role had been powerfully reinforced by victory in the 1948 election in which he had defied a Republican-controlled Congress, had ignored the pessimistic predictions of public opinion analysts, and had triumphed over a hostile press in a "fighting" campaign. They were tempered by the President's recognition that one of the salutary effects of a free election upon a democratic leader was to demonstrate that nearly as many voters as those who supported him would have preferred someone else in office.

Mr. Truman's views about the meaning and uses of history were important elements in his behavior as President. For him, today's problems were largely yesterday's implications. But if the past thrust forth problems for decision it also promised to reveal appropriate solutions for them. Thus he held that for "almost all" present problems there were precedents that would provide clear guides to right principles of action.[4] With history as an unambiguous moral teacher, decision making became an exercise in applying its lessons. An occasion for decision became a stimulus to search for past analogy. "When we are faced with a situation," the President later explained, "we must know how to apply the lessons of history in a practical way."[5]

In addition to frequent reference to history, another characteristic feature of the President's pattern of making decisions was the

---

3. E.g., *Memoirs*, I, pp. 99, 529-30; II, p. 315.
4. *Memoirs*, I, p. 121.
5. *Ibid.*

way in which he sought to base them upon group deliberations among his advisers. He deliberately sought to avoid the practice of his predecessor who had demoralized staffs and had heightened conflict both within and among departments by confronting formal meetings with informally reached conclusions. When faced with a major occasion for decision, the President's customary practice was to gather his principal advisers, to state or to have someone else state the matter for decision, to elicit individual expressions of opinion, to encourage further discussion for the clarification of issues, and then to decide or to delay decision.[6] In this way he sought both to improve the quality of his decisions and to avoid jealous hostilities among his advisers.

The President's advisers greatly admired his ability to make crucial decisions without tormenting afterthoughts. This ability seemed to grow with experience. Early in office, on May 8, 1945, the President had revealed in a letter to his mother some apprehension that some day he might make a mistake "too great to remedy."[7] A month later, as he became more accustomed to his role, he explained to her, "I have to take things as they come and make every decision on the basis of the facts as I have them and then go on from there; then forget that one and take the next."[8] After four months in office, the President showed in a letter to his sister that he was learning to live with difficult decisions. "Nearly every crisis seems to be the worst one," he wrote on August 12, 1945, "but after it's over, it isn't so bad. . . ."[9] Years later he was to explain, "When I had a decision to make I made it; if it was wrong, I changed it."[10]

The way in which the President related himself to the principal officers of his administration showed that he was a stickler for "channels."[11] Just as he was wary lest any Cabinet officer encroach upon presidential prerogatives, he made it clear that he would not interfere with his subordinates as long as they did not overstep the bounds of his general policies. The President's sensitivities on this

---

6. E.g., *Memoirs*, I, p. 19.
7. *Ibid.*, p. 293.
8. *Ibid.*
9. *Ibid.*, p. 433.
10. Interview, July 30, 1957.
11. Dean G. Acheson, "Responsibility for Decision in Foreign Policy," *Yale Review* (Autumn, 1954), p. 8.

point, while tempered with political considerations, were shown by his dismissal of Secretary of Commerce Henry A. Wallace in 1946 and by his request for the resignation of Secretary of State Byrnes in 1947. In the latter case the President had become suspicious that the politically experienced Secretary of State was beginning to regard himself as president.[12] The President later explained, "The Secretary of State should never at any time come to think that he is the man in the White House, and the President should not try to be the Secretary of State."[13]

A close observer of the deterioration of the relationship between President Truman and Secretary Byrnes during 1945-47 had been the then Under Secretary of State, Dean G. Acheson. He had worked intimately with the Chief Executive during the long absences of the Secretary of State in overseas negotiations and had won the President's respect and confidence.

The Secretary of State

In June 1950, Secretary of State Dean G. Acheson, then fifty-seven years old, had been in office for nearly a year and a half. The Harvard-trained lawyer from Connecticut had been called from private life to succeed General George C. Marshall when the latter had been forced to retire by failing health in January 1949. Secretary Acheson inherited the rediscipled State Department organization that General Marshall had built upon the legacy of Secretary Byrnes whose extended absences from Washington (350 days out of 562 days in office) had not permitted relief of the indiscipline and professional frustrations that had been bequeathed by the tenure of circumvented Secretary Cordell Hull.[14]

Mr. Acheson's views on the role of the Secretary of State had been developed in the course of a career that had alternated high-level government service with the private practice of law. After service as a Navy ensign in World War I and as private secretary

12. *Ibid.*, pp. 546ff.
13. *Ibid.*, p. 330.
14. An insightful account of departmental morale and procedures under the three secretaries is given in Joseph M. Jones, *The Fifteen Weeks: February 21-June 5, 1947* (New York: The Viking Press, 1955), pp. 100ff.

to Associate Justice Louis Brandeis of the Supreme Court, he had
served as Under Secretary of the Treasury in 1933; as Assistant Secretary of State for Economic Affairs from 1941 to 1944; as Assistant
Secretary of State for Congressional Relations from December to
July 1944; and as Under Secretary of State from 1945 to 1947 when
he returned once again to his legal career.

Secretary Acheson conceived of his role as being that of the
President's "first minister,"[15] "the senior member of the Cabinet."[16]
The concept of primacy among other presidential advisers stemmed
from the historical precedence of the Secretary of State as the first
cabinet officer created under the Constitution, the pressing importance of American involvement in world affairs in the postwar
era, and the warm personal working relationship that existed between the Secretary and the President. Secretary Acheson knew
that the President understood that he was completely loyal to him
and that the President had great confidence in his judgment. He had
learned that when disputes among advisers were carried to the
President for resolution the President almost invariably decided in
his favor.

Mr. Acheson's views on the distinctive and complementary nature of the roles of the President and the Secretary of State were
virtually identical with those held by Mr. Truman. The Secretary,
who thought of himself as having a "lively sense of power," was
keenly appreciative of presidential authority and responsibility. For
him the President was "the pivotal point, the critical element in
reaching decisions on foreign policy."[17] "The decisions are his," he
later wrote, "ultimately he must decide."[18] The Secretary further
cautioned, "No good comes from attempts to invade the authority
and responsibility of the President." For his part, Mr. Acheson
thought that the Secretary of State should be the "principal, unifying, and final source of recommendation" to the President on foreign
policy.

In order to carry out his responsibilities to the President, the

15. Secretary Acheson, Interview, October 25, 1955.
16. Acheson, p. 8.
17. *Ibid.*, p. 6.
18. *Ibid.*, p. 12.

Secretary considered that his role should be to marshal expert knowledge about foreign affairs within the State Department; to stimulate discussion among the experts (who could be expected to disagree) so that issues might be clarified and consequences of alternative courses of action appreciated; to contribute to the discussions a sense of the broader issues with which the President would be concerned; to promote interdepartmental consultation for the enhancement of mutual understanding among presidential advisers; to give the President the "real issues, honestly presented, with the extraneous matter stripped away"; and to inform the President continuously about the policy formulation process so that he might both contribute his own ideas and avoid belated entrapment in "narrowed choices."[19]

In dealing with his own staff the Secretary of State translated into action the role he conceived for himself as a presidential adviser and at the same time demonstrated a pattern of decision making that had much in common with that of the President. As described by a close associate,

> Meeting with members of his own staff, Acheson never stated an opinion or conclusion until everyone present had an opportunity to give his own ideas about the subject and suggest a remedy. By questions he stimulated others to talk, while he listened and took occasional notes. When every aspect of the matter had been carefully and fully considered he would summarize what he had heard, point out conflicts in points of view, attempt to reconcile them, introduce facts and reasoning that might not have appeared and finally suggest a solution.[20]

Secretary Acheson regarded the capacity for decision as an uncommon human attribute and the nature of decision making as being so subtle as almost to elude human understanding. For him, the more difficult the problem, the rarer the capacity for decision. "The choice becomes one between courses all of which are hard and dangerous," he has explained. "The 'right' one, if there is a right one, is quite apt to be the most immediately difficult one. . . . In

---

19. *Ibid., passim.*
20. Jones, p. 111.

these cases the mind tends to remain suspended between alternatives and to seek escape by postponing the issue."[21] Summarizing
the process of decision, the Secretary has explained further, "The
facts have to be mastered, the choices and their consequences
understood—so far as consequences can be understood; and then
upon 'judgments more subtle than any major premise,' the decision
made."[22] Thus Secretary Acheson expressed skepticism of the "too
facile and pat,"[23] shunned the idea that American foreign policies
could be based on readings taken from a piece of moral "litmus
paper,"[24] and doubted that decisions could be analyzed or really
understood at all by techniques short of psychoanalysis.[25]

Although an important component of Mr. Acheson's conception
about an appropriate role for a secretary of state was the idea that
he should serve as a catalyst in achieving interdepartmental collaboration in matters of foreign policy, it was common knowledge
in Washington during the spring of 1950 that relationships between
the Departments of State and Defense were very seriously impaired.
"It may seem extraordinary, but it is neverthless true," Secretary
Acheson subsequently explained, "that not until General Marshall's
tenure as Secretary of Defense [i.e., not until September 1950] did
the Secretary of State and his senior officers meet with the Secretary
of Defense and the Joint Chiefs of Staff for continuous discussion
and development of policy."[26] Mr. Acheson attributed this breakdown in State-Defense relationships to a tendency for officials in
government departments "to isolate themselves from other departments and to regard persons outside their ranks with something
amounting on occasion to suspicion and hostility." But other observers, noting the more harmonious relationship that had existed
between Secretary of State Marshall and Secretary of Defense For-

---

21. Acheson, p. 7. The omitted portion of this passage is the sentence: "It was
certainly so in reaching a decision regarding Korea in June 1950." It has been
omitted in order to recapture the Secretary's general orientation toward decision
making without prejudging the Korean decision.

22. *Ibid.*, p. 12.

23. *Ibid.*, p. 10.

24. Dean G. Acheson, "Total Diplomacy to Strengthen U.S. Leadership for
Human Freedom," *Department of State Bulletin*, XXII, No. 559 (March 20, 1950)
p. 428.

25. Secretary Acheson, Interview, October 25, 1955.

26. Acheson, "Responsibility for Decision in Foreign Policy," p. 11.

restal, tended to attribute the rupture to a clash of personalities compounded by policy differences and vice versa. According to Senator Harley M. Kilgore, Democrat of West Virginia, the Secretary of Defense "undercut Acheson at every opportunity [and] went around Washington saying, 'I'll keep asking what our China policy is until I find out.' "[27] Stories circulated that the Defense Secretary was supplying anti-Acheson materials to hostile Republican Senators Owen Brewster of Maine and Styles Bridges of New Hampshire.[28]

"I don't know why the President surrounded himself with such intellectually incompatible people," later puzzled an official just below the highest levels who was able to observe the presidential advisers.[29] At least part of the answer seems to have been that the President deliberately did this so that he could benefit from a divergence of views. Thus each of his cabinets contained a spread of "liberal" and "conservative" opinion. In this sense, Secretary Acheson was regarded as being liberally inclined while the Secretary of Defense was known as a "conservative."

The Secretary of Defense

When Korean events called for decision, the Secretary of Defense, Louis A. Johnson, lawyer-politician from West Virginia, then fifty-nine years old, had been in office for sixteen months. As the second Secretary of Defense since the office was first established in 1947, Mr. Johnson had not inherited a well-established and smoothly functioning organization when he took over from Secretary Forrestal in March 1949 but was confronted with the task of creating one. This was not Secretary Johnson's first experience as a military administrator; previously he had served as Assistant Secretary of War from 1937 to 1940.

Secretary Johnson shared with the President at least two main interests: military affairs and politics. Both had served overseas in World War I, Johnson as captain of infantry, Truman as commander of an artillery battery. Both had continued their military interests

---

27. Alfred Steinberg, *The Man from Missouri* (New York: G. P. Putnam's Sons, 1962), p. 354.
28. *Ibid.*, p. 381.
29. Interview.

into the interwar years and beyond. By 1950 Mr. Johnson was a reserve lieutenant colonel and Mr. Truman held the rank of reserve colonel. In addition, Mr. Johnson had served as national commander of the American Legion during 1932-33.

Although the Defense Secretary differentiated sharply between "political" and "military" factors in his administrative philosophy, the two had been related closely in his own career. Secretary Johnson's interest in politics went back at least to his election in 1916 to the West Virginia House of Delegates where he quickly became majority leader and chairman of the judiciary committee before he left to serve in World War I. Active later in veterans' activities, Secretary Johnson first came to national political attention as national commander of the American Legion. In this post he had worked with President Roosevelt to prevent a veterans' march on Washington to protest the lowering of veterans' benefits that the President had adopted as an anti-Depression measure. Having forestalled the march, he worked successfully with the President to restore the benefits. In the 1936 campaign he continued his national political activity as chairman of the Democratic National Veterans Committee. After the Roosevelt victory, he was given what he regarded as a "temporary" appointment as Assistant Secretary of War under Harry Woodring, whom he had been led to believe would retire in four months and thus allow the President to appoint him as Secretary. The expected resignation did not occur until three years later. In the interim, Mr. Johnson worked closely with the President in the shadow of impending war to improve the nation's military preparedness. In matters such as the rendering of surreptitious aid to beleaguered Britain he was often used to circumvent the pacifist-minded Secretary Woodring. When the President chose Republican Henry L. Stimson to succeed Secretary Woodring, Mr. Johnson resigned in bitter disappointment. Recalled to serve briefly as a presidential emissary in India during World War II, he dropped out of national political life until 1948.

As chairman of the Democratic Party's finance committee during the 1948 campaign, Colonel Johnson, as he was known to his associates, was credited with having played a key role in the Truman electoral triumph. In view of the anticipated defeat at the polls, the post was not a popular one among the Democratic financial leaders whom the President had called upon to help with his campaign. Virtually drafted for the post by his colleagues, Mr. Johnson responded by raising a million and a half dollars for the bankrupt party and pledged more than $100,000 of his own funds at critical junctures. Having been offered a number of lesser posts in the aftermath of victory, he finally accepted the coveted post of Secretary of Defense where his long-standing interests in politics and military affairs could be combined. Despite his publicly expressed agreement with a contemporary cartoon that advised him to leave politics outside the door of his office, there were persistent rumors, consistently denied, that his ambitions reached beyond the secretaryship to the Democratic presidential nomination in 1952.

For many who knew him ambition was regarded as the key to his behavior. "Louis is overambitious," critically remarked former Secretary Woodring under whom he had served impatiently on the eve of American participation in World War II, "with him it's sort of like being oversexed."[30] Another critic characterized him as "a bull who carries his own china shop with him." In response to his critics Secretary Johnson once said, "I am reminded of the bleacher fans at the Yankee Stadium who credited the victories of the team to the players and always blamed Casey Stengel for temporary setbacks. So it has often been with me."[31]

When he came to office in 1949, Secretary Johnson was charged with executing two principal presidential policies: to strengthen the new office of the Secretary of Defense in the face of vigorous interservice rivalries and to hold defense spending below a ceiling of $15 billion. With the strengthening of the National Security Act of 1947 by amendment in August 1949, he was given statutory assistance in carrying out the first task. This legislation created a separate Department of Defense organization over which he had direct control, deprived the Service Secretaries of membership on the National Security Council, and created a voting chairmanship

---

30. James A. Bell, "Defense Secretary Louis Johnson," *The American Mercury,* LXX (June 1950) p. 646. The foregoing review of Secretary Johnson's career seems to represent a consensus of this source and two other interpretations: Jack Alexander, "Stormy New Boss of the Pentagon," *Saturday Evening Post,* CCXXII (July 30, 1949) pp. 26ff., and Walter H. Waggoner, "Louis Johnson Tackles It," *New York Times Magazine,* April 3, 1950, pp. 15ff.

31. *New York Times,* April 25, 1966, p. 31.

for the Joint Chiefs of Staff. By the summer of 1950, after a year of vigorous efforts to assert authority over the armed services by the Defense Secretary and after intense interdepartmental conflict, some progress had been made toward creating a unified defense establishment, but the Department of Defense was still far from being an effectively integrated organization.

In his second task of maintaining defense spending below the given ceiling, the Defense Secretary had the firm support of the President, who had developed strong convictions about defense economy during his chairmanship of the wartime Senate Committee to Investigate the National Defense Program from 1941 to 1944. By the time of Secretary Johnson's appointment in 1949 the defense budget for the year beginning July 1 already had been established at $14 billion and the Bureau of the Budget had given guidelines that anticipated expenditures for fiscal year 1951 at a level of $13 billion.[32]

Secretary Johnson had approached his tasks with a reputation for being a contentious, tough administrator, and with a concept of administration that emphasized the "implied powers" of his office. In twelve months after assuming office he had accepted the resignations of the Secretary of the Navy, two Secretaries of the Army, the Secretary of the Air Force, the Chief of Naval Operations, and other officers, especially officers of the Navy in what became known as the "Revolt of the Admirals."

In his approach to interdepartmental policy making the Secretary of Defense maintained a sharp distinction between "military" and "political" factors. Thus he vigorously defended his young department against what he viewed as "the political domination of Defense in many ways by State."[33] Early in his tenure he had ordered that there should be no contacts between officials of his Department and those of the Department of State except through his office and had obtained a presidential directive that upheld his position. As interdepartmental liaison officer on the Defense side he appointed his Assistant for Foreign Military Affairs, Major

32. Paul Y. Hammond, *Organizing for Defense* (Princeton: Princeton University Press, 1961), p. 244.

33. Walter Millis, *Arms and the State* (New York: Twentieth Century Fund, 1958), p. 235.

General James H. Burns, an old friend and associate. The State Department counterpart was Mr. H. Freeman Matthews.

THE DECISION MAKERS AND THE DOMESTIC POLITICAL SETTING

When the occasion for decision in Korea was abruptly thrust upon them, the President, the Secretaries of State and Defense, and other Administration leaders were caught up in the complex network of reciprocal influences and expectations that characterize executive-legislative relationships, competitive party relations in a midterm election year, and the subtle linkages between political leadership and public opinion in American politics.

The Decision Makers and the Congress

In the Eighty-first Congress, elected with the President in 1948 and approaching a recess in the summer of 1950, the Administration was favored by Democratic control that derived from majorities of twelve seats in the Senate and ninety-two seats in the House of Representatives. Although the Democratic legislators demonstrated over the long run sufficient cohesion to be identified as a majority congressional party,[34] the absence of a clear-cut system of party responsibility in American government meant that the President could not count upon automatic majority support for his programs and policies. Thus on some issues the President's wishes were neglected; on others, he was given firm support. Sometimes he was confronted with demands for modifications; sometimes he was at least temporarily defeated. On a few issues he was pressed to take action different from that which he considered desirable; on some crucial tests he could evoke a solid phalanx of Democratic power; on others, he could be decisively defeated.

The Eighty-first Congress largely ignored some of the key issues of the President's Fair Deal platform on which he had campaigned in 1948: the repeal of the Taft-Hartley labor law, the passage of the

---

34. David B. Truman, *The Congressional Party* (New York: John Wiley and Sons, 1959), demonstrates the existence of such a party in a case study of the Eighty-first Congress.

Brannan farm plan, and the establishment of a national health insurance program. At least part of the lack of Congressional enthusiasm for the Fair Deal among the members of the President's own party seems to have been that many of them had polled more votes than he had in the election and thus felt no strong sense of loyalty to his program. But on some issues the President received firm support not only from his own party but from the Republicans as well. An example is the strong bipartisan support given to the Foreign Economic Assistance Act of 1950, signed by the President on June 5, which included extension of the European Recovery Program (Marshall Plan) for a third year. Other provisions of the Act were $100 million for Korea, $94 million for non-Communist China, $27 million for Arab refugees from Palestine, $15 million for United Nations children's relief, and $35 million for the first technical assistance program under Point Four. The measure had passed by votes of 287 to 86 in the House and 60 to 8 in the Senate.

Congressional reluctance to provide without modification authority requested by the President as well as Congressional jealousy of its Constitutional powers was illustrated by the debate over the extension of the Selective Security Act of 1948 that took place in the six months prior to its expiration date of June 23, 1950. In his State of the Union address in January the President had requested a three-year extension of the Act that would allow him to induct men into the armed services to keep them at their authorized strength. On May 24, the House approved a two-year extension by a vote of 216 to 11 but had attached the prohibition that the President could not exercise his authority to induct without a prior joint declaration of national emergency by the Congress. On June 22, a day before the expiration date, the Senate passed by voice vote a two-year extension that would allow the President to invoke his authority under two conditions: if the Congress found that this was necessary to keep the military services at their authorized levels, or if the President found it to be of national necessity during a period when the Congress was not in session. Because of the conflict between the House and the Senate versions, both houses agreed on June 22 to extend the life of the existing law until July 9; in the interim it was hoped that a conference committee could work out an acceptable compromise.

On one issue of foreign policy, the President and his Administration suffered an embarrassing, if temporary, defeat on January 19, 1950. This was the defeat in the House of Representatives by a vote of 192 to 191 of a bill to provide $60 million in supplementary economic assistance to the Republic of Korea to be expended prior to the end of the fiscal year on June 30. After alarmed pleas by the President and the Secretary of State, the invocation of Democratic Party discipline by House Speaker Sam Rayburn, and the acceptance of a compromise whereby the additional aid for Korea would be coupled with extension of the deadline for the expenditure of funds already allocated for Nationalist China from mid-February to the end of June, the bill was revived and passed on February 9 as the Far East Assistance Act of 1950 by a vote of 240 to 134. It was approved without dissent by the Senate on the following day. Analysis of the persisting opposition to the bill in the House revealed the coalition of Midwestern Republicans and Southern Democrats that the Administration often found to be the core of "reaction" at home and "isolationism" abroad. Fifty-nine of the 91 opposing Republicans were from the Midwest; 32 of the 42 objecting Democrats were from the South. Although the defeat of the separate Korean aid bill in January was interpreted by some as a protest against the Administration's decision not to provide additional assistance to Nationalist China, Secretary Acheson interpreted it, even in the light of its subsequent passage, as evidence of a very slim margin of Congressional and popular support for the State Department in its Korean policies.[35]

A clear indication of Congressional intent in favor of executive action beyond that approved by the President and the Secretary of Defense was given on October 18, 1949, when the Congress authorized for the Air Force $738 million more than the Administration had requested. This action was but another indication of dissatisfaction over defense policies by Congressional supporters of a seventy-group Air Force in a dispute that had been growing since 1945. When the President signed the appropriations bill for fiscal

---

35. The Secretary later suggested that the defeat of the Korean aid bill would "bulk large" as one of the factors that encouraged the Communist attack upon the Republic of Korea. Dean G. Acheson, *A Citizen Looks at Congress* (New York: Harper and Brothers, 1957), pp. 83ff. Critics cited his own January 12 defense perimeter speech, to be recalled in the following chapter, as an invitation to invasion.

year 1950 on October 29, 1949, he indicated that he would not follow the Congressional initiative but would hold the additional funds "in reserve."[36] This gave further evidence of the strong determination of the President, the Secretary of Defense, and the Director of the Bureau of the Budget to hold down defense spending.

Two issues brought a sharpening of partisan conflict and growing bitterness within the Congress throughout the spring of 1950. On one of them the President was able to benefit from a solid wall of Democratic resistance to Republican opposition in the Senate. This was the issue of Administration policy toward the Chinese Nationalist Government on Formosa (Taiwan). The second source of deepening controversy was the charge that Communist subversives and their sympathizers had infiltrated the Department of State. The President and the Secretary of State benefited from a virtually unanimous expression of partisan support for their Formosan policy when the members of the Senate Democratic Conference emerged from a caucus on the morning of January 17, 1950, and announced that the Democratic members of the Senate had reached a unanimous consensus in support of the Administration on this issue. Administration policy, as announced by the President on January 5, was to avoid further involvement in the Chinese "civil conflict."

The declaration of partisan solidarity by the Democratic senators on January 17 precipitated a day of angry debate that lasted into the early evening hours and eventually demonstrated the futility of a direct Republican assault on the issue of Formosa as well as its shortcomings as a political weapon. The debate contained mutual recriminations over responsibility for an alleged breakdown in the bipartisan approach to foreign policy that had been developed in the postwar years largely under the leadership of Republican Senator Arthur H. Vandenberg of Michigan. During the Eightieth Congress this had meant that 82 per cent of Republican legislators had joined with 92 per cent of their Democratic col-

---

36. Warner R. Schilling, "The Politics of National Defense: Fiscal 1950," in Warner R. Schilling, Paul Y. Hammond, and Glenn H. Snyder, *Strategy, Politics, and Defense Budgets* (New York: Columbia University Press, 1962), p. 88.

leagues in support of key measures ranging from ratification of the United Nations Charter to the Marshall Plan.[37] On the issue of Formosa itself critics of the policy of disengagement were challenged to advocate openly what was portrayed as the only way to prevent a Communist victory in the Chinese civil war. In the view of the State Department, as expressed in its report on American-Chinese relations of July 1949, this could be only "full-scale intervention in behalf of a Government which had lost the confidence of its own troops and its own people."[38] "Intervention of such magnitude," it was argued, "would have been resented by the mass of the Chinese people, would have diametrically reversed our historic policy, and would have been condemned by the American people."[39] In the aftermath of this debate, although there were individual expressions of disgruntlement over present and past China policies, there was no concerted Republican assault upon them.

Charges of Communist sympathy in the State Department, that were made by Republican Senator Joseph R. McCarthy of Wisconsin in February and subsequently linked by him in March to the idea of betrayal in China, contributed both to the intensification of partisan conflict within the Congress and to the exacerbation of factionalism within the Republican Party. The Senator's assault upon the State Department was begun on February 9, amidst Republican criticisms that the Democrats had "sold out" the East European democracies to Communism at Yalta in 1945, that they had been "soft" on Communism in China, and that this lack of resolution had caused the "loss" of China. As the spring months passed, the Senator alleged that as many as 280 Communists and their sympathizers had infiltrated the Department of State. Personal attacks were leveled against Secretary Acheson, especially in criticism of a statement by him on January 25 that he would not "turn his back on" his long-time friend and former State Department associate

---

37. Robert A. Dahl, *Congress and Foreign Policy* (New York: Harcourt, Brace, and Company, 1950), p. 228.

38. Department of State, *United States Relations with China* (Washington: Government Printing Office, 1949), p. xv.

39. *Ibid.*, p. xvi. An excellent study of American policy toward China is Tang Tsou, *America's Failure in China: 1941-50* (Chicago: University of Chicago Press, 1963).

Alger Hiss who had just been convicted of perjury in an espionage case.[40] Suspicions of Communist sympathy were also aroused against Ambassador-at-large Philip C. Jessup and other State Department officials.

The Democratic response took several forms. The President firmly defended the Secretary of State and his department, deplored the irresponsible damage to personal reputations, and argued that Senator McCarthy had not uncovered anything that was not already known to the executive branch as a result of the Federal Employee Loyalty Program that he had begun in 1947. On April 24, in a major address on the issue before the Federal Bar Association in Washington, the President called the Communists "noisy" and "troublesome" but declared that they were "not a major threat." With characteristic firmness he defended his decision not to give confidential loyalty files to Congressional investigating committees. "The decision was mine to make and I made it," he declared. "I am confident that no President whatever his party would have acted otherwise. I'd do it again if necessary." Calling upon Americans to report any information they might have about subversive activity to the Attorney General and the Federal Bureau of Investigation, the President gave assurances that he was not going to let the issue of Communism put an end to American democracy. "We are not going to turn the United States into a Right-Wing totalitarian country in order to deal with a Left-Wing totalitarian threat."[41]

In the Congress, Democratic strategy was to have Senator McCarthy's allegations investigated by a subcommittee of the Senate Foreign Relations Committee under the chairmanship of Democratic Senator Millard Tydings of Maryland, and to complete the investigation as far in advance of the forthcoming Congressional elections as possible. The committee proceedings evoked criticism from Republicans, even from those who were not in sympathy with the tactics of the Wisconsin Senator, as a whitewash of the Administration's record on security matters.

Among Secretary Acheson's own responses was to make what he

---

40. The Hiss issue was not a new one. It had been raised by critics at the time of Mr. Acheson's nomination as Secretary of State. See New York Times, January 8, 1949, p. 1.

41. New York Times, April 25, 1950, p. 4.

called a "humiliating" statement before Senator Bridges, Senator William F. Knowland of California, and other Republican antagonists on the Senate Appropriations Committee in connection with departmental budgetary hearings on February 28. "I will accept the humiliation of stating what should be the obvious," the Secretary read with what reporters described as bitterness from a prepared statement, "that I did not and do not condone in any way the offenses charged [against Alger Hiss], whether committed by a friend or by a total stranger, and that I would never knowingly tolerate any disloyal person in the Department of State."[42] The Secretary made two other major presentations during the spring that seemed to have been designed in part to strengthen confidence in the Department of State and to build support for Administration policies. On May 31, he appeared before what was believed to be a historically unprecedented, informal joint session of 250 members of the House and Senate held in the auditorium of the Library of Congress. There, as arranged by the President,[43] he reported upon a recent NATO Council meeting in London and stressed the need for American support of a European collective defense system. This confrontation, which seemed to Washington observers to be an attempt to replicate the public policy dialogue of the British parliamentary system,[44] produced no harsh clashes over China policy or security issues. A month later, on June 20, Secretary Acheson made what was reported to be a highly sucessful policy presentation and defense of the State Department at the annual Governors' Conference in White Sulphur Springs, West Virginia. The Secretary was said to have "converted" both his Democratic and Republican critics. "[He] swept them all," a Republican governor commented.[45] "He scared the hell out of us," remarked one Democratic governor about Secretary Acheson's discussion of the international situation in a closed session. The only obstacle to a resolution expressing confidence in the Secretary and the Depart-

---

42. *New York Times,* March 1, 1950, p. 1.

43. Dean G. Acheson, *A Citizen Looks at Congress* (New York: Harper and Brothers, 1956), p. 80.

44. After this experience, in which few questions of relevance to the London talks were asked, the Secretary found himself less enthusiastic than before about the interpellation system. *Ibid.*

45. W. H. Lawrence, *New York Times,* June 21, 1950, p. 1.

ment the next day seemed to have been that some Midwestern Republican governors were reluctant to give a blanket endorsement to a Democratic administration in an election year.[46] During the conference the Secretary of State was observed frequently in friendly discussion with Governor Thomas E. Dewey of New York, who had been the Republican opponent of President Truman in the 1948 election. They were observed at lunch together and were known to have held a private evening meeting. When asked earlier about his reaction to Senator McCarthy's charge, Governor Dewey had said that his feelings were "mixed," declining to define the mixture.[47] At the Governors' Conference, Governor Earl Warren of California, Republican vice presidential candidate in 1948, commented openly in praise of the Secretary of State.

Within the State Department, officials took advantage of the pages of the State Department *Bulletin* to issue detailed refutations of the allegations against departmental personnel. They concluded on June 19, "Senator McCarthy has utterly failed to show that there is a single Communist or pro-Communist in the State Department."[48] Ambassador Jessup reportedly was so annoyed by Senator McCarthy's insinuations about him that he reversed an earlier decision to resign in favor of returning to his academic career.

The responses of Congressional Republicans to the issue of subversion in government and the manner in which it had been raised by their colleague from Wisconsin were varied. As the spring months passed, the divergences in response became clearer and there were signs of growing conflict among national Republican leaders.[49] A few legislators were enthusiastically supportive both of the charge and of the mode of attack upon the Administration. Some influential leaders, such as Senator Robert A. Taft of Ohio, sensing that an effective political issue had been raised, were at least permissive. By early summer, at least some Republicans identified with the "liberal wing" of the Republican Party, felt the necessity of dis-

---

46. W. H. Lawrence, *New York Times*, June 22, 1950, p. 28.

47. *New York Times*, June 19, 1950, p. 2.

48. "Analysis of Senator McCarthy's Public Statements," *Department of State Bulletin*, XXII, No. 572 (June 19, 1950), p. 107.

49. An analysis of Republican Party reactions is contained in H. Bradford Westerfield, *Foreign Policy and Party Politics: Pearl Harbor to Korea* (New Haven: Yale University Press, 1955).

associating themselves from the tactics of "personal smear" and "character assassination" being employed by Senator McCarthy, if not from the general issue he had raised. On June 1, 1950, Republican Senator Margaret Chase Smith of Maine and six colleagues (Senators Irving M. Ives of New York, Charles M. Tobey of New Hampshire, George M. Aiken of Vermont, Robert C. Hendrickson of New Jersey, Edward L. Thye of Minnesota, and Wayne L. Morse of Oregon) issued a "Declaration of Conscience" in which they repudiated the Senator without naming him and at the same time criticized the Administration for "lack of effective leadership, by its contradictory grave warnings and optimistic assurances, by its complacency to the threat of communism here at home, by its oversensitiveness to rightful criticism, [and] by its petty bitterness against its critics." "But," added Senator Smith in a comment on the joint statement, "I don't want to see the Republican Party ride to a political victory on the Four Horsemen of Calumny—Fear, Ignorance, Bigotry, and Smear."[50] Two weeks later, Republican governors James H. Duff of Pennsylvania, Earl Warren of California, and Earl M. Driscoll of New Jersey joined in the public repudiation of Senator McCarthy's techniques.

Secretary Johnson was also subject to Congressional attack throughout the spring of 1950 over the issue of the size of the defense budget. The President in his annual budget message to Congress in January had asked for $13.5 billion for fiscal year 1951. Congressional and military critics had argued that this was insufficient for the nation's security requirements. The Defense Secretary replied that by cutting waste out of the military budget he could keep it low without reducing combat effectiveness. But on March 23, General Dwight D. Eisenhower, then president of Columbia University, complained that the defense economy program already had reduced the armed forces in some respects below the level that he would have considered a desirable safety point.[51] Later he urged before Congressional committees an additional $500 million in defense appropriations. On April 4, Representative Carl Vinson, Democrat of Georgia and chairman of the Armed Services Committee, declared on the floor of the House, "I regret deeply

---

50. *New York Times*, June 2, 1950, p. 11.

51. *New York Times*, March 24, 1950, p. 1.

that in his zeal for economy, Secretary Johnson has weakened the national security in very important respects." "It is an open secret in Washington," he revealed, "that the Secretary actually requested a considerably smaller budget than was decided upon by the President." ". . . We are again encouraging war through weakness," he warned.[52] Apparently responding to criticism, Secretary Johnson supported in April an increase of $350 million. But on May 4, the President defended the defense budget as he had done consistently throughout the year and promised that the budget for fiscal year 1952 would be even smaller.[53] On May 9, the House voted an increase of $383 million for 1951.

Thus in June 1950 the relationships between the Administration and the Congress were characterized by a complex set of conflictful, supportive, avoidant, and hortative relationships. The President, the Secretary of State, and the Secretary of Defense were all under critical attack—the President for his overall leadership, Secretary Acheson for his China policies and for harboring subversives, and Secretary Johnson for sacrificing military needs to budgetary compression. The President, product of a lifetime of political controversy, supported by relationships with a Democratic Congress that were much improved over the acrimonious ties that had bound him to the Republican Eightieth Congress in 1948, consistently defended his subordinates.

The Secretary of State, supported by a politically skillful and permissive President, worked under the impression that he must inevitably be viewed as something of a pariah by the Congress since his role would often require him to ask its members to make unpopular decisions.[54] In his view there were deep-seated Congressional tendencies to "interfere with administration and attempt to control it."[55] The Secretary had found it necessary to spend about a sixth of his total time in office in testimony before Congressional committees.[56] This had led him to expect in executive-legislative relations "a good deal of wear and tear on the executive side."[57] In

52. *Congressional Record*, Vol. 96, Part 4 (April 4, 1950), p. 4681.

53. Anthony Leviero, *New York Times*, May 5, 1950, pp. 1, 5.

54. Acheson, "Responsibility for Decision in Foreign Policy," p. 9.

55. Dean G. Acheson, *A Citizen Looks at Congress*, p. 124.

56. *Ibid.*, p. 65.

57. *Ibid.*, p. 84.

the Senate he had learned to expect the general support and under-
standing of the Democratic and Republican members of the Foreign
Relations Committee, under the chairmanship of Texas Senator Tom
Connally, as well as the constant criticism of the six Republican
Senators who had opposed his nomination in the first place—Sena-
tors Styles Bridges of New Hampshire, Homer E. Capehart and
William E. Jenner of Indiana, William F. Knowland of California,
William Langer of North Dakota, and Kenneth S. Wherry of
Nebraska, minority floor leader, who in 1949 had called him "an
appeaser of Russia."[58] Less than a third of the members of the
Senate ever entered into the public discussion of his merits or
shortcomings.[59]

The Secretary of Defense, backed by an economy-conscious
President and tax-conscious legislators, seemed to thrive in the
midst of controversy.

The Impending Congressional Election

Executive-legislative relationships on the eve of the Korean
decision took place within the broader context of the electoral party
competition that had developed throughout the spring in anticipation of the Congressional election to be held in November. Then
all of the seats in the House of Representatives and more than a
third of those in the Senate, including vacancies, would be subject
to contention.

Early in March, Senator Robert A. Taft, powerful leader of the
"conservative wing" of the Republican Party, had declared that the
1950 electoral campaign would center around three issues: "socialism," "spending," and "softness toward communism."[60] Senator
Taft's specification of the campaign issues came in the wake of a
wave of partisan charges that President Truman, under the influence of "socialistic advisers," was leading the nation toward the

58. *New York Times*, January 19, 1949, p. 1.

59. James N. Rosenau has shown on the basis of content analysis of the *Congressional Record* that of the 121 senators who served between 1949 and 1952 only
34 ever expressed themselves in praise or criticism of the Secretary. James N. Rosenau, *The Senate and Dean Acheson*, Ph.D. dissertation, Princeton University, May,
1957. For a discussion of terms of praise and abuse see pp. 166ff. and pp. 130ff.

60. *New York Times*, March 5, 1950, p. 16.

suppression of economic and individual freedom by "Big Government." It also came after the McCarthy assault on the State Department. But among the three issues, Senator Taft thought, "The deficit and the further increase in spending proposed by the Truman Administration is the best issue and the soundest."[61] On the other hand, he thought that criticism of the state of the national economy was not a "very appealing platform." "Cutting the deficit is a better one," he said. Nearly four months later, on June 20, 1950, Dr. Leon H. Keyserling, chairman of the President's Council of Economic Advisers, emerged from a White House conference and announced that "the national economy has reached its highest point of prosperity in the nation's history."[62]

In apparent response to the growing Republican campaign activity, the President devoted a large part of May 1950 to an extensive "nonpolitical" speaking tour of the midwestern and mountain states. Ridiculing the issue of "socialism," the President argued that only government spending and initiative since the Great Depression had saved American business from real socialism. Emphasizing domestic economic and welfare issues, the President repeatedly called for support of his labor, farm, and health programs. On international issues, the President attacked what he described as a new upsurge of "isolationism," an issue singled out for emphasis by the Democratic National Committee. The President did not make a major address on the issue of subversion in government. As the President started on his speaking tour Republican critic Harold E. Stassen, who had aspired to the Republican presidential nomination in 1948, described him as the "worst President" and one of the "cleverest politicians" ever to occupy the White House.[63]

The Decision Makers and Public Opinion

As the political campaigning gained momentum in the spring and early summer of 1950 the Gallup Poll organization conducted a series of studies of public opinion on the various personalities and issues involved. Although the President tended to have little confidence in polling results after his 1948 experience, and though there is little evidence either that the polls were brought to the attention

---

61. *New York Times,* March 5, 1950, p. 16.
62. *New York Times,* June 21, 1950, p. 3.
63. *New York Times,* May 3, 1950, p. 24.

of the President and his advisers or of what their reactions to them were,[64] these public opinion findings may be regarded as some evidence of the environment of opinion that surrounded both the Executive and the Congress when the time came for decision in Korea. In his swing across the country in May, of course, the President must have made his own soundings in his own way.

In April 1950, the polls showed that the President's overall personal popularity had dropped to one of its lowest points since he had taken office in 1945, a point almost exactly comparable to the low points it had reached just before the 1946 Congressional election and in the spring prior to the 1948 presidential election. The Gallup Poll analysts, aware of the sensitivity to events of this kind of political opinion, speculated that the decline in the President's popularity might have been associated with the prolonged coal strike that had occurred during the winter, with increased international tension, with "Communist gains in Asia," and with "constant criticism leveled at the State Department."[65] Some past fluctuations in the level of presidential popularity are summarized below.

Public Approval of the President's Leadership[66]

Date	Approve	Disapprove	No Opinion
July 1945	87%	3%	10%
October 1946	32	53	15
March 1947	60	23	17
April 1948	36	50	14
January 1949	69	17	14
January 1950	45	40	15
June 1950 (Pre-decision)	37	45	18

Thus in April 1950, the Gallup Poll estimated that 60 per cent of American voters would have preferred General Eisenhower to Mr. Truman as President if an election were to be held at that time. President Truman would have been preferred by 31 per cent.[67] Among Democratic voters, however, President Truman was by far the most attractive prospective candidate for the 1952 nomination:

---

64. An exception, on war expectations, will be cited at the end of the next chapter.

65. *Public Opinion News Service,* April 11, 1950.

66. Compiled from the *Public Opinion News Service* (Gallup Poll) by W. W. Rostow, *The United States and the World Arena* (New York: Harper and Brothers, 1960), p. 278. Used by permission.

67. *Public Opinion News Service,* April 22, 1950.

45 per cent approved him, whereas only a little more than ten per cent each would have favored Vice President Alben W. Barkley or Franklin D. Roosevelt, Jr., the second- and third-place favorites. Virtually no support was expressed for Secretary Johnson as a presidential candidate.

Despite the President's apparent decline in popularity, a series of polls directed toward anticipating the outcome of the forthcoming Congressional election in November indicated that it was unlikely that the Democrats would lose control of the Congress. In key areas outside the South, where shifts in attitudes had been found to be decisive, support for the Republican Party was recorded as being slightly higher than it had been in the spring of 1948 but markedly lower than it had been at the time the Republicans gained control of the Congress in 1946.[68] The national estimate of voting preference was that 42 per cent of the voters would prefer Democratic representation while 37 per cent would have favored Republicans in the Congress.[69] In March, with respect to domestic campaign issues, most of the voters expected that government finances and taxes would outrank in importance all other issues in the coming election.[70]

In May 1950, the polls showed that public knowledge of Senator McCarthy's charges against the State Department was more widespread than that about any other domestic issue. Only 14 per cent of the persons questioned were uninformed. Of the remainder, 39 per cent thought that the charges would be beneficial for the country; 29 per cent considered them harmful; 16 per cent had no opinion about their effects. Republican voters tended to have attitudes more favorable to the charges (50 per cent considered them good; 22 per cent thought them harmful) while Democratic voters were more evenly divided in their judgments (35 per cent thought them good; 33 per cent considered them injurious).[71]

On foreign policy issues, the polls showed that there was moderate support for American commitments in Europe and that there were sharp divisions among the knowledgeable minority on Asian

---

68. *Public Opinion News Service,* April 15, 1950.
69. *Public Opinion News Service,* April 27, 1950.
70. *Public Opinion News Service,* March 19, 1950.
71. *Public Opinion News Service,* May 20, 1950.

policy. Although only 53 per cent of the respondents knew about the $3-billion extension of the European Recovery Program that had been approved by the Congress, only 27 per cent considered the amount of aid too much.[72] It was estimated that 36 per cent of the voters thought that a closer federal union among the Atlantic Pact nations was a good idea; that four per cent accepted it as a "fair" suggestion; and that 41 per cent were opposed to it.[73] Thus while the magnitude of supporting opinion for American policy in Europe by no means reached the level of 80 per cent that favored the acceptance of the risk of war during the Berlin blockade of 1948-49 or the 74 per cent that had supported the North Atlantic Treaty in 1949, there was still considerable backing for it.

With respect to Formosa policy, 51 per cent of a sample of voters questioned in February had no knowledge about it. Of those who were informed on the issue, only 10 per cent favored military action to prevent the extension of Communist control over the island. Another 14 per cent were recorded to be in favor of rendering financial aid and indirect military assistance to the Chinese Nationalist Government. Those who favored a policy of "wait and see" constituted 21 per cent of the knowledgeable sample.[74]

One of the findings that analysts of the Gallup Poll found most striking in the spring of 1950 was the growing public anxiety about the threat of war. On May 5 they reported, "The proportion of people singling out war as the chief worry [facing the entire country today] is the highest (40 per cent) at any time since the end of World War II five years ago." "It is almost as if time had turned back," they recalled, "and we were again in the world of 1939. The worries of the general public today closely parallel those of 1939, on the eve of the second world war [when] a 'cold war' against the western democracies was being waged by Hitler instead of the Russians." On May 30, 1950, it was estimated that 22 per cent of the American people expected war within one year and that 57 per cent expected war within five years.[75] As further evidence of

---

72. *Public Opinion News Service,* May 25, 1950.
73. *Public Opinion News Service,* May 23, 1950.
74. *Public Opinion News Service,* February 3, 1950.
75. *Public Opinion News Service,* May 30, 1950.

popular anxiety, it was reported that a small margin of Americans thought that the Russians were "winning the cold war" and that this opinion had increased since 1948.[76]

In view of their increased anxiety over the threat of war, Americans were asked about their opinions on the adequacy of the response that the United States Government was making to it. On June 13 it was reported that 50 per cent of those questioned thought that "Washington" was doing all that it could to avert another war; 31 per cent were dissatisfied; 19 per cent had no opinion.[77] Of the dissatisfied, only three per cent suggested that the Administration should act with greater firmness toward the Soviet Union; only two per cent recommended increased military preparedness; and only one per cent advocated an intensified campaign against Communists within the United States.

But two months earlier, on April 29, the Gallup organization had reported that 63 per cent of its voting sample, in a decisive bipartisan majority, held the opinion that defense spending ought to be increased. It was reported that only seven per cent favored a decrease, while 24 per cent were satisfied with the present level of defense spending. Reflectively, the Gallup analysts commented:

> In the 1930's when the nation was faced with Hitler's aggressive attitude and growing power, the Institute surveys found public sentiment in much the same mood concerning defense as it is today. . . . Looking back on those surveys in the light of what subsequently happened in Europe, students of government have pointed out that the collective judgment of the public on defense spending proved sound.[78]

Although the April findings of dissatisfaction with defense spending suggested that there was a substantial basis of popular support for critics of the Administration's budgetary policies, they also illustrated the rapid shifts in opinion that could occur on many issues. A month earlier in March, for example, 44 per cent of a sample of voters had said that they were satisfied with the defense budget; at

76. *Public Opinion News Service*, March 27, 1950.
77. *Public Opinion News Service*, June 13, 1950.
78. *Public Opinion News Service*, April 29, 1950.

that time only 23 per cent supported increased expenditures.[79]

Even though American opinion seemed apprehensive about the coming of war, there was still considerable support for the United Nations in spite of disappointment over the organization's record since 1945. In early June 1950, it was reported that 45 per cent of the sample questioned expected that the United Nations would be more important five years in the future; 28 per cent thought that it would be less important; 15 per cent did not give an opinion.[80] There was a rather close division of opinion over whether the United Nations would be more or less effective if the Soviet Union would end the boycott of the organization that it had begun in January 1950 in protest over the failure to eject the representatives of the Republic of China from the Security Council in favor of a Chinese Communist delegation. Forty-one per cent of those questioned thought that the organization would be more capable of keeping the peace if the Russians would resume their participation; 39 per cent thought that a Russian return would make the United Nations less effective.

"The American foreign policy mood is permissive," wrote one American scholar a few months before the Korean decision and after a study of the foreign policy implications of change in public opinion from 1946 to 1949, "it will follow the lead of the policy elites if they demonstrate unity and resolution. The decline of isolationism has widened the scope of discretion of the policy and opinion elite. The problem of contemporary foreign policy is not so much one of mass traditions and resistances as it is one of resolution, courage, and the intelligence of leadership."[81]

---

79. *Public Opinion News Service,* March 24, 1950.
80. *Public Opinion News Service,* June 3, 1950.
81. Gabriel A. Almond, *The American People and Foreign Policy* (New York: Harcourt, Brace and Company, 1950), p. 88.

THE EXTERNAL SETTING

A WORLD DIVIDED

By June 1950 American policy makers had generally come to view the nations of the world as being divided into two contending camps. One was regarded as being based on a combination of Russian national power, a universal revolutionary ideology, and an international political movement. The other was seen as a coalition, centered on American power, of nations determined to escape Communist subversion and Soviet political domination. The organization of the world was said to be "bipolar"; its condition was described as that of "cold war." The Secretary of State, however, did not like the "cold war" imagery. "It is not a good phrase and might as well be dropped," he advised journalists futilely on June 5, explaining

CHAPTER 3

THE EXTERNAL SETTING

A WORLD DIVIDED

By June 1950 American policy makers had generally come to view the nations of the world as being divided into two contending camps. One was regarded as being based on a combination of Russian national power, a universal revolutionary ideology, and an international political movement. The other was seen as a coalition, centered on American power, of nations determined to escape Communist subversion and Soviet political domination. The organization of the world was said to be "bipolar"; its condition was described as that of "cold war." The Secretary of State, however, did not like the "cold war" imagery. "It is not a good phrase and might as well be dropped," he advised journalists futilely on June 5, explaining that he considered it unfortunate to apply a term originally descriptive of Russian behavior to American actions. "We are not engaged in war," he cautioned, "but in peace."[1]

PERCEPTIONS OF THE INTERNATIONAL ENVIRONMENT

The President, in foreign policy speeches given during the spring of 1950, described for the American people the nature of the international environment and explained the role he thought the United States should play in it. In his view, the United States of America stood as the leader of an international moral crusade against an evil and aggressive foe. On May 9, 1950, at Laramie, Wyoming, the President defined Communism as "a compound of evils," "the newest form of tyranny," and a "new powerful imperialism." "Communism," he declared, "denies all that we have come to know as democracy. It denies freedom and liberty and human dignity. It denies God."[2] For him, Communism was on an offensive designed to "penetrate," "divide," "confuse," "subvert," and "weaken" free peoples. At St. Louis, on June 10, the President reminded the American people, "By means of infiltration, subversion, propaganda, and indirect aggression, the rulers of the Soviet Union have sought to extend their totalitarian control."[3]

In order to cope with the ominous international environment in which "oppression, tyranny, and aggression," threatened "democracy, freedom, and peace," the President called for two main courses of action.[4] "First, we cannot compromise our own moral and ethical beliefs," he declared. "Second, we cannot isolate ourselves." "The people of the world," he explained, "look to the United States of America as a strong bulwark of freedom, and to them we pledge that we shall work side by side with other free nations in order that men the world over may live in freedom and in peace." Thus the President summoned the American people to demonstrate

---

1. *New York Times*, June 6, 1950, p. 3.
2. Raymond Dennett and Robert K. Turner, eds. *Documents on American Foreign Relations*, (Princeton: Princeton University Press, 1951), XII, p. 4.
3. *Ibid.*, p. 7.
4. *Ibid.*, p. 4f.

the "moral and material superiority" of the free world over Communism. "As the strength and effectiveness of the system of freedom are made clear on the globe," he predicted, "as the peoples who now stand in doubt turn to democracy—the danger of Communist domination will dwindle and finally disappear."

For Secretary of State Acheson, the central task of American diplomacy in the postwar era was to create a balance of power such that Soviet leaders might gradually be brought to the genuine acceptance of a "live and let live philosophy."[5] In his view, wherever the United States and the free world showed weakness, a "political vacuum" would be created into which Soviet power would flow. Therefore, the Secretary explained in early March 1950, American policy should be to create "situations of strength" through "total diplomacy" in order to demonstrate to the Soviet leaders that the free world would neither "collapse" nor "appease." The more realistic the Russian leaders became in their estimates of American power, he predicted, the greater would be the probability that they would engage in "genuine negotiation." "Someday perhaps," the Secretary suggested, "it might be possible to get them to accept a live and let live philosophy."

POSTWAR INTERNATIONAL POLITICAL LEARNING: COLLABORATION TO CONTAINMENT

The American perceptions of the international environment as essentially dichotomous, threatening, and requiring the application of countervailing power, had been learned in the course of events since 1945. They were strikingly different from the expectations about Soviet-American peaceful collaboration that had predominated at the highest levels of American policy making as World War II drew to an end. "The Russians had proved that they could be reasonable and far seeing," explained President Roosevelt's adviser Harry Hopkins about the Yalta Conference of February 1945, "and there wasn't any doubt in the minds of the President or any of

---

5. Dean G. Acheson, "Total Diplomacy to Strengthen U.S. Leadership for Human Freedom," *Department of State Bulletin*, XXII, No. 559 (March 20, 1950) pp. 427ff. For other examples of the Secretary's emphasis upon balance-of-power theory see Dean G. Acheson, *A Democrat Looks at His Party* (New York: Harper and Brothers, 1955), pp. 91, 102.

us that we could live with them and get along with them peacefully for as far into the future as any of us could imagine."[6] In this optimistic assessment, there was only one imponderable factor. "I think we all had in our minds the reservation," Mr. Hopkins later explained, "that we could not foretell what the results would be if anything should happen to Stalin. We felt sure that we could count on him to be reasonable and sensible and understanding— but we could never be sure who or what might be back of him there in the Kremlin."[7]

Only six months later at Potsdam, with Stalin still the chief negotiator, American hopes for harmonious postwar cooperation with the Russians had already been virtually dissipated. "You never saw such a pig-headed people as are the Russians," wrote President Truman to his mother in July 1945. "I hope I never have to hold another conference with them—but, of course, I will."[8] At Potsdam the President had heard Stalin declare that politics should not be based on "feelings" but rather on "calculation of forces."[9] Thus by the end of 1945, as Soviet controls were imposed over Bulgaria, Rumania, and Poland, as the Four Power Control Commission for Germany broke up, and as Soviet pressures on Iran and Turkey intensified, the President's tone stiffened. "Unless Russia is faced with an iron fist and strong language," he wrote to Secretary Byrnes on January 5, 1946, "another war is in the making. Only one language do they understand—'how many divisions have you?'"[10]

The early establishment of the language of power as the terms of the postwar Soviet-American discourse was followed by three crucial confrontations that were perceived by American policy makers as successful contests of strength and will. These were in Iran (1946), in Greece (1947-48), and in Berlin (1948-49).[11] In each

---

6. Robert E. Sherwood, *Roosevelt and Hopkins* (New York: Harper and Brothers, 1948), p. 870.

7. *Ibid.*

8. *Memoirs*, I, p. 402.

9. *Ibid.*, p. 346.

10. *Ibid.*, p. 552.

11. These three cases are singled out in Truman, *Memoirs*, II, p. 340 as instances of successful resistance to aggression. They are also cited as cases of "determined and effective resistance to aggression" by the director of the Policy Planning Staff, Department of State, Paul H. Nitze, "The United States in the Face of the Communist Challenge," in C. Grove Haines, ed., *The Threat of Soviet Imperialism* (Baltimore: The Johns Hopkins Press, 1954), p. 374.

instance the United States was favored by a monopoly of atomic weapons. In each case American policy makers seem to have agreed eventually that some degree of war risk had to be accepted in order to discourage further Soviet aggression. In the aftermath, all of these resistances to Soviet pressure had generally been considered a success: The extension of Communist power did not take place by violence or the threat of violence; a direct Soviet-American military clash did not occur. Thus each of these tests of strength were considered to be contributions to the achievement of a peaceful world. In one way or another each of the confrontations eventually became linked to the United Nations. Finally, each case seemed to indicate that the Soviet leaders did not intend to engage the United States in a major war.

The specific conflicts over Iran, Greece, and Berlin, took place within the context of increasingly more articulate and comprehensive American programs for countering perceived Soviet expansionism in the postwar years. The first of the major American policy innovations, after participation in the United Nations, was the program of economic and military aid for Greece and Turkey that was created by the Executive and approved by the Congress under crisis conditions in the spring of 1947. The Greek-Turkish aid program was largely created during the period from February 21 when the British Government announced its inability to continue the aid that had helped avert economic collapse and Communist subversion in Greece to March 12 when President Truman appealed to a joint session of Congress for supporting appropriations for a policy that was immediately labeled the Truman Doctrine. The President explained after reviewing the difficulties facing Greece and Turkey,

> At the present moment in world history nearly every nation must choose between alternative ways of life. The choice is often not a free one.
> One way of life is based upon the will of the majority, and is distinguished by free institutions, representative government, free elections, guaranties of individual liberty, freedom of speech and religion, and freedom from political oppression.
> The second way of life is based upon the will of a minority forcibly imposed upon the majority. It relies upon terror and oppression, a controlled press and radio, fixed elections, and the suppression of individual freedoms.

The President then continued with the basic policy statement, "I believe that it must be the policy of the United States to support free peoples who are resisting attempted subjugation by armed minorities or outside pressures. I believe that we must assist free peoples to work out their destinies in their own way."[12]

Within the State Department, the Administration's assumption of international responsibilities thrust upon it by the decline of British power was recognized as a "revolution in American foreign policy." The President saw it as the "turning point" in American policy after World War II.[13]

The articulation of the Truman Doctrine was followed almost immediately by a proposal for a bold, cooperative program for the economic reconstruction of Europe based on American economic assistance. The European Recovery Program, soon to gain world attention as the Marshall Plan, was suggested most authoritatively by Secretary of State Marshall in a Harvard commencement address on June 5, 1947. This was the American response to the intensifying economic distress of a war-crippled Europe that, among other things, seemed to portend electoral victories for the French and Italian Communist parties. A month later, in July 1947, an anonymous article by the diplomat-scholar George F. Kennan, one of the nation's chief interpreters of Russian affairs, set forth a strategy of "containment" for dealing with the Soviet leadership.[14] This famed article publicized, gave further intellectual coherence to, and stimulated the further elaboration of some of the ideas that had emerged among American policy makers since 1945 and that had undergirded both the Truman Doctrine and the Marshall Plan. Thus from 1945 to 1947 American leaders and the policy-attentive public self-consciously made the transition from collaboration to containment as the basic concept underlying Soviet-American relations.

The shocks of the Communist coup in Czechoslovakia and the blockade of Western land-access routes to Berlin in 1948 seemed both to affirm the correctness of the earlier analysis of the Soviet threat and to call for a stiffening of response. One response was to

12. *Congressional Record*, Vol. 93, Part 2 (March 12, 1947), p. 1981.
13. *Memoirs*, II, p. 106.
14. X, "The Sources of Soviet Conduct," *Foreign Affairs*, July 1947, pp. 566-82.

organize the collective military defense of Western Europe. The Senate ratification of the North Atlantic Treaty in July 1949 by a vote of 83 to 13, with Republican Senator Robert A. Taft opposed, put an end to the historic policy of avoiding entangling military alliances in Europe. A logical corollary to the attempt to create a collective security system centered on Europe was the Mutual Defense Assistance Program of 1949 by which American policy makers began to provide military arms and equipment to principal allies throughout the world. By the end of 1949, the Soviet-American antagonism thus had assumed a more organized and military character on a widening international basis.

Although given relatively little attention at the time, the year 1949 saw a significant attempt by the President to articulate a positive concept for shaping the international environment in peaceful directions in a way that would step outside the framework of "cold war" confrontation. This was the suggestion of a program of technical and economic assistance to underdeveloped areas of the world that the President included in his Inaugural Address of January 1949. The program became identified by its position in his speech as "Point IV." This suggestion seemed to reflect both the President's reservations about the concept of "containment" as being too negative an approach to the international environment and his sensitivity to criticisms made by Henry A. Wallace and others during the 1948 campaign that he had been responsible for precipitating the "cold war" by being too hostile toward the Russians. For the President, the Point IV program if accepted would be a fitting complement to American efforts to seek a peaceful world through the United Nations.

But by the spring of 1950 two unsettling international events had overshadowed the Point IV initiative, had created an increased sense of anxiety about the general trend of international politics, and had stimulated American policy makers to undertake a fresh reassessment of the situation and its requirements. These events were the Soviet explosion of an atomic bomb in August 1949, announced by the President on September 23, and the proclamation of the Chinese People's Republic on October 1, which formalized the Communist victory on the mainland of China. The impact of the Soviet atomic explosion was the more shaking because it came as a surprise; American policy makers had not expected a Soviet breakthrough in atomic technology until about four years later. The victory of the Chinese Communists was no surprise but it was still disturbing. In Secretary Acheson's view, the collapse of the Chinese Nationalists had added weight to the Communist side of the scales in the world balance of power.[15]

POLICY REAPPRAISAL ON THE EVE OF DECISION: NSC-68

On January 30, 1950, the President responded to the increased apprehension about the trend of the nation's security position with a major decision and a request for a general policy reappraisal. The decision was to proceed with the development of a hydrogen bomb despite expert and interdepartmental differences about its feasibility, costs, and timing. Appended to the presidential directive on the hydrogen bomb was a letter to the Secretaries of State and Defense that reportedly requested them to make a joint review of the requirements for overall national strategy in view of the fall of China, the Soviet atomic tests, and the anticipated American possession of a fusion bomb.[16] The request for a policy reappraisal had been initiated in the State Department and in fact the President's letter had been drafted there. This initiative stemmed from uneasiness about the American international position that had been growing since the fall of 1949.

The studies called for in the presidential letter were undertaken within a six-week period from the middle of February to the end of March. The results of the study were submitted to the President on April 7, 1950, over the signatures of Secretaries Acheson and Johnson. On April 12, the President forwarded the report to the Executive Secretary of the National Security Council, with a request that studies be made as to the costs of implementing the strategy that had been recommended. The President expressed

15. Dean G. Acheson, *A Democrat Looks at His Party*, p. 93.
16. The following account of NSC-68 is based on the excellent case study by Paul Y. Hammond, "NSC-68: Prologue to Rearmament," in Warner R. Schilling, Paul Y. Hammond, and Glenn H. Snyder, *Strategy, Politics and Defense Budgets* (New York and London: Columbia University Press, 1962), pp. 271-378.

neither approval nor disapproval of the report itself. Within the National Security Council the State-Defense study report was given the title of NSC-68. When the Korean crisis came, the cost studies requested by the President were in process.

Although the paper was read by only a few top officials, NSC-68 became widely known at the higher levels of government for its principal conclusion: Because of recent Soviet advances, American military spending had to be increased substantially over the current Administration ceiling of $15 billion.[17] The report of the joint State-Defense committee did not include any cost estimates since the committee chairman, Paul Nitze, head of the State Department's Policy Planning Staff, wished to have ideas in the report considered on their merits rather than to have them dismissed summarily as economically infeasible.[18] During the committee deliberations, however, certain figures had been discussed: military officers had talked in terms of $17 or $18 billion; the State Department officials had spoken of a level of $35 to $50 billion.

The preparation of what was to become NSC-68 illustrated both the difficulties in the relationships between the departments of State and Defense and the political sensitivity of the issue of the size of the defense budget. The chief military representative on the Nitze committee was Air Force Major General Truman H. Landon, a member of the Joint Strategic Survey Committee of the Joint Chiefs of Staff. While the State Department members of the joint committee worked with the full support and knowledge of Secretary Acheson, General Landon worked without the same fullness of understanding and support within the Defense Department. On about March 20, just before the final draft of the paper was prepared, a formal briefing on the work of the committee was arranged

---

17. The chairman of the committee that prepared NSC-68 later explained, ". . . The necessity of developing, in support of our world position, a stronger and more flexible military posture than was being provided became clear as early as 1946 or 1947. The dilemma involved in choosing between an unbalanced budget, higher taxes, and more stringent economic controls on the one hand, and a more adequate military posture on the other was not resolved at the policy decision level until some three months prior to the outbreak of the North Korean aggression. Those decisions were translated into specific action only after the aggression into South Korea had given concrete and bloody confirmation to the conclusions already produced by analysis." Nitze, p. 374.

18. Hammond, p. 321.

for Secretary Johnson through the State Department's defense liaison officer H. Freeman Matthews and Major General Burns in the Defense Secretary's office. When the work of the committee was presented to Secretary Johnson by Mr. Nitze, "the abruptness and severity of his reaction startled everyone present, even though there had been forebodings of it."[19] In an unpleasant scene, the Defense Secretary questioned the authority under which the study had been made, accused all those present of trying to undermine his policies, reproached General Burns for having failed to perform his duties as interdepartmental liaison officer, declared that the paper was against established policy, and abruptly left the room for a private discussion with Secretary Acheson. Secretary Acheson indicated that the study was being conducted under the authority of the President and that he would take the matter to him. Apparently he did not do so, but the incident was reported to the President by Admiral Sidney W. Souers of the National Security Council who received presidential authorization to continue the study.

In the aftermath of this incident, the Nitze-Landon paper was endorsed by the Joint Chiefs of Staff, the Service Secretaries, and other key advisers in the Department of Defense. Thus the Defense Secretary eventually chose to add his signature also rather than carry the fight against an increased defense budget before the President where he would be confronted not only by the opposition of Secretary Acheson but also of the members of his own department.

The policy recommendations of NSC-68 apparently were based primarily on the analysis of Soviet capabilities and intentions. Thus the reported discussion of these matters in drafting the paper provides important evidence about American perceptions of the Soviet Union just prior to June 1950. The Nitze committee estimated that the Soviet Union would not have an operational stockpile of atomic weapons that could effectively challenge the American monopoly until 1954.[20] When this happened, it was anticipated that American atomic strength could no longer serve as a deterrent against the employment of superior Soviet conventional forces. Therefore it was predicted that atomic stalemate would probably make limited con-

---

19. Hammond, p. 324.
20. Hammond, p. 313.

ventional wars more likely. Consequently the need for strengthening conventional forces for this kind of fighting was appreciated. NSC-68 reportedly concluded that the Soviet Union had no master plan for world domination, a conclusion strongly supported by Counselor George F. Kennan. The paper apparently portrayed the Soviet leaders as having three main objectives that, in order of priority, were "(1) to preserve the internal power position of the regime and develop the U.S.S.R. as a base for that power; (2) to consolidate control over the Soviet satellites and add them as support for that base; and (3) to weaken any opposing centers of power and aspire to world hegemony."[21] Reportedly there was some controversy over the order in which these priorities should be listed. Chairman Nitze had favored emphasis on the Soviet goal of world hegemony as the first priority both for rhetorical effect and to spur action on the paper's recommendations. Counselor Kennan had favored the final order of priorities. Secretary Acheson apparently had become bored with the disagreement over priorities and had stated that "'he thought it was of little practical consequence in which order the Soviet objectives were listed, so long as they were all there."[22]

It is not known to what extent NSC-68 discussed major policies in force that would be relevant for the Korean decision but some of the major policy emphases of the time can be recalled.

MAJOR POLICIES IN FORCE

The United Nations

In June 1950, as a matter of general policy, the United States Government was committed to the support of the United Nations. "As long as I am President," Mr. Truman declared on May 10, "we shall support the United Nations with every means at our command."[23] On May 4 he had stated that both as President and as an individual he supported the United Nations, adding his opinion

---

21. Hammond, p. 305.
22. Hammond, p. 309.
23. Dennett and Turner, p. 5.

that on the whole it was functioning well.[24] On June 22 Secretary
Acheson assured a Harvard commencement audience, ". . . We shall
continue to give unfaltering support to the United Nations."[25]

Europe

In mid-1950 the basic strategic, military, industrial, and economic counterweight to Soviet power was considered to be Western
Europe. "I knew," the President later wrote, "that in our age,
Europe, with its millions of skilled workmen, with its factories and
transportation network, is still the key to world peace."[26] The
potential of Asia was still regarded as of lesser importance.

China

In Asia, American policy makers had decided to accept the
Chinese Communist conquest of Formosa without further involvement in the Chinese civil war. The decision not to intervene in the
defense of Formosa had been made by the President after a
Defense-State disagreement in late 1949. The decision was made
public in a policy statement by the President on January 5: "The
United States . . . [does not] have any intention of utilizing its
armed forces to interfere in the present situation. The United States
Government will not pursue a course which will lead to involvement in the civil conflict in China." He continued, "Similarly, the
United States Government will not provide military aid or advice
to Chinese forces on Formosa. . . . The United States Government
proposes to continue under existing legislative authority the present
ECA program of economic assistance."[27]

As later explained by the Assistant Secretary of State for Far
Eastern Affairs, the controversy over Formosan policy between the
Departments of State and Defense had not been over the question
of the desirability of denying the island to Communist control, but

24. *New York Times,* May 5, 1950, p. 1.

25. Dean G. Acheson, "Achieving a Community Sense Among Free Nations—A
Step Toward World Order," *Department of State Bulletin,* XXIII, No. 574 (July 3,
1950) p. 17.

26. *Memoirs,* II, p. 380.

27. Harry S. Truman, "United States Policy Toward Formosa," *Department of
State Bulletin,* XXII, No. 550 (January 16, 1950) p. 79.

rather over what could and should be done to prevent it.[28] The State Department was willing to agree that it was important to hold Formosa, but when it recommended the commitment of the necessary military equipment and forces to repel the invasion, the Defense Department, in view of its limited capabilities and global responsibilities, was not prepared to make such a committment. The Department of Defense position apparently was that the State Department ought to attempt to deter the invasion by employing all the diplomatic and economic techniques at its disposal; otherwise it would be encouraging the attack. The State Department replied that its estimate was that such techniques could not be successful and that unless diplomatic action could be backed by military power the prestige of the United States should not be exposed to further damage through almost certain defeat.

By late spring of 1950 intelligence reports indicated that the invasion of the island was still contemplated by the Chinese Communists and that it would probably be launched sometime in the summer.

But in the third week of June 1950, there was renewed speculation that the Department of Defense was preparing to press for a reversal of the President's Formosan decision.[29] The speculation arose especially in connection with an Asian inspection tour that Secretary Johnson and General Omar N. Bradley, chairman of the Joint Chiefs of Staff, had begun in mid-June and that was centering on talks with General MacArthur in Tokyo. Since General MacArthur was then reported to be a strong advocate of the strategic importance of Formosa, the Tokyo conferences were watched with considerable interest. But when Secretary Acheson was questioned in his news conference on June 23 about the rumors of possible change in Administration policy, he replied that the policy announced by the President on January 5 remained unchanged: The United States would continue to provide economic assistance to the Chinese Nationalist Government but would provide neither military equipment nor military advice.[30]

28. Assistant Secretary Rusk, Interview, August 22, 1955.
29. *Washington Post*, June 22, 1950, p. 4. Homer Bigart, *New York Herald Tribune*, June 24, 1950, p. 1.
30. *New York Times*, June 24, 1950, p. 18.

Japan

American policy toward Japan in the late spring of 1950 had taken a definite turn in the direction of formulating a treaty of peace that would end the American Occupation. The nature and timing of such a treaty had been discussed within the Government at least since 1947. Since the fall of 1949 it had become a matter of increasing contention between the Departments of State and Defense.[31] The general view of the State Department, based mainly upon psychological and political analysis, was that prolongation of the Occupation would exacerbate anti-American feelings and might favor efforts of the Japanese Communist Party to keep Japan out of any alignment with the United States. General MacArthur supported the State Department in its advocacy of an early peace treaty and believed that a long-range harmony of interests would make Japan a reliable future partner of the United States. In the Department of Defense, however, proponents of prolonging the Occupation based their arguments mainly on strategic military requirements. For them it was essential not to jeopardize the retention of American military bases in Japan that would help to deter Soviet aggression by confronting Russian leaders with the prospect of a dreaded two-front war. The strategic importance of Japan was evidenced by its inclusion within the Pacific "defense perimeter" announced by Secretary Acheson in January. The problem of the treaty, if not the conflict between the two departments, was further complicated by the question of Soviet participation. Technically, the Soviet Union was still at war with Japan. Some analysts feared that if the Soviet Union was excluded as a signatory to a peace treaty, Soviet leaders might invoke the rights of belligerency to take actions that would threaten Japanese security.

In a press conference on May 18, 1950, President Truman announced the responsibility for conclusion of a treaty of peace with Japan rested in the hands of the Secretary of State. In effect, this meant that the President had decided in favor of the State Department's advocacy of an early treaty. It meant also that a key role in formulating such a treaty would be played by Ambassador John

---

31. The following summary of American policy calculations during 1949-50 is based on Frederick S. Dunn, *Peace Making and the Settlement with Japan* (Princeton: Princeton University Press, 1963), pp. 83ff.

Foster Dulles, lawyer and leading Republican spokesman on foreign affairs, who had been appointed as Foreign Policy Adviser to the Secretary of State on April 6. The principal objective of the Dulles appointment was to restore the sense of bipartisanship in foreign policy that had been largely dissipated in the controversy over Formosa. There is "no clear evidence"[32] that the Administration intended that Ambassador Dulles should assume responsibility for a Japanese peace treaty at the time of his appointment. But two days after his appointment the Ambassador asked to be briefed on the background of thinking about a treaty of peace with Japan. He soon recommended to Secretary Acheson that someone be given primary responsibility for breaking the deadlock over a treaty and was given the assignment himself on May 18. On June 6, 1950, he submitted his first memorandum on the subject in which he suggested a preliminary international conference on the treaty in Hawaii later in the summer, a regular conference in the fall, and a draft of some recommended treaty provisions.

In order to gain direct knowledge about factors affecting a treaty, Ambassador Dulles left Washington on June 14 for a two-week trip to Japan and Korea. At the invitation of President Syngman Rhee he planned first to visit Korea during June 17-20 and then to confer in Tokyo with General MacArthur and Japanese leaders. Leaving Washington, he said, "I emphasize that the purpose of my trip is only for the purpose of getting first-hand information and that I have no mission to negotiate about anything."[33]

Even though Ambassador Dulles had no mission to negotiate, he had a special mission to perform in Korea. Taking advantage of an opportunity to speak before the Korean National Assembly, he had decided, with the approval of the Assistant Secretary of State for Far Eastern Affairs, to make a statement that would "firm up" the public American policy position in Korea.

Korea

American policy toward Korea in mid-1950 lacked the firmness and clarity of its policies toward China and Japan but it was

---

32. *Ibid.*, p. 97.
33. *Department of State Bulletin*, XXIII, No. 573 (June 26, 1950), p. 1061. Also *New York Times*, June 15, 1950, p. 20.

markedly different from the policy of disengagement in Formosa. The United States was substantially committed to the support of the Republic of Korea. As explained by Secretary Acheson in testimony before the Senate Foreign Relations Committee on March 7, "The United States hopes to achieve the objective of strengthening the Republic of Korea to the point where it can: (1) successfully withstand the threat of expanding Communist influence arising out of the existence in North Korea of an aggressive Soviet-dominated Communist regime and (2) serve as a nucleus for the eventual peaceful unification of the entire country on a democratic basis."[34] The American commitment in Korea was based on three years of American military government from 1945 to 1948 and assistance in the formation of the Republic of Korea under United Nations supervision in 1948. In June 1950, the United States was supporting the Republic politically in the international arena and in the United Nations, economically under the Far Eastern programs of the Economic Cooperation Administration, and militarily through provision of the services of a military advisory group and certain military equipment.

Field control over the execution of American policy in Korea rested in the hands of the Ambassador in Seoul, John J. Muccio. Under his operational control was a five-hundred-man Korean Military Advisory Group (KMAG), commanded until late June 1950 by Brigadier General William L. Roberts. On "strictly military" matters KMAG was authorized to report directly to the Department of the Army in Washington, to keep General MacArthur's headquarters in Tokyo informed as necessary, and to coordinate its activities with the American Embassy in Seoul. Thus General MacArthur's responsibility for American military activities in Korea was limited to the provision of logistical support as far as Korean ports.[35]

Despite declarations of support for the Republic of Korea, American words and actions in early 1950 gave the impression both in Korea and abroad that the United States Government was not

---

34. "Continued Aid to Korea Requested," *Department of State Bulletin*, XXII, No. 559 (March 20, 1950), p. 454.

35. Roy E. Appleman, *South to the Naktong, North to the Yalu* (Washington: Government Printing Office, 1960), p. 13.

deeply committed to its survival. In his major speech on Asian policy before the National Press Club on January 12, 1950, Secretary Acheson publicly declared that the American defense perimeter in the Pacific ran from the Aleutians to the Philippines, enclosing Japan and the Ryukyus. By omission he excluded both Korea and Formosa from within the perimeter. "So far as the military security of other areas of the Pacific is concerned," he explained,

it must be clear that no person can guarantee these areas against military attack. But it must also be clear that such a guarantee is hardly sensible or necessary within the realm of practical relationship.

Should such an attack occur—one hesitates to say where such an attack should come from—the initial reliance must be on the people attacked to resist it and then upon the commitments of the entire civilized world under the Charter of the United Nations which so far has not proved a weak reed to lean on by any people who are determined to protect their independence against outside aggression. But it is a mistake, I think, in considering Pacific and Far Eastern problems to become obsessed with military considerations. Important as these are, there are other problems that press, and these other problems are not capable of solution through military means. These other problems arise out of the susceptibility of many areas, and many countries of the Pacific area, to subversion and penetration. That cannot be stopped by military means.[36]

In another part of the same speech, Secretary Acheson dealt more specifically with Korea, declaring support for the Korean Republic even though it lay beyond the protective confines of the defense perimeter. "In Korea," he explained,

we have taken great steps which have ended our military occupation, and in cooperation with the United Nations we have established an independent and sovereign country recognized by nearly all the rest of the world. We have given that nation great help in getting itself established. We are asking the Congress to continue that help until it is firmly established and that legislation is now pending before the Congress. The idea that we ought to scrap all of that, that we should stop half way through the achievement of the establishment of this

---

36. Dean G. Acheson, "Crisis in Asia—An Examination of U.S. Policy," *Department of State Bulletin*, XXII, No. 556 (January 23, 1950), p. 116.

country seems to me to be the most utter defeatism and utter madness in our interests in Asia.[37]

This plea was designed to win support for a $60 million supplemental Korean aid bill then before the House of Representatives. But the appeal failed. A week later, on January 19, the measure was defeated by a vote of 192 to 191 in what was described as "the first major setback" to the Administration on a foreign policy issue since the end of World War II. "Pique" over Administration failure to aid Nationalist China was cited as "the decisive factor" in defeating the Korean aid bill.[38] Although the question of additional assistance was reconsidered and passed on February 9, and although $100 million in further Korean aid for fiscal year 1951 was approved by both houses in early May, the impression persisted that economic assistance to Korea did not have a firm basis of Congressional support.

"Do you think the suggestion that we abandon Korea is going to be seriously considered?" Senator Tom Connally, chairman of the Senate Foreign Relations Committee, was asked in an interview published on May 5, 1950. The Senator replied,

I'm afraid it's going to be seriously considered because I'm afraid it's going to happen, whether we want it to or not. I'm for Korea. We're trying to help her—we're appropriating money now to help her. But South Korea is cut right across by this line [the Thirty-eighth Parallel]—north of it are the Communists with access to the mainland—and Russia is over there on the mainland. So that whenever she takes a notion she can overrun Korea just like she will probably overrun Formosa when she gets ready to do it. I hope not, of course.[39]

This statement contributed further to the impression that the Administration was prepared to accept the loss of the Republic of Korea as well as the Republic of China on Formosa.

Underlying both the public exclusion of Korea from the Pacific

37. *Ibid.*, p. 117.
38. Clayton Knowles, *New York Times*, January 20, 1950, p. 1. Voting against: 131 Republicans, 60 Democrats, American Labor Party; voting for—170 Democrats and 21 Republicans.
39. *U.S. News and World Report*, XXVII (May 5, 1950) p. 40.

defense perimeter by Secretary Acheson and the open admission of the peninsula's indefensibility by Senator Connally were the repeated secret findings of the Joint Chiefs of Staff that in the event of a major war with the Soviet Union, the Korean peninsula would not be of strategic importance in the defense of the United States. The low military significance accorded to Korea had been a basic factor ever since 1945 in decisions to avoid a drain of men and materiel on the peninsula that would weaken American capabilities elsewhere, especially in vital Europe. Such considerations, aided by the removal of Soviet troops from Korea in December 1948, contributed to the decisions to withdraw American forces by the end of June 1949. An earlier military disengagement had been planned for 1948 but it had been postponed at the request of the State Department and President Syngman Rhee after guerrilla warfare had threatened the stability of the new Republic during the fall and winter of 1948-49. When the final decision to withdraw was being made, the Joint Chiefs of Staff solicited the views of General MacArthur. The General reportedly advised that since the United States was incapable of strengthening the Korean forces to such an extent that they could both resist a full-scale invasion and suppress an internal Communist insurrection, the Republic of Korea would have to be abandoned if a serious threat developed.[40]

The limited buildup of the Republic of Korea Army that took place in the year prior to June 1950 was also related to the low strategic value attached to the Korean peninsula. Other factors were KMAG's assessment of Korea's needs, the Administration's defense economy program, and Congressional fiscal reluctance. Although President Rhee had alarmed some American officials with talk of invading North Korea, such as in a comment to Secretary of the Army Kenneth C. Royall in February 1949, and in his Independence Day speech of March 1, 1950, fear of South Korean aggressiveness apparently was not an important consideration in decisions that affected the size and equipment of the Republic of Korea Army.[41]

---

40. Robert K. Sawyer, *Military Advisers in Korea: KMAG in Peace and War* (Washington: Government Printing Office, 1962), p. 37, citing Msg CX67198, CINCFE to DA, 19 Jan 49.

41. Sawyer, p. 100. This conclusion of the KMAG historian parallels the recollection of Assistant Secretary Rusk Interview, August 22, 1955.

By June 1950 an anxious Korean Government had expanded the manpower of the Republic of Korea Army beyond its material capabilities and had received less than $1000 worth of military equipment under the Mutual Defense Assistance Act of 1949.[42] Between March 1949 and June 1950, the ROK Army was expanded from 65,000 to about 98,000 men; the total strength of the Republic's security forces grew from about 114,000 to about 154,000. When the United States Army withdrew from Korea in mid-1949 it left behind equipment for an army of 50,000 men, except for tanks and other heavy weapons. In March 1949, the National Security Council had approved the provision of additional equipment that would supply an army of 65,000 men by the end of the year. On October 6, 1949, President Truman signed the Mutual Defense Assistance Act which contained $10,200,000 for Korea. This sum was to be expended according to a set of priorities established by KMAG; maintenance items for equipment already in Korean hands, ammunition, and equipment required by normal replacement needs. The formal agreement to provide this assistance was signed between the United States and the Republic of Korea on January 6, 1950, but implementation of the program was delayed by a review of military requirements in the Pacific that was carried out by the defense establishment in the aftermath of the major policy statements of the President and the Secretary of State in January. During this review, a request from Ambassador Muccio and General Roberts for $10 million in supplementary assistance for fiscal year 1950 was set aside.[43] On March 15, 1950, the Congress finally approved a revised appropriation of $10,970,000 under the Mutual Defense Assistance Act. Because the Joint Chiefs of Staff had assigned a low priority to Korea for procurement from existing military stocks, the execution of the Korean program had to await deliveries under new contracts. Thus by June 1950, only $50,000 in signal equipment and $298,000 in spare parts were en-

---

42. The following review of military assistance to Korea is based largely on Sawyer, *op. cit.*

43. This supplement would have provided such items as F-51 fighter aircraft, three-inch guns for coast guard vessels, longer range 105 howitzers for the ROK Army, machine guns, mortars, and signal equipment. Sawyer, p. 100.

route to Korea; only a few hundred dollars worth of signal equipment actually had reached the peninsula.[44]

The dominant KMAG estimate of the capabilities of the Republic of Korea Army was that it was a match for the North Korean People's Army as long as there was no foreign military intervention. The official Army historian has recorded that "there was the general feeling, apparently shared by Brig. Gen. William L. Roberts, chief of KMAG, that if attacked from North Korea the ROK Army would have no trouble in repelling the invaders."[45] This optimism, while dominant, apparently was not completely shared within KMAG, within the Korean military establishment, or within the American Embassy in Seoul. For some time Korean leaders, apprehensive about the military buildup in North Korea, had sought to obtain heavier equipment. In October 1949, for example, the Korean Defense Minister had requested 189 tanks but had been told by the acting chief of KMAG that it was the opinion of the advisory group that the Korean terrain, roads, and bridges would make tank operations ineffective.[46] Thus despite continued reports of increases in the offensive strength of the North Korean Army, the ROK Army in June 1950, was still without tanks, heavy artillery, or supporting combat aircraft.

On June 9, 1950, Ambassador Muccio submitted a statement to Congress that contained an estimate of relative Korean military capabilities sharply at variance with the prevailing consensus. "Although the threat of North Korean aggression seems temporarily at least to have been contained," the Ambassador wrote,

> the undeniable material superiority of the North Korean forces would provide North Korea with a margin of victory in the event of a full-scale invasion of the Republic. Such superiority is particularly evident in the matter of heavy infantry support weapons, tanks, and combat aircraft with which the USSR has supplied and continues to supply its Korean puppet. It has been aggravated also by the recent Communist successes in China which have increased considerably the military potential of the North, particularly by releasing undeter-

---

44. Sawyer, p. 103.
45. Appleman, *South to the Naktong*, p. 16.
46. Appleman, *South to the Naktong*, p. 17.

mined numbers of Korean troops from the Chinese Communist armies for service in Korea. The threat to the Republic will continue as long as there exists in the North an aggressive Communist regime desiring the conquest and domination of the south.[47]

At the State Department the Ambassador's assessment was discounted somewhat as a normal case of special pleading by a field officer who was deeply concerned about his local responsibilities and who could be expected to do everything possible to increase support and understanding of them at home.[48] The statement was not given special attention at the highest levels of national policy making and did not lead to a revision of the prevailing estimate of the relative capabilities of the Korean armies.

In Seoul, however, throughout the spring of 1950 there was a continuing dialogue between Korean and American officials about the adequacy of the South Korean defense establishment, and over the question of whether an invasion from the North was imminent. On May 5, President Rhee told a news conference, "May and June may be a crucial period in the life of our nation. We lack adequate defense."[49] On May 10, the Korean Defense Minister announced that the ROK Army had been on an invasion alert during the night of May 7. The Minister's concern reached the American public the next day in the form of a brief news dispatch inconspicuously carried on page 14 of the *New York Times:*

South Koreans Warned

SEOUL, Korea, May 10 (AP)—Defense Minister Sihn Sung Mo warned South Korea today that invasion by Communist North Korea was imminent. Mr. Sihn said intelligence reports indicated the North Koreans were moving in force toward the South.[50]

"Threats of invasion make us nervous," President Rhee told reporters on May 12, "but we are getting used to it. We don't get hysterical or panicky any more. We know we haven't the planes nor the

---

47. John J. Muccio, "Military Aid to Korean Security Forces," *Department of State Bulletin*, XXII (June 26, 1950) p. 1049. For a comment by General Bradley consult *Hearings* II, p. 1053.

48. Assistant Secretary Rusk, Interview, August 22, 1955.

49. O. H. P. King, *Tail of the Paper Tiger* (Caldwell, Idaho: Caxton, 1961), p. 331. Mr. King was an Associated Press correspondent in Seoul at the time.

50. *New York Times,* June 11, 1950, p. 14.

weapons we need but we don't wish to sound complaining. . . . You understand our concern. Our life is threatened and our people are imperilled."[51] On the other hand, General Roberts reportedly said on April 25 that North Korean raids across the Thirty-eighth Parallel had decreased from 60 or 70 a month to about seven or eight and that it was as safe in Korea as in the United States.[52] On May 28 he reportedly told newsmen who had arrived to cover the May 30 elections for the Korean National Assembly, "There is no buildup of North Korean military forces along the thirty-eighth parallel at the present."[53]

The Korean-American dialogue about military matters was paralleled by interchanges on political and economic matters. There was concern both in Seoul and in Washington over the development of political democracy and a viable economy in Korea. When President Rhee announced on March 31 that the legislative elections scheduled for May would be postponed until November, the Department of State replied on April 7 with a note that sought both to persuade the Korean Government to hold the elections on schedule and to undertake certain anti-inflationary measures. Otherwise, the State Department warned in a blunt statement, "it will be necessary to reexamine, and perhaps to make adjustments in, the Economic Cooperation Administration's assistance program in Korea."[54] The elections, the results of which were interpreted as an expression of a loss of confidence in the Rhee Administration, were held on May 30. Only 30 of 210 incumbent legislators were reelected. Both supporters and opponents of President Rhee lost, while the number of independents in the National Assembly rose to 130. The North Koreans denounced the results as fraudulent and called for general elections throughout Korea. A dramatic aftermath to the North Korean response took place on June 10 when an American official of the United Nations Commission on Korea walked alone across the Thirty-eighth Parallel after a severe firefight to receive the North Korean election proposals. The North Koreans

---

51. King, p. 331.
52. *Ibid.*, p. 330.
53. *Ibid.*, p. 331.
54. "U.S. Concerned Over Korea's Mounting Inflation," *Department of State Bulletin*, XXII, No. 503 (April 17, 1950) p. 602.

refused to accept copies of the U.N. unification plans.[55]

It was against a background of apparent American irresolution and Korean anxiety that Ambasador Dulles visited Korea in late June 1950. Secretary Acheson later recalled that he thought the visit to Korea had been Ambassador Dulles' own idea.[56] He did not see the text of the speech that the Ambassador was to give in Korea. "It was a case," he recalled, "where you had a fellow out in the field who wanted to do something, and you couldn't say no." The speech had been cleared by Assistant Secretary Rusk and had received his full support. In fact, the last paragraph had been drafted by him and by the director of the State Department's Policy Planning Staff, Paul Nitze.[57] On June 19, after a visit to the Thirty-eighth Parallel on the previous day, Ambassador Dulles told the Korean National Assembly that just as the United States had served the world as an inspiring moral example in the nineteenth century, the Republic of Korea could serve the same function in the twentieth century. Referring to the "Great Korean Experiment," he predicted that the "peaceful influences" of a "wholesome society of steadily expanding well-being" would eventually "disintegrate the hold of Soviet Communism on your fellows to the north and irresistibly draw them into unity with you." In the last paragraph, which had been drafted in Washington to "firm up" the public American policy position toward Korea,[58] the Ambassador assured the Korean legislators, "You are not alone. You will never be alone so long as you continue to play worthily your part in the great design of human freedom."[59]

For American policy makers Korea was one of a number of recognized danger spots in the global confrontation of Soviet power. Recognition of its danger is illustrated by a radio report to the American people that was made on April 13 by a close adviser to the Secretary of State, Ambassador-at-large Philip C. Jessup, after a three-month Asian inspection tour that had included a trip to the Thirty-eighth Parallel which he described as a "front line in an

55. *New York Times,* June 11, 1950, p. 26.

56. Secretary Acheson, Interview, October 25, 1955.

57. Assistant Secretary Rusk, Interview, August 22, 1955.

58. *Ibid.*

59. John Foster Dulles, "The Korean Experiment in Representative Government," *Department of State Bulletin,* XXIII, No. 574 (July 3, 1950) p. 12.

actual shooting war." "There is constant fighting between the South Korean Army and bands that infiltrate the country from the North," he reported. "There are very real battles, involving perhaps one or two thousand men. When you go to this boundary, as I did, you go very well protected. You see troop movements, fortifications, and prisoners of war. And you can feel the tension."[60]

As a potential source of trouble, Korea had been included in intelligence studies that were conducted in connection with the preparation of NSC-68. Other potential danger spots that were studied included Finland, Berlin, Yugoslavia, and Iran. For the intelligence analysts there was a sense of growing tension in the international environment and even a "hunch" that something important was about to happen somewhere along the Soviet periphery. Yet the predominant conclusion of studies of Korea were that an all-out invasion was not then likely. The North Korean Communists were viewed as being under the direct control of the Soviet Union; North Korea was seen as having been transformed into "virtually a republic of the U.S.S.R."[61] Since it was generally believed that the Soviet Union was not prepared to engage the United States in general war, and since the Korean Communists were believed to be favored by a great subversive potential in the Republic of Korea it was considered that the latter would be favored as a technique for gaining power in South Korea rather than an all-out invasion.[62] In Asia it was considered that Communist expansion into Southeast Asia and invasion of Formosa were more likely immediate prospects.

In late June 1950 then, Korea was only one of the problems that confronted American policy makers as a result of the expanded

---

60. Philip C. Jessup, "Report to the American People on the Far East," *Department of State Bulletin*, XXII, No. 564 (April 24, 1950) p. 627.

61. Department of State, *North Korea: A Case Study in the Techniques of Takeover* (Washington: U.S. Department of State, 1961), p. 120.

62. Secretary Acheson later testified, "The view as generally held that since the Communists had far from exhausted the potentialities for gaining their objectives through guerrilla and psychological warfare, political pressure and intimidation, such means would probably continue to be used rather than overt military aggression." United States Senate, *Military Situation in the Far East*, Hearings Before the Committee on Armed Services and the Committee on Foreign Relations, 82nd Congress, 1st Session, to Conduct an Inquiry into the Relief of General of the Army Douglas MacArthur from His Assignments in that Area, Part III, p. 1991. Hereafter cited as *Hearings*, Part, and page.

American involvement in international affairs and the breakdown of Soviet-American collaboration after World War II. It was tucked down somewhere below the surface of crucial attention. It was subsumable under a broader view of the world such as President Truman had been called upon to express during a press conference on June 1 when he had been asked to give his reaction to the reported Gallup Poll finding that a majority of Americans expected war within five years. "He did not agree with the poll at all," it was reported in the style of the days in which it was forbidden to quite directly presidential remarks in press conferences. "He said this country was doing everything to avoid war and that the situation was better now than in five years." When a reporter rephrased the question to ask if the President thought the world was closer to peace than at any time since 1945, "Mr. Truman replied that he did." "In past references to the Gallup Poll," an observer noted, "Mr. Truman has been derisive, recalling its erroneous prediction of his defeat in 1948. Today, however, he referred to it with serious demeanor."[63]

Now, the Korean decision.

---

63. *New York Times*, June 2, 1950, p. 3.

PART III

NARRATIVE

CHAPTER 4

SATURDAY, JUNE 24

The President Leaves Washington

It was the morning of Saturday, June 24, 1950.

At about 11 A.M., Harry S. Truman, President of the United States, left the city of Washington on board the Presidential aircraft *Independence*, namesake of his home town in Missouri where he planned to spend a quiet weekend with his wife and daughter. But before the airplane turned westward to chase the sun across the American continent, the President had one last duty to perform in Baltimore, Maryland. He had promised to dedicate the new Friendship International Airport. When within minutes the plane returned to earth, the President received a welcoming ovation by

the assembled citizens of Baltimore and their guests. After the cere-
monial preliminaries, the President stepped to the microphone on
the speaker's platform and gave his dedicatory address. It was
devoted for the most part to the subject of federal financing of local
projects as exemplified by the construction of the airport. At the
end of his remarks, however, he directed the attention of his
listeners to the theme of world peace. He reminded them that the
magnificent air facility stretching out before their eyes was concrete proof of America's faith in a "peaceful future." If the American
people had not been animated by such a faith, he explained, they
would not have embarked upon such an elaborate commercial
undertaking. The President's final statement was, "I dedicate this
airport to the cause of peace in the world."[1] Soon afterward the
Independence was winging west, carrying the President home to
Missouri. He was scheduled to return to Washington on Monday.

Secretary Johnson and General Bradley Return from the Far East

While the President was leaving the Washington area, the Secretary of Defense, Louis A. Johnson, and the Chairman of the Joint
Chiefs of Staff, General Omar N. Bradley, were just returning from
a thirteen-day inspection tour of the Far East. As they deplaned at
approximately noon, reporters asked them about the results of their
trip: "Are the rumors true that the Department of Defense is going
to press for a change in the Administration's policy toward Formosa?" But neither the Secretary nor the General would comment
upon this or any other question. They said that they would not
discuss their tour until after they had reported to the President.
The only statement Secretary Johnson would make was, "We have
seen all our important commands in the Far East and I think we've
got the facts."[2] In connection with the return of the two key defense
officials, Senator Tom Connally, chairman of the Committee on
Foreign Relations, said that although the Far East was still the
most dangerous area in the worldwide conflict with Communism,
he felt that on the whole there had been a general lessening of

---

1. Carl Levin, *New York Herald Tribune,* June 26, 1950, p. 3.
2. *Washington Post,* June 25, 1950, p. 3.

international tension. He indicated that his assessment was based on private, diplomatic, and military reports.[3]

The North Koreans Attack

At 3 P.M. Eastern Daylight Time, while the President was still homeward bound in flight, the North Koreans struck. It was 4 A.M. Sunday, in Korea.[4] None but the Pyongyang leadership and their intimate advisers knew the exact strength and battle plans of the well-drilled forces which charged across the Thirty-eighth Parallel into the border defenses of the Republic of Korea. Only they knew that nearly 110,000 soldiers, over 1,400 artillery pieces, and 126 tanks were directly committed to the southward stab.[5] Only they knew that the First and Sixth divisions of the People's Army and the Third Constabulary Brigade would keep South Korean units pinned down on the Ongjin peninsula and in the Kaesong-Korangp'o area, while the main attacking force, consisting of the Third and Fourth divisions and the One Hundred Fifth Tank Division, would strike in the Uijongbu-Tongduch'on area—intent upon a blitzkrieg-type advance down the corridor to Seoul. Only they knew that while the Second and Twelfth divisions attacked in central Korea, other units and local guerrillas would be advancing down the east coast aided by amphibious landings from sailboats and motor launches beginning at 6 A.M. (5 P.M. Saturday, Washington time).

The Situation Unfolds in Seoul

In Seoul, capital of the Republic of Korea, the full extent of the military action then in progress along the Thirty-eighth Parallel was

---

3. *New York Times*, June 25, p. 18.

4. Korean time during this period was thirteen hours in advance of Eastern Daylight Time. All times in this and following chapters have been converted into Eastern Daylight Time except in a few instances where Korean time is clearly indicated in the text.

5. Kim Wonyong, "Chont'u kaehwang" (Battle Situation), in Military History Committee, Political Training Section, National Defense Ministry, Republic of Korea, *Hanguk chollan illyon chi* ("Korea in War, 1950-1951") (Seoul: 1951), pp. A32ff.

not immediately apparent. Less than 50 miles from the villages, rice fields, denuded hills, and muddy roads over which the northern legions swarmed, knowledge of the situation grew but gradually. United States Ambassador John J. Muccio received his first news of the attack shortly after 8 A.M.—about four hours after it had been launched—when he was called on the telephone at his residence by his chief deputy, E. F. Drumright.[6] "Brace yourself for a shock," Drumright warned, "the Communists are hitting all along the front!" Thus the American Ambassador learned of the onslaught about one and one-half hours after the Korean President had received the first news of the fighting at 6:30 A.M.[7] Ambassador Muccio told Mr. Drumright that he would meet him in the Embassy Chancery right away. The Ambassador later recalled that as he was enroute to the Chancery, a five-minute walk from his residence, he met United Press correspondent Jack E. James, who asked him why he was stirring so early on a Sunday morning. "I'm checking on a report I've received that the Communists are striking all along the Parallel," the Ambassador replied.[8]

This was not the first information about the attack that Mr. James had obtained. Having some work to do, and still unaware of the fighting, he had driven through the rain at about eight o'clock to the press room, located in the American Embassy building.[9] There was a mail story to finish and a report, written on his desk-pad, to be investigated. The gist of the mail story was to be "Despite a quickened propaganda campaign by North Koreans and their continuing threatening that zero hour would be on such and such a date, the best opinion did not believe there would be any invasion at least before the Fall." The report to be checked was that the North Koreans would invade the South on June 25. He had checked this report with an Army Intelligence officer some-time after midnight, Saturday, but had received a "negative re-

6. Ambassador Muccio, Letter, June 20, 1957.

7. Robert T. Oliver, *Syngman Rhee: The Man Behind the Myth*, (New York: Dodd Mead and Company, 1954), pp. 300-01.

8. Ambassador Muccio, Letter, June 20, 1957.

9. The following account of how Mr. James obtained a "world beat" on the North Korean invasion is based mainly upon the account given by him in *Editor and Publisher*, July 22, 1950, p. 10.

ply." Nevertheless, he had made a note to check again later in the morning. "We had heard the North Koreans cry 'Wolf' so many times," Mr. James recalled, "that none of us took it really seriously when we heard the real one."

Parking his jeep at the curb, he dashed through the rain to the entrance of the Embassy just as a friend of his—a military intelligence officer—was hurriedly leaving the building.

"What do you hear from the border?" the officer asked.

"Not very much yet," Mr. James replied. "What do you hear?"

"Hell, they're supposed to have crossed everywhere except in the Eighth Division Area," the officer explained.

"That's more than I've heard," admitted Mr. James as he bolted for the press room to start telephoning his contacts in an attempt to confirm the story.

For more than an hour and a half, Mr. James tried in every possible way to determine the nature of the reported attack. He telephoned Embassy officials for reports from their own sources; he alerted an Embassy public affairs officer, asking him to check the most recent monitor reports of Pyongyang radio broadcasts for information about the fighting—there were as yet "no references to war." He drove to ROK Army headquarters to learn what he could there. "First reports were spotty, and difficult to pin down," he recalled. "Most of them were police reports which usually are extremely exaggerated."

Returning to the Embassy, he kept close to the military specialists. When one of them said, "I think we'd better let Washington know about this," Mr. James responded, "If it's good enough for you to file, it's good enough for me."[10]

At about 9:50 A.M. (8:50 P.M. Saturday in Washington), he quickly drafted an "urgent" press cable; it would be costly, but would receive the most rapid handling by his news organization. Moments later, by jeep he had covered the short three blocks to the international cable facilities of the Ministry of Communications, in the center of Seoul. As the operator there typed out Mr. James' cable, it was received almost simultaneously in San Fran-

---

10. Jack E. James, Letter, October 18, 1963.

cisco where it was relayed automatically to United Press headquarters in New York.[11]

"Rather than start a war where there was not one," Mr. James
had handled the reported attack cautiously, holding the report
until he had obtained reasonable confirmation. He appended to the
main body of his cable item a precautionary note that information was still "fragmentary." He warned his colleagues on the
UP cables desk in New York that "they should not beat the drums
too hard on the story." "However, I sent the message at urgent
rates," he later recalled, "which was an indication that I felt it
was extremely important."[12] At 10:30 A.M. (forty minutes after his
first dispatch), on the basis of further confirming evidence, Mr.
James filed a second report "without qualifications."

Moments after his early morning encounter with Mr. James,
Ambassador Muccio reached the Chancery and learned that Mr.
Drumright had received several reports of fighting along the
border from Korean Military Advisory Group headquarters, begin-
ning at about seven o'clock. These messages had been relayed from
KMAG liaison officers who were with Korean units in the field.
Since there had been constant skirmishes along the Parallel during
the past two years, it was important to determine whether the
reports indicated just another border clash or something different.
Thus Mr. Drumright had checked them for about an hour before
alerting the Ambassador. After studying all available information
Ambassador Muccio drafted his first official cable on the situation
for transmission to Washington. The report consisted of two para-
graphs the wording of which was "crucial."[13] The intent of the
first paragraph was to convey the factual information which was
available to him at the time of drafting; the second paragraph,
consisting of a single sentence, stated his appraisal of the available
information.[14]

Ambassador Muccio's cable was dispatched at about 9:30 A.M.

---

11. The speed of world news transmission at that time is shown by the fact
that the cable returned to Seoul at 11 A.M. (one hour and ten minutes after drafting), via the UPI world distribution network. It had gone from New Work to
Tangier where it was morsecast to Manila and relayed back to Seoul. The UPI
report thus was published in Seoul's Sunday newspapers.

12. Jack E. James, Letter, October 18, 1963.

13. Ambassador Muccio, Letter, June 20, 1957.

14. See p. 91 following for the complete text of this cable.

Sunday, Korean time (i.e., about 8:30 P.M. Saturday in Washington). It was transmitted over the official circuits of the American Mission in Korea which tied in at Tokyo with Washington.[15] At about the same time the Military Attache of the Embassy submitted his first report on the fighting to the Assistant Chief of Staff G-2 (Intelligence), Department of the Army, in Washington.[16] Copies of the Ambassador's message and of all subsequent reports emanating from the Embassy were sent simultaneously to the headquarters of General Douglas MacArthur, the American military commander in the Far East and Supreme Commander for the Allied Powers, in Tokyo.

Uncertainty about the nature and weight of the attack and optimism about the ability of the South Korean Army to repel it characterized the reactions of other officials in Korea to the first reports of fighting along the Parallel. Major Walter Greenwood, Jr., KMAG Deputy Chief of Staff, first learned of the attack at 5:30 A.M.[17] He did not feel sure until three hours later that the North Koreans had launched an attempt to invade the Republic whose army he had helped to train. By noon (11 P.M. Saturday, Washington time)—some eight hours after the attack began—both the operations and intelligence officers of KMAG were agreed that a full-scale invasion was on.[18] Mr. John C. Caldwell, deputy director of the United States Information Service, at home in Seoul, was alerted to the invasion attempt in a telephone call from a friend about noon. Although his friend's first thought was to escape with his family to Pusan, Mr. Caldwell later recalled that "nothing but optimism prevailed among the Koreans and optimism was the official tone of the American Embassy."[19] One of the apparent bases of this optimism, aside from earlier estimates of

15. There were two other major channels of communication out of Korea during the summer of 1950: regular commercial radiotelegraph facilities and international radiotelephone circuits. These were open only for limited periods each day.

16. Roy E. Appleman, "The United States and the United Nations Intervene in Korea," MSS, Chapter IV of *Korean Combat History*, Vol. I, in preparation by the Office of the Chief of Military History, Department of the Army.

17. Keyes Beech, *Tokyo and Points East* (Garden City: Doubleday and Company, 1954), p. 11.

18. Appleman, "The U.S. and the U.N. Intervene in Korea," p. 3.

19. According to Mr. Caldwell, this optimism persisted for "many" of the hours preceding the capture of Seoul on Wednesday, Korean time. John C. Caldwell, *The Korea Story* (Chicago: Henry Regnery Company, 1952), p. 166.

the capabilities of the opposing armies, was the reported strength of the attackers. Sometime on Sunday, Korean time, Major General Ch'oe Pyongdok, chief of staff of the Republic of Korea (ROK) Army, reported that the invasion force consisted of from forty to fifty thousand ground troops and 94 tanks.[20]

The timing of the attack had taken both Korean and American military leaders by surprise. About one third of the ROK Army was on leave and most of the KMAG advisers were spending the weekend in Seoul. Brigadier General William L. Roberts, until recently commander of KMAG, had just embarked on a transport from Yokohama, Japan, enroute to reassignment in the United States. The acting chief of KMAG, Colonel W. H. Sterling Wright, chief of staff, was in Tokyo, after seeing his wife off for the United States aboard the same ship. Colonel Wright expected to follow her within a few days.[21] The chief of the ROK Navy, Admiral Son Wonil, and the deputy chief of staff of the ROK Army, Brigadier General Chong Ilgwon, were enjoying an aloha party in Honolulu, Hawaii, after having effected the transfer of some converted PC boats from the United States Navy to the ROK naval forces.[22]

The Situation Unfolds in Tokyo

The slow unfolding of the military situation in Korea to officials in Seoul was paralleled by the gradual revelation of the seriousness of the conflict to American military leaders in Japan. Officials in Tokyo had three main sources of information on the fighting: The American Embassy in Seoul, KMAG, and the Air Force officers who were assisting Northwest Airlines in the operation of Kimpo Airfield. Major General Edward M. Almond, General MacArthur's chief of staff, had gone to his Tokyo office in the Daiichi Building early Sunday morning (Saturday evening, Washington time) to complete some work that had been postponed because of the past

---

20. National Defense Ministry, Republic of Korea, *Hanguk chollan illyon chi* ("Korea in War, 1950-1951"), p. B11.

21. Colonel Wright returned to Korea on Monday. Appleman, "The U.S. and the U.N. Intervene in Korea," p. 21.

22. *New York Times*, June 26, 1950, p. 5.

week's conferences with Secretary Johnson and General Bradley.[23] He had been in his office for about twenty minutes when he received a report from KMAG that there had been a "border incident" on the Ongjin peninsula. About thirty minutes later he received a similar message. Within the next three hours he received five more reports of fighting stretching roughly all across the Thirty-eighth Parallel. Only when it had become apparent that the North Koreans had launched an attack in "great force" did one of the duty officers at General Headquarters telephone General MacArthur in his American Embassy bedroom.[24] The first report of the North Korean attack reached the headquarters of the Far East Air Forces (FEAF) in Tokyo at 9:45 A.M. and was relayed to all subordinate units. It was not possible to inform acting FEAF commander, Major General Earle M. Partridge, until 11:30 A.M.[25]

Author John Gunther, who was on a Sunday morning sightseeing excursion with a key member of General MacArthur's staff, subsequently reported that up until noon (11 P.M. Saturday, in Washington) the Korean conflict had been characterized by American officers in Japan as an "incident."[26] By 3 P.M. (2 A.M., Sunday, in Washington), however, top Army and Air Force officers in Tokyo who had been comparing notes on the basis of their own sources of information since mid-morning had concluded that the attack represented something far more grave than a border skirmish.[27] Important indicators were the loss of Kangnung at 9 A.M., and amphibious landings south of Kangnung.[28] But more than twenty-four hours after the attack began, Major General William F. Dean, commander of the Twenty-fourth Infantry Division—encouraged by reports of a South Korean counterattack—thought

23. U.S. Senate, Committee on the Judiciary, *Interlocking Subversion in Government Departments*, 83rd Congress, 2nd Sess., (1954) Part XXV, 2059.

24. Courtney Whitney, *MacArthur: His Rendezvous with History* (New York: Alfred A. Knopf, 1956), p. 315. Marguerite Higgins, *War in Korea* (Garden City: Doubleday and Company, 1951), p. 15.

25. Robert Frank Futrell, *The United States Air Force in Korea* (New York: Duell, Sloan and Pearce, 1961), p. 8.

26. John Gunther, *The Riddle of MacArthur* (New York: Harper and Brothers, 1951), p. 166.

27. Appleman, "The U.S. and the U.N. Intervene in Korea," p. 2.

28. Futrell, p. 8.

that "perhaps this would turn out to be only a slightly larger version of the many border incidents that had occurred since the Thirty-eighth Parallel had been established as a dividing line across Korea."[29]

The First News of the Fighting Reaches Washington

No inkling of the attack upon the Republic of Korea reached officials in the United States until about seven hours after the first blows had been struck. Then it came as an unconfirmed news flash. At 9:04 p.m. Saturday in Washington, W. Bradley Connors, public affairs officer of the State Department's Bureau of Far Eastern Affairs, received a telephone call at his home from Mr. Donald Gonzales of the United Press, requesting confirmation of a dispatch that had just been filed by Seoul correspondent Jack James.[30] At the same time, United Press was seeking similar confirmation from the chief watch officer at the State Department, Mr. Frank Duvall. Mr. James had cabled:

URGENT PRESS UNIPRESS NEWYORK
25095 JAMES FRAGMENTARY REPORTS EXTHIRTY EIGHTH PARALLEL INDICATED NORTH KOREANS LAUNCHED SUNDAY MORNING ATTACKS GENERALLY ALONG ENTIRE BORDER PARA REPORTS AT ZERO NINETHIRTY LOCAL TIME INDICATED KAESONG FORTY MILES NORTHWEST SEOUL AND HEADQUARTERS OF KOREAN ARMYS FIRST DIVISION FELL NINE AYEM STOP ENEMY FORCES REPORTED THREE TO FOUR KILOMETERS SOUTH OF BORDER ON ONGJIN PENINSULA STOP TANKS SUPPOSED BROUGHT INTO USE CHUNCHON FIFTY MILES NORTHEAST SEOUL STOP LANDING EXSEA ALSO REPORTED FROM TWENTY SMALL BOATS BELOW KANGNUNG ON EASTERN COAST WHERE REPORTEDLY OFFCUT HIGHWAY ENDITEM NOTE SHOULD STRESSED THIS STILL FRAGMENTARY AND PICTURE VAGUE SYET JAMES[31]

29. William F. Dean (as told to William L. Worden), *General Dean's Story* (New York: The Viking Press, 1954), p. 14.

30. Based on the Special Collection of Materials on the Korean Decision in the Historical Office, Department of State; hereafter cited as SCDS.

31. Original copy in files of Jack E. James. The United Press system was to number each day's cables with the day of the month and the hour, broken up into

"Was this report true?" the State Department officials were asked. No one knew.

Mr. Connors soon reached by telephone the Assistant Secretary of State for Far Eastern Affairs, Dean Rusk, who was at dinner that evening in Georgetown, District of Columbia, at the home of the nationally known journalist Joseph Alsop.[32] Upon learning of the press report from Korea, Secretary Rusk asked Mr. Connors to send an immediate inquiry to Ambassador Muccio, and said that in the meantime he would be going straight to the State Department. Mr. Connors attempted to establish telephone contact with the Embassy in Seoul, but found to his dismay that the radiotelephone circuits to Korea had closed at nine o'clock. He then began to prepare a cable which could be transmitted by radiotelegraph.

Another guest at the Alsops' dinner party that evening was the Secretary of the Army, Frank Pace, Jr. Thus he received his first warning of the attack at the same time as Secretary Rusk. Together with the State Department official, Mr. Pace excused himself from the gathering and hastened to his office at the Pentagon. After alerting the staff in the huge nerve center of the nation's military affairs, he telephoned Secretary of Defense Johnson at home.

The Defense Secretary had heard the surprising news when a member of his staff had telephoned him a few minutes earlier. Secretary Johnson's surprise had been accentuated by the fact that in the intelligence briefings which he had just attended throughout the Far East, there had been no indication that a North Korean Communist assault was imminent.[33] During the earlier conversation, he had issued an order that all incoming information concerning the situation in Korea should be directed to Secretary Pace. When Mr. Pace called, the Secretary of Defense told him that he was delegating to him temporary responsibility for acting for the Defense Department in the matter. Secretary Johnson had decided to do this because the Army had a primacy of

---

ten-minute intervals. Thus, 25095 indicates that the cable was written at about 9:50 A.M. on June 25.

32. Albert L. Warner, "How the Korea Decision Was Made," *Harpers,* CCII (June 1951), p. 99.

33. *Hearings,* Part IV, 2572.

interest in Korea growing out of the presence of KMAG, and because the top military commander in the Far East, General Mac-
Arthur, was an Army officer.[34] The Secretary of Defense later
recalled that as the night progressed he engaged in a number of
other telephone conversations, but that since there was very little
to go on he finally went back to bed for much needed rest after his
long journey home from Japan.[35]

Ambassador Muccio's Official Report Is Received

At 9:26 P.M., approximately two hours after it had been drafted
in Seoul,[36] Ambassador Muccio's first report on the Korean fighting
reached the Department of State.[37] Shortly after the cable arrived,
Mr. Lincoln White, the Department's press officer, announced to
reporters that a telegram had arrived from the American Ambassador in Korea, that it presumably dealt with the fighting, but
that it had not yet been decoded. The reporters attempted to get
further information from the Korean Embassy but were told there
that no official notification of the attack had been received.[38]

At about ten o'clock, while Ambassador Muccio's cable was still
being decoded, Mr. Connors, now at the State Department, dispatched his request to Seoul for confirmation of the United Press
reports. At 10:15 P.M., the chief watch officer delivered the clear
text of Ambassador Muccio's report to Mr. Connors and to Mr.
White in the latter's office.[39] The report was relayed to the Department of the Army within the next fifteen minutes, and two copies
of it were sent to the White House at eleven o'clock.

Key Officials Gather at the State Department

At half-past ten o'clock, Assistant Secretary for Far Eastern
Affairs Rusk and Secretary of the Army Pace met at the State

---

34. Secretary Johnson, Interview, October 27, 1955.
35. *Hearings*, Part IV, 2572.
36. Ambassador Muccio, Letter, June 20, 1957.
37. Department of State, *United States Policy in the Korean Crisis*, Far Eastern Series, No. 34 (Washington: Government Printing Office, 1950), p. 1.
38. *New York Times*, June 25, 1950, p. 20.
39. Based on SCDS.

Department.[40] Assistant Secretary Rusk immediately telephoned Secretary Acheson who was at his farm in Sandy Spring, Maryland, not far from Washington, and read him the text of Ambassador Muccio's cable:

> SEOUL, June 25, 1950
> According to Korean Army reports which are partly confirmed by Korean Military Advisory Group field adviser reports, North Korean Forces invaded Republic of Korea territory at several points this morning. Action was initiated about 4 A.M. Ongjin was blasted by North Korean artillery fire. About 6 A.M. North Korean infantry commenced crossing the (38th) parallel in the Ongjin area, Kaesong area, and Chunchon area, and an amphibious landing reportedly was made south of Kangnung on the east coast. Kaesong was reportedly captured at 9 A.M. with some ten North Korean tanks participating in the operation. North Korean forces, spearheaded by tanks, are reportedly closing in on Chunchon. Details of the fighting in the Kangnung area are unclear, although it seems that North Korean forces have cut the highway. I am conferring with Korean Military Advisory Group advisers and Korean officials this morning concerning the situation.
>
> It would appear from the nature of the attack and the manner in which it was launched that it constitutes an all-out offensive against the Republic of Korea.   MUCCIO[41]

Assistant Secretary Rusk's telephone call to the Secretary of State at this time was purely informational in nature; no recommendations were made or agreed upon.[42] Virtually everything that was known about the fighting in Korea was contained in the cable from Seoul. The fact that Ambassador Muccio had submitted the report was considered to be significant for evaluating its contents.[43] The Ambassador had the reputation of being a cautious and careful observer; since he had concluded that apparently an "all-out offensive" was in progress, the very least that one could say was that a "considerable fracas" was taking place in Korea—not just another minor border clash. Thus the two officials agreed that

---

40. Based on SCDS.
41. Department of State, *United States Policy in the Korean Crisis*, p. 1.
42. Assistant Secretary Rusk, Interview, August 22, 1955.
43. *Ibid.*

an attack had apparently come in force and that the situation was "serious."[44]

At about 10:45 P.M., the Assistant Secretary of State for United Nations Affairs, John D. Hickerson, joined Secretaries Rusk and Pace. He had received an urgent summons to appear at the Department but had not been told the nature of the emergency. Now he knew. A few minutes earlier, as his taxi was speeding through Washington's Rock Creek Park, he had come to the conclusion that the Chinese Communists probably had launched their long-anticipated invasion of Formosa.[45] After reading Ambassador Muccio's report and discussing the situation briefly with the two high officials at the Department, Assistant Secretary Hickerson also conferred by telephone with the Secretary of State.

"What are your suggestions?" asked Secretary Acheson.[46] Mr. Hickerson replied that both he and Assistant Secretary Rusk[47] thought that as a general policy the United States should react to the attack through the United Nations. They suggested that the United States bring the matter to the attention of the Security Council in emergency session. Since it was a weekend there might be some delay in mobilizing the United Nations Secretariat; therefore they recommended that the Secretary-General be alerted immediately to the possibility that the United States might call for an extraordinary meeting of the Council. Mr. Hickerson added that he, Mr. Rusk, and other officials who were expected to arrive at the Department would remain at work throughout the night, continuing to gather information from the Embassy in Seoul, from KMAG, from the Department of Defense, and from the press. These suggestions sounded reasonable to the Secretary of State.[48]

While approving the preliminary moves required to alert the United Nations Secretariat, Mr. Acheson further instructed the

44. Secretary Acheson, Interview, October 25, 1955.

45. Assistant Secretary Hickerson, Interview, November 6, 1958.

46. Secretary Acheson, Interview, October 25, 1955.

47. Mr. Rusk had served as Assistant Director of the Office of International Security Affairs in 1946, as Director of the Office of the United Nations Affairs in 1947, as an alternative delegate to the United Nations General Assembly in 1948, and as the first Assistant Secretary of State for United Nations Affairs from 1949 to the spring of 1950.

48. Secretary Acheson, Interview, October 25, 1955.

group at the Department to work closely with the Pentagon in assessing the North Korean attack and its implications. It was understood that although none was contemplated, the group at the State Department would make no further commitment until more information became available and a more specific course of action had been worked out for approval by the President.

Secretary Acheson and President Truman Confer by Telephone

At 11:20 P.M. Secretary Acheson telephoned the President,[49] who received the call in the library of his Independence, Missouri, home. "Mr. President, I have very serious news. The North Koreans have invaded South Korea," reported Mr. Acheson.[50] He explained the situation as it appeared from Ambassador Muccio's cable and news dispatches. The President's first thought was that he should return to Washington at once, but Mr. Acheson assured him that since there was so little information to go on there was no need to make a hasty journey back to the capital in the middle of the night. Mr. Acheson then suggested the possibility of calling for an emergency meeting of the Security Council and said he had already authorized some preliminary moves in that direction which could be canceled, however, if the President so desired.[51] Mr. Truman was in complete agreement with the recommendation to bring the invasion before the United Nations. It was understood that the Secretary should call again to submit the details of that action to him for final approval.

Since it was his belief that Secretary Johnson was still absent from Washington on his inspection tour of the Far East, Mr. Acheson further recommended that the President authorize the Secretary of State to assume major responsibility for dealing with the situation.[52] The President agreed. Mr. Acheson then telephoned Mr. Hickerson at the State Department and informed him that the

49. Based on SCDS.
50. *Memoirs*, II, 332.
51. Secretary Acheson, Interview, September 24, 1957.
52. Based on notes of a conference of former officials of the Truman Administration, held at the Institute of Advanced Study, Princeton, N.J., in 1953-54 to review major problems that had faced them in office. Hereafter cited as "Princeton conference."

President approved taking action preliminary to the submission of a formal request for a meeting of the Security Council.[53]

By half-past eleven, the group at the State Department had been joined by two more top officials: Deputy Under Secretary of State H. Freeman Matthews, liaison officer with the Defense Department, and Ambassador-at-large Philip C. Jessup. Other important members of the State Department who had arrived by this time were Theodore Achilles, director of the Office of Western European Affairs; David Wainhouse, deputy director of the Office of United Nations Political and Security Affairs; and Miss Ruth Bacon of the Bureau of Far Eastern Affairs.[54] Before the night was over, a full operating staff was on duty in the bureau of Far Eastern Affairs[55]—including Niles Bond, a foreign service officer specializing in Korean affairs.[56] Also at work were five members of the Office of United Nations Political and Security Affairs.[57]

Sometime before midnight, the Ambassador of the Republic of Korea, John M. Chang, visited the Department of State. After conferring with Secretary Rusk for twenty minutes he told reporters, "I don't think the United States will abandon us at all."[58] Explaining that the invasion was "decidedly an aggressive act," Ambassador Chang declared: "They [the North Koreans] are the ones who crossed the border and started all the trouble. This could not have been done without Soviet direction."[59] Mr. Rusk also discussed the situation with newsmen, telling them that the Department had received an official report of heavy fighting in Korea and that he was keeping the Secretary of State fully informed. The press representatives who had rushed to the Department saw

---

53. Secretary Acheson, Interview, September 24, 1957.
54. Based on SCDS.
55. Dean G. Acheson (McGeorge Bundy, ed.), *The Pattern of Responsibility* (Boston: Houghton Mifflin, 1952), p. 246.
56. *Chicago Tribune*, June 25, 1950, p. 2.
57. Testimony of Assistant Secretary of State Hickerson in U.S. Senate, Appropriations Committee, *Appropriations for the Departments of State, Justice, Commerce, and the Judiciary for the Fiscal Year Ending June 30, 1952*, 82nd Congress, 1st Sess., Part I, 1087. By Sunday morning nearly the entire thirty-man staff was on duty.
58. *Washington Star,* June 25, 1950, p. 1.
59. *Chicago Tribune,* June 25, 1950, p. 2.

no indication that the United States planned to undertake direct military action against the attackers.[60]

Preliminary Steps Are Taken to Alert United Nations Secetariat

Shortly after 11:30 P.M. Assistant Secretary Hickerson telephoned the home of the Deputy United States Representative to the United Nations, Ernest A. Gross, in Manhasset, New York. The chief American delegate, Ambassador Warren R. Austin, was vacationing at his home in Vermont. Failing to contact Ambassador Gross, who had not yet returned from a dinner engagement in Port Washington, New York, Mr. Hickerson telephoned the home of the Secretary-General of the United Nations, Trygve Lie.

"My God, Jack," exclaimed Mr. Lie on learning the news, "that's a violation of the United Nations Charter!"[61] Mr. Hickerson told him about the report received from Ambassador Muccio. Mr. Lie concluded that the information concerning the fighting in Korea seemed to indicate "much more than a border skirmish."[62] Since the North Korean attack appeared to be a blatant act of aggression, Mr. Lie considered bringing it to the attention of the Security Council on his own initiative under the provisions of Article 99 which states: "The Secretary-General may bring to the attention of the Security Council any matter which in his opinion may threaten the maintenance of international peace and security." He felt, however, that he could do this only on the basis of a report from the United Nations Commission on Korea. Accordingly, after Mr. Hickerson's call, he cabled a request for full information from the United Nations observers on the scene in Korea.[63] Assistant Secretary Hickerson had also explained to Mr. Lie that the United States—through Ambassador Gross—would probably call for a meeting of the Security Council within hours, the American request to be addressed to the President of the Security Council,

60. *New York Times*, June 25, 1950, p. 20.

61. Assistant Secretary Hickerson, Interview, November 6, 1958.

62. Trygve Lie, *In the Cause of Peace* (New York: The Macmillan Company, 1954), p. 327.

63. U.N. Security Council, Fifth Year, *Official Records*, No. 15, 473rd Meeting (June 25, 1950), p. 3.

Sir Benegal N. Rau of India, who alone had the authority to invoke the emergency session.

After conferring with Secretary-General Lie, Mr. Hickerson succeeded in contacting Ambassador Gross. He asked him to return home and await further orders. When Ambassador Gross arrived in Manhasset, he immediately telephoned Mr. Lie, reviewed the situation with him, and discussed the various measures which might be taken in the Security Council. As they completed their conversation, the Ambassador told the Secretary-General that he would call again as soon as he had received further instructions from Washington.[64]

Calculations at the Department of State

At the State Department, Saturday became Sunday as the group of officials who had hastily gathered there worked out the American response to the North Korean onslaught. The information from the fighting front along the Thirty-eighth Parallel was "fragmentary";[65] neither the ultimate intentions of the attackers nor the extent of their immediate gains were clear.[66] The kind of information available in Washington at this time is suggested by the content of the second cable sent by United Press correspondent Jack James only forty minutes after his original dispatch:

PRESS UNIPRESS NEWYORK
25103 JAMES ADD 25095 REPORTS SAID ATTACKS
LAUNCHED IN HEAVY RAIN AFTER MORTAR ARTILLERY
BARRAGES WHICH BEGAN FOUR AYEM SUNDAY MORN-
ING STOP KAESONG WHICH LIES PRACTICALLY ON PAR-
ALLEL ONLY MAJOR CITY REPORTED TAKEN STOP TANKS
SUPPOSEDLY BROUGHT INTO PLAY THERE PARA KAE-
SONG ABOUT FIFTY MILES ALONG ONE KOREAS BEST
ROADS FROM SEOUL STOP MILITARYERS HERE HOW-
EVER SAID NORTHERN FORCES COULD PROBABLY
STOPPED AT IMJIN RIVER WHICH CAN CROSSED BY VE-
HICLES EITHER ALONG SINGLE RAILWAY BRIDGE OR BY

---

64. Lie, p. 328.
65. Secretary Pace, Letter, September 18, 1959.
66. Secretary Pace, Interview, October 24, 1955.

HANDPOWER FERRY PARA THERE APPARENTLY NONO
ACTION DIRECTLY NORTH SEOUL AT CHOSONGNI WHICH
PROVIDES SHORTEST ROUTE FOR INVASION SUDKOREAN
CAPITAL AND IS ONE OF TRADITIONAL ROUTES
THROUGHOUT KOREAN HISTORY STOP THERE SOME
OPINION HERE THAT ATTACKS WHICH BEEN HEAVIEST
IN EAST AND WESTERN PORTIONS OF PENINSULA MIGHT
BE FEINTS DESIGNED DRAW SUDKOREAN STRENGTH
AWAY FROM THIS ROUTE PARA NORTH KOREAS SUPE-
RIOR AIRFORCE NOTNOT USED STOP WEATHER TOO
BAD IF USE INTENDED PARA OBSERVERS SEOUL SAY
MAJOR ATTACK THIS TIME NOTNOT IN NORTHS FAVOR
STOP RAINY SEASONS JUST BEGINNING RICE PADDYS
ARE FULL WATER ROADS CAN BECOME MORASS MAKING
TRANSPORT SUPPLY AND OPERATIONS OF TANKS AND
AIRFORCE DIFFICULT TO IMPOSSIBLE PARA STILL NOT-
NOT CERTAIN WHAT SCOPE OR STRENGTH OF ATTACKS
ARE BUT ONE OFFICER SAID QUOTE THIS LOOKS LIKE
REAL THING UNQUOTE PARA THERE BEEN NONO UN-
USUAL ACTIVITY REPORTED RECENTLY FROM NORTH
OF PARALLEL REGARDING TROOP MOVEMENTS OR CON-
CENTRATIONS SUPPLYS WHICH WOULD INDICATE
MAJOR ATTACK STARTING HOWEVER ENDS JAMES

Yet there was little doubt in the minds of these officials that
the North Koreans, in a "calculated act of aggression," had
launched a military operation of considerable scope. A rough first
estimate of the defensive capabilities of the ROK Army which the
officials shared was that it could hold its own unless Soviet forces
were actively supporting the invaders.[67] If the invasion really
were serious, they had no doubt but that it was a Soviet-directed
operation—whether Soviet troops directly participated or not. "It
was fully realized," Secretary Acheson later explained, "that the
timing of any move in Korea would be ordered from the Kremlin."[68] But at the moment Soviet intentions were "fuzzy."[69] Ambassador Jessup's first assessment of the attack was that it was a So-

---

67. This view was expressed publicly on Sunday afternoon by Secretary Johnson. Bert Andrews, New York Herald Tribune, June 26, 1950, p. 4.

68. Hearings, Part III, 1991.

69. Assistant Secretary Rusk, Interview, August 22, 1955.

viet "probing action." He readily recalled that State Department experts on the Soviet Union often referred to Lenin's dictum that when one is bayonetting and strikes concrete he should withdraw; but if he strikes a soft belly, he should continue the thrust.[70]

The officials also shared a strong sense of the emergency of the situation—the need to do something and to do it without delay. The North Korean invasion had caught them by surprise.[71] There was no "position paper" that dealt with the present crisis and that could be employed as a basis for policy determination.[72] It had been previously decided that Korea would not be of strategic importance to the United States in the event of a global war, but the question of what the American response should be if the Republic of Korea became the victim of aggression in the absence of a general conflagration hitherto had not been answered.[73]

Despite the absence of a predetermined plan, the officials at the State Department, the President, and the Secretary of State had all agreed immediately that the correct initial response to the North Korean invasion should be to bring it to the attention of the United Nations. In fact, this appeared to be the only reasonable course of action.[74] There is no evidence that they considered any

---

70. Ambassador Jessup, Interview, July 28, 1955.

71. All the officials interviewed were in unanimous agreement on this point. One later explained in a letter to the author: "The question of the intelligence warnings on Korea has been complicated by politics of bureaucracy. Our intelligence agencies were frightened by the Roberts Commission which investigated Pearl Harbor and have gotten into the habit of warning about everything all the time. The result is useless to policy makers because a large percentage of their warnings turn out to mean nothing. During the week of the attack nothing was called to the attention of the policy makers pointing a finger toward Korea. It would be interesting to know where key intelligence officers were on the weekend of the attack, to ascertain whether they were sufficiently impressed by their own warnings to be on any special duty."

72. KMAG, of course, had worked out a defense plan with the ROK Ministry of National Defense. Secretary Pace, Interview, October 24, 1955.

73. This distinction was clarified by Secretary Rusk, Interview, August 22, 1955; and by Counselor Kennan, Interview, August 1, 1955.

74. This was the view of all officials concerned with the decision to respond within the framework of the United Nations. This view was not shared by Counselor George F. Kennan who did not participate in it. He was spending the weekend at his farm (80 miles from Washington) which had no telephone; he did not learn of the invasion until he returned to the capital late Sunday afternoon. Counselor Kennan, Interview, August 1, 1955.

other alternative for meeting the crisis facing them, including that of doing nothing. Since the United States had previously dealt with the Korean problem within the United Nations and since the very government under assault had come into being under United Nations supervision, the policy makers thought that it was only "natural" that the attack should be met within the United Nations framework. Secretary Pace, for example, considered it to be "the only logical course."[75] Furthermore, they felt an "obligation" to do so—an obligation stemming from the ideal of collective security and the desire to strengthen the United Nations as an instrument of peace. As Secretary Acheson explained a few days later, ". . . It was the view of the President and of the entire Government of the United States that our first responsibility was to report this to the United Nations."[76]

According to Assistant Secretary Rusk—although no one was relying on it—there was some faint hope that the North Koreans might be induced to withdraw by a Security Council resolution if their invasion attempt were not a major one.[77] "We knew they wouldn't do it, but you go through that procedure," was the later explanation of Assistant Secretary Hickerson.[78]

Whatever the North Koreans did, the United States would be serving notice to the world of the grave view it took of the situation and would be putting the moral force of the United Nations behind the American position.[79] Moreover, the move to bring the North Korean invasion before the Security Council would be working toward achieving a collective response to it—a mode of response which was immediately considered to be far more preferable than unilateral American action.[80] Furthermore, the decision to call for an emergency meeting of the Security Council would not prejudice the alternatives for action that might

75. Secretary Pace, Interview, October 24, 1955.

76. *New York Times,* June 29, 1950, p. 10.

77. Assistant Secretary Rusk, Interview, August 22, 1955.

78. Senate Appropriations Committee, *Appropriations for the Departments of State, Justice, Commerce, and the Judiciary for the Fiscal Year Ending June 30, 1952,* 82nd Congress, 1st Sess., Part I, 1087.

79. Interviews, Assistant Secretary Rusk, August 22, 1955; Secretary Pace, October 24, 1955.

80. Ambassador Jessup, Interview, July 28, 1955.

develop in the future.[81] Normal diplomatic techniques and procedures, including consultation with major American allies, could still be employed. While American officials waited for further information on the military situation in Korea, flexibility of action would still be preserved. If the situation were less serious than it appeared, or if it rapidly improved, no further commitment might be needed. If, however, the situation were much more grave than it seemed, or if it rapidly deteriorated, the resolution which the United States would place before the Security Council would be a necessary preliminary for any further commitment that might be made.

As summarized later by Ambassador Jessup, the calculations of those American officials in Washington who first reacted to the North Korean assault were, "We've got to do something, and whatever we do, we've got to do it through the United Nations."[82]

Thus the officials at the State Department whom crisis had called to duty on a summer Saturday evening worked on drafting a request for an emergency meeting of the Security Council, a resolution that Ambassador Gross would introduce, and an accompanying statement that he would make.

81. Interviews, Secretary Pace, October 24, 1955; Assistant Secretary Rusk, August 22, 1955.

82. Ambassador Jessup, Interview, July 28, 1955.

CHAPTER 5

SUNDAY, JUNE 25

The President Gives Final Approval to a Request
for an Emergency Meeting of The Security Council

At two o'clock on Sunday morning Secretary Acheson again telephoned President Truman.[1] He reported that the fighting in Korea still seemed serious but that in his opinion the situation was not grave enough to warrant the President's immediate return to Washington. He informed the President that all was in readiness for taking the United Nations action that they had discussed previously. The group at the State Department had drafted an outline of a resolution which charged the North Koreans with a "breach

---

1. Secretary Rusk, Interview, August 22, 1955. Warner, p. 100. The President recalled only the earlier conversation with Mr. Acheson.

of the peace" and an "act of aggression" and asked the Security
Council to take action to end the fighting. The United Nations
Secretariat had been alerted. All that was needed to set the planned
action in motion was the final approval of the President. He gave it.

The Secretary of State immediately contacted Assistant Secretary Hickerson at the State Department, telling him to go ahead
with the projected meeting of the Security Council. Mr. Acheson
added that he would come back to Washington later in the
morning. The group at the Department hastened to implement the
decision that had been taken on the basis of Ambassador Muccio's
first report. A second communication from him had been received
at 11:47 P.M., but it "contained no new details."[2] A final draft of the
request for the meeting was cleared for transmission to the United
States Mission to the United Nations. A circular telegram was dispatched to American missions in Security Council member states
instructing them to request that the governments to which they
were accredited give immediate instructions to their respective dele-
gations at Lake Success. The American Embassy in Seoul was informed of the action about to be taken by the United States and
was instructed to continue the submission of the fullest possible
reports on further developments.

Ambassador Gross Officially Notifies Secretary-General Lie

At 2:30 A.M. Ambassador Gross in Manhasset received the
instructions for which he had been waiting.[3] Assistant Secretary
Hickerson dictated to him by telephone the text of the official
note which he was to communicate at once to the Secretary-
General of the United Nations. At three o'clock Ambassador Gross
telephoned Secretary-General Lie and read him the American
request:

> The American Ambassador to the Republic of Korea has in-
> formed the Department of State that North Korean forces invaded
> the territory of the Republic of Korea at several points in the early
> morning hours of June 25 (Korean time).

---

2. Based on SCDS.
3. Based on SCDS.

Pyongyang Radio under the control of the North Korean regime, it is reported, has broadcast a declaration of war against the Republic of Korea effective at 9 P.M. e.d.t. June 24.

An attack of the forces of the North Korean regime under the circumstances referred to above constitutes a breach of the peace and an act of aggression.

Upon the urgent request of my Government I ask you to call an immediate meeting of the Security Council of the United Nations.[4]

The Ambassador then arranged for a late morning meeting with the Secretary-General. After his conversation with Mr. Lie, he notified his colleagues on the Security Council of the American request. Carlos P. Romulo, President of the United Nations General Assembly, was also notified. A spontaneous sense of the gravity of the situation characterized the initial reactions of delegates from lands throughout the world as the news of an invading army on the march broke their sleep.[5]

Events Continue to Unfold in Korea

While the initial news of the North Korean invasion swept the world, events continued their progressive unfolding on the battle-stricken Korean peninsula. At 3 A.M. Sunday, Washington time—twelve hours after the outbreak of fighting—Ambassador Muccio made his first broadcast to the American community over Seoul's English language radio station WVTP.[6] The Ambassador announced:

At four o'clock this morning North Korean armed forces began unprovoked attacks against defense positions of the Republic of Korea at several points along the thirty-eighth parallel.

Korean forces are taking up prepared positions to resist the Northern aggression.

Both Korean officials and Security Forces are handling the situation calmly and with ability. There is no reason for alarm. As yet it cannot be determined whether the northern Communists intend

---

4. Department of State, *United States Policy in the Korean Crisis,* pp. 11ff.

5. Ambassador Gross, Interview, October 28, 1955.

6. John C. Caldwell, *The Korea Story* (Chicago: Henry Regnery Co., 1952), p. 167.

to precipitate all out warfare. New developments will be reported regularly over WVTP.

Mission personnel are advised to travel about as little as necessary. The Ambassador requests American Mission personnel . . . to remain at home or at their posts as the situation dictates.[7]

An hour later the Ambassador appeared before an emergency meeting of the United Nations Commission on Korea where he stated that he expected that the ROK Army would give a "good account" of itself.[8]

Korean officials also took to the airwaves to inform the citizens of the Republic of the fighting. Broadcasts were made by the Minister of Foreign Affairs, Ben C. Limb, and officials of the Ministry of National Defense. In response to incessant North Korean broadcasts which followed the launching of the invasion, Defense Minister Shin Songmo told his people at 7:30 A.M. Sunday, Washington time, ". . . In a move to shift the responsibility to us for their inhuman activities, ["the North Korean Communist gang"] spread propaganda to the effect that our National defense Army crossed the Parallel first. I am convinced that the world and our thirty million fellow countrymen will never fail to judge the situation correctly."

In Washington, at 4 A.M., Assistant Secretary Rusk sought further information on the developing situation from American officials in Tokyo. By international radiotelephone he conferred with John M. Allison, director of the Office of North Asian Affairs, then accompanying John Foster Dulles on his current Japanese peace treaty mission; and with William Sebald, State Department political adviser on General MacArthur's staff. Nothing more was known in Tokyo than in Washington. These officials were unable to confirm the rumor that the North Koreans had broadcast a declaration of war.[9]

At 8 A.M. Washington time, the Korean Military Advisory Group released one of its first public reports on the progress of the fighting.[10] According to KMAG, by this time the ROK Army

---

7. *New York Times,* June 25, 1950, p. 21.
8. United Nations Document S/1946, June 25, 1950.
9. Based on SCDS.
10. *Asahi,* (Tokyo) June 26, 1950, p. 1.

had lost the entire area east of Kaesong and west of the Imjin River. Kaesong itself, 40 miles northwest of Seoul, had been occupied by a North Korean regiment. A tank regiment accompanied by a regiment of armored infantry, having captured P'och'on, 25 miles northwest of Seoul, was advancing toward Uijongbu. An entire North Korean division with its supporting artillery was reportedly attacking Ch'unch'on, ten miles south of the Thirty-eighth Parallel in central Korea. On the east coast, KMAG reported that a reinforced North Korean battalion had captured Ingu near the Thirty-eighth Parallel and was advancing toward Chumunjin, ten miles south of the Parallel. This particular statement did not contain a general assessment of the military situation, but KMAG officers at this time were widely quoted by correspondents in Korea as having stated that the North Korean drive had been "virtually stopped" by Sunday afternoon, Korean time.[11] At about the same time, an official of the army information section of the ROK National Defense Ministry was telling the same thing to the Japanese newspaper *Asahi* in an exclusive radiotelephone interview. Among the questions asked by the *Asahi* representative was, "What about the strength and equipment of the Communist army?" The unnamed Korean official answered, "It is still green and inexperienced. Since the North Koreans have just begun their premeditated surprise attack, we do not have any further information, but by tomorrow morning we shall have defeated them completely. Our only cause for dissatisfaction is that there has been no order to advance into the North."[12] This interview took place between 8:30 and 9 P.M. Sunday, Korean time (between 7:30 and 8 A.M. Sunday, in Washington).

The U.S. Mission Prepares for the Security Council Meeting

Into the daylight hours of Sunday morning the United States Mission to the United Nations worked under great pressure in preparation for the Security Council meeting which Secretary-General Lie had arranged for 2 P.M. Between the hours of four-thirty and six-thirty Ambassador Gross had tried to rest. Shortly

11. E.g., *Chicago Tribune*, June 25, 1950, p. 1.
12. *Asahi*, (Tokyo), June 26, 1950, p. 1.

after eight o'clock, he and John McVane, press officer of the
American Mission whom he had called to his home, drafted a formal letter of transmittal for the note which he had communicated
earlier to Mr. Lie.[13] This detail had been overlooked in the rush
of the night's activities. Later in the morning Ambassador Gross
conferred at Lake Success with the Secretary-General and with
Abraham Feller, general counsel of the United Nations. During
their discussion of procedural matters connected with the Security
Council session, the possibility that the Soviet Union might paralyze the Council with a veto was mentioned. Ambassador Gross
was of the opinion that this would not entail a delay of more than
24 hours in obtaining United Nations action to meet the North
Korean aggression.[14] In case of a Soviet veto, the General Assembly
would be called into emergency session to consider the American-
sponsored resolution. Although the customary rules of procedure
required a rather lengthy period of prior notification before such
a meeting could be convened, the Ambassador thought that this
delay could be avoided by making the first item on the agenda
of the emergency session the question of waiving the notification
requirement. Also working on the problem of an American response to a Soviet veto were officials in the State Department's
Office of United Nations Affairs.[15]

Late in the morning the Ambassador returned to the Park
Avenue headquarters of the American Mission, reporting at once
to the Assistant Secretary of State for United Nations Affairs over
the secret telephone circuit that linked the Mission and the State
Department. They discussed in general terms the way in which the
Security Council meeting was to be handled and exchanged views
on the resolution which the United States was to introduce. Each
had prepared a draft resolution. The basic problem confronting
them was whether the resolution should take the form of an
"order" or a "recommendation." This problem involved legal ques-

13. Phillip Hamburger, "Letter From Lake Success," *New Yorker*, June 29,
1950, p. 46.

14. Ambassador Gross, Interview, October 28, 1955.

15. Testimony of Assistant Secretary of State John D. Hickerson, in U.S.
Senate, Appropriations Committee, *Appropriations for the Departments of State,
Justice, Commerce and the Judiciary for the Fiscal Year Ending June 30, 1952*,
Part I, 1086.

tions related to Chapter VII of the United Nations Charter, "Action with Respect to Threats to the Peace, Breaches of the Peace, and Acts of Aggression." They finally decided to use "calls upon" language, standard phraseology that had been found a convenient formula in past United Nations practice for use in situations where for one reason or another it was considered desirable to leave the precise legal implications of a resolution somewhat in doubt.[16] Until 10 A.M. on Sunday another important problem had been that of a factual basis for the preamble of the American-sponsored resolution. Although the report from Ambassador Muccio might have been used, it was considered far more preferable to have a report from the United Nations body at the scene of the fighting. Sole reliance on American sources might have meant trouble with some members of the Council. At mid-morning such a report came—a message from the United Nations Commission on Korea (UNCOK).[17] In its report the Commission passed on the information concerning the fighting which it had received from the Government of the Republic of Korea, reported the approval of President Rhee for a "cease fire" broadcast to be made by the Commission, repeated Ambassador Muccio's estimate of the defensive capabilities of the ROK Army, and stated that "yak-type aircraft" had strafed installations in the vicinity of Seoul. In conclusion, the Commission cabled:

> Commission wishes to draw attention of Secretary General to serious situation which is assuming character of full-scale war and may endanger the maintenance of international peace and security. It suggests that he consider the possibility of bringing matter to the notice of the Security Council. Commission will communicate more fully considered recommendations later.[18]

A reference to this report thus became an important part of the

---

16. Ambassador Gross, Interview, October 28, 1955. Edwin C. Hoyt, who also interviewed Ambassador Gross, explains: "The wording 'calls upon' was used because it was diplomatically strong without being a legal order." Hoyt, "The U.S. Reaction to the Korean Attack: A Study of the Principles of the U.N. Charter as a Factor in American Policy Making," *American Journal of International Law*, LV (January, 1961) p. 51.

17. The Commission was composed of representatives from Australia, China, El Salvador, France, India, the Philippines, and Turkey.

18. United Nations Document S/1946, June 25, 1950.

preamble of the resolution which Ambassador Gross laid before the
Security Council later in the day. Having reached agreement on
basic principles, the two officials ended their discussion with the
notification by Assistant Secretary Hickerson that he was sending
David Wainhouse, acting head of the Office of Political and
Security Affairs and long-time personal friend of Ambassador
Gross, to New York to further assist in developing the American
resolution. Mr. Wainhouse, accompanied by foreign service officer Niles Bond, had already left Washington at 8:30 A.M. in an
Army airplane, bringing the draft of the resolution that had been
prepared at the Department and an outline of a speech to be
presented with it.[19] The responsibility for the final text of the
resolution, however, was now in the hands of Ambassador Gross
and the United States Mission.[20]

Initial American Press Reaction

Sunday morning readers of the nation's leading newspapers
found the headlines of the day devoted to a terrible tragedy. Life
had ended for fifty-eight persons when a Northwest Airlines DC-4
plunged into Lake Michigan. The early dispatches from Korea
were carried in positions which indicated that they were being
treated as the second-place news of the day. Deep within the
New York Times under the heading of "Washington Holds Russia
to Account" were carried the observations of reporters at the State
Department on Saturday night.[21] Editors of the early Sunday edi-
tions did not foresee that the Korean story would demand banner
headlines for days to come.

Secretary Johnson and General Bradley Go to Norfolk

Early Sunday morning in Washington, while Pentagon walls
were breaking out with maps of Korea, Secretary of Defense Johnson and General Bradley decided to participate in a previously
scheduled Defense Department orientation conference for sixty

---

19. Based on SCDS.
20. Ambassador Gross, Interview, October 28, 1955.
21. New York Times, June 25, 1950, p. 20.

civilian leaders in Norfolk, Virginia. Secretary Johnson gave instructions that he was to be kept fully informed about further developments in Korea while he was absent from the capital. In Norfolk, speaking in his shirt sleeves on the hangar deck of the aircraft carrier Midway, the Secretary of Defense named Russia as "the one country which might take an aggressive role and bring on war with the United States."[22] He assured his audience that American battle plans had been "signed and sealed" for just this eventuality. Commenting on the reported outbreak of fighting in Korea, Secretary Johnson explained that the forces of the Republic of Korea would defeat the North Koreans unless the latter had received substantial aid from beyond Korean frontiers. "If South Korea fails to come through," he declared, "it will be evidence of outside assistance."[23]

A Joint State-Army Conference Is Held

Other key defense leaders worked directly upon the problems posed by the North Korean invasion. In his Pentagon office, the Secretary of the Air Force, Thomas K. Finletter—having made a flying return from an interrupted Maine weekend—immersed himself in a day-long study and review of the capabilities of the Republic of Korea, the North Koreans, and the United States.[24] Late in the morning Secretary of the Army Pace, Assistant Secretary of the Army Karl Bendetsen, and General Thomas S. Timberman, chief of the Department of the Army Operations Division, went to the State Department for a conference on the developing military situation.[25] The joint State-Army conference commenced at 11:30 A.M. Forty-five minutes later General J. Lawton Collins, Army chief of staff, joined the conferees. Among the State Department officials who participated were Under Secretary James E. Webb, Assistant Secretary Rusk, Assistant Secretary Hickerson, and Ambassador Jessup. Secretary of State Acheson joined the group at 12:15 P.M.

---

22. *New York Times*, June 26, 1950, p. 12.
23. *Washington Post*, June 26, 1950, p. 2.
24. Secretary Finletter, Interview, October 24, 1955.
25. Based on SCDS.

Further Reports Are Received from Seoul and Tokyo

Secretary Acheson had arrived at the State Department shortly after eleven o'clock.[26] Reporters observing his arrival noted that he had arrived coatless, driving his convertible with the top down. They interpreted this deviation from the Secretary's normally impeccable attire[27] as evidence that the fighting in Korea was developing into a matter of great urgency for American policy makers. Upon reaching his office, the Secretary of State learned that telephone communications had been established with Ambassador Muccio and that additional cables had been received from him. The military situation seemed much worse than it had during the night.[28] Previously, at 2:05 A.M. on Sunday, Washington time, Ambassador Muccio had urged the Department to support a request by KMAG to General MacArthur's headquarters that a ten-day emergency supply of ammunition for the South Korean forces be shipped immediately to Pusan. Two hours later the Department had relayed to Tokyo the Ambassador's support of the appeal from the American advisers in Korea.[29]

Now, at 11:32 A.M., Ambassador Muccio reported that he had decided to evacuate American women and children from the Seoul area through the port of Inch'on. An hour and a half earlier he had alerted the Far East Command in Tokyo to prepare for the air evacuation of American dependents from Korea. "My whole motivation in regard to evacuation," the Ambassador later explained, "was to hold on as long as possible to bolster Korean morale to the best of our ability, and at the same time not to be trapped."[30] The Ambassador's policy of calculated delay had been opposed within the military advisory group. About ten hours earlier, certain KMAG officers had urged him to call for the implementation of the Korean evacuation plan—only the Ambassador had the formal authority to make this decision. But at that time Muccio and his diplomatic advisers had decided to delay its implementation

---

26. *New York Herald Tribune,* June 26, 1950, p. 2.
27. Secretary Acheson had been named Best-Dressed Man of the Year in 1949.
28. Secretary Acheson, Interview, October 25, 1955.
29. Based on SCDS.
30. Ambassador Muccio, Letter, August 27, 1959.

because of the adverse effect it would have on South Korean morale.[31]

According to Army sources, about six hours earlier the Ambassador had suggested the possibility that the American Mission might surrender and depend upon diplomatic immunity for its protection. Major Greenwood, de facto chief of KMAG,[32] had considered this proposal so "unrealistic" that he had issued verbal instructions that preparations be commenced at once to enable the military personnel of the Mission to withdraw by rail or by road toward Pusan. According to Ambassador Muccio, however, he at no time had any thought of surrendering, but had only mentioned during a staff meeting—which had included KMAG officers—that the members of the American Mission in Korea should not overlook the possibility of being trapped. In such a case, he advised, "we should make an all-out effort to identify ourselves."[33] At 10 A.M. (11 P.M. in Korea), Ambassador Muccio, over radio station WVTP, ordered the dependents in the American community to assemble for evacuation to Inch'on. The first buses left Seoul at noon Sunday, Washington time (1 A.M. Monday in Korea).

Meanwhile at the State Department, Secretary Acheson learned that a cable bearing on the course of events in Korea had been received at 10:30 A.M. from Ambassador John Foster Dulles and Mr. John M. Allison in Japan. Mr. Dulles had returned to Tokyo hurriedly from a sightseeing trip to the ancient Japanese capital of Kyoto for conferences with General MacArthur and other high officials.[34] The Dulles-Allison cable advised:

> It is possible that the South Koreans may themselves contain and repulse the attack and, if so, this is the best way. If, however, it appears that they cannot do so, then we believe that United

31. Appleman, "The U.S. and the U.N. Intervene in Korea," pp. 16ff.

32. Colonel W. H. S. Wright, in Japan at the time of the attack, had designated Lt. Col. William J. Maloney to be acting head of KMAG in his absence, but it seems that Lt. Col. Carl H. Sturies assumed command because of seniority. According to Lt. Col. Appleman, Major Greenwood—deputy chief of staff—made most of the decisions for KMAG prior to the return of Colonel Wright on June 26. See Appleman, "The U.S. and the U.N. Intervene in Korea," p. 17.

33. Ambassador Muccio, Letter, August 27, 1959.

34. *Asahi*, June 26, 1950, p. 1.

States force should be used. . . . To sit by while Korea is overrun by unprovoked armed attack would start a disastrous chain of events leading most probably to world war. We suggest that Security Council might call for action on behalf of the organization under Article 106 by the five powers or such of them as are willing to respond.[35]

The Secretary of State did not interpret this telegram as being an expression of General MacArthur's views.[36]

At 12:26 P.M., Washington time, shortly after Secretary Acheson had joined the State-Army conference, Ambassador Muccio reported that President Syngman Rhee had decided to move the Government of the Republic of Korea from Seoul to Suwon, twenty miles to the south. This report was added to the information already available to the conferees as they discussed "possible courses of military action preparatory to laying the matter before the President."[37] All agreed that a full-scale invasion was underway in Korea. Military intelligence estimates emanating from General MacArthur's headquarters were confirming Ambassador Muccio's initial characterization of the North Korean attack as an "all-out offensive." All agreed also that the military situation appeared to be getting worse. "The South Koreans seemed to be disintegrating," Secretary Acheson later recalled.[38] In the course of the discussion the Army reported that prompt approval had been given to the KMAG appeal for the emergency shipment of supplies to the ROK army. A ten-day emergency supply of ammunition and other expendables of war was already being flown from Japan to Korea under air escort.[39] This material was being delivered under the existing provisions for Korea which were contained in the Mutual Defense Assistance Program Act of 1949.[40]

---

35. *Memoirs*, II, 336, and Beverly Smith, "The White House Story: Why We Went to War in Korea," *Saturday Evening Post*, November 10, 1951, p. 76. The Truman version does not include the ellipsis. The Smith version lacks the final sentence.

36. Secretary Acheson, Interview, October 25, 1955. In fact, the General did not see the cable until several years later. Whitney, p. 322.

37. Based on SCDS, but no minutes of the meeting are available.

38. Secretary Acheson, Interview, October 25, 1955.

39. Based on SCDS.

40. *New York Times*, June 26, 1950, p. 1.

The President Decides to Return to Washington

In view of the ominous trend of events, the Secretary of State decided to confer again with the President. Mr. Truman was at his home in Independence, Missouri, when Secretary Acheson telephoned him at 2:45 P.M., Washington time.[41] Earlier on Sunday morning the President had visited his brother Vivian's farm in Grandview, but before noon he had returned home to await reports of further developments in Korea.[42] Secretary Acheson briefed the President on the latest available information and read to him the text of the draft resolution which had been prepared for submission to the Security Council. He added that although the Council would probably approve the resolution, it was not expected that the North Koreans would comply with the request that they cease fire and withdraw to the Thirty-eighth Parallel. The President agreed that the "complete disregard" which they and their "big allies" had demonstrated toward United Nations actions in the past left little hope of their compliance now. Since he felt that "some decision would have to be made at once as to the degree of aid or encouragement which our government was willing to extend to the Republic of Korea," the President decided to fly back to Washington without delay.[43] As they completed their conversation, President Truman instructed Secretary Acheson to collaborate with the Service Secretaries and the Joint Chiefs of Staff on recommendations to be presented to him on his return to the capital.

The crew of the *Independence* had the President's airplane ready for the return flight within an hour after they had been alerted. The President ate a hasty lunch and hurried to the Kansas City Municipal Airport. His quick decision to return to Washington came as a surprise to the reporters who had accompanied him to Missouri. Only a half-hour prior to Secretary Acheson's telephone call, the President's press secretary, Eben A. Ayers, had informed them that there would be no change in the President's weekend plans; he would return to Washington on Monday as previously

41. Based on SCDS.
42. Smith, p. 23.
43. *Memoirs*, II, 332.

scheduled. With this assurance some of the reporters had left
Independence for Kansas City. Now Mr. Ayers was trying to
locate them in order to tell them that "the President has three or
four important decisions to make and he feels he should go back
to Washington right away."[44]

Reporters at the airport as the President boarded the *Independence* noted that he was "stern faced." Anthony Leviero of the
New York Times[45] also reported that Mrs. Truman appeared
"calm but serious" and recalled that her mood seemed similar to
her demeanor at the time her husband had assumed the presidency after the death of President Roosevelt. The President's
daughter, Margaret, Mr. Leviero noted, was "absorbed in a sub-
conscious, prayerful attitude." In his remarks to reporters the
President said that he was sure that there had been no formal
declaration of war by the North Koreans[46] and that he would
have nothing further to say about the fighting in Korea until he had
conferred with the Secretary of State. In parting, the President
asked the reporters not to magnify the seriousness of the situation.
"Don't make it alarmist. It could be a dangerous situation, but I
hope it isn't," he cautioned.[47] One of the President's aides privately
told a reporter, "The boss is going to hit those fellows hard."[48] A
last-minute pickup of two presidential assistants was made just
before take-off, but two more were left behind as the *Independence*
climbed and banked eastward at 4:12 P.M. Washington time.

The President spent most of the journey to the capital alone
in his compartment. As a devoted student of history who was
confirmed in the belief that the "lessons of history" offered clear
guides to "right principles" of action to those who knew them, he
naturally weighed the North Korean invasion in the balance of
past experience.[49] Later he recorded some of his thinking as the
Independence droned steadily toward Washington.

44. Carl Levin, *New York Herald Tribune*, June 26, 1950, p. 1.

45. *New York Times*, June 26, 1950, p. 7.

46. This was reported by a number of news agencies, but no official confirmation of the rumored declaration of war reached the State Department. According
to Kim Wonyong, such a declaration was broadcast at 8:30 A.M., Sunday, Korean
time. Consult Republic of Korea, National Defense Ministry, p. A34.

47. Anthony Leviero, *New York Times*, June 26, 1950, p. 7.

48. The President's statement was not printed until a week later. *New York
Times*, July 2, 1950, p. E 1.

49. President Truman, Interview, July 30, 1957.

In the President's view, the North Korean attack was the same in nature as the German, Italian, and Japanese aggressions that had led to World War II. For him it was another case in which a strong state was attempting to overpower a weaker one. If the international Communist leaders were appeased, then gradually the scale of violence and the number of participating states would gradually increase to global dimensions. A third world war between Communist and non-Communist states would inevitably ensue. Thus the President considered it right to resist promptly and effectively the North Korean aggression. Communist belligerency would be deterred and small states everywhere would be encouraged to resist coercion by more powerful Communist nations. Also the principles of the United Nations, founded in 1945 with great hopes that it would serve as an instrument of world peace, could be affirmed by a collective response to the act of aggression.[50]

In flight, the President had the radio operator of the *Independence* send a message to Secretary Acheson, notifying him of his estimated time of arrival and requesting that he have a designated group of advisers meet the President at Blair House for a dinner conference later in the evening.[51] Secretary Acheson was told that he might add to the list of conferees as he desired.[52]

While the President was enroute, intelligence experts in Washington grappled with the central problems that had been raised by the North Korean invasion. Why had the Korean Communist leaders risked the dangers of open aggression at a time when their potential ability to subvert the Republic of Korea seemed so great? How did their move fit in with broader Soviet and Chinese Communist plans? Did the invasion indicate that the Soviet Union was now willing to risk an open "shooting war"? What was the relationship between recent maneuvers along the Balkan periphery of the Soviet bloc and the sudden thrust in the Far East? Had the North Korean blow been coordinated with the plans of the Chinese Communists to invade the last refuge of the Nationalists on Formosa?

50. *Memoirs,* II, 332ff.
51. *Ibid.,* p. 333.
52. Secretary Acheson, Interview, October 25, 1955.

Twenty-four hours earlier when President Truman had last been in flight aboard the *Independence*, North Korean officers had ordered their men southward to kill their fellow Koreans and thus smash the fragile peace of the world. Now, as the President returned to Washington, a convocation of diplomats at the United Nations was coming to agreement on a collective appeal—vigorous in language but faint in hope—that would call for an end to the bloodshed.

The United Nations Security Council Meets

The emergency session of the Security Council which had been requested by the United States had convened at Lake Success at 2 P.M. The Soviet Union, apparently continuing the boycott it had begun six months earlier of all United Nations organs where Nationalist China was represented, was absent. The representatives of China, Cuba, Ecuador, Egypt, France, India, Norway, the United Kingdom, the United States, and Yugoslavia were present.

Shortly after the Council came to order, Secretary-General Lie, having decided earlier that it was his duty to make a statement concerning the invasion, said that he believed the North Koreans had violated the United Nations Charter. He explained that he had come to this conclusion on the basis of the report of the United Nations Commission in Korea and other information from the peninsula. He expressed the opinion that the Security Council was the competent body to deal with the matter: "I consider it the clear duty of the Security Council to take steps necessary to re-establish peace and security in that area."[53]

Ambassador Gross was next to address the Council. He reported the gravity with which the United States viewed the aggression in Korea and briefly reviewed the past record of attempts to achieve a peaceful solution of the Korean problem. He then read aloud the text of the resolution that had emerged from the efforts of the State Department and the United States Mission in the past sixteen hours:

53. U.N. Security Council, Fifth Year, *Official Records*, No. 15, 473rd Meeting, June 25, 1950, p. 3.

The Security Council

Recalling the finding of the General Assembly in its resolution of 21 October 1949 that the Government of the Republic of Korea is a lawfully established government having effective control and jurisdiction over that part of Korea where the United Nations Temporary Commission on Korea was able to observe and consult and in which the great majority of the people of Korea reside; and that this Government is based on elections which were a valid expression of the free will of the electorate of that part of Korea and which were observed by the Temporary Commission; and that this is the only such government in Korea;

Mindful of the concern expressed by the General Assembly in its resolutions of 12 December 1948 and 21 October 1949 of the consequences which might follow unless Member States refrained from acts derogatory to the results sought to be achieved by the United Nations in bringing about the complete independence and unity of Korea; and the concern expressed that the situation described by the United Nations Commission on Korea in its report menaces the safety and well being of the Republic of Korea and of the people of Korea and might lead to open military conflict there;

Noting with grave concern the armed invasion of the Republic of Korea by armed forces from North Korea,

Determines that this action constitutes a breach of the peace,

I. *Calls upon* the authorities in North Korea
   (a) To cease hostilities forthwith; and
   (b) To withdraw their armed forces to the 38th parallel;

II. *Requests* the United Nations Commission on Korea
   (a) To observe the withdrawal of the North Korean forces to the 38th parallel; and
   (b) To keep the Security Council informed on the execution of this resolution.

III. *Calls upon* all Members to render every assistance to the United Nations in the execution of this resolution and to refrain from giving assistance to the North Korean authorities.[54]

Neither the Ambassador's introductory statement nor the resolution charged the Soviet Union with responsibility for the North Korean aggression. This was the official American public position. But Edward W. Barrett, Assistant Secretary of State for Public

---

54. Department of State, *U.S. Policy in the Korean Crisis*, p. 15.

Affairs, on a trip away from Washington and not yet cognizant of the Department's policy, soon expressed publicly what officials were thinking privately. Secretary Barrett told reporters that the North Korean invasion demonstrated the "rank hypocrisy of the Kremlin's so-called peace offensive."[55] He further explained that the relationship between the Soviet Union and the North Koreans was the same as that between "Walt Disney and Donald Duck." He soon received a urgent telegram from the State Department telling him to "pipe down."[56]

The next speaker to follow Ambassador Gross was John M. Chang, Korean Ambassador to the United States and observer of the Government of the Republic of Korea at the United Nations. He owed his place at the Security Council table to a split-second improvisation by Ambassador Gross, who suddenly realized as he rose to present the American position that in the rush of events no one had arranged to have him there.[57] Ambassador Gross had quickly moved that the Council invite the Republic of Korea to sit with it while it discussed the breach of the peace in Korea, and the motion had carried.[58] Thus the Korean representative gravely could petition, "I appeal to the Security Council to act forthwith in removing this threat to international peace. I also appeal to the Security Council to direct the invaders of my country to cease fire and to withdraw from our territory."[59] Ambassador Chang did not call for armed assistance.

Among other members of the Council who spoke after the Korean ambassador was Sir Terence Shone of the United Kingdom. He counseled caution in exceeding the bounds of the evidence

---

55. *New York Times,* June 26, 1950, p. 9.

56. Secretary Barrett later apologized to Secretary Acheson. "He told me to forget it, that the idea of pressuring the Soviet to stop the war was a long shot at best, and that events had proved I had done no harm." Edward Barrett, *Truth Is Our Weapon* (New York: Funk & Wagnalls Company, 1953), p. 157.

57. Ambassador Gross, Interview, October 28, 1955.

58. The seating of Ambassador Chang at this time had important implications for the future. The Council was unable to adopt an agenda throughout the month of August, the tenure of Soviet delegate Malik as president, because of a dispute over the legality of seating the Republic of Korea. President Malik refused to recognize it; Ambassador Warren R. Austin, the American representative, maintained that it already had been duly approved.

59. U.N. Security Council, p. 8.

which had been presented in the first report from the United Nations Commission. "It seems to me," he advised, "that the draft resolution presented by the representative of the United States meets this case pretty well and goes as far as the Security Council properly can go at this stage."[60]

The Council recessed its public discussion at 4:15 P.M. to deliberate upon the terms of the American resolution in closed session. Ambassador Gross had known that his work was just beginning when he arrived at Lake Success earlier in the afternoon and now he was sure of it.[61] The American delegation had to work hard to defend the wording of its resolution; sometimes effort alone could not prevent defeat. Ambassador Gross wanted to call the North Korean assault an "armed invasion," others wanted to call it an "armed attack." The latter view prevailed. Ambassador Gross wanted to strengthen the resolution by calling upon the North Koreans to "cease aggression"; others insisted that the phrase "cease hostilities" be retained. Their view again prevailed. One member of the Council wanted to refer to the "Korean People's Democratic Republic"; Ambassador Gross successfully defended the reference to merely the "authorities" of North Korea. At least two delegates wanted to move an adjournment until Monday; Ambassador Gross strenuously and successfully opposed the suggestion. Shortly after five o'clock the delegates reached agreement. They had decided to change the American draft resolution in three respects: First, they decided to change "armed invasion of" to "armed attack upon"; second, they inserted a general call for an "immediate cessation of hostilities" directed at both parties to the conflict just before the resolution's specific call for a North Korean withdrawal; and third, they added a request for the "fully considered recommendations" of the United Nations Commission on Korea.[62] According to Ambassador Gross, the primary reason for the final wording of the resolution was the fact that several delegates had not yet received instructions from their governments.

At half-past five the Council reconvened. Fifteen minutes later it adopted the revised resolution by a vote that would have been

---

60. *Ibid.*
61. Ambassador Gross, Interview, October 28, 1955.
62. United Nations Document S/1501, June 25, 1950.

unanimous save for one abstention—that of Yugoslavia. The delegates of China, Cuba, Ecuador, Egypt, France, India, Norway, the
United Kingdom, and the United States signified approval. Yugoslavia's abstention from the voting was signified by its deputy representative, Djura Nincic, who earlier had attempted unsuccessfully
to get the Council to adopt an alternative resolution which called
for a cease-fire and invited North Korea to voice its complaint
before the United Nations. Mr. Nincic had argued that there
was not enough information to support the draft resolution
introduced by the United States. The chief Yugoslav delegate,
Ambassador Ales Bebler, vacationing at a remote mountain retreat
beyond telephone contact, could not be notified about the Security
Council meeting. There were those on the Council who regretted
his absence, believing that if he had been present he could have
been induced to make the vote unanimous. This belief in part grew
out of the strong sense of the historic significance of the occasion
which was shared by the delegates. The United Nations was
viewed as fighting for its very life. Some of the delegates, giving
concrete expression to their deep concern, actually had risked
their political fortunes by deciding to vote in the absence of instructions from their governments. Independent voting of this nature
was most unusual.[63]

The President of the Council, Sir Benegal N. Rau of India,
gaveled to a close the first formal deliberations of the United Nations in the Korean crisis at 6 P.M. Just before declaring the
emergency session at an end, he provisionally had set the next
meeting of the Council for three o'clock on the afternoon of
Tuesday, June 27. By that time he hoped that the recommendations of the United Nations Commission in Korea would be available for consideration.[64]

To some informed observers of the international scene the
behavior of the American delegation in the Security Council on
Sunday afternoon seemed to indicate that the United States would
not do anything really effective to cope with the disaster in

---

63. Ambassador Gross, Interview, October 28, 1955.
64. U.N. Security Council, p. 18.

Korea. Not only had there been no appeal for military sanctions against the North Koreans, but as far as anyone could tell, the Council had not even been asked to arrive at a specific determination of aggression against them. The story soon reached the ears of American officials that one friendly diplomat from a British Commonwealth nation had cabled his government, "The time has come for the United States to put up or shut up in Korea, but in my opinion it will do neither."[65] Yet there was no doubt among the American officials at Lake Success that the resolution adopted by the Security Council provided ample basis for whatever additional measures might be needed to secure North Korean compliance with it. In radio interviews from Lake Success immediately after the meeting, Ambassador Gross said, "If unhappily our assumption [of North Korean compliance with the resolution] proves to be unwarranted, then the measures which are available to the Security Council . . . include the possibility of economic measures and the use of military force or sanctions of various kinds."[66]

On the basis of conversations with American spokesmen in New York, reporters concluded that the resolution just passed "carried with it the clear implication that the United Nations would move to take stronger measures if North Korea flouted the Council."[67]

Members of Congress Comment on the Fighting

In Washington on Sunday afternoon members of Congress were beginning to comment upon the surprising turn of events in Korea.[68] Senator H. Alexander Smith, Republican of New Jersey and a member of the Foreign Relations Committee, stated his belief that the United States had a "moral responsibility" for the

---

65. Assistant Secretary Rusk, Interview, August 22, 1955.

66. ABC interview with Pauline Frederick, June 25, 1950; CBS interview with Larry Lesueur, June 25, 1950. See also Hoyt, "The U.S. Reaction to the Korean Attack," p. 51.

67. *New York Times*, June 26, 1950, p. 1.

68. *Ibid.*, p. 4.

"infant Korean Republic." He recommended that the United
States continue its efforts to try to bring about a cease-fire through
shipments of arms and ammunition. Senator Richard B. Russell,
the United Nations, while bolstering South Korean defenses with
Democrat of Georgia, a member of the Armed Services Committee,
agreed that military supplies should be rushed to Korea and
thought that existing legislation provided ample authority to cover
the measure; but he found it "incomprehensible" that Defense and
State Department intelligence groups had not warned the Government of the impending invasion.

Senator Alexander Wiley, Republican of Wisconsin, second
ranking minority member of the Foreign Relations Committee,
wanted to know whether the struggle in Korea was "a fight between Koreans or a Communist assault egged on by the Russians."
The United States, he said, would have to decide this question
before it would know how to deal with the situation. Republican
Senator Kenneth E. Wherry of Nebraska inveighed: "The whole
thing is a result of our China policy. The Administration should
stand up and do something and then we'll stop those Commies."
Representative Paul W. Shafer, Republican of Michigan, charged
that Korea had been "flung into the soviet orbit" by State Department policies: "If the department's policies have not been activated
by Red spies and fellow travelers, then it is being directed by a
prize package of dupes and incompetents and should be thoroughly housecleaned."[69]

Representative John Kee of West Virginia, Democratic chairman of the House Foreign Affairs Committee, told reporters: "My
view is, from what I know of the situation at the moment, that the
government of South Korea is in a fairly good position to take care
of itself. I don't see anything that the United States can do at the
moment other than to press the case before the U.N. Security
Council."[70] At 3 p.m., Mr. Livingston Merchant of the State Department's Bureau of Far Eastern Affairs discussed the Korean crisis
with the members of the Far Eastern Subcommittee of the Senate
Foreign Relations Committee.[71]

---

69. Walter Trohan, *Chicago Tribune*, June 26, 1950, p. 4.
70. *Washington Post*, June 26, 1950, p. 1.
71. Based on SCDS.

Ambassador Muccio Reports Evacuation of Americans in Progress

At 5:05 P.M., Ambassador Muccio reported to the State Department that more than 700 dependents and female employees of the American Mission in Korea had been evacuated from Seoul to Ascom City near Inch'on, and that he was conducting negotiations with a Norwegian ship in the Inch'on harbor for their evaculation to Japan; the freighter Reinholt, loaded with fertilizer, had a normal passenger capacity of twelve, but about thirteen hours later (7 P.M. Monday in Korea), Ambassador Muccio learned with "tremendous relief" that the crowded freighter with all 700 aboard had safely sailed.

At six o'clock Sunday evening in Washington, the State Department informed the Ambassador that a decision was expected within hours on granting General MacArthur full authority to furnish at his discretion arms and equipment outside of existing military assistance legislation. The Ambassador also was assured that he would be notified shortly of decisions with respect to the actions which General MacArthur might take directly to insure the safety of American citizens in Korea. He was further notified that the policy of the Government at this time was that American military advisers should remain actively associated with the South Korean forces as long as possible.

Premier Kim Ilsong Appeals to the Korean People

As the *Independence* with President Truman aboard neared the Washington area, Marshal Kim Ilsong, North Korean premier, was making an inflammatory radio appeal to the people of Korea from the northern capital of Pyongyang.[72] He charged that the "Rhee puppet army," following American directives, had first attacked northward all along the Thirty-eighth Parallel and reported that the People's Army, sweeping the enemy from the north, already had penetrated from ten to fifteen kilometers into southern territory. He railed against the "reactionary fascist Rhee

---

72. The speech was delivered at 7 P.M., Eastern Daylight Time (8 A.M. Monday in Korea). The account below is derived from the text published in the *Jen-min jih-pao* (*People's Daily*, Peking), June 28, 1950, p. 1.

system" which sought to make Koreans the "colonial slaves of American imperialism." He alleged that the efforts of Korean patriots to achieve peaceful unification had now been brought to nought by a "Rhee-instigated civil war." To the rhetorical question, "What are the Korean people going to do about this?" Marshal Kim replied with detailed instructions for militant activity by all segments of the southern population to aid the People's Army offensive and to establish the hegemony of the Korean People's Democratic Republic. The guerrillas of the south were to hit the enemy from the rear, disrupting communications and destroying roads and bridges. All citizens of the south were to disobey the government. Workers were to strike, but were to protect their factories from destruction. Farmers were enjoined to refuse food to the "enemy" and to help the guerrillas. Small businessmen were called upon to "liberate" the Korean economy from American control. The intellectuals of the south were called upon to engage in political propaganda and to agitate for a mass uprising. The Republic of Korea military forces were told that their "real enemy" was President Syngman Rhee and were asked to join the ranks of the People's Army. In closing, Marshal Kim declared, "History tells us that people who resolutely fight for freedom and independence must be victorious. Our cause is a just cause. Victory is ours. The time has come to unify our country. . . . Forward!"

The President Arrives in Washington

The *Independence* landed at Washington National Airport at about 7:20 P.M. The President was met by Secretary Acheson, Secretary Johnson, and Under Secretary of State Webb. Reporters noted that he was in a "grim mood."[73] His displayed none of his usual patience and good humor when press photographers clamored, "Just one more shot, Mr. President!" "That's enough!" he snapped, "We've got a job to do!" As the presidential limousine departed for Blair House, the first thing the President said was that he was not going to let the attack succeed and that he was going to "hit them hard." In a voice broken with emotion, Secretary Johnson reportedly responded, "I thank you, Mr. President."

---

73. Walter Trohan, *Chicago Tribune*, June 26, 1950, p. 1.

The First Blair House Conference Is Held

Upon reaching Blair House, at about twenty minutes to eight, the President first notified Mrs. Truman of his safe arrival, as was his custom.[74] Then, in the Blair House living room, he joined the group of advisers whom he had asked Secretary Acheson to assemble for dinner and discussion. Thirteen of the nation's top diplomatic and military leaders had promptly responded to the President's summons.[75] Representing the State Department, in addition to Secretary Acheson and Under Secretary Webb, were Assistant Secretaries Hickerson and Rusk, and Ambassador Jessup. Civilian and military officials who represented the Department of Defense, in addition to Secretary Johnson, were the three Service Secretaries—Secretary Pace of the Army, Secretary Francis P. Matthews of the Navy, Secretary Finletter of the Air Force; and the Joint Chiefs of Staff—General Bradley, chairman; General J. Lawton Collins, Chief of Staff of the Army; Admiral Forrest P. Sherman, Chief of Naval Operations; and General Hoyt S. Vandenberg, Chief of Staff of the Air Force.

There was some preliminary conversation as the group waited in the living room for dinner to be served. Secretary Acheson reported on the action that had been taken by the Security Council two hours earlier. President Truman, sitting on a window seat, declared softly, "We can't let the U.N. down!"

Secretary Johnson wanted the group to hear a memorandum containing General MacArthur's views on the strategic importance of Formosa which he and General Bradley had just brought back from Tokyo. He considered the General's presentation on the subject to be both "brilliant and to the point."[76] Strictly in terms of American military security the Secretary had long considered Formosa to be more important than Korea. But in presenting the MacArthur memorandum at this time he said he was not attempting to prejudge the American reaction to the situation in Korea.

---

74. Smith, p. 76.

75. Testimony of General Omar N. Bradley, *Hearings*, Part II, 1049. An accurate list of the conferees was also reported in the *New York Times*, June 26, 1950, p. 10.

76. Testimony of Secretary of Defense Louis A. Johnson, *Hearings*, Part IV, 2579.

At Secretary Johnson's request, General Bradley read the paper aloud in full without interruption.[77]

Dinner was announced shortly after eight o'clock by the White House maitre d'hotel, Alonzo Fields. As the President waved the others to precede him into the dining room, Under Secretary Webb reportedly took advantage of the opportunity to draw him aside and suggested that although everyone seemed in agreement with him, "Let's not do it too fast."

"Don't worry, I won't," the President apparently replied. When the group was seated, the President requested that all discussion be postponed until the meal was over and the domestic staff had withdrawn. After dessert, the table was cleared and the conferees settled down to the business of the evening.[78]

The President opened the discussion with a statement which in substance was that he was there with an "open mind" and wanted to hear everything his advisers had to say about the situation. He further indicated that for the present he was not planning to make any crucial decisions.[79] Then he called upon the Secretary of State to open the discussion with a "detailed picture of the situation."[80]

Secretary Acheson reviewed the developments of the past 24 hours, beginning with the receipt of Ambassador Muccio's first report. He noted that subsequent information from Korea supported the conclusion that the North Koreans had launched an all-out invasion, and that the Department had received a still unconfirmed report that the North Koreans had broadcast a declaration of war. The Secretary then continued with a detailed account of the emergency meeting of the Security Council and the passage of the American-sponsored resolution. Although no one was relying heavily upon the resolution as an effective instrument for

77. Sometime after the conference Secretary Johnson provided copies of the paper for the President, Secretary Acheson, the Service Secretaries, and the Joint Chiefs. *Ibid.*, p. 2580.

78. Secretary Johnson later recalled that as dinner ended, a "violent discussion" took place between him and Secretary Acheson over the subject of Formosa. According to Secretary Johnson, the President intervened and the subject was not raised again during the evening. (*Ibid.*, p. 2580.) None of the conferees interviewed recalled this incident. According to notes made at the time, Secretary Acheson presented the recommendations with respect to Formosa which are discussed below.

79. Secretary Finletter, Interview, October 24, 1955.

80. *Memoirs*, II, 333.

inducing the invaders to withdraw, there was still an "outside chance" that the United Nations might be able to handle the situation.[81] Secretary Acheson might have reported that at 4 P.M.[82] the State Department had instructed the American Embassy in Moscow to deliver a note to the Soviet Government which requested assurances that the Union of Soviet Socialist Republics disavowed responsibility for the attack and that it would use its influence with the North Koreans to secure their withdrawal.[83]

Then, speaking from his own notes and not a formal Defense-State draft, Secretary Acheson advanced the following suggestions for consideration by the conference: (1) That General MacArthur be authorized to furnish the South Koreans with military equipment over and above that already authorized under the Mutual Defense Assistance Program, (2) that American airplanes be employed to cover the evacuation of the American women and children from Inch'on, (3) that the Air Force be authorized to destroy North Korean tanks and airplanes interfering with the evacuation, (4) that consideration be given to what further assistance might be given to Korea pursuant to the Security Council resolution just passed or to any supplementary resolution, and (5) that the Seventh Fleet be ordered to prevent a Chinese Communist invasion of Formosa as well as to prevent operations by the Chinese Nationalists against the mainland.[84]

Following Secretary Acheson's presentation, the President asked each of his advisers in turn around the table to comment on the proposals advanced by the Secretary of State and to contribute any further suggestions he might have.[85] He first called upon Secretary Johnson to present the views of the Department of

---

81. Assistant Secretary Rusk, Interview, August 22, 1955.

82. Based on SCDS.

83. This note was not delivered until June 27. A full explanation for the delay is not available at this time; part of the reason seems to have been that the Soviet authorities were reluctant to accept the note. Reportedly, when Embassy officials tried to deliver it they found that Soviet officials to whom the note should be delivered were "out of town." Another explanation given is that the note was not received in Moscow until early June 26 and required a special appointment for delivery. The note finally delivered on June 27 was the same as that dispatched on Sunday.

84. Based on SCDS.

85. All participants interviewed agreed that this was the President's mode of conducting the conference.

Defense. Mr. Johnson stated that the Defense Department, without
a war plan for Korea and having come to no specific conclusions
during the day, had no departmental recommendations to make.[86]
He had deliberately come to the conference without a predetermined set of recommendations ". . . so that each [of the civilian
Secretaries and the Joint Chiefs of Staff] would feel that there
was no inhibition on the President having the benefit of whatever
he honest to God thought of the situation."[87] Thus the Joint
Chiefs presented neither a formal estimate of the military situation
in Korea nor a formal estimate of the requirements for American
military operations there.[88] They did however discuss these and
other problems orally.[89] On the basis of rather meager information
from the combat area the military leaders discussed the difficulties
inherent in the Korean peninsula as a field of battle for American
arms and examined the possibility of a commitment there in the
light of the worldwide responsibilities of American military power.
The sudden turn of events had not changed their previous opinion
that under conditions of global war Korea was not of strategic
importance to the United States.[90] Secretary Johnson later recalled
that the remainder of the conference was devoted to ". . . the individual, unrehearsed, unprepared and uncoordinated statements
of the several Chiefs and the Secretaries, the President asking a
number of questions that showed he had a great knowledge of
where our troops were and the military situation."[91]

With respect to the fighting, there was a general feeling that
the available information concerning its progress was rather "limited."[92] The conflict had been raging for only 33 hours, and the
conferees did not feel confident that the information they had
garnered from piecemeal reports added up to a clear understanding

---

86. *Hearings*, Part IV, 2580, 2671 f.
87. *Ibid.*, pp. 2621 f.
88. *Ibid.*, p. 2632. See also the testimony of General Omar N. Bradley, *Ibid.*,
Part II, 949.
89. Testimony of General Hoyt S. Vandenberg, *ibid.*, Part II, 1490.
90. Testimony of General Bradley, *ibid.*, pp. 1110 f.
91. *Ibid.*, Part IV, 2580.
92. Although an exact record of the information about the military situation in
Korea which was brought to the attention of the conferees at this time is not available, its major outlines remain in their memories; some of its details may be inferred from contemporary and later published reports.

of military developments. Despite this feeling they were agreed that the situation was "serious in the extreme."[93]

Having lashed across the Thirty-eighth Parallel at eleven places, the North Koreans had now penetrated the Republic of Korea to depths at some places of from ten to twenty miles.[94] Northwest of Seoul the invaders who had taken Kaesong were now attacking Munsan, twenty-five miles from the capital. Further to the northwest on the coast, the Seventeenth Regiment of the South Korean First Infantry Division was executing a withdrawal by sea from the Ongjin peninsula in accordance with a previous decision that its position there would be untenable if a full-scale invasion came. Northwest of Seoul, the invaders, having captured Tongduch'on and P'och'on situated along the twin road arteries which converged just north of Uijongbu, were sweeping down on that town only twelve miles from the capital. In central Korea the northerners were continuing to press the attack on Ch'unch'on. On the east coast, after taking Chumunjin, the invaders were advancing on Kangnung, twenty miles south of the Parallel. Forty miles further south, the North Koreans had made a bold amphibious landing with air support in the P'ohang area. North Korean aircraft had been reported in several other actions; they had bombed and strafed both Seoul and Kimpo airports, setting fire to oil storage tanks, and had machine-gunned the capital.[95]

The information from the fighting front, however, was not all bad. The ROK Army was stirring to action after the first shocking blows of the surprise invasion and was mustering its strength for a counterattack. An American correspondent in an exclusive eye-witness account from the Uijongbu area directly in the path of the North Koreans' main line of attack, reported that two South Korean divisions were moving up to stem the advance.[96] At about the same time it was reported that the invasion had "bogged down"

---

93. *Memoirs*, II, 335.

94. The following reconstruction is based on Republic of Korea, National Defense Ministry, p. B11.

95. This action was taking place on Sunday night, Washington time. Walter Simmons, *Chicago Tribune*, June 26, 1950, p. 1.

96. An account of the collapse of this counterattack, which apparently stemmed in part from failure to follow orders, is contained in Robert Leckie, *Conflict: The History of the Korean War* (New York: G. P. Putnam's Sons, 1962), pp. 47ff.

in this area. Some of the 60,000 refugees who earlier had clogged
the muddy road to Seoul in the Uijongbu valley were now reported
returning to their homes as confidence rose. Other reports indicated that American military advisers had confirmed the capture
by troops of Brigadier General Paik Sun Yup's First ROK Division,
of Haeju, capital city of Hwanghae province, one mile north of
the Thirty-eighth Parallel northeast of Seoul.[97] South Korean units
had encircled the troops who had made the amphibious landing
in the Samch'ok area, and were beginning to "exterminate" them.[98]

Thus, at this first Blair House conference, the consensus of the
President and his advisers, based on the general trend of earlier
calculations, was that the South Koreans could probably contain
the attack unless the North Koreans had received extensive outside assistance.[99] This appraisal was shared by Korean and American officials who had been closely associated with the development
of the South Korean military forces. In Seoul the Chief of Staff
of the ROK Army, General Ch'oe, reportedly stated after an
inspection of the front that the defenders were "more than holding
their own."[100] Brigadier General William L. Roberts, former
KMAG Commander, enroute to the United States, made a similarly
optimistic statement at about this time. The *New York Times*
reported: "General Roberts was inclined to discount North Korean
superiority in numbers, asserting that the many skirmishes of the
past had demonstrated that one South Korean regiment was easily
a match for one North Korean brigade. A full-scale attack, he said,
was just what was needed to complete the training of the South
Korean Army." Although the General expressed "some nervous-
ness" over the defenders' lack of air power, he considered their lack
of tanks to be but a "slight disadvantage because the Korean
terrain is not suited to them."[101]

---

97. An Associated Press dispatch from Seoul, *Chicago Tribune,* June 26, 1950,
p. 1, also reported a "town" had been taken five miles north of the Parallel.

98. Republic of Korea, National Defense Ministry, p. B11.

99. According to one of the President's advisers they "completely overestimated" South Korean capabilities and "completely underestimated" those of the
North Koreans at this time. All participants interviewed agreed on the earlier estimate of the South Korean fighting potential.

100. *Chicago Tribune,* June 26, 1950, p. 1.

101. *New York Times,* June 26, 1950, p. 3.

In estimating North Korean capabilities, the conferees also relied heavily on previous assessments. The People's Army was believed to be essentially a constabulary type military organization similar in size to the army in the south, although somewhat heavier in weight. The information they had on Sunday evening about the strength of the invasion force is suggested in a statement made at this time by the South Korean Minister of Defense, Shin Songmo, who reported that it consisted of 50,000 men out of a total trained reserve of 170,000. Minister Shin also said that the North Koreans were equipped with 173 tanks, an equal number of airplanes, and 32 naval vessels.[102] The state of knowledge in Washington on Sunday about the weapons in the hands of the People's Army is suggested by an article based on the "latest intelligence summaries" published two days later by Hanson Baldwin, military editor of the *New York Times*. He reported that no Russian-made tanks had been identified in the attacking forces and that although some Soviet equipment had been found in use, there was probably less of it than that of Japanese manufacture.[103] To the President and his advisers in the Blair House dining room, the strength, equipment and fighting ability of the aggressors were only partially known.[104]

In order to obtain more information about the military situation and the ways in which the United States might render assistance to the South Koreans, the conferees agreed that General MacArthur should be directed to send a reconnaissance party to Korea for a firsthand report from the battle area.[105] General MacArthur later ordered to the front Major General John H. Church, thirteen officers and two enlisted men from General Headquarters in Tokyo.[106] The group reached the town of Suwon, twenty miles south of Seoul, on the night of Tuesday, June 27 (6 A.M., Tuesday, in Wash-

---

102. *Chicago Tribune*, June 26, 1950, p. 2.

103. *New York Times*, June 28, 1950, p. 12.

104. Nearly a year later General MacArthur paid high professional tribute to the North Korean People's Army as being "as smart, as efficient, and as able a force as any I have seen in the field." Testimony, General MacArthur, *Hearings*, Part I, 230.

105. *Memoirs*, II, 335.

106. Testimony of Major General Edward M. Almond, *Interlocking Subversion in Government Departments*, Part XXV, 2059.

ington).[107] They were met by Ambassador Muccio and President Syngman Rhee.

The President and his advisers had no doubt whatever that the North Korean invasion had been inspired and controlled by the Soviet Union.[108] No one interpreted the absence of the Soviet delegate from the deliberations of the Security Council earlier in the afternoon as evidence that the attack had caught Soviet leaders by surprise; some, however, thought that these leaders had not expected Security Council action. Counselor George F. Kennan, who had discussed the Korean crisis with Secretary Acheson and others just before the Blair House conference began, thought that "the Russians were surprised that the United Nations would regard it as within its competence to take cognizance of what was, in the formal sense, a civil war."[109] Ambassador Jessup attributed Soviet absence from the Council—once it became known that it would meet—to a general lag in Soviet processes of decision. He further conjectured that even if Soviet leaders had contemplated the possibility that the United Nations might take action, they had decided that it would be ineffectual and invalid.[110]

The premonitioned Soviet action which intelligence experts had begun to feel was imminent as spring went and summer came had now apparently materialized. But the precise implications of the invasion in terms of Soviet world strategy were not entirely clear. The general trend of earlier thinking had been that the contemporary posture of the Soviet Union did not indicate a willingness to engage in a "hot" war with the United States, either directly or indirectly through any of the satellite nations. The sudden strike into South Korea evidently caused this earlier conclusion to be questioned.[111] But the consensus reached by the

---

107. Appleman, *South to the Kaktong*, p. 43.

108. Consult for example the testimony of Secretary of State Acheson, *Hearings*, Part III, 1936.

109. Counselor Kennan, Letter, September 4, 1959.

110. Ambassador Jessup, Interview, July 28, 1955.

111. In intelligence circles the invasion reportedly touched off a real dispute as to whether it was a "localized civil war" or a "big Soviet trial balloon." Correspondingly, it was disputed whether the U.S. should react in Korea or elsewhere. Some analysts reportedly were puzzled as to why the Soviet leaders had taken such a great risk as armed aggression in view of the "low importance" of Korea. Other problems apparently considered on Sunday were the world political effects of the invasion, and probable responses to U.S. inaction or resistance.

Blair House conferees was that the Soviet Union was using its Korean satellite as a pawn and probably was still not ready to wage a global war. President Truman expressed the view that Soviet leaders had gambled that the United States would do nothing in Korea and therefore expected to achieve a victory by default.[112] General Bradley was of the opinion that the Soviet Union, although unprepared for war, was "obviously testing" the United States.[113] In his view the North Korean invasion was a "limited challenge" but a challenge which evidenced a greater proclivity toward risk taking on the part of the Soviet leadership than they had hitherto demonstrated.[114] Ambassador Jessup thought that Soviet strategists were "probing for a soft spot."[115]

Although their estimates of Soviet intentions at this time did not bring them to the firm conclusion that World War III was imminent, nevertheless the conferees did consider the possibility that the invasion of the Republic of Korea might be accompanied by moves at other critical points along the periphery of the Soviet bloc, or by Communist expansion in the Far East.[116] Would the Soviets now move in Iran or Yugoslavia, for instance? The conferees believed that the plans of the Chinese Communists to invade Formosa were still in effect. Intelligence reports indicated that they had completed their invasion preparations by June 15.[117] Secretary Johnson had information that a buildup of Communist forces on the mainland opposite the island, from slightly over 40,000 to about 156,000 had coincided with his two-week trip to the Far East.[118] Would the mainland Chinese leaders now launch their invasion in conjunction with the North Korean attack? Evidently the Chinese Nationalist leaders thought so, for as soon as they had received reports of the fighting in Korea they had established an emergency round-the-clock invasion alert.[119] Chinese Communist expansion into Southeast Asia, especially into Indo-

112. *Memoirs*, II, 335.
113. *Ibid.*
114. Testimony of General Omar N. Bradley, *Hearings*, Part II, 942, 1070.
115. Interview, July 28, 1955. Also reported by Albert Friendly, *Washington Post*, June 28, 1950, p. 2.
116. Ambassador Jessup, Interview, July 28, 1955.
117. Hanson Baldwin, *New York Times*, June 28, 1950, p. 12.
118. *Hearings*, Part IV, 2621.
119. Associated Press dispatch from Taipeh, *Chicago Tribune*, June 26, 1950, p. 3.

china, was also considered by the Blair House conferees to be a possibility.

Another site of potential danger was the Philippines. The Communist-led Hukbalahap guerrillas had for long threatened the Philippine Government, and there was a possibility that a large-scale uprising might now take place. The North Korean invasion was also seen as a threat to Japan; all of Korea in hostile hands would be a menace to Japanese security. If there were an internal disturbance sparked by the North Korean invasion or an additional threat from without, American forces there might be pinned down.[120] There was some concern that in the absence of a Japanese peace treaty, the Soviet Union might invoke the right of belligerency to land troops on the Japanese home islands.[121]

To have the benefit of a fresh estimate of Soviet and Asian Communist "bloc intentions" the President ordered a worldwide intelligence recheck of the intentions of the Soviet Union and its allies.[122] Consequently, before midnight the State Department cabled an alert to key American diplomatic and military leaders throughout the world which read in part: "Possible that Korea is only the first of series of coordinated actions on part of Soviets. Maintain utmost vigilance and report immediately any positive or negative information. . . ."[123]

Other subjects of discussion that Sunday evening were the relative capabilities of the United States and the Soviet Union, the strength and disposition of American and Soviet forces in the Far East, and questions related to the contingency of American or Soviet intervention in Korea. In terms of overall military potential, the President later recalled, "I thought that we were still holding the stronger hand, although how much stronger, it was hard to tell."[124] Though the United States Army had only 592,000 men in its ranks,[125] the conferees saw no need for general mobilization.

---

120. Secretary Acheson, Interview, October 27, 1955.
121. Assistant Secretary Rusk, Interview, August 22, 1955.
122. Smith, p. 78.
123. Malcolm W. Cagle and Frank A. Manson, *The Sea War in Korea* (Annapolis: United States Naval Institute, 1957), p. 34.
124. *Memoirs*, II, 335.
125. Testimony of General J. Lawton Collins, *Hearings*, Part II, 1309. Eleven months later the ranks of the Army had swelled to 1,600,000.

The President asked the Joint Chiefs of Staff to report the latest information they had concerning Soviet forces in the Far East[126] and requested an estimate of the measures that would be required to neutralize Soviet bases there if the Soviet Union openly intervened in Korea.[127] He also questioned Admiral Sherman about the Seventh Fleet, asking how long it would take to bring it into the Straits of Formosa.[128] The Fleet—the major combatant units of which were the aircraft carrier *Valley Forge,* the heavy cruiser *Rochester,* and eight destroyers—was then deployed in Hong Kong and at Sangley Point and Subic Bay in the Philippines.[129] Admiral Sherman estimated that the move would take from one and a half to two days.[130] Other naval units available in the Far East were those in Japanese waters under the command of Vice Admiral C. Turner Joy, General MacArthur's naval chief, and included the light cruiser *Juneau* and four destroyers.[131] The President asked General Collins ". . . how many divisions we had in Japan and how long it would take to move two or three of them to Korea."[132] The American ground force then in the Far East totaled about 123,000 men and was the largest of its kind outside of the continental United States.[133] However, there were only four understrength combat divisions in Japan—the Seventh, Twenty-fourth, and Twenty-fifth Infantry Divisions, and the First Cavalry Division—which were engaged primarily in occupation duties. "Next," the President later recalled, "I asked Secretary of the Air Force Finletter and General Vandenberg what the present disposition of the Air Force was and how long it would take to reinforce our air units in the Far East."[134] Although it was not considered large, the United States had a powerful air armada based in and around Japan under Lt. General George E. Stratemeyer, General MacArthur's air commander. This force included three hundred and

126. *Memoirs,* II, 335.
127. Smith, p. 78.
128. *Memoirs,* II, 335.
129. Cagle and Manson, p. 31.
130. *Memoirs,* II, 335.
131. Austin Stevens, *New York Times,* June 28, 1950, p. 13.
132. *Memoirs,* II, 335.
133. *New York Times,* July 9, 1950, p. 7.
134. *Memoirs,* II, 335.

seventy-five F80 jet fighters, thirty F82 twin Mustang fighters, thirty-two B26 light bombers, and thirty B29 super-fortresses.[135] There was a difference of opinion among the Blair House conferees as to the nature of the military assistance that the Republic of Korea would require if its defensive forces really were shattered. Admiral Sherman and General Vandenberg thought that American airpower could be decisive. General Bradley and General Collins thought that American ground forces definitely would be required.[136] Some of the conferees stated that they did not wish to see ground troops committed in Korea.[137]

Despite the fact that the conferees discussed the possibility of an American military commitment in Korea additional to the provision of arms and ammunition, the question before them was not so black and white as, "To intervene, or not to intervene?"[138] They later recalled that the main reason why the problem was not thus sharply delineated was the sparsity of information from the battle area.[139] "No one could tell what the state of the Korean army was on that Sunday night," the President later explained.[140]

As each of the President's advisers expressed his opinion on the implications of an appropriate response to the North Korean

135. Austin Stevens, *New York Times*, June 28, 1950, p. 13.

136. *Memoirs*, II, 335.

137. Based on SCDS. While the exact record of the calculations of the nation's military leaders on the courses of military action which the U.S. might take in Korea is not available, existing evidence tends to confirm the accuracy of a report published within twelve hours by Harlan Trott of the *Christian Science Monitor*. The salient points of Mr. Trott's conclusions, reached on the basis of conversations with defense officials, were as follows: (1) Although the Army estimated that the South Koreans could repel the invaders unless they had been heavily reinforced, the Navy was somewhat doubtful because of North Korean air superiority and wanted an immediate "fly-over" of American airplanes for psychological effect while the aggressors pondered the terms of the Security Council resolution; (2) the Air Force favored bombing strategic targets in the rear of the invaders, but the Navy opposed this on the grounds that "saturation bombing" of these targets would involve undesirable nonmilitary destruction; (3) the Air Force was considering the possibility of sending tactical air units to South Korean airfields, a move which would involve the commitment of ground forces to protect the bases, but the Navy believed that the situation was "made to order" for carrier-based air power. Harlan Trott, *Christian Science Monitor*, June 26, 1950, p. 3.

138. All participants interviewed agreed that this was not the issue at this time.

139. E.g., Interviews, Secretary Acheson, October 27, 1955; Secretary Pace, October 24, 1955.

140. *Memoirs*, II, 335.

Communist challenge to world peace and American interests, it became evident that each of them shared a common conviction. As interpreted by the President, there emerged ". . . the complete, almost unspoken acceptance on the part of everyone that whatever had to be done to meet this aggression had to be done. There was no suggestion from anyone that either the United Nations or the United States could back away from it. This was the test of all the talk of the last five years of collective security."[141] General Bradley thought that the United States would have to "draw the line somewhere" against Communist aggression and expressed the opinion that it "ought to be drawn now."[142] At least one of the conferees drew a historical parallel between what was happening in Korea and the aggressions that had preceded World War II.[143] It was the "same old business" as the German, Japanese, and Italian aggressions of the 1930's.[144]

After listening to his advisers discuss Secretary Acheson's recommendations and questioning them about the points of information he felt were necessary for decision, the President announced his conclusions. First of all, General MacArthur was to be authorized to furnish the South Koreans whatever arms and equipment he could spare from the stocks of the Far East Command. This was to be a crash program of military aid over and above the provisions of the Mutual Defense Assistance Program. General Collins reported on the basis of a teletype conference with General MacArthur that he was ready to begin shipment of the material to Korea at once.[145] In long-range terms the military strengthening of the Republic of Korea would be all to the good, but since it would take some time before the arms-aid injection took effect, there was no certainty that it would halt the invaders.[146] The conferees hoped that the impact of American military supplies on the

---

141. *Ibid.*, p. 334. There is evidence, however, that all conferees did not share this conviction to the same degree, especially when it came to the question of the nature of the consequences which the U.S. was willing to accept as a result of "doing something" in Korea. See below, p. 224.

142. *Ibid.*, p. 335.

143. Based on SCDS.

144. One participant told this to reporter Ferdinand Kuhn earlier in the day. *Washington Post*, June 26, 1950, p. 5.

145. *Memoirs*, II, 335.

146. Ambassador Jessup, Interview, July 28, 1955.

battle situation could be accelerated by delivering some of them by airdrop.[147] They agreed that General MacArthur should be authorized to use the air and naval forces under his command to ensure their delivery.[148] The shipment of additional arms to the South Koreans was a positive measure that could be implemented quickly and publicized. Assistant Secretary Rusk's later characterization of the measure was, "If you can give them something, well go ahead and give it to them."[149] As Secretary Pace later explained, "It was one of those things you do anyway in a crisis."[150]

The President and his advisers were in unanimous agreement with Secretary Acheson's second recommendation that naval and air units of the Far East Command should be employed as necessary to insure the safe evacuation of American civilians from Korea. By this time the removal of American women and children from Korea had been Ambassador Muccio's "first preoccupation" for many hours.[151] The protection of American citizens with American military power was not only a measure rich in historical precedent,[152] but also was an integral part of the worldwide planning of the Department of Defense.[153] An evacuation plan for Korea had been in readiness since June 21, 1949.[154] There was no doubt in the minds of the conferees that General MacArthur would take whatever steps were necessary to guarantee the safe implementation of the evacuation plan that Ambassador Muccio had invoked without waiting for further instructions from Washington. To Secretary Johnson the measure was more of an "assumption" than a "decision."[155] To Secretary Pace it was "a normal and automatic thing to do."[156]

But the discussion of Secretary Acheson's third recommendation—that the covering forces be authorized to attack North Korean

147. Based on Princeton conference.
148. *Memoirs*, II, 336.
149. Assistant Secretary Rusk, Interview, August 22, 1955.
150. Secretary Pace, Interview, October 24, 1955.
151. Ambassador Muccio, Letter, August 27, 1959.
152. Ambassador Jessup, Interview, July 28, 1955.
153. Testimony of General Omar N. Bradley, *Hearings*, Part II, 1011.
154. Appleman, "The U.S. and the U.N. Intervene in Korea," p. 15. The Air Force evacuation plan for Korea and its execution is described in Futrell, p. 8.
155. *Hearings*, Part IV, 2574.
156. Secretary Pace, Interview, October 24, 1955.

tanks and airplanes which interfered with the execution of their mission—made of his second one something more than a foregone conclusion. The consensus of the conference was that American fighters should have fairly wide discretion in hitting the aircraft and the armor which were spearheading the invasion in the Seoul area.[157] General Bradley, however, did not wish to see this authorization explicitly stated in the orders which would be sent to American pilots in the Far East. Since he thought that they would get the idea without being told to do so, he did not want to give orders that might be subject to a broader interpretation than that which had been intended.[158] Secretary Acheson stated that in attacking the North Korean tanks the United States would be acting as a belligerent under the terms of the Security Council resolution.[159] Military protection of the evacuation of American civilians from Korea—justified by precedent, initiated by prearranged plan, and capable of implementation without delay—might also influence the military situation. Clearly, this was the view of the Blair House conferees at this time. The later testimony of some members of the Joint Chiefs of Staff shows that they had regarded the decision to employ American forces to cover the evacuation as the distinguishing feature of the conference.[160]

Secretary Acheson's fourth proposal, that further aid to the United Nations be discussed, had been more of a suggestion for the conference agenda than a recommendation for action, and the conferees had discussed it in that light. The President stressed the fact that whatever assistance the United States rendered to the Republic of Korea would be given under the banner of the United Nations. The United States in this crisis was "working for" the United Nations. He said that he would wait until the Security Council resolution was flouted before taking any action additional to that already decided upon.[161] Since the President expected the North Koreans to demonstrate their contempt of the international

---

157. Smith, p. 78.

158. Based on Princeton conference.

159. Secretary Finletter, Interview, October 24, 1955.

160. Testimony of General Omar N. Bradley, *Hearings,* Part II, 933. Testimony of Admiral Forrest P. Sherman, *Ibid.,* p. 1643.

161. Based on SCDS.

body, he thought the Security Council ". . . would have to apply force if it wanted its order obeyed," and asked the Joint Chiefs of Staff to "prepare the necessary orders" which would make American forces available if the United Nations requested them.[162]

Secretary Acheson's final recommendation had been to interpose the Seventh Fleet between the island of Formosa and the Chinese mainland, and to issue a statement of American intentions in making this move. Previously, both the departments of State and Defense had considered armed American military intervention in the impending final struggle in China to be undesirable as a general policy. Now, however, it was considered necessary, possible, and correct. Just before the conference began, Secretary Johnson had made clear his agreement with General MacArthur's position that the island bastion should not be allowed to fall into the hostile hands of the Chinese Communists. Secretary Acheson had come to the conference with a recommendation that not only encompassed this position but also sought to restrain the Chinese Nationalists—as well as the Chinese Communists—from military operations that would spread war in East Asia. The movement of the Fleet to the Straits of Formosa would serve the purpose also of bringing naval air power closer to Korea,[163] and would provide flank protection for a possible American military commitment on the peninsula.[164] The President decided that the Fleet should be put under the operational control of Admiral Joy and that it should be ordered to the southwestern Japanese port of Sasebo, some 700 miles from Formosa and less than 150 miles from the Korean port of Pusan.[165] He did not comment on the merits of Secretary Acheson's proposals with respect to Formosa as a whole.[166] He stated that he wished to "sleep on" a final decision in the matter,[167] since in any case he would not want to make any announcement about

---

162. *Memoirs*, II, 335. No evidence that orders of this kind were prepared prior to the Monday evening Blair House conference has been found.

163. Secretary Acheson, Interview, October 27, 1955.

164. Assistant Secretary Rusk, Interview, August 22, 1955.

165. Later, as the Fleet steamed toward Japan, Admiral Joy ordered it diverted to Okinawa where it would be close to both Korea and Formosa and not too close to Soviet or Chinese air bases. Cagle and Manson, pp. 31, 34.

166. Secretary Acheson, Interview, October 27, 1955.

167. Ambassador Jessup, Interview, July 28, 1955.

it until the Fleet was in the area.[168] Otherwise the United States would be merely advertising a military maneuver. Although the conferees had discussed the problem of Formosa as well as the crisis in Korea, they were later agreed that the latter was the main focus of attention at the time.[169]

As the discussion neared an end, Under Secretary of State Webb said, "I'd like to talk about the political aspects of the situation." The President snapped back, "We're not going to talk about politics. I'll handle the political affairs."[170] Thus the conference did not consider any questions dealing with domestic politics.

At about 11 P.M., the President and his advisers completed their deliberations. As the conferees departed, Secretary Acheson showed the President the cable that had been received earlier in the day from Ambassador Dulles in Japan. The President later recalled, "[Ambassador Dulles] too seemed to have little doubt about the course of action we had to take."[171] While the Presidential counselors quietly slipped out of the rear exit at Blair House to execute the decisions of the conference, reporters waited across from the White House on Pennsylvania Avenue for further news. About fifteen minutes later, the President's press secretary, Eben Ayers, announced that there would be no statement from the President that night. In effect, Mr. Ayers explained, the conference was still continuing, since the President planned to meet again with his advisers sometime on Monday.[172]

The Decisions of the Conference Are Transmitted to General MacArthur

Leaving Blair House, the civilian Secretaries and the Joint Chiefs of Staff hurried to the Pentagon to convey the decisions of

---

168. *Memoirs*, II, 334.

169. According to Secretary Johnson, the President also approved at this time the movement of American aircraft to some unidentified islands off Formosa. Secretary Johnson suggested this, he recalled, because the conference showed some reluctance to basing American planes on Formosa itself. Testimony of Secretary of Defense Louis A. Johnson, *Hearings*, Part IV, 2581.

170. Interview. This incident is also reported in Louis Fischer, *This Is Our World* (New York: Harper and Brothers, 1956), p. 162.

171. *Memoirs*, II, 336.

172. *Chicago Tribune*, June 26, 1950, p. 1.

the evening to General MacArthur in Tokyo. General Collins was principally in charge of the communications with the American commander in the Far East. Since no written directive had been produced during the conference with the President, one had to be improvised. The officials at the Pentagon were keenly aware of the grave responsibility entrusted to them as they sought to convey the sense of the Blair House conference that American aircraft were to have wide leeway in striking the aggressor tanks.[173] The public record contains some fragmentary paraphrased excerpts of the orders that were flashed to Japan at this time:

> On 25 June 1950 General MacArthur was informed that, to assist in evacuating United States dependents and noncombatants (names to be furnished by the United States Ambassador in Korea) he could take action by Air and Navy to prevent the In-chon-Kimpo-Seoul area from falling into enemy hands.[174]
>
> CINCFE is authorized to dispatch a survey party to Korea for purposes outlined . . . CINCFE is authorized to send any ammunition and equipment deemed necessary to prevent loss of Seoul-Kimpo-Inchon area . . . Appropriate air and naval cover authorized to ensure safe arrival . . . CINCFE authorized to take such action by air and Navy to insure safe evacuation U.S. dependents and noncombatants . . . Seventh Fleet ordered to proceed immediately to Sasebo and to report to COMNAVFE for operational control . . . While foregoing decisions are geared to the protection of dependents and noncombatants further high level decisions may be expected as military and political situations develop. . . .[175]

Just as the State Department had been the center of activity on Saturday night, now it was the Department of Defense. Twenty-four hours earlier a handful of men at the State Department had worked out an American response to the North Korean aggression within the framework of the United Nations. Now at the Pentagon another handful of men were sending out the orders that would implement further measures to cope with the continued attack. Much had transpired during the summer Sunday that intervened,

---

173. Secretary Finletter, Interview, October 24, 1955.

174. Appendix K, *Hearings*, Part V, 3192.

175. Walter Karig, Malcom W. Cagle, and Frank A. Manson, *Battle Report: The War in Korea* (New York: Rinehart, 1952), pp. 31ff.

but for the additional responses the United States might make to the crisis across the Pacific, nothing was more important than the deliberations of the fourteen men who had gathered in the dining room of historic Blair House. In their later memories two things stood out.[176] First, there was a sense of very limited information about the course of battle in Korea and about its specific implications for American policies. Thus the conference was remembered primarily as a meeting called by the President at which his advisers might share their information and views.[177] Questions were raised and answers were given—except to the question of whether the United States would undertake direct military intervention to repel the aggressors. Since information was felt to be meagre, that issue was not sharply posed. But despite the information about the actual progress of the fighting, the conferees agreed that the North Korean attack constituted a clear case of aggression. Thus the second major impression of the conferees was that they were immediately, strongly, and unanimously agreed that the aggression should not go unchallenged. In the view of one Presidential adviser, the conference was characterized by the manifestation of a "hard core of resolve" from which would emanate inexorably and logically all further measures that would be required to repel the invasion.[178] He further maintained that on the basis of this conference, the United States—under the banner of the United Nations—was prepared to accept the catastrophe of World War III if it proved to be unavoidable because of American refusal to accept the intolerable evils of "appeasement."

---

176. Secretary Acheson, Letter, August 24, 1959.
177. Assistant Secretary Rusk, Interview, August 22, 1955.
178. Ambassador Jessup, Interview, July 28, 1955.

CHAPTER 6

MONDAY, JUNE 26

The President Finds Press Opinion Parallels His Own Views

The President was ready for a strenuous day at an early hour on Monday morning. The newspapers which he customarily read after breakfast *(New York Times, New York Herald Tribune, Washington Post* and *Baltimore Sun)* were discussing the crisis in Korea with great concern. In the editorial of the *Washington Post* the President read: "This country is committed to repel the aggressor by every reason of prestige in Asia and of moral obligation to the Koreans."[1] He also read the exhortation to firmness published by the editors of the *New York Times:* "Thus far we have temporized and improvised. Our time for that ran out when North Korean tanks crossed the border. We can lose half a world at this

---

1. *Washington Post,* June 26, 1950, p. 8.

point if we lose heart."[2] The President was interested in these expressions of editorial opinion because they paralleled his own conclusion that the United States should make a determined positive response to the North Korean aggression.[3]

By 8:40 A.M. the President was at work in his White House office. He ordered all government departments to refrain from commenting upon the crisis in Korea. The explanation given for this injunction was that the United States was merely a "third nation" in the conflict and should not give the impression of being an "active participant."[4] He conferred with two early visitors, key staff members of the National Security Council—James S. Lay, executive secretary, and Sidney W. Souers, consultant. After this conference, the White House press secretary, Charles G. Ross, announced that although there would be no meeting of the National Security Council, President Truman would probably confer with Secretary of Defense Johnson later in the day.[5]

Secretaries Acheson and Johnson Testify Before the Senate Appropriations Committee

Secretary Johnson and Secretary Acheson appeared before a closed morning session of the Senate Appropriations Committee to urge quick Congressional passage of a bill to amend the Mutual Defense Assistance Program Act of 1949 which was then before the committee. This bill authorized sixteen million dollars for use in Korea and the Philippines, and provided for additional funds to be allocated at the discretion of the President. Secretary Acheson reportedly told the committee that "the situation in the Far East was never more than today a matter of the gravest concern to this government."[6] However, on the grounds that the problem was then under consideration by the President, neither he nor Secretary Johnson would comment upon the possible courses of action that

---

2. *New York Times,* June 26, 1950, p. 26.
3. President Truman, Interview, July 30, 1957.
4. James Reston, *New York Times,* June 27, 1950, p. 5.
5. *Washington Star,* June 26, 1950, p. 3.
6. *New York Times,* June 27, 1950, p. 4.

the United States might adopt to cope with the situation. The Senators especially wanted to know why the nation had not been forewarned of the invasion. A few hours later, Republican Senator Bridges of New Hampshire reported to the Senate, "The answer we got was that we would have to talk to Rear Admiral Hillenkoetter, Director of Central Intelligence."[7] The Admiral was called before the Committee later in the afternoon.

Soviet Intentions Are Assessed

After their appearance before the Appropriations Committee, Secretaries Johnson and Acheson returned to their offices. At the Pentagon, Secretary Johnson plunged into a full-scale conference with key leaders of the military establishment—including Deputy Secretary of Defense Stephen T. Early, the civilian secretaries, the Joint Chiefs of Staff, and Major General James H. Burns, Special Assistant to the Secretary of Defense for Military Affairs and Assistance.[8] Although the details of the agenda of this conference are not now available, the general trend of the deliberations was imparted to reporters in "off-the-record discussions" as the day wore on. Defense officials cautioned reporters that despite the very serious crisis that had arisen in Korea "they were not losing sight of what they regarded as the larger theater of the 'cold war'— Europe."[9] At the Department of State, Secretary Acheson engaged in a series of conferences with his advisers. The studies of overall Soviet intentions which had been requested by the President on Sunday night at Blair House were being prepared. Secretary Acheson discussed them in a conversation which continued through the noon hour with his foremost adviser on Soviet affairs, Counselor George F. Kennan. All the evidence available at this time seemed to point to the conclusion that the North Korean invasion was a "local affair," not connected to a wider pattern and not indicative of a Soviet desire to precipitate a third world war.[10]

---

7. *Congressional Record*, Vol. 96, Part 7, June 26, 1950, p. 9160.
8. Group photograph in *Christian Science Monitor*, June 28, 1950, p. 2.
9. *New York Times*, June 27, 1950, p. 4.
10. Counselor Kennan, Interview, August 1, 1955.

Ambassador Gross Reports on Opinion at the United Nations

An active participant in the discussions at the State Department throughout the day was Ambassador Ernest A. Gross, who had arrived in Washington early in the morning by special military airplane from his post at the United Nations.[11] The Ambassador had come to Washington to familiarize himself with the latest policy thinking at the State Department and to report his evaluations of the reactions to the Korean crisis by the Secretary-General and the various delegates to the United Nations. On Sunday, within the course of a few hours, because of the compact grouping in New York of the diplomatic representatives of scores of nations, Ambassador Gross had been able to discuss the Korean situation with many of his colleagues, both singly and in groups. On the basis of these conversations the Ambassador now reported with great emphasis that there was strong support among the delegates for sterner measures to enforce North Korean compliance with the Security Council resolution. To illustrate the attitude of determined resistance to the North Korean aggression which he had found at the United Nations, Ambassador Gross pointed to the assumption of personal responsibility for voting by some Security Council members on Sunday afternoon.

At the White House, President Truman pointed to Korea on the large globe that stood under a picture of George Washington in his office and said to an aide, "This is the Greece of the Far East. If we are tough enough now there won't be any next step."[12] The members of the White House staff were impressed by the President's attitude of grim resolution. When Senator Tom Connally, chairman of the Foreign Relations Committee, paid a late morning call upon the President, he gained the impression that the Chief Executive had not made up his mind as to what specific course of action the United States would take.[13] According

---

11. Ambassador Gross, Interview, October 28, 1955.

12. Smith, p. 80.

13. Senator Tom Connally (as told to Alfred Steinberg), *My Name is Tom Connally* (New York: Thomas Y. Crowell Company, 1954), p. 346. Secretary Acheson later pointed out that at this time "the material for specifics simply was not available." Thus the President was not to be viewed as hesitating between alternative courses of action. Secretary Acheson, Letter, August 24, 1959.

to Senator Connally, the President said that he wanted to review every possible alternative before he took any steps that might involve the nation in war. Senator Connally later recalled that although the President expressed some dismay over the fact that Soviet leaders had picked such a difficult place for the United States to defend, he declared emphatically, "I'm not going to tremble like a psychopath before the Russians and I'm not going to surrender our rights or the rights of the South Koreans." The Senator also recalled that the President asked his opinion as to whether or not he would have the authority to commit American forces in Korea without the prior approval of the Congress.[14] Senator Connally replied, "If a burglar breaks into your house you can shoot him without going down to the police station and getting permission. You might run into a long debate in Congress which would tie your hands completely. You have the right to do it as Commander-in-Chief and under the U.N. Charter."

The President Issues a Formal Statement

At 11:45 A.M., following a telephone conversation with Secretary Acheson, the President issued his first formal statement on the Korean crisis:

> I conferred Sunday evening with the Secretaries of State and Defense, their senior advisers, and the Joint Chiefs of Staff about the situation in the Far East created by the unprovoked aggression against the Republic of Korea.
> The Government of the United States is pleased with the speed and determination with which the United Nations Security Council acted to order a withdrawal of the invading forces to positions north of the 38th parallel. In accordance with the resolution of the Security Council, the United States will vigorously support the effort of the Council to terminate this serious breach of the peace.
> Our concern for the lawless action taken by the forces from North Korea, and our sympathy and support for the people of Korea in this situation, are being demonstrated by the cooperative

---

14. The President does not recall this incident. Others of his advisers have cautioned that it should not be construed as evidence of hesitancy on his part since he characteristically stood for a strong executive.

action of American personnel in Korea, as well as by steps taken to expedite and augment assistance of the type being furnished under the Mutual Defense Assistance Program.

Those responsible for this act of aggression must realize how seriously the Government of the United States views such threats to the peace of the world. Willful disregard of the obligation to keep the peace cannot be tolerated by nations that support the United Nations Charter.[15]

Following the lead of the President's statement, the Economic Cooperation Administration announced that it was placing its aid to Korea on an emergency basis; useful nonmilitary goods would be shipped to Korea in conjunction with the shipments of military materiel from Japan. A typical comment on these two announcements was that published by the *New York Times:* "Thus the pattern of action appeared to be to keep South Korea supplied with all the arms that General MacArthur could rush to the beleaguered country, as well as with new types of essential civilian goods under current aid programs, but to avoid any semblance of direct military intervention by this country."[16] Ferdinand Kuhn of the *Washington Post* interpreted the President's statement in this way: "Behind these strong words was an evident desire to temporize until the U.N. had acted, and until the President had made up his mind about the enormous issues raised by the Korean invasion."[17]

At a quarter past twelve, forty-five minutes earlier than usual, the President walked to Blair House accompanied by his Secret Service escort. He did not return to the White House until midafternoon.[18]

The Senate and House React

Just at noon the Reverend Frederick Brown Harris opened the first session of the Senate since the Korean crisis had gripped the attention of the nation. "Standing in these epochal days in the valley of decision," the Senate chaplain prayed, "strengthen our will to choose that which is morally excellent rather than that

---

15. Department of State, *U.S. Policy in the Korean Crisis*, pp. 15ff.
16. *New York Times,* June 27, 1950, p. 3.
17. *Washington Post,* June 27, 1950, p. 6.
18 *New York Times,* June 27, 1950, p. 4.

which is politically expedient. May we never hesitate when the choice is between honor and calculation. Our hearts and sympathy leap the seas this morning with the solemn realization that this very hour, under eastern skies, men are dying for freedom rather than to live as slaves."[19] The bulk of the ensuing session was devoted to the routine consideration of the Senate's normal business—committee reports, a prolonged discussion of the Magnuson-Morse amendment to a bill increasing the borrowing power of the Commodity Credit Corporation, and a number of other matters, such as the registration of foreign ships under American flags, and a boundary agreement between Missouri and Kansas. However, six Senators (five Republicans and one Democrat) addressed themselves to the problem of Korea.

Republican Senators Styles Bridges of New Hampshire and William F. Knowland of California vigorously criticized the apparent indecisiveness of the Democratic Administration. Senator Bridges, invoking the fateful memories of Manchuria, Poland, Czechoslovakia, Rumania, and Bulgaria, declared that he saw two ways in which the United States could cope with the disaster in Korea:

> First. We can continue our present course. It is the way of appeasement. It is surrender on the installment plan. We postpone war and we finally become the largest slave state.
> Second. We can call communism's bluff. I think it would work. I believe the Cominform is too crafty to risk a full scale armed conflict with the free world. But it is a calculated risk. Let us be frank. It might lead to war.
> But it is the only course open to America to preserve its freedom.[20]

Senator Knowland stressed the cruciality of the time factor in what he perceived to be a rapidly worsening military situation: "Time is of the essence. We must constantly keep in mind that Holland was overrun by Nazi Germany in five days and Denmark in two." Seconds later he declared gravely, "Time is rapidly running out. Difficult decisions cannot be permanently pushed aside.

---

19. *Congressional Record*, Vol. 96, Part 7, June 26, 1950, p. 9146.

20. *Ibid.*, p. 9155. It is probable that the Senator expressed similar ideas to Secretaries Acheson and Johnson when they appeared before a closed session of the Senate Appropriations Committee earlier in the day.

In these closing days of June 1950, the Congress, the American people, and the free world must be prepared to make a prompt decision."[21]

The only Democratic spokesman, Senator Tom Connally of Texas, followed his two critical colleagues on the Senate floor. Since he did not have a clear idea of the specific measures that would be undertaken to cope with the crisis—after his morning conversation with the President—he could only speak in "general hypothetical terms."[22] Senator Connally emphasized that the United States was seeking a solution to the Korean problem, peacefully if possible, but in any case firmly, under the United Nations. "We have set up the United Nations, and when it decides upon the course that ought to be pursued, we will then be in a better position to judge our responsibility, and what we should do, than we are today. If it takes more than resolutions, the United Nations can take actions beyond resolutions," he explained. Senator Knowland questioned what the United States would do if the Soviet Union crippled the Security Council with a veto on Tuesday afternoon. ". . . Does the Senator from Texas believe that we should sit back and twiddle our thumbs and do nothing?" he asked. The Chairman of the Foreign Relations Committee replied, "If the United Nations cannot act, they might pursue a course over and above the powers of the United Nations." Senator Knowland agreed that this was a possibility. The two Senators had clashed from the moment the Democratic spokesman had begun his remarks. Senator Connally pleaded that he be allowed to finish answering one question before being "shot in the ribs" by another. Senator Knowland berated him for "continual attempts to throw harpoons into Members on this side of the aisle." Senator Connally charged that his antagonist had "never contributed to bipartisan cooperation in the Senate"—and then apologized; Senator Knowland failed to rise when answering a question—then tendered his apologies.

When harmony had been restored and Senator Connally had finished his remarks, Senator Alexander L. Wiley, second ranking minority member of the Foreign Relations Committee,[23] gained

---

21. *Ibid.*, pp. 9157ff.
22. Connally, p. 347.
23. Republican Senator Arthur H. Vandenberg of Michigan, ranking minority member of the Committee, was ill at this time.

the floor. "Mr. President, now that everything has been smoothed out in such a lovely fashion between the two distinguished Senators, and love once more rules on the floor of the Senate, I feel that perhaps . . . I should say a few words," he began.[24] The Senator reported that he had been in touch with Secretary Acheson—as had Senator Connally—and that he had been assured that he would be informed of the latest information concerning developments in Korea. He said that he felt a need for more facts about the situation and that he thought the thing to do was to "keep calm" until they became available. In Senator Wiley's opinion the central question facing the nation was, "Where do we go from here?" He did not favor ". . . dwelling on the past with the present so full of challenges." "I do not think that the practice of examining into the past and of constantly dwelling on mistakes is going to be of assistance at this particular moment, in this particular crisis, unless we can profit from our mistakes and can determine how best to meet the present situation," he explained. Other questions which Senator Wiley thought needed to be answered were: "Is it a crisis of major or minor importance?" "Does it mean war?" "Will the invasion of South Korea provide another proving ground, as Spain did when two forces tested and proved their weapons?" "Is Russia bluffing?" and, "Should we call her bluff?" The Republican Senator cautioned, "One thing we want to make sure, and that is we do not focus all our attention on Korea, important as that may be. The Russian technique has always been to divert attention."

As the Senate session neared adjournment, two Republican senators charged unrefuted that the turn of events in Korea had stemmed from the premeditated calculations of American officials whose loyalty belonged to international Communism. From the past they drew ominous lessons of betrayal. Senator George W. Malone of Nevada inserted a few reflections on this subject in some extended remarks about the background of the Korean conflict. "It is fairly clear that what happened in China and what is now happening in Korea were brought about deliberately by the advisers of the President at Yalta and by the advisers of the State Department since then," he asserted.[25] Senator William E. Jenner

24. *Congressional Record,* Vol. 96, Part 7, June 26, 1950, pp. 9610ff.
25. *Ibid.,* p. 9184.

of Indiana joined in this denunciation. "Mr. President," he charged, "the front paging of the present plight of Korea is a grim reminder that the Russian bear is sprawled across the Eurasan continent biding its time, digesting its prey, and digging itself in for a long and cruel international winter. The Korean debacle also reminds us that the same sell-out-to-Stalin statesmen, who turned Russia loose, are still in the saddle, riding herd on the American people."[26] Republican Senator Joseph R. McCarthy of Wisconsin, while introducing into the *Congressional Record* a severe attack upon Secretary Acheson, did not comment upon the situation of the moment in Korea.

After the Senate session ended at about 5:45 P.M., there was a caucus of the Senate Republican Policy Committee. When they had completed their deliberations their spokesman, Senator Eugene D. Millikin of Colorado, announced to the press that they had come to a formal decision that the United States should give maximum aid to the Republic of Korea in the form of weapons and other military supplies but should not let the fighting drag it into a war.[27] The consensus of the meeting had been that the United States was under a "moral commitment" to help the Koreans help themselves, but was under "no obligation" to go to war.[28] Nevertheless, veteran Washington correspondent Arthur Krock reported on the basis of the afternoon activities in the Senate that it had become evident that "the President will have firm bipartisan support for any firm policy that is linked to plain national security."[29]

During the afternoon, the House of Representatives gave even less attention to the problem of Korea than had the Senate. Only two representatives mentioned the subject at all. Representative Laurie C. Battle, Democrat of Alabama, commended the American officials at the United Nations and the President and his

26. *Ibid.*, p. 9188.
27. *Christian Science Monitor*, June 26, 1950, p. 3. This seems to support Senator Connally's morning advice to the President that a move to secure prior Congressional approval for direct military action might provoke lengthy debate.
28. *New York Times*, June 27, 1950, p. 12. It is probable that this action and other Senate activities were communicated to the President by Senate secretary Leslie Biffle with whom the President kept in close touch about Senate affairs. On his desk Mr. Biffle had a red, white, and blue wrapped telephone that was connected directly to one on the President's desk in the White House.
29. *New York Times*, June 29, 1950, p. 28.

advisers for their "speedy action" and "alert response" to the crisis.[30] Republican Representative A. L. Miller of Nebraska attacked the State Department for "softness toward communism in the Far East."[31] At 3 P.M., Mr. Livingston Merchant of the State Department's Bureau of Far Eastern Affairs discussed the situation with the House Foreign Affairs Committee.[32]

There is no evidence that statements made in either the House or the Senate at this time came to the attention of any of the policy makers who had conferred with the President on Sunday night. But Secretary Acheson, upon whose department much of the invective of the afternoon had been heaped, needed no special notice to know that certain of his Republican opponents were constantly critical.[33]

President Truman returned to the White House shortly before three o'clock for a busy afternoon schedule. His first callers were Rear Admiral Roscoe H. Hillenkoetter, director of the Central Intelligence Agency, and the two staff members of the National Security Council with whom he had conferred earlier in the day. After his meeting with the President, Admiral Hillenkoetter appeared at 4 P.M. before the Senate Appropriations Committee to testify about intelligence warnings of the North Korean invasion. The Admiral had stated publicly on Sunday that the CIA had been aware that ". . . conditions existed in Korea which could have meant an invasion this week or next."[34] According to contemporary press accounts of his secret testimony, the Admiral told the senators that the CIA had received reports of unusual military activity by the North Koreans, beginning as early as the summer of 1949 and including fresh reports of tank and troop movements in April 1950.[35] After the interpellation, one of the senators told a representative of the *New York Times* that the Committee was satisfied that the CIA had passed on to top officials whatever information it had obtained with respect to the North Korean invasion —information that was not the responsibility of the CIA to

---

30. *Congressional Record*, Vol. 96, Part 7, June 26, 1950, p. 9197.
31. *Ibid.*, p. 9197.
32. Based on SCDS.
33. Secretary Acheson, Interview, October 27, 1955.
34. Robert F. Whitney, *New York Times*, June 26, 1950, p. 3.
35. Walter Trohan, *Chicago Tribune*, June 27, 1950, p. 4.

evaluate.[36] Although his views were not published in the last week
of June, the chairman of the Appropriations Committee, Senator
Kenneth McKellar (Democrat of Tennessee) later revealed that
he understood from Admiral Hillenkoetter's testimony that the CIA
had warned the President, the Secretary of State, and the Secretary of Defense on June 19 that northern forces were about to
invade the Republic of Korea. When he questioned Secretaries
Acheson and Johnson about this understanding, they both acknowledged that officials of their departments had signed receipts for
an intelligence document of that date. But, with the text in hand,
they both denied that it forewarned of impending invasion.
"There is not a word in the report to that effect," testified Secretary Acheson.[37] "There is not a thing in that report that inferred
that the invasion of South Korea was imminent," agreed Secretary
Johnson.[38] On the contrary, Secretary Acheson maintained that
the intelligence appreciation contained therein concluded that the
reported events in Korea were but a continuation of the wearing-
away-by-border-raids strategy which the North Koreans had been
pursuing for some time.[39]

Ambassador Chang Delivers Appeals from President Rhee
and the Korean National Assembly

At 3:50 P.M. the Ambassador of the Republic of Korea, John M.
Chang, arrived at the White House bearing an urgent appeal for
assistance from President Syngman Rhee. He was also officially
delivering an appeal from the Korean National Assembly which
had been quoted in a dispatch from Seoul that had arrived at the
State Department at 6:02 A.M.[40] The Korean legislature had peti-
tioned :

Seoul, June 26, 1950
Beginning in the early morning of 25 June the North Korean Com-

---

36. *New York Times*, June 27, 1950, p. 3. According to Arthur Krock, *New York Times*, August 20, 1950, the unidentified Senator must have misunderstood the Admiral; the CIA does evaluate raw reports.

37. Senate Committee on Appropriations, *Supplemental Appropriations for 1951*, 81st Congress, 2nd Sess., p. 291.

38. *Ibid.*, p. 290.

39. *Ibid.*, p. 291.

40. Based on SCDS.

munist Army began armed aggression against the South. Your Excellency and the Congress of the United States are already aware of the fact that our people, anticipating an incident such as today's, established a strong national defense force in order to secure a bulwark of democracy in the east and to render service to world peace. We again thank you for liberating us and in establishing our Republic. As we face this national crisis, putting up a brave fight, we appeal for your increasing support and ask that you at the same time extend effective and timely aid in order to prevent this act of destruction of world peace.[41]

Eight hours later, at 2 P.M., the situation had become so desperate that President Rhee placed a personal telephone call to Ambassador Chang.[42] Gone was the calm confidence with which he had viewed the invasion twenty-four hours earlier. Now with an impassioned expression of deep despair the Korean President informed the Ambassador that complete disaster seemed near and instructed him to carry his personal request for assurance of support to President Truman. At this time the Korean Government was withdrawing from Seoul to Suwon, 20 miles to the south across the Han River, as the invaders continued their unrelenting advance. The armored column spearheading their drive in the Uijongbu corridor was voraciously chewing its way through the two full South Korean divisions which hopefully had gone forth to bring it to a halt.[43] Along the invasion route to Seoul the blood of heroes and cowards together with the blood of those bewildered ones to whom circumstance did not provide a conscious choice between courage or cowardice stained the damp Korean earth the same bright red. "The suddenness of the catastrophe caught even the keenest of military observers with their predictions down," wrote eyewitness Walter Simmons from the front.[44] Estimates of the strength of the invaders had now risen to 75,000.[45] As he arrived at the White House, Ambassador Chang seemed glum to reporters. In a prepared statement he expressed regret that a negligible amount of the military aid which Congress had authorized for

41. Department of State, *U.S. Policy in the Korean Crisis,* p. 17.
42. Conversation with an official of the Korean Embassy, 1957.
43. Associated Press dispatch from Seoul, *Chicago Tribune,* June 27, 1950, p. 4.
44. *Chicago Tribune,* June 27, 1950, p. 1.
45. *Chicago Tribune,* June 27, 1950, p. 4.

Korea in 1949 had been delivered. "I am sorry that none of it has reached Korea to date at the time when we needed it most," the Ambassador sadly commented.[46]

Secretary of State Acheson also had come to the White House to participate in Ambassador Chang's conference with the President. Since one o'clock he had been engaged in intensive consultations with his advisers, including Assistant Secretaries Rusk and Hickerson, Under Secretary Webb, Deputy Under Secretary Matthews, Ambassador Jessup, and Counselor Kennan. He had conferred also with Army Secretary Pace and Admiral Hillenkoetter.[47] A sense of the rapid deterioration of the South Korean forces had permeated the discussions.[48] At about half-past three Secretary Acheson had terminated the deliberations in his office and had requested that he be given time to think in private and to write out his position.[49] At the start of this contemplation, he left for the White House.

When Ambassador Chang entered his office President Truman thought he looked "downhearted to the point of tears."[50] The President tried to cheer him up by reminding him that the battle was still young and that other men had successfully defended their freedoms "under much more discouraging circumstances." By way of illustration the President referred to two historical examples—examples in which help to the defenders of liberty ultimately came —the defeated Americans at Valley Forge in the winter of 1777-78, and the embattled Allies in Europe in 1917.[51] The President informed Ambassador Chang that orders had been issued for the delivery of certain arms and ammunition to the Republic of Korea[52] and that this equipment should soon tell upon the military situation. But he did not promise the commitment of American forces in Korea and the Korean Ambassador in fact did not specifically ask for them.[53]

---

46. *New York Times*, June 27, 1950, p. 4.
47. Based on SCDS.
48. Secretary Acheson, Interview, October 27, 1955.
49. *Ibid.;* Counselor Kennan, Interview, August 1, 1955.
50. *Memoirs*, II, 336.
51. Conversation with an official of the Korean Embassy, 1957.
52. Based on SCDS.
53. Conversation with an official of the Korean Embassy, 1957.

As the Ambassador left the White House he appeared to be more cheerful. "I think those arms will be coming soon," he told reporters. Speaking extemporaneously, Ambassador Chang voiced the limited scope of Korean expectations of American assistance: "We don't expect American soldiers to give their lives for us. We will do the fighting and the dying. Our boys are fighting their best. They're not afraid to die. A lot of them are dying already."[54]

A few minutes after the Korean Ambassador had departed, Secretary Acheson emerged from the President's office and without comment returned to the State Department.

Hope Diminishes for the Survival of the Republic of Korea

With the deepening shadows of the late afternoon the prospects for the survival of the Republic of Korea became darker and the anxiety of the nations of the Western world became more intense. The day had heard the anguished cry of Korea's President that American military aid was "too little and too late."[55] It had seen a report from the United Nations Commission on Korea which came to the unhappy conclusion that in view of "past experience" and the "present situation" it was convinced that the North Koreans would neither heed the resolution passed by the Security Council on Sunday nor accept the good offices of the Commission in putting an end to the fratricidal bloodshed. Therefore, the Commission somberly concluded, the resolution might soon "prove academic."[56] The day had also witnessed uneasy restlessness in European capitals as heads of state turned to fix their inquiring gaze on Washington. French eyes fearful for Indochina watched to see whether the United States would save its "Korean protege" from destruction.[57] The Cabinet of the Netherlands came out of conference with a collective stare which apparently meant that ". . . it is up to the United States to take a hand in Korea or Western prestige will drop all over the world."[58] An observer of British

54. *New York Times*, June 27, 1950, p. 4.
55. *Ibid.*, p. 1.
56. United Nations Document S/1503, June 26, 1950.
57. *New York Times*, June 26, 1950, p. 9.
58. *Ibid.*

politics reported that "Britain was waiting to throw her full support behind the United States once the United States Government had decided what it was going to do."[59]

But in Washington it appeared to many thoughtful men both within and outside the Government that it would do nothing. Informed officials, "usually in the know," were telling reporters privately that given the low strategic value of Korea, the risks of American military intervention were too great; therefore Korea had to be "written off."[60] As evening fell there was abroad in the city "a feeling of apathetic fatalism. . . . The belief that the Administration was unable or impotent to act in the sudden crisis was so widespread as to approach certainty."[61] James Reston, perceptive Washington correspondent of the *New York Times*, mulled over the conversations he had held with various officials and concluded: "There are some officials here who argue that Korea, established by the United Nations, and attacked without provocation, furnishes the best possible moral basis for challenging the Communist campaign of aggression, but the majority seems to believe that it would be unwise to choose a battleground and a time more favorable to the Communists than to the Western nations."[62] Virtually alone, Joseph C. Harsch of the *Christian Science Monitor* ventured a personal prediction which departed from the prevalent mood among officials: "It is not yet official policy that force will be met by force. There remain many interim problems and questions. One is that Korea is so singularly unfavorable for a military operation by western forces. However, it will be surprising, I think, if in the end Washington does not decide that the danger of giving way to pressure is far greater than the difficulties of supporting the South Koreans in South Korea."[63]

In the city of Washington this was "the night of the big gloom."[64] To the small group of advisers who had met with the President at Blair House almost twenty-four hours earlier, how-

---

59. *New York Times*, June 27, 1950, p. 2.

60. *New York Herald Tribune*, June 29, 1950, p. 4.

61. Richard L. Strout, *Christian Science Monitor*, June 29, 1950, p. 4.

62. *New York Times*, June 27, 1950, p. 5.

63. *Christian Science Monitor*, June 26, 1950, p. 1.

64. Phrase attributed to Joseph C. Harsch by Richard L. Strout, *Christian Science Monitor*, June 27, 1950, p. 1.

ever, there was nothing especially "gloomy" about their thinking.[65] As Ambassador Jessup later recalled, "We were simply faced with a particularly tough problem." Earlier in the day, on the basis of the Sunday Blair House conference, Admiral Sherman had told Vice Admiral Arthur D. Struble, commander of the Seventh Fleet who was about to leave Washington to return to the Far East, that "U.S. forces would definitely be committed in Korea."[66]

Secretary Acheson Drafts a Plan of Action

At 6:30 P.M. the Secretary of State, who had been working alone in his office since his return from the White House, called in his chief advisers and announced that he had drafted a paper embodying a recommended course of action for meeting the intensifying crisis in Korea.[67] The group worked on the draft in Secretary Acheson's office until a little after seven o'clock when they all went over to Washington's Metropolitan Club for dinner. During the meal, another of the President's advisers informed them that General MacArthur apparently had not understood the intent of the message sent to him on Sunday night because the Air Force pilots seemed to be limiting their mission to protecting the evacuation and were not hitting the North Korean tanks. "Oh my God, no!" exclaimed one of the State Department officials. At 7:29 P.M. Secretary Acheson telephoned the President. They agreed that the situation had now become so serious that another full-scale conference of the President's military and diplomatic advisers was in order. "Have them here at 9:00 P.M.," the President instructed.[68]

The Second Blair House Conference Is Held

The President's advisers assembled once again at the appointed hour. The conferees were substantially the same as those who had met the previous night. From the State Department came Secre-

---

65. Ambassador Jessup, Interview, July 28, 1955.
66. Cagle and Manson, p. 32.
67. Counselor Kennan, Interview, August 1, 1955.
68. Smith, p. 80.

tary Acheson, Assistant Secretaries Rusk and Hickerson, and Ambassador Jessup. As the meeting ended, Deputy Under Secretary H. Freeman Matthews arrived; he was to substitute for Under Secretary Webb, then on duty at the Department. The Defense Department contingent consisted of Secretaries Johnson, Pace, and Finletter, Generals Bradley, Collins and Vandenberg, and Admiral Sherman. Navy Secretary Matthews arrived at Blair House shortly after the meeting adjourned.[69]

To open the conference President Truman first called for the latest estimate of the military situation. General Bradley presented General MacArthur's most recent assessment of the course of the battle.[70]

> . . . Piecemeal entry into action vicinity Seoul by South Korean Third and Fifth Divisions has not succeeded in stopping the penetration recognized as the enemy main effort for the past 2 days with intent to seize the capital city of Seoul. Tanks entering suburbs of Seoul. Govt transferred to south and communications with part KMAG opened at Taegu. Ambassador and Chief KMAG remaining in the city. FEC mil survey group has been recalled under this rapidly deteriorating situation.
>
> South Korean units unable to resist determined Northern offensive. Contributory factor exclusive enemy possession of tanks and fighter planes. South Korean casualties as an index to fighting have not shown adequate resistance capabilities or the will to fight and our estimate is that a complete collapse is imminent.[71]

"There was now no doubt! The Republic of Korea needed help at once if it was not to be overrun," President Truman later recalled.[72] The conferees agreed that the ROK Army was apparently in a "rout"[73] and that unless the United States came to its support within a few hours there might be no more decisions to make concerning the preservation of the Korean Republic. In Korea[74] the situation had appeared so desperate by this time that the KMAG com-

69. Based on SCDS.
70. Smith, p. 80.
71. *Memoirs*, II, 337.
72. *Ibid.*
73. Assistant Secretary Rusk, Interview, August 22, 1955.
74. The rapid deterioration of the military situation in Korea in the twelve hours preceding the Blair House conference can be appreciated from the following

mander, Colonel W. H. S. Wright, with Ambassador Muccio's approval, actually had ordered his men to leave Korea, except for a group of 33 officers who were to remain to work with ROK Army headquarters. At about this time, however, or perhaps while the Blair House conference was in progress, he received a message to the following effect: "Personal MacArthur to Wright: Repair to your former locations. Momentous decisions are in the offing. Be of good cheer."[75] Apparently the originator of these hopeful tidings was General Collins, Army Chief of Staff.

Continuing the discussion of the combat situation, General Vandenberg reported that in executing its mission of covering the evacuation, an American fighter had shot down the first North Korean airplane, a Soviet-built YAK-3 fighter. "I hope it's not the last," the President said.[76] Possibly while the President and his advisers deliberated, or shortly thereafter, his wish came to fulfillment. Three North Korean aircraft attacked four American fighters providing air cover for the evacuation of American and other foreign nationals from the airfields at Kimpo and Suwon, and all three were destroyed.[77] The President was informed that the withdrawal of American civilians had not yet been completed.[78]

After considering the objective military situation, the President called upon Secretary Acheson to open the discussion of what further action the United States might take to save the Republic of Korea. The Secretary of State, reading from the draft which he

---

recollection by Ambassador Muccio: "Monday afternoon [i.e. Monday A.M. in Washington] the situation continued to deteriorate. At about 6:00 P.M., we requested CINCFE for sufficient air lift to evacuate all women plus less essential male members of the staff, and around midnight Monday we requested CINCFE to increase the air lift to include all members of the staff, including U.N. and diplomatic corps personnel. The final busload left the American Embassy building at about eleven o'clock Tuesday morning.

"Shortly thereafter my Deputy Drumright, with four members of the staff, proceeded to Taejon by car to maintain contact with the Korean Government. Accompanied by four other members of the staff, I personally went to the Korean Army headquarters and finally left Seoul at 4:00 P.M." Letter, August 27, 1959.

75. Appleman, "The U.S. and the U.N. Intervene in Korea," p. 24. Lieutenant Colonel Appleman was unable to discover the original text of this message, but KMAG officers remembered two substantially similar versions of it.

76. Smith, p. 80.

77. Appleman, "The U.S. and the U.N. Intervene in Korea," p. 19.

78. Smith, p. 80.

had prepared in the late afternoon, made five recommendations for decision by the President.[79] These proposals were as follows: (1) that the Navy and Air Force be instructed to give the fullest possible support to the South Korean forces and that such support be limited to the area south of the Thirty-eighth Parallel; (2) that orders be issued to the Seventh Fleet to prevent an attack upon Formosa, that the Chinese Nationalist Government be told to desist from operations against the mainland, and that the Fleet be ordered to secure the compliance of the latter; (3) that American forces in the Philippines be strengthened and that increased military assistance be rendered to the Philippine Government; (4) that military assistance to Indochina be accelerated and that a military mission be sent there; and (5) that Ambassador Austin be instructed to report any action taken under the above recommendations to the United Nations. Secretary Acheson also proposed that continuing scrupulous study be made of Soviet activities in places other than Korea. Elaborating on his first recommendation, Secretary Acheson explained that there was strong support within the Security Council for military sanctions against the North Korean aggressors.[80] He further stated that when the Council reconvened on Tuesday afternoon the United States would be prepared to introduce a resolution calling for additional assistance to the Republic of Korea.

Just as he had done on the previous evening, the President next asked for the opinions of each of his advisers, beginning with the Secretary of Defense. Once again Secretary Johnson reported that the Defense Department had no specific recommendations of its own to present.[81] As he later explained, "Neither I nor any member of the Military Establishment in my presence recommended we go into Korea. The recommendation came from the Secretary of State, but I want to repeat that it was not opposed by the Defense Department all the members of which had severally pointed out the trouble, the trials, tribulations, and the difficulties."[82]

---

79. The first four of these recommendations are based on SCDS. The fifth was recalled by Secretary Acheson: Interview, October 27, 1955.

80. Secretary Acheson, Interview, October 27, 1955.

81. Secretary Johnson later recalled that he knew of the recommendations to be introduced in the conference prior to its convening, but only through the President. Interview, October 27, 1955.

82. *Hearings*, Part IV, 2584.

The ensuing discussion, with all of the President's advisers having the opportunity to voice their opinions, centered around the recommendations that Secretary Acheson had presented. Although the present state of the ROK Army was alarming, the conferees agreed that with the support of American air power it could probably throw back the invaders.[83] American fighter strikes against enemy armor should cripple the aggressor advance. The reassuring presence of white-starred American airplanes over the battle area also might help to raise the morale of the shocked defenders, while diminishing the confidence of the invaders. The North Koreans were not known to have anything comparable to the sea and air power which the United States had available in the Far East to throw against them. Austin Stevens of the *New York Times* reported on Tuesday that Defense leaders had estimated that the North Koreans had about 100 aircraft of "inferior performance characteristics," and about 30 small naval vessels. Therefore American naval and air support would give the South Koreans "overwhelming superiority."[84] As Secretary Finletter later pointed out, ". . . The enemy came right down under our noses where we had the greatest concentration of American military power outside the United States."[85]

Despite the prevailing confidence in the impact of air and sea power on the fighting, Generals Bradley and Collins perhaps still entertained the reservations they had expressed on Sunday that American ground troops might be needed if the ROK Army had really lost its fighting effectiveness. But no one seems to have recommended that they be committed.[86] Apparently Secretary Johnson said that he did not wish to see ground troops sent to Korea. One of the President's advisers expressed the view that if a decision to employ ground forces were taken, mobilization would be required; otherwise the United States could not meet its obliga-

---

83. The participants subsequently agreed that at this time they "overestimated" the impact of airpower upon the military situation, "overestimated" South Korean capabilities, and "underestimated" those of the North Koreans; e.g., Interview, Secretary Finletter, October 24, 1955.

84. *New York Times*, June 28, 1950, p. 13.

85. Testimony of Secretary of the Air Force Thomas K. Finletter, House of Representatives, Committee on Appropriations, *The Supplemental Appropriation Bill for 1951*, 81st Congress, 2nd Sess., p. 230.

86. Based on SCDS.

tions elsewhere throughout the world[87]—especially in vital Europe.[88] The United States was limited in whatever help it could give Korea to its airplanes and ships in Far Eastern skies and waters and to the four understrength divisions deployed in Japan. However, as indicated above, the conferees did not formally consider at this time the possible commitment of ground soldiers to combat on the Korean peninsula.

Aside from the limitations of available strength, the President's advisers considered other difficulties connected with the military support of the South Koreans. The United States would have to operate a supply line some 5,000 miles in length. Moreover, looking at American defense requirements from a global point of view, the Joint Chiefs of Staff had long considered Korea to be of no strategic importance to the United States. As the chairman, General Bradley, later explained: "We had always hoped that we would not have to fight in Korea, and that's why we were in favor of getting out of Korea as far as our occupation was concerned. Because strategically it is a poor place to fight."[89]

The conferees were in complete agreement with that part of Secretary Acheson's recommendations pertaining to military support of the South Koreans which stipulated that American aircraft and ships should be limited in their combat action to the territory south of the Thirty-eighth Parallel. There were two main reasons why such a restriction was thought desirable. First, it was not contemplated at this time that more extensive operations in the enemy's rear would be required to repulse him. Second, it was hoped that by limiting the scope of American military operations, the possibility of direct Soviet or Chinese Communist intervention in Korea might be minimized. The conferees were in basic accord that the United States should do only what was necessary to repel the invaders; any provocation which might enlarge the conflict was to be avoided. There was a general understanding that the United States should act in such a way as to assure the Soviet

---

87. Based on SCDS.

88. James Reston wrote on Tuesday: "Some of the soldiers naturally hesitated to disperse United States forces too much. General Bradley, in particular, has been warning that we must keep our eye on the central target, which in his judgment, still lies in Europe." *New York Times*, June 28, 1950, p. 4.

89. Testimony of General Omar N. Bradley, *Hearings*, Part II, 753.

Union that it was "not looking for trouble."[90] An aspect of the proposed commitment of air and naval forces which was related to the desire to keep the conflict limited was its perceived flexibility. If, unhappily, the South Korean forces had deteriorated to such an extent that they were overwhelmed before effective help could arrive on the scene, then it would be advantageous for the United States to be able to make a rapid disengagement.[91] Furthermore, if—unknown to the Blair House conferees—Soviet or Chinese forces were already engaged in combat, or later became committed, a clash with American ships or airplanes would not carry the same psychological overtones for the American people as would the mutual slaughter of infantrymen. The pressure to plunge into an ill-considered war would thus be lessened.[92] There was also some feeling that from the domestic point of view the commitment of air and naval units would be more natural and normal than the dispatch of ground forces which would carry the strong connotation of "war."[93] The desire of the President and his advisers to keep the conflict limited reflected not only the conviction that the Korean peninsula was no place to fight a major war, but also the determination that the United States should not let the fighting there drag it into a general war elsewhere.

There was no opposition to Secretary Acheson's repeated proposal that the Seventh Fleet be ordered to guarantee the security of Formosa from invasion and to ensure that the Nationalist garrison did not assault the Communist-held mainland. Secretary Acheson's main objectives in advancing this proposal were to try to keep the Korean conflict limited, to try to avoid the possible loss of both Korea and Formosa, and to contribute to the general stability of the Far East.[94] There is no evidence that the Secretary of State included this recommendation in his set of proposals in order to gain military approval of intervention in Korea. As President Truman later explained, "The purpose of this move was to prevent attacks by the Communists on Formosa as well as forays by Chiang

90. Secretary Acheson, Interview, September 24, 1957.
91. Assistant Secretary Rusk, Interview, August 22, 1955.
92. Secretary Pace, Interview, October 24, 1955.
93. Ambassador Jessup, Interview, July 28, 1955.
94. Secretary Acheson, Interview, September 24, 1957.

Kai-shek against the mainland, this last to avoid reprisals by the Reds that might enlarge the area of conflict."[95] One of the President's advisers mentioned that the island of Formosa might serve as a "staging area" for American military operations in Korea. The use of Formosa as a base would be especially convenient when transferring air units. Another conferee regarded its defense as "flank protection" for American efforts to repel the North Korean invaders. Because it was understood that most members of the United Nations would be willing to support American action in Korea but not in Formosa, the conferees agreed that the United States should assume sole responsibility for flinging a naval cordon around the island to insure its military neutralization.

There was no disagreement on the proposal to strengthen the military potential of the Philippines. The islands had long been considered a vital link in the American Pacific defense chain. There was every assurance that this assistance would be warmly received in Manila. On Sunday, as soon as he had received news of the North Korean invasion, influential Senator Camilo Osias, former Resident Commissioner of the Philippines in Washington, had stated publicly: "The whole orient is watching American commitments regarding Pacific defenses. The oriental people will base their judgment on what the American government and people will do in aid for the Philippines."[96] Similarly, the conferees expressed unanimous approval of the proposed extension of military aid to Indochina beyond that already provided for under the Mutual Defense Assistance Program. Thus, except for the sending of a military mission, this measure represented no change in American policy toward Indochina which was to support the Bao Dai government as an alternative preferable to that of rule by Communist-supported Ho Chi Minh. Augmented assistance to the Southeast Asian land also fitted in with American hopes that the Vietnamese army could assume more responsibility for the security

---

95. *Memoirs*, II, 337. In his speech to Congress on July 19, 1950, the President explained, "Our action in regard to Formosa was a matter of elementary security. The peace and security of the Pacific area had been violently disturbed by the attack on Korea. Attacks everywhere in the Pacific area would have enlarged the Korean crisis, thereby rendering much more difficult the carrying out of our obligations to the United Nations in Korea."

96. David Boguslav, *Chicago Tribune*, June 27, 1950, p. 6.

of their country so that French forces could be freed for the protection of metropolitan France.

There was full agreement that whatever action the United States took in Korea would be carried out within the framework of the United Nations. The President's diplomatic advisers were certain that the Sunday Security Council resolution could be "stretched" to cover the air and sea support of the South Koreans that Secretary Acheson had proposed. In any case, it would be surprising—given Ambassador Gross' report of strong opinion in favor of the application of military sanctions—if the Security Council on Tuesday afternoon did not adopt the resolutions calling for them, which the United States was prepared to introduce. One of the conferees mentioned the possibility that the Soviet Union might paralyze the Council with its veto power. But the opinion was expressed that a Soviet veto, in itself, would not change the American position.

The problem of Soviet intentions and the probable reaction Soviet leaders might make to American intervention in Korea were topics of discussion. Earlier in the day, one of the President's chief advisers in the State Department had made an analysis of the factors that had probably motivated Soviet leaders to give their blessing to the invasion of South Korea at this particular time. First of all, the North Korean invasion had been launched in the aftermath of the emergence of Georgi Malenkov over Andre Zhadanov within the Soviet hierarchy—a power realignment which had been accompanied by a shift in Soviet policy attention to the Far East. Second, the attack was interpreted as being partly a response to indications that the United States was prepared to proceed with the conclusion of a Japanese peace treaty without Soviet participation. Soviet leaders undoubtedly had been disturbed by the discussions concerning the treaty which revealed for the first time that the United States intended to maintain some sort of military establishment in Japan for an indefinite length of time. Third, in the well-trained, heavily armed North Korean People's Army, Soviet leaders had at hand an instrument which offered the tempting prospect of an easy victory over the lightly armed defense forces of an area in which American prestige was deeply involved. A fourth major consideration in the Soviet decision to trigger the invasion, this analyst held, was the fact that since 1949 the five bright new stars of Communist China had risen triumphant in the East to rival in brilliance the red star of the Soviet Union. Soviet leaders, having achieved no comparable success since the end of World War II, were deeply in need of a victory that would counterbalance the ascent of Chinese Communist prestige, power, and influence in the Orient. Where, then, could they act? Outside of the Soviet-Afghanistan border, including the Pamir Mountains, the rest of the Soviet Asian frontiers nestled against China and Mongolia—except for Korea. On the basis of these considerations, this analyst had concluded that the Soviet venture in Korea was a limited, local undertaking, not immediately connected to a wider pattern of aggressive action the aim of which was to engage the United States in World War III. The Soviet Union, therefore, could be expected to avoid direct involvement in the Korean fighting. Soviet leaders probably would remain content with manipulating their Korean puppet from behind the eleven-mile Soviet-Korean border.

On the basis of this analysis and other results of the worldwide intelligence recheck of Soviet intentions which the President had ordered on Sunday night, the participants in the second Blair House conference were in general agreement that—although the possibility could never be ruled out completely—Soviet leaders for the present did not intend to precipitate a global war. The invasion of South Korea was considered to be what General Bradley later termed a "limited challenge."[97] Although the analysis outlined above was an important contribution to the thinking of the President and his advisers, it was not the only interpretation of Soviet intentions which was offered during their deliberations. President Truman later recalled: "I told my advisers that what was developing in Korea seemed to me like a repetition on a larger scale of what had happened in Berlin. The Reds were probing for weakness in our armor; we had to meet their challenge without getting embroiled in a world war."[98] Ambassador Jessup held to the similar interpretations he had placed upon the attack

----

97. "We accepted a limited challenge . . . with the hopes that it would be limited to Korea and would not develop into a world war." Testimony of General Omar N. Bradley, *Hearings,* Part II, 1070.

98. *Memoirs,* II, 337.

when he first learned of it on Saturday night; namely, that Soviet leaders were "probing for a soft spot."[99] General Bradley thought that the Soviet move in Korea was a "softening-up operation"[100]— the first stop on a "timetable" of aggressions the final destination of which, if uninterrupted, would be World War III.[101] The weight of opinion in the conference was that the invasion of South Korea was part of a Soviet strategic master plan.[102] But lest the question of Soviet motivations and intentions be given undue emphasis, Secretary Acheson later cautioned that the crux of the problem confronting the conference was not that of abstract speculations about Soviet strategy. It was "This is what they are doing in Korea. What, within the limits of our capabilities, are we going to do about it?"[103]

But the secondary question remained: "What would Soviet leaders do if the United States ordered its air and naval forces into combat against the invading North Koreans?" The consensus of the conference was that direct Soviet counterintervention was possible, but improbable. General Bradley later described its probability as "rather remote."[104] To General Vandenberg it was "very doubtful" and "relatively small."[105] Secretary Acheson subsequently explained that intelligence studies had concluded it was ". . . improbable, barring Soviet decision to precipitate global war."[106] Although there had been no official reports of Soviet forces actively participating in the Korean fighting,[107] Secretary Johnson later recalled that the conferees had no definite assurance that they were not.[108] A few newspaper accounts based on South Korean sources had indicated that they were. The Associated Press had reported a statement by Korean Defense Minister

99. Ambassador Jessup, Interview, July 28, 1955.

100. General Omar N. Bradley, "A Soldier's Farewell," *Saturday Evening Post,* August 22, 1950, p. 62.

101. *Hearings,* Part II, 896, 942, 971.

102. Based on SCDS.

103. Secretary Acheson, Interview, October 25, 1955.

104. *Hearings,* Part II, 949.

105. *Ibid.,* p. 1491.

106. *Ibid.,* Part III, 1832.

107. Based on SCDS. Also letter from the Chief of Military History, Dept. of the Army, August 20, 1958.

108. *Hearings,* Part IV, 2586.

Shin Songmo that Russian crewmen had manned ten of twenty tanks which had been captured on the Seoul front and that the Korean Navy had sunk a Soviet naval vessel off the east coast.[109] In Korea the Taehan News Agency also had reported that Soviet officers were leading the People's Army and that "large numbers" of Soviet soldiers were riding the invading tanks northeast of Seoul.[110] It was the unanimous view of the Blair House conferees that Soviet leaders would be greatly surprised by American military intervention to save the Republic of Korea.[111] Since Soviet leaders apparently had concluded that the United States had "washed its hands" of Korea,[112] and since their North Korean minions seemingly had a "walkover" in their invasion,[113] they probably had not worked out a definite plan of reaction to the contingency of firm American resistance. Therefore the problem of estimating the response they might make was important, but not crucial.[114]

The President and his advisers also discussed the possibility that the Chinese Communists might intervene in the Korean fighting, but this too was held to be unlikely. Some of the reasons advanced in support of this conclusion were that they were already engaged militarily in a "pacification campaign" in northeastern China and that their present troop dispositions did not indicate that they were poised to lunge across the Korean-Manchurian frontier.[115] General Vandenberg subsequently recalled that it was estimated at this time that the Chinese Communists in the immediate future would be incapable of organizing, training, equipping, and transporting a large ground army which could be committed to the Korean conflict.[116] If they moved offensively it was much more likely that they would push into Southeast Asia or launch their long-anticipated invasion of Formosa.[117] Nevertheless the policy makers considered the possibility that if the Chinese did

109. *Chicago Tribune*, June 26, 1950, p. 2.
110. National Defense Ministry, Republic of Korea, p. B11.
111. Testimony of General Bradley, *Hearings*, Part II, 970.
112. Testimony of Secretary of Defense Johnson, *Ibid.*, Part IV, 2585.
113. Ambassador Jessup, Interview, September 21, 1958.
114. *Ibid.*
115. Assistant Secretary Rusk, Interview, August 22, 1955.
116. *Hearings*, Part II, 1504.
117. By late August, however, Secretary Acheson was referring to the possibility of Chinese Communist intervention in Korea as the "chief danger" to world peace

intervene, the United States might have to approach the Soviet Union in order to get them to withdraw.[118]

Despite the conclusions that the Soviet Union was not prepared to fight a general war and that neither it nor Communist China would intervene directly in Korea, the Blair House conferees knew that the risk of war would be involved in a decision to repel the North Korean aggressors with American men and arms. "We of the military recognized it as a calculated risk," Secretary Johnson subsequently explained.[119] General Bradley later wrote, ". . . If the defense of South Korea was risking an all-out war the choice was not ours, for the Communists had thrown down the gauntlet."[120] According to Ambassador Jessup, "The invasion had to be met even if it meant the beginning of World War III."[121] Secretary Pace, while agreeing on the necessity for repelling the aggression and willing to accept the risk of war, was concerned lest Soviet counterintervention evoke in the American people a strong emotional reaction that might carry the nation into a global conflict before its full implications could be assessed.[122] In another participant's view, a decision to resist militarily in Korea would not necessarily be a decision to accept a general war with the Soviet Union.[123] State Department records of the conference, however, reportedly indicate that the danger of all-out war was "not seriously discussed" and was "not a deterrent factor" in the decisions that were taken.[124]

During the discussion of Secretary Acheson's recommendations,

---

and American security: "I think we cannot emphasize the seriousness of that situation." Testimony of Secretary of State Dean G. Acheson, *Supplemental Appropriations for 1951*, p. 292.

118. According to Albert L. Warner, p. 103, Secretary Johnson took the position that if either Chinese or Soviet forces were committed in Korea, the U.S. itself would have to withdraw. The Defense Secretary has also maintained, however, that even if the conferees had known that Chinese or Soviet troops were fighting in Korea this knowledge would not have altered substantially the decisions of the evening. Testimony of former Secretary of Defense Johnson, *Hearings*, Part IV, 2586.

119. *Hearings*, Part IV, 2585.

120. General Omar N. Bradley, "U.S. Military Policy: 1950," *Reader's Digest*, (October, 1950), p. 146.

121. Ambassador Jessup, Interview, July 28, 1955.

122. Secretary Pace, Interview, October 24, 1955.

123. Letter, August 20, 1959.

124. Based on SCDS.

not one of the President's advisers took the position that the United
States should not undertake military intervention to save South
Korea. There were difficulties and there were risks, but American
refusal to repel the aggression would be nothing but "appeasement." And appeasement, as history has shown, would ultimately
lead to war. Ever since their first awareness that the North Korean
People's Army had launched an invasion of the Republic of
Korea, President Truman and some of his advisers had drawn
three historical parallels from the fateful decade which had preceded the horror of World War II: Adolph Hitler's disdainful,
violent, piecemeal conquests; Benito Mussolini's rape of Ethiopia;
and Japan's arrogant seizure of Manchuria. While sharing these
historical memories, although differing slightly in the specific additional instances which the North Korean invasion called to mind,[125]
the conferees at once had identified it as a case of blatant "aggression."

In the catastrophic consequence of the League of Nations'
failure to thwart the aggressive actions of German, Italian, and
Japanese leaders in the 1930's, the policy makers found a grave
lesson for the United Nations in 1950. They subsequently agreed
that General Bradley expressed the consensus of the conference
when he later explained: "Well, the decision was made that here
was another act of aggression that, if we appeased in this case, something else would come along, and either you appeased again or
took action in the next one, and I think it was fully realized by
everyone and it seemed to meet the approval of the people at
the time, that one appeasement leads to another until you eventually make war inevitable."[126] The conferees also identified the
situation confronting them with similar crises which the United
States had faced in the postwar period—the Greek crisis of 1947,
and the Berlin crisis of 1948.[127] Resolute American resistance to
Soviet pressure in these earlier situations had been successful. "No
appeasement" was the dominant theme of the conference.

The President and his advisers agreed that the consequences of

125. Secretary Finletter, for example, also identified it with the Chaco War
between Paraguay and Bolivia which broke out in 1933.
126. *Hearings*, Part II, 890.
127. Composite Questionnaire. See also *Memoirs*, II, 337.

an American failure to save the Republic of Korea would be intolerable. Not only would the United States and the free world lose a friend and an ally, but also, as President Truman later explained, "More seriously, a Communist success in Korea would put Red troops and planes within easy striking distance of Japan, and Okinawa and Formosa would be open from attack from two sides."[128] Although there had been no "eleventh-hour" shift in the opinion of the Joint Chiefs of Staff that Korea was not of strategic importance as far as the United States was concerned, they did agree that a Communist Korea would be a threat to Japanese security.[129] The Blair House conferees calculated that if they stood idly by while South Korea was bludgeoned into submission, American prestige and the reputation of the United States as a dependable friend and ally would sink lower with every blow. According to General Vandenberg, ". . . Recognizing the very evident risks, we all believed that somewhere, sometime, we had to stop being pushed around, and to afford some hope to those people who lined themselves up with us, that they could expect some assistance from the United States."[130]

The conferees also believed that a failure to repel the aggression against the Republic of Korea would mean the negation of five years of American efforts to build up a viable system of collective security. As explained later by Secretary Acheson:

> The attack on Korea was . . . a challenge to the whole system of collective security, not only in the Far East, but everywhere in the world. It was a threat to all nations newly arrived at independence. This dagger thrust pinned a warning notice to the wall which said: "Give up or be conquered."
>
> This was a test which would decide whether our collective security system would survive or would crumble. It would determine whether other nations would be intimidated by this show of force. . . .

---

128. *Memoirs*, II, 337.

129. Testimony of General Bradley, *Hearings*, Part II, 1110ff. The General also cautioned, ". . . You have to stop your front line somewhere." On June 30 Ambassador Dulles explained the implications of a Communist success in Korea for Japan as follows: "Thus, if the Communists not only have Sakhalin to the north but also Korea to the south, Japan would be between the upper and lower jaws of the Russian bear." *Department of State Bulletin*, Vol. 23, No. 575, (July 10, 1950), p. 50.

130. *Hearings*, Part II, 1504.

As a people we condemn aggression of any kind. We reject appeasement of any kind. If we stood with our arms folded while Korea was swallowed up, it would have meant abandoning our principles, and it would have meant the defeat of the collective security system on which our own safety ultimately depends.[131]

Thus, while the loss of Korea as a piece of real estate would not have meant a direct threat to American military security, the President and his advisers perceived a logical progression of consequences stemming from it which would inevitably menace the safety of the United States. From the outset, having in mind the experience of the League of Nations, they had recognized the grave implications which the Korean crisis held for the future of the United Nations. The defiant North Korean aggression threatened to destroy its effectiveness. The effectiveness of the United Nations as a collective security system was considered to be one of the bases of American security. Therefore, the North Korean invasion was perceived to threaten the security of the United States.[132]

Ambassador Jessup later explained the dominant concerns of the Blair House conference partly in terms of the organizational affiliations and primary responsibilities of the conferees. "Well, the military here probably reacted to the military challenge," he recalled, "while those of us from the State Department who were handling United Nations affairs were reacting to the U.N. and to the whole system of collective security. All had in mind the ultimately dangerous consequences to the United States if this aggression was not resisted."[133]

Concern for the United Nations, however, was not the exclu-

---

131. *Hearings*, Part III, 1715.

132. Questioned about the reasons for American intervention in Korea, Secretary Acheson later explained: "It is motivated by the security of the U.S., because this whole question of collective security is one of the bases of our own security; and, therefore, when this attack occurred in Korea and Korea appealed to the U.N. for assistance against an unprovoked armed attack, it was of the greatest importance that the collective security system should work, the U.N. should come to the assistance of Korea, and that this attack should be repelled, because, if that is not done, then I think the whole system of collective security will begin to disintegrate." Testimony of Secretary of State Acheson, *Hearings*, Part III, 1818f. See also *Hearings*, Part V, 3381.

133. Fischer, p. 163.

sive preserve of the President's diplomatic advisers. The President himself had expressed a deep sense of obligation toward the international body as the first Blair House conference began. This had been noted and shared by Air Force Secretary Finletter.[134] And Army Chief of Staff Collins, from youth a supporter of collective efforts to end "damnable wars," subsequently declared, "[The United Nations] may not be effective, but, by God, until it is proven completely ineffective, I think we ought to do everything in our power to make it work."[135] Therefore James Reston might have described the attitudes of all the conferees when he wrote with particular reference to the Secretary of State: "Mr. Acheson, from the moment of the attack on South Korea, argued that the whole moral basis of American policy, and the confidence of the world in the United States, in the United Nations, and in the whole collective security system was at stake."[136]

In a later statement Secretary Johnson summarized several of the considerations which had stiffened the resolve of the Blair House conferees and had made the prospects of American inaction so unacceptable to them:

> The fairest statement I can make as to the general approach was that if you let this one happen, others would happen in more rapid order; that the whole world looked to the majesty of strength of the United States to see what we were going to do about this picture. The impression was abroad, very widespread, it seemed to us in the world as well as the United States we were not going to do anything about it. There were signs if we did nothing about it American stock would drop pretty low and where we needed friends on the Japan question we would not have friends.
>
> Moreover, we have joined the United Nations, which had certain commitments contained in its Charter, and this was a direct violation of that Charter. But at the time it was a question of resisting aggression and not absolutely a question of then fighting communism.[137]

The crucial importance of the "resistance to aggression" theme

---

134. *Ibid.*
135. Testimony of General J. Lawton Collins, *Hearings*, Part II, 1225.
136. *New York Times*, June 28, 1950, p. 4.
137. *Hearings*, Part IV, 2585.

which marked the deliberations of the President and his advisers
at this time was also later heavily underscored by Assistant Secretary Rusk who held that the decision emerging from the conference had almost nothing to do with Korea or with Communist
ideology per se. In his view the decision had been in the making
ever since the infamous Japanese grab of Manchuria in 1931. All
the arguments in favor of American military intervention in
Korea, he maintained, would have applied equally as well to
aggression elsewhere by a nation capable of exploiting it seriously
—except for the singular threat a Communist victory in Korea
would have posed to American interests in Japan.[138]

Having heard once again the opinions of his advisers, having
pondered the difficulties and the risks of both action and inaction, President Truman, who had set a tone of resolution and
determination from the very outset of the Sunday conference,
unhesitatingly announced his decisions. He approved without substantial modification all five of Secretary Acheson's recommendations.[139] American airplanes and naval vessels would be ordered
into combat against the aggressors south of the Thirty-eighth
Parallel. Formosa would be insulated from military involvement.
The Philippines and Indochina would receive augmented military
assistance. And the American action in Korea would be reported
to the United Nations in whose name it would be taken. In making
these decisions the President and his advisers sought to save the
friendly Korean Republic and to restore the status quo which had
existed prior to the invasion; to limit the scope of the conflict to
the Korean peninsula; to avoid the loss of Formosa to the Chinese
Communists; to ward off a threat to American interests in Japan;
to contribute to the general political-military stability of East and
and Southeast Asia; to preserve the United Nations and the collective security system; to protect American prestige in Europe and
throughout the world; to minimize the probability of a direct military collision with the Soviet Union; and, to prevent World War
III by nonappeasement of aggression. Questions of a domestic
political nature had not entered into the deliberations that had preceded the President's decisions.

138. Secretary Rusk, Interview, August 22, 1955.
139. Secretary Acheson, Interview, October 27, 1955.

There was a unanimous sense of satisfaction among the President's advisers with the decisions he had taken. There had been no major disagreement during the conference, just as there had been none on Sunday night. Secretary Johnson, in effect, was expressing the sentiments of all the advisers when he subsequently explained, "If we wanted to oppose it, then was our time to oppose it. Not a single one of us did. There were some pointing out of the difficulties . . . and then the President made his decision, which . . . I thought was the right decision."[140] Another participant described the general atmosphere of the conference at the time as "the finest spirit of harmony I have ever known."[141] "I felt proud of President Truman," Ambassador Jessup later recalled.[142] The President's military and civilian advisers alike stood solidly behind him in his decision, fully agreed on the dominant goals to be achieved—to resist military aggression and to uphold the United Nations. As Admiral Sherman later explained, "We went into Korea to assist the South Koreans in resisting aggression."[143] According to General Bradley, "We did it so we wouldn't have one appeasement lead to another and make war inevitable."[144] Secretary Finletter later wrote, "In this more than any other act of postwar policy in Asia we took the path of principle, [i.e.] to honor our promises in the United Nations Charter."[145]

The Decisions of the Conference Are Transmitted to General MacArthur

It was ten o'clock Monday evening when President Truman accepted Secretary Acheson's recommendations. The conference had been in session for about one hour. Just before it ended, the President asked Secretary Johnson to convey the conclusions of the meeting to General MacArthur. The Secretary of Defense delegated this responsibility to Secretary of the Army Pace.[146] The President

---

140. *Hearings,* Part IV, 2585.
141. *New York Times,* June 28, 1950, p. 4.
142. Fischer, p. 163.
143. *Hearings,* Part II, 1528.
144. *Ibid.,* p. 1070.
145. Thomas K. Finletter, *Foreign Policy: The Next Phase The 1960's* (New York: Frederick A. Praeger, 1960), pp. 138ff.
146. Secretary Johnson, Interview, October 27, 1955.

also indicated that he wanted Secretary Acheson's draft worked over into a form suitable for public announcement. He asked Secretaries Acheson and Johnson to collaborate on seeing that this was accomplished. President Truman further stated that he wanted to discuss the decisions he had made with Congressional leaders before announcing them to the public. The White House staff was instructed to begin immediate preparations for a Tuesday morning meeting of the President and 14 selected legislators. As his advisers hurried out to execute the decisions of the conference, the President was heard to remark, "Everything I have done in the last five years has been to try to avoid making a decision such as I had to make tonight."[147] Later he wrote, "This was the toughest decision I had to make as President."[148]

The President's diplomatic advisers went directly to the State Department where they engaged in further consultations beginning at 10:20 P.M., with Counselor Kennan also participating.[149] By half-past ten, Secretaries Pace and Finletter, Generals Collins and Vandenberg, and Admiral Sherman had returned to the Pentagon to to communicate the latest decisions of the President to General MacArthur.[150] Summoning the General in person to the General Headquarters end of a Washington-Tokyo telecon circuit,[151] they began a conference with him which lasted until nearly midnight.

---

147. Smith, p. 80.

148. *Memoirs*, II, 463. Entries apparently made in the diary of the President's daughter on Sunday and Monday suggest both that he was prepared to order military intervention if necessary on Sunday and that he had communicated the decisions of at least one of the Blair House conferences privately to his family. On June 25, she wrote, "Everybody is extremely tense. Northern or Communist Korea is marching in on Southern Korea and we are going to fight." For June 26, she entered, "Last night Dad said we would resist the aggression of Northern Korea. Tonight he sent the 7th Fleet to guard Formosa and he is going to send planes and troops." Margaret Truman (with Margaret Cousins), *Souvenir* (New York: McGraw-Hill, 1956), p. 275.

149. Based on SCDS.

150. *New York Herald Tribune*, June 28, 1950, p. 4. *Washington Post*, June 28, 1950, p. 6.

151. "It was the first time I had ever in person been summoned to such a conference." Testimony of General Douglas MacArthur, *Hearings*, Part I, 231. A telecon is a device by which the writing of a typewriter at one end is recorded and projected upon a screen at the other. In this way a group at each end can participate in and have a record of the discussion.

Again as on Sunday night the Defense leaders had no written directive upon which to base their instructions to the American commander in the Far East. Once more they improvised their orders to him. One of the Pentagon officials wanted to make absolutely sure there was no misunderstanding of the central decision which had been taken at Blair House. "Your mission is to throw the North Koreans out of South Korea," he instructed the General. The following is a paraphrased excerpt of the orders that were sent to the General at this time:

> In order to clear South Korea of North Korean military forces, all military targets south of the thirty-eighth parallel were cleared for attack by the Air Force. Similarly naval forces were authorized to operate against forces engaged in aggression against South Korea without restriction in coastal waters and sea approaches south of the thirty-eighth parallel.[152]

General MacArthur's initial reaction to these instructions was one of surprise and satisfaction.[153] Subsequent events did not alter his agreement with the basic decision that had been made. As he explained in the spring of 1951, "If there is anything I have said to lead you to believe I was critical of the decision to defend Korea, I would correct it immediately."[154] The General's subordinate commanders shared his initial reaction. According to Vice Admiral C. Turner Joy, his naval commander, "When the word of the invasion of South Korea reached us, I felt that we should oppose the aggression, but I didn't think we would. Consequently, when the United Nations took action, and American forces were ordered into Korea, I was quite surprised. This was the general impression among all of us in Japan. General MacArthur was likewise surprised, and commented that this was a complete reversal of our Far Eastern policy. He and I agreed that opposing the invasion was the correct action, but we were surprised that it happened. As a consequence, we had no plans for this type of

---

152. *Hearings,* Part V, 2581.

153. The General's official biographer implies that he was dissatisfied with the manner in which the decision had been taken; namely, that neither he nor Congress had been consulted prior to its making. Whitney, p. 324.

154. *Hearings,* Part I, 81. See also *ibid.,* p. 277.

war."[155] During the teletype conference, the military leaders at the Pentagon asked the General if he had any recommendations to submit. He replied that he had none.[156] He did not ask for air, sea, or ground reinforcements to help him carry out his mission at this time.[157]

While his advisers worked on into the night at the Departments of State and Defense, the President worked with his staff at Blair House. At a very late hour he telephoned Senator Connally and informed him of the decisions he had made and of the actions to implement them that his advisers were undertaking.[158] Then, while the orders went out that would summon American sailors and airmen to battle stations in the Far East—orders that would soon bring the direct force of American military power to bear against the invaders of the Republic of Korea—the President retired.

---

155. Statement made in Tokyo in October 1950, and quoted in Cagle and Manson, p. 31.

156. Testimony of Secretary of Defense Johnson, *Hearings,* Part IV, 2574.

157. *New York Times,* June 28, 1950, p. 13.

158. Connally, p. 347.

CHAPTER 7

TUESDAY, JUNE 27

President Chiang Kai-shek Is Notified

Having dispatched the necessary orders to the Far East, the President's advisers turned to the secondary problem of drafting a public announcement of the decisions he had made. When the officials at the State Department had composed a statement with which they were satisfied—an announcement substantially the same in outline as the set of recommendations Secretary Acheson had laid before the second Blair House conference—they transmitted it by telephone to the Department of Defense so that the President's military counselors might suggest any revisions that they considered desirable.[1]

---

1. Counselor Kennan, Interview, August 1, 1955.

Then the diplomatic advisers turned to the urgent problem of notifying the President of the Republic of China, Chiang Kai-shek, about the decisions concerning Formosa. To have the leader of Nationalist China receive from unofficial sources his first news of an American decision vitally affecting Chinese interests would be most undesirable. Consequently, by 1:30 A.M. they had prepared a message to President Chiang and had made arrangements for its delivery by the American Chargé d'Affaires on Formosa, Robert Strong. A few hours later, early Tuesday evening on the Nationalist-held island, Mr. Strong delivered the note in person to President Chiang in his suburban home outside the capital city of Taipeh. In Mr. Strong's presence, Foreign Minister George K. C. Yeh translated the text of the American communication for the President. After conferring with President Chiang for about twenty minutes, Mr. Strong returned to Taipeh; the President continued in conference with Minister Yeh, Prime Minister Ch'en Ch'eng, and other officials. On Wednesday, Formosan time, after the Chinese President had conferred with General Chou Chih-jou, chief of the Joint General Staff, and other key military and civilian advisers, Foreign Minister Yeh announced that the Nationalist Government had decided to order its army and navy to cease attacks upon the Chinese mainland. Minister Yeh further stated that the Chinese Government considered President Truman's decision to protect Formosa "a most welcome sign of comradeship in the fight against communism."[2] It was reported that one of the reasons why the Chinese Nationalist leadership accepted the restriction placed upon their military activity by the American decision was that they believed it would be of short duration.[3]

General MacArthur Requests Immediate Publicity to Bolster Korean Morale

Meanwhile, as the President's advisers at the Department of State continued to work into the small hours of Tuesday morning, another ticklish problem developed—General MacArthur requested

2. Associated Press dispatch from Taipeh, *Chicago Tribune*, June 28, 1950, p. 4.
3. *New York Times*, June 28, 1950, p. 1.

permission to make an immediate announcement to the Republic of Korea that American military assistance was on the way, in order to bolster sagging Korean morale. A three-way telecon discussion began between Under Secretary of State Webb, Secretary Pace at the Pentagon, and the General in Tokyo. On behalf of the President, Under Secretary Webb, who was himself keenly sensitive to political considerations, insisted that no announcement could be made until the Chief Executive had discussed his decisions with members of the Congress. Premature revelation of them might be highly damaging to the strong Congressional support which they required. Just as firmly, however, General MacArthur insisted that if he were to accomplish his mission, there could be no delay in the employment of any measure that could nourish the will to fight of the ROK Army. The South Koreans had to be told at once that the Americans were coming to help them. Under Secretary Webb held fast; the Far East commander's request could not be granted. Nevertheless, a compromise was finally reached that Counselor Kennan later described as "a triumph of American ingenuity."[4] While the impending American military involvement was to be announced in Korean, nothing was to be said in English. Shortly after 3 A.M. Tuesday, Washington time,[5] the chief of the ROK Army information service in person broadcast the following message in the Korean language over South Korean radio stations:

> At 4:00 P.M. June 27 an official notification was received from General MacArthur's Headquarters that a combat command post of General MacArthur's Headquarters will be immediately established in Seoul.
>
> From tomorrow morning American Air Force planes will directly participate in the fighting and American troops will gradually participate in the fighting.
>
> The National Defense forces will resolutely hold their present positions. All citizens are requested to carry out their tasks calmly and march to crush the Communist bandits.

---

4. Counselor Kennan, Letter, May 17, 1957.

5. I.e., sometime after 4 P.M. Tuesday in Korea. These boadcasts were reported later by Maurice Chanteloup of the French News Agency who claimed to be the last Western reporter in Seoul. *Washington Post*, June 28, 1950, p. 2.

This message was rebroadcast every ten minutes between intervals of martial music. Thus, while the American nation slept, Koreans within radio range of Seoul learned that direct American military assistance was on the way. General MacArthur had found in the Korean language a convenient means for circumventing Under Secretary Webb's position. Both General Headquarters in Tokyo and the Department of Defense subsequently denied Korean reports that American ground forces would fight on the peninsula.[6]

When the nation stirred on Tuesday morning, none but a handful of men in the United States knew that for the first time since World War II American fighting men had been ordered into battle. They kept their secret well; there were no leaks to the press. Nevertheless, the "broadest hints" as to the nature of the President's decisions were given to reporters after 9:30 A.M., when White House press officers informed them that he would have a very important announcement to make at noon.[7]

The President and His Advisers Work Out a Public Statement

The President's advisers began gathering at the White House at an early hour. About 8 A.M., Secretary Johnson, Deputy Secretary of Defense Early, General Bradley and General Collins arrived at the President's office to discuss his announcement. Secretary Johnson and General Bradley were not satisfied with the statement as it stood after the middle-of-the-night drafters had finished their work. The Defense Secretary later could not recall the specific details of the changes he wished to see made, but he remembered, "They were in the interest of clarification pretty much on the Formosa picture."[8] Entering the President's office, they found that he had been at work on the draft for some time and had already incorporated some of the changes they desired. The early arrivals at the White House were followed by Secretaries Acheson, Pace, and Finletter, Deputy Under Secretary Matthews, the Joint Chiefs of Staff, and other State and Defense officials.

6. *Ibid.*

7. Richard H. Rovere, "Letter from Washington," *New Yorker*, July 8, 1950, p. 72.

8. *Hearings*, Part IV, 2710.

The President Meets with Congressional Leaders

By late morning, Vice-President Alben W. Barkley and the group of 14 Congressmen whom the President had invited to confer with him at 11:30 A.M. had arrived. This group consisted of nine Democrats and five Republicans, including Senate majority leader Scott W. Lucas of Illinois; House speaker Sam Rayburn of Texas; and House majority leader John W. McCormack of Massachusetts. From the Senate Foreign Relations Committee came its chairman, Senator Tom Connally of Texas, and Senators H. Alexander Smith, Republican of New Jersey; Elbert D. Thomas, Democrat of Utah; and Alexander Wiley, Republican of Wisconsin. Representing the Senate Armed Services Committee were its chairman, Senator Millard E. Tydings of Maryland, and Senator Styles Bridges, Republican of New Hampshire. From the House Foreign Affairs Committee came its chairman, Representative John Kee of West Virginia; Representative Charles A. Eaton, Republican of New Jersey; and Representative Mike Mansfield, Democrat of Montana. On behalf of the House Armed Services Committee came its chairman, Representative Carl Vinson of Georgia, and Representative Dewey Short, Republican of Missouri.[9] Upon the advice of Secretary Acheson, the President had decided not to ask the Congress for a joint resolution supporting his decisions.[10] With the morale of the American combat forces in mind, the Secretary of State did not want to risk exposing the decisions to possible attacks by legislators such as Republican Senator William E. Jenner of Indiana, or to precipitate a general discussion of the ultimate costs or consequences of military intervention in the Korean fighting.

Promptly at half-past eleven, President Truman joined the assembled group of Congressional leaders and advisers waiting for

9. Smith, p. 82. *Memoirs,* II, 338, omits Senator Lucas and Representative Mansfield, and lists instead Senators Ernest W. McFarland, Democrat of Arizona, and Walter F. George, Democrat of Georgia. The *New York Times,* June 28, 1950, p. 2, reports that Senator Lucas attended the meeting. The *Congressional Record* shows that Senator George was absent by leave of the Senate from all of its deliberations during the week under study. The evidence seems to favor Mr. Smith's listing.

10. Secretary Acheson, Interview, September 24, 1957.

him in the White House Cabinet Room. The bright cheerful bow
tie around his neck was in striking contrast to the grim expression
on his face as he walked around the room shaking hands with
each Senator and Representative without engaging in the light-
hearted banter for which he was noted.[11] Then taking his seat
next to Secretary Acheson at the middle of the conference table,
the President asked him to give a summary of the Korean crisis
as it had unfolded since the first reports of the North Korean invasion had been received on Saturday evening. In his review Secretary Acheson pointed out how desperate the military situation had
become by the time of the second Blair House conference on
Monday night, and how anxious many nations throughout the
world had been lest the United States fail to take the strong measures necessary to repel the aggression. He reminded the Congressmen that aggression unopposed would surely lead to World War
III. This, he concluded, was the crux of the problem that had confronted the President and his advisers fourteen hours earlier.

"But Dean, you didn't even mention the U.N.!" the President
exclaimed as Secretary Acheson finished his remarks.[12] In an extended statement President Truman then dwelt with strong emphasis upon the important role of the United Nations in removing the
threat to world peace that had been posed by the arrogant invasion of South Korea. He explained that if the North Korean aggression went unchallenged it would mean the end of the effectiveness
of the international organization, and that for this reason
the United States could not act unilaterally in repelling the invasion. Then the President read aloud the text of the announcement
of his decisions which, minutes later, was to be released to the
nation and the world:

> In Korea the Government forces, which were armed to prevent
> border raids and to preserve internal security, were attacked by in-
> vading forces from North Korea. The Security Council of the United
> Nations called upon the invading troops to cease hostilities and to
> withdraw to the 38th parallel. This they have not done but on the
> contrary have pressed the attack. The Security Council called upon

11. Accounts of this meeting may be found in *Memoirs*, II, 338, Connally, pp.
347ff, and Smith, p. 82.
12. Interview with a participant.

all members of the United Nations to render every assistance to the United Nations in the execution of this resolution. In these circumstances I have ordered United States air and sea forces to give the Korean Government troops cover and support.

The attack upon Korea makes it plain beyond all doubt that Communism has passed beyond the use of subversion to conquer independent nations and will now use armed invasion and war. It has defied the orders of the Security Council of the United Nations issued to preserve international peace and security. In these circumstances the occupation of Formosa by Communist forces would be a direct threat to the security of the Pacific area and to the United States forces performing their lawful and necessary functions in that area.

Accordingly I have ordered the Seventh Fleet to prevent any attack upon Formosa. As a corollary of this action I am calling upon the Chinese Government on Formosa to cease all air and sea operations against the mainland. The Seventh Fleet will see that this is done. The determination of the future status of Formosa must await the restoration of security in the Pacific, a peace settlement with Japan, or consideration by the United Nations.

I have also directed that United States Forces in the Philippines be strengthened and that military assistance to the Philippine Government be accelerated.

I have similarly directed acceleration in the furnishing of military assistance to the forces of France and the Associated States in Indochina and the dispatch of a military mission to provide close working relations with those forces.

I know that all members of the United Nations will consider carefully the consequences of this latest aggression in Korea in defiance of the Charter of the United Nations. A return to the rule of force in international affairs would have far-reaching effects. The United States will continue to uphold the rule of law.

I have instructed Ambassador Austin, as the Representative of the United States to the Security Council, to report these steps to the Council.[13]

After reading this statement the President invited questions and general discussion. Each Congressman had an opportunity to express his views. There seemed to be unanimous agreement that the course of action which had been decided upon was the only

---

13. Department of State, *U.S. Policy in the Korean Crisis*, p. 18.

one that could have been taken under the existing circumstances. There was no criticism of the President's decisions.[14] Much of the discussion centered around the United Nations. Senators Wiley and Smith, as well as Representative Short, wanted to be reassured—and they were—that the actions of the United States were fully in accord with the principles, purposes, and directives of the United Nations. The President pointed out, however, that the United States naturally was assuming sole responsibility for its decisions with respect to Formosa. Senator Connally reemphasized a point made earlier by the President that since the invasion was the "first major test" of the United Nations, the United States could not act independently in Korea. The President later recalled that Secretary Acheson, Senator Connally, and Representative Kee made "several suggestions" for the wording of the new resolution that the United States was to lay before the Security Council later in the day.[15]

Military matters also came up for discussion. In response to a question from Senator Wiley, Secretary Johnson announced that General MacArthur had already ordered naval and air units into combat. Senator Tydings reported that his committee had just cleared a bill extending the Selective Service Act of 1948 for an additional year and giving the President authority to call up the National Guard. Representative McCormack asked if the Navy might not have to be expanded to enable it to bear the additional burdens placed upon it by the conflict in Korea. Secretary Johnson replied that the Joint Chiefs were already at work on a plan for the balanced expansion of the armed services if that were deemed necessary. During this discussion of military questions the Con-

14. Some Congressmen later recalled that the question was raised as to why the Administration had not consulted the Congress before undertaking the military commitment in Korea. However, Beverly Smith, who had access to a memorandum of the meeting, has reported that it did not indicate that this question had arisen. Smith, p. 82. See also the testimony of Secretary of Defense Johnson, *Hearings*, Part IV, 2677. The question was raised, however, during a similar meeting on the morning of June 30.

15. *Memoirs*, II, 338. Since President Rau of the Security Council received his draft of the American resolution at 10:30 A.M., there is some doubt that any of these suggestions actually were incorporated in it. U.N. Security Council, Fifth Year, *Official Records*, No. 16, 474th Meeting, June 27, 1950, p. 16.

gressional conferees specifically were informed that the Administration did not plan to commit American ground troops in Korea.[16] The joint Executive-Congressional conference ended shortly after twelve o'clock. As each participant left the Cabinet Room he was handed a mimeographed copy of the President's announcement which had been released to the press a few minutes earlier.

American Allies Are Briefed

While the President had been informing the Congressional group of his decisions, officials at the State Department had been conducting special briefing sessions for the representatives of European and Latin American nations.[17] At one of these meetings Assistant Secretary for European Affairs George Perkins and Counselor Kennan explained the latest American response to the Korean crisis to the envoys of eleven member states of the North Atlantic Treaty Organization and of other European nations. After Secretary Perkins read the President's announcement, Counselor Kennan gave an impromptu explanation of the American action.[18] He had been brought into the briefing without forewarning, unable to confer in advance with the Secretary of State. Sketching in the background of the American decisions, the Counselor stressed Soviet motivations in launching the invasion, the importance for the timing of the thrust of the emergence of the well-trained People's Army, the fact that the United States had no strong convictions about the strategic importance of Korea, and the relevance of the North Korean aggression for the international political situation in Europe and Asia as well as for world peace. Then, interpreting the President's decisions, Mr. Kennan explained that the United States had no ambitions in Korea beyond restoring the

16. *New York Times,* June 28, 1950, p. 2. This report subsequently was confirmed by the testimony of Secretary of Defense Johnson, *Hearings,* Part IV, 2609. Assistant Secretary Rusk later cautioned that the statement that there were no plans to commit ground forces should be distinguished from a decision not to commit them. At this time no such decision had been taken. "Everything was on an hour-to-hour basis," he recalled. Letter, August 20, 1959.

17. *Washington Star,* June 27, 1950, p. 1.

18. Counselor Kennan, Interview, August 1, 1955.

status quo ante and did not plan to occupy North Korea; that a clear distinction would have to be maintained between the localized military conflict on the Korean peninsula and the possibility of a wider clash with the Soviet Union—the latter contingency would precipitate an entirely new occasion for decision; that an American failure to act in the Straits of Formosa would have increased the danger of war; that in addition to its responsibilities to the United Nations, the United States had special international obligations in Japan, for which a successful North Korean invasion would be a grave liability; that the United States was the only nation with forces at hand for repelling the invasion; and that because of these special circumstances, the responsibilities of the United States to the international community for checking the aggression differed somewhat from those of other members of the United Nations.[19] This interpretation, representing what Mr. Kennan believed to be the views of the President and the Secretary of State at the time, appeared to have been received very sympathetically by the friendly diplomats. As the official State Department interpretation later became firm, however, it did not emphasize to the same degree the peculiar American responsibilities for Japan that Counselor Kennan had stressed in his extemporaneous remarks.

At a similar meeting the Acting Assistant Secretary for Inter-American Affairs, Willard F. Barber, briefed representatives of twenty member states of the Organization of American States. American diplomatic representatives overseas also began to explain President Truman's decisions to the leaders of the nations to which they were accredited. According to the President, the gist of the basic explanation which they gave was as follows:

> Our allies and friends abroad were informed . . . that it was our feeling that it was essential to the maintenance of peace that his armed aggression against a free nation be met firmly. We let it be known that we considered the Korean situation vital as a symbol of the strength and determination of the West. Firmness now would be the only way to deter new actions in the other portions of the world. Not only in Asia but in Europe, the Middle East, and elsewhere the confidence of peoples in countries adjacent to the Soviet Union would

---

19. Based on Princeton conference.

be very adversely affected, in our judgment, if we failed to take action to protect a country established under our auspices and confirmed in its freedom by action of the United Nations. If, however, the threat to South Korea was met firmly and successfully, it would add to our successes in Iran, Berlin, and Greece, a fourth success in opposition to the aggressive moves of the Communists. And each success, we suggested to our allies, was likely to add to the caution of the Soviets in undertaking new efforts of this kind. Thus the safety and prospects for peace of the free world would be increased.[20]

Immediate Public Reactions to the President's Decisions

The first public comments on the United States decision to intervene in Korea were made to waiting reporters by departing participants in the White House conference. "I think it is a damned good action," declared Senator Bridges.[21] His reaction was the keynote of the day. "The statement is full and complete and speaks for itself if anything did," Secretary Acheson explained. "We are doing over there what the U.N. asked us to do," said Secretary Johnson. He added that there were no plans for committing American soldiers or marines to combat on the Korean peninsula.[22] "I am very pleased," said Senator Smith. "The President's decision has untied a thousand knots," an unidentified participant declared.[23] Of the President's role in making the decisions that had just been announced, another participant in the Blair House conferences explained at the time, "He pulled all of us together . . . and the indisputable facts persuaded everyone that his decisions were both inevitable and right."[24] As the President walked to Blair House for lunch with eight members of his Cabinet, the corre-

---

20. *Memoirs,* II, 339f.
21. *New York Times,* June 28, 1950, p. 4.
22. "While Secretary of Defense Johnson and other officials said no soldiers or marines would be thrown into the ground fighting there is no absolute bar against this being done later, if necessary." *Washington Post,* June 28, 1950, p. 6. "Secretary Johnson said, as the President's statement indicated, that none of our ground troops would be committed in the Korean conflict." Arthur Krock, *New York Times,* June 28, 1950, p. 2.
23. James Reston, *New York Times,* June 28, 1950, p. 4.
24. *New York Times,* July 2, 1950, p. E2.

spondent of the *Chicago Tribune* noted that he was "grinning broadly," but that his advisers "wore long faces."[25] Later, under the broiling afternoon sun, the President dedicated a new $15 million federal courthouse for the District of Columbia, without mention of Korea, and good-humoredly helped workmen lower the cornerstone into place.[26]

No characterization of the impact of the President's decisions upon official Washington was more vivid than that written by Joseph C. Harsch of the *Christian Science Monitor* who expressed in personal terms the consensus of virtually all informed observers of the capital scene:

> I have lived and worked in and out of this city for 20 years. Never before in that time have I felt such a sense of relief and unity pass through this city.
>
> The most curious thing about the affair was the June 27 gloom from a belief that the administration would miss the boat and do something idle or specious. The decision to act already had been taken, yet almost everyone was assuming there would be no action. When it came there was a sense first of astonishment and then of relief. Mr. Truman obviously did much more than he was expected to do, and almost exactly what most individuals seemed to wish he would do. I have never seen such a large part of Washington so nearly satisfied with a decision of the government.[27]

One of the first communications received by the President following the announcement of his decisions was a telegram from Governor Thomas E. Dewey of New York, his Republican opponent in the 1948 presidential campaign and Franklin D. Roosevelt's opponent in the election of 1944. After a lengthy telephone conversation with Secretary of State Acheson, the Governor cabled the President: "I whole-heartedly agree with and support the difficult decision you have made today to extend American assistance to the Republic of Korea in combatting armed Communist aggression. Your action there, in Formosa, the Philippines and Indo-China was necessary to the security of our country and the free world. It should be supported by a united America." President Truman im-

25. Walter Trohan, *Chicago Tribune*, June 28, 1950, p. 5.
26. Lewis Wood, *New York Times*, June 28, 1950, p. 3.
27. *Christian Science Monitor*, June 29, 1950, p. 1.

mediately wired in reply: "I am grateful for your message and hasten to assure you that I shall find strength and courage in your brave words. The wholehearted pledge of support which you give will be a source of inspiration and fortitude as we gird ourselves for the difficult tasks ahead. We have taken our stand on the side of Korea and our pledge of faith to that nation is a witness to all the world that we champion liberty wherever the tyranny of Communism is the aggressor."[28]

Coincident with the revelation of the President's decisions there was a rise in the stock market, which had been depressed by selling waves on Monday. The fall in prices had been reported in the press under such headlines as "War Nerves Cause Record Slump on Stock Exchange."[29] After the Tuesday noon announcement, the market began to revive, and this phenomenon was reported as "Stocks Recover After Big New Losses in War Scare; Sales Near 5 Million."[30] Later in the afternoon the National Security Resources Board, headed by W. Stuart Symington, announced that it had drafted legislation, which could be introduced in the event of a national emergency, that gave extensive economic controls over prices, wages, manpower, and materials to the President.

Responses in the Senate and House

According to one observer, "one of the great scenes in Senate history" took place Tuesday afternoon on Capitol Hill as the legislators of that body were informed of the President's decisions.[31] Another likened the crowded galleries and air of excitement to the Senate scene on the day after Pearl Harbor.[32] But in the opinion of still another observer, "If it weren't for the fact that there simply isn't much Congress can do at a time like this, the scene in the House and Senate . . . might have seemed a great tableau of indifference and unawareness."[33] Senate majority leader Lucas and the other Senators who had conferred with the President hurried over

28. *New York Times*, June 28, 1950. p. 4.
29. *Washington Post*, June 27, 1950, p. 1.
30. *New York Times*, June 28, 1950, p. 1.
31. Richard L. Strout, *Christian Science Monitor*, June 28, 1950, p. 3.
32. Walter Trohan, *Chicago Tribune*, June 28, 1950, p. 5.
33. Richard H. Rovere, "Letter from Washington," *New Yorker*, July 8, 1950, pp. 72-73.

from the White House and were on the Senate floor to answer the roll call shortly after twelve o'clock. When the routine initial business of the Senate had been administered, the lawmakers turned their attention to the consideration of a bill to amend the Mutual Defense Assistance Act of 1949. Senator Ernest W. McFarland (Democrat, Arizona) moved that a vote on the bill be set for four o'clock. Senator Kenneth S. Wherry (Republican, Nebraska) objected on the grounds that he thought the measure should be subjected to a full-scale debate. Senator Connally expressed opposition to the proposed delay, pointing out that since the bill had been under consideration for several days his colleagues had had ample opportunity to make known their positions. Senator James P. Kem (Republican, Missouri) gained the floor from the Senator from Texas and launched an attack upon the State Department. At last Senator Lucas achieved recognition and, reading from the mimeographed statement he had brought from the White House, finally informed his colleagues of the decisions President Truman had made.

The first reaction to the announcement came from Senator Kem who, failing to mention Korea at all, centered attention on the President's instructions to the Seventh Fleet. "I notice that in the President's statement he says, 'I have ordered the fleet to prevent any attack on Formosa.' Does that mean he has arrogated to himself the authority of declaring war?" he asked.[34] Senator Lucas, while refusing then to be drawn into an extended debate on the question of the President's Constitutional authority, replied, ". . . History will show that on more than 100 occasions in the life of this Republic the President as Commander in Chief has ordered the fleet or the troops to do certain things which involved the risk of war." Republican Senator William F. Knowland of California, determined foe of past Far Eastern policies of the Administration, rose at once to speak briefly in support of the President's decisions which he thought had "drawn" a long-needed "line" in the Far East. "I believe that in this very important step which the President of the United States has taken in order to uphold the hands of the United Nations and the free peoples of the world, he should have the overwhelming support of all Americans regardless of their partisan affiliation," he declared.[35] Republican Senators Leverett Saltonstall of Massachusetts, H. Alexander Smith of New Jersey, Wayne Morse of Oregon, and Robert C. Hendrickson of New Jersey joined Senator Knowland in unequivocal expressions of support. Senator Henry Cabot Lodge, Jr., Republican of Massachusetts, also applauded the firm leadership of the President and stated further, "I merely wish to add the hope that he will not shrink from using the Army, if the best military judgment indicates that is the effective course to take."[36] Spokesmen from the Democratic side of the Senate who registered their approval of the President's decisions, in addition to Senators Lucas and Connally, were Senators Estes Kefauver of Tennessee and Herbert H. Lehman of New York. Democratic Senator Hubert H. Humphrey of Minnesota declared, "I believe this is a fatal hour. I believe the decision the President has made may save the lives of millions of people, and may ultimately save the peace of the world. I pray God in all reverence that all the people will give their support to this policy, so that we shall not find ourselves driven by our indecision and our own inaction into the cataclysm of a third world war. This may be the greatest move for peace in the twentieth century."[37]

Although no Senator directly opposed the President's decisions themselves, a few joined Senator Kem in questioning the President's authority to make them. Republican Senator Arthur V. Watkins of Utah, expressing disapproval of the President's failure to include Congress in the decision-making process, explained, "I would have sent a message to the Congress setting forth the situation and asking for the authority to go ahead and do whatever was necessary to protect the situation."[38] Senator John W. Bricker, Republican of Ohio, asked some questions related to the United Nations aspects of the President's decisions but expressed neither approval nor disapproval of them. Republican Senator George W. Malone of Nevada delivered a long oration stating his often repeated position that the State Department had "no foreign policy" and that it should specify those areas in the world which were

---

34. *Congressional Record,* Vol. 96, Part 7, June 27, 1950, p. 9228.
35. *Ibid.,* p. 9229.
36. *Ibid.,* p. 9230.
37. *Ibid.,* p. 9233.
38. *Ibid.*

essential to American security so that the nation could build up its armed forces and take a firm stand to protect them. His colleagues apparently were puzzled about what his positions on the decisions of the day were, for in the middle of his remarks Senator Warren R. Magnuson, Democrat of Washington, asked him whether he objected to the President's statement and whether he objected to having the United States act in support of the United Nations. No clear answers were ever given, but as Senator Malone neared the end of his speech he announced at last, ". . . If the executive department decides that the integrity of Korea is important to our ultimate safety let us now send jet planes, fighter planes, bombs, munitions, and men to protect Korea and fight back the aggressor. Let us be strong and use strong means."[39] By 2:30 P.M. most of the speeches on the subject of the President's announcement were over, and after three o'clock not more than a dozen Senators were on the Senate floor at one time.

In the House of Representatives the general pattern of events was much the same. After House majority leader McCormack read the President's statement, the members of the House—except for Congressman Vito Marcantonio, American Labor Party representative from New York—rose and cheered.[40] Following declarations of support by his colleagues, Representative Marcantonio attacked directly the President's decisions as interfering in what he regarded as two legitimate civil wars—in China and in Korea—and as "acceptance of the doctrine of the inevitability of war." Charging that the Republic of Korea was "a government imposed upon the people of Korea by force of arms, a police state," he complained, "Here now we are sending American aviators to lay down their lives, and who knows how long it will be before our infantry will be sent to lay down their lives to defend, aid, and abet tyranny and perpetrate aggression against the Korean people who strive for a united and independent nation."[41] In reply Democratic Representative Abraham A. Ribicoff of Connecticut, a member of the Foreign Affairs Committee, denied that the President's decisions would make war inevitable. "The gentleman from New York talks as if this were an action

---

39. *Ibid.*, p. 9243.
40. Harold B. Hinton, *New York Times*, June 28, 1950, p. 1.
41. *Congressional Record*, Vol. 96, Part 7, June 27, 1950, p. 9269.

by Korean patriots; this is an action by pawns of Soviet imperialism. What difference is there in the action of northern Koreans today and the actions which led to the Second World War? Talk about parallels!" he exclaimed.[42]

The final declaration before the House voted on the conference report on the Selective Service Act then before it, was delivered by Representative Short of Missouri, who had participated in the morning White House conference. Press observers agree it was one of the most eloquent speeches of the afternoon on Capitol Hill.[43] "Mr. Speaker," he began, "most of the Members of this House know that I have up to this hour at all times violently opposed peacetime military conscription. Perhaps I have not been the most intelligent, but certainly I have been one of the most vigorous and consistent opponents of peacetime draft because it is repugnant to free men." He then explained that the North Korean invasion had removed any doubts as to the intentions of the Soviet Union which ". . . has been nibbling here, grabbing there, eating away, gnawing under, winning every round of this fight since the shooting stopped in 1945, winning every round in the cold war without firing a shot." "Heavens," he queried, "where will there be an end and when shall we call a halt?" The Missouri Republican continued, "Now the big issue at stake in this thing is the supreme and severe test of the United Nations. Mr. Speaker, either it is going to be a going and successful concern from here out or it is going to crash and fall to pieces. For my part I want it to succeed." Then, recalling some remarks made by the President in the course of the White House conference, Representative Short declared, ". . . Let us hope and pray that by taking bold, positive, firm action now we can stave off world catastrophe." He concluded, "Much as I dislike a peacetime draft, we must realize that while we are not perhaps in a shooting war at this minute . . . we are not living in peacetimes, we are living in dangerous and perilous times. We are living in times that try men's souls, and I hope that our souls will prove to have the mettle capable of standing up sounding and showing a clear challenge to the forces of aggression wherever they might rear their ugly heads." After this dramatic expression of a change of

42. *Ibid.*
43. *Ibid.*, pp. 9289ff.

heart by one of the most determined opponents of the measure, the House went on to agree by the overwhelming vote of 315 to 4 to extend the Selective Service Act for one year without restriction on the President's authority except that he should not exceed authorized ceilings on strength.

Responses in the British Parliament

In London, at about this same time, there was parliamentary cheering as Prime Minister Clement Attlee, after an emergency two-hour Cabinet meeting on the Korean crisis, read before the House of Commons the part of President Truman's announcement which dealt with his decision to intervene in the fighting. The British legislators listened in silence to the remaining portions of the statement. The British Government had been informed of the President's decisions prior to their publication.[44] In remarks accompanying the President's statement, the Labour Government leader stated: "The situation is of undoubted gravity, but I am certain that there will be no disagreement, after our bitter experiences in the past 35 years, that the salvation of all is dependent on prompt and effective measures to arrest aggression wherever it may occur, using for this purpose the international machinery which the peace-loving nations have set up for this very purpose. The fact is that the authorities in Northern Korea have invaded the territory of the Government of the Republic of Korea. This is naked aggression and it must be checked. We can only hope that all concerned will recognize this simple fact. If they do, there is hope for the future."[45] The Prime Minister further explained that the British representative on the Security Council, Sir Terence Shone, had been instructed to support the new resolution to be introduced, it was understood, by the United States. The Member from Woodford, Winston S. Churchill, leader of the Conservative opposition, responded, "Naturally I only intervene for the purpose of expressing our thanks to the Prime Minister for making us acquainted with these grave matters and the sense of unity which dominates the whole house when ques-

---

44. 476 *H. C. Deb.* 5s., June 27, 1950, 2159.
45. *Ibid.*, 2159-60.

tions of this gravity seem to touch the principles of freedom and law for which we stand."[46] French, Italian, and other European officials also expressed support of President Truman's decisions.

An American Note Is Delivered in Moscow

There is no evidence of the spontaneous reaction of Soviet leaders in Moscow to the news of the President's decisions. Late Tuesday afternoon, almost two days after it had been drafted in Washington, they received an additional communication from the United States in the form of a note handed to Soviet Foreign Minister Andre Gromyko by American Ambassador Alan G. Kirk:

> My Government has instructed me to call your attention to the fact that North Korean forces have crossed the 38th parallel and invaded the territory of the Republic of Korea in force at several points. The refusal of the Soviet Representative to attend the Security Council meeting on June 25, despite the clear threat to peace and the obligations of a Security Council member under the Charter requires the United States to bring this matter directly to the attention of the Government of the Union of Soviet Socialist Republics. In view of the universally known fact of the close relations between the Union of Soviet Socialist Republics and the North Korean regime, the United States Government asks assurance that the Union of Soviet Socialist Republics disavows responsibility for this unprovoked and unwarranted attack, and that it will use its influence with the North Korean authorities to withdraw their invading forces immediately.[47]

The consensus at the Department of State on Sunday was that this note was good from every point of view. There was notable dissent within the Department, however, since one top official considered it a worthless gesture from which nothing could be expected. Nevertheless, the predominant opinion had been that any measure that conceivably might contribute to ending the fighting was worth trying. In accordance with the public fiction of Soviet

---

46. *Ibid.*, 2161.
47. Department of State, p. 65. Embassy officials tried to deliver this note in Moscow on June 25. Based on SCDS.

noninvolvement in Korea that American diplomatic officials sought to maintain, the note did not charge the Soviet Union with direct complicity in launching the North Korean invasion. There was some hope, however slight, that when Soviet leaders found themselves faced by strong and unexpected opposition and presented with an opportunity to "save face," they might call off the attack.[48] It was also hoped that by its moderate tone the note might serve to assure the Soviet leaders that the United States did not desire an enlargement of the conflict unless Soviet behavior made it unavoidable.[49] The decision to approach the Soviet Union directly did not signify any change in the United Nations focus of American policy; it was regarded as being peripheral to it.

The possibility of Soviet participation in the Korean fighting was the subject of Defense-State consultations throughout the day. Strong minority sentiment was developing among certain key members of both Departments that the American commitment in Korea should be thoroughly reconsidered if the military might of the Soviet Union were thrown into direct combat support of the North Koreans.[50] In the early evening the President's State Department advisers terminated their discussions and returned to their homes for the first good night's rest enjoyed by many of them since the first alarming news of the invasion had summoned them to duty on Saturday night.

The United Nations Security Council Meets Again

The representative of the Soviet Union was absent when the United Nations Security Council met at 3 P.M. in a dramatic session witnessed by 1,200 visitors, while 5,000 more, concerned and disappointed, were turned away. Ambassador Yakov A. Malik's absence confirmed the calculations of those State Department officials who had predicted that cumbersome Soviet processes for reaching decisions would preclude the possibility of his taking his

---

48. Assistant Secretary Rusk, Interview, August 22, 1955.

49. *Ibid.* According to Secretary Acheson this "might have been" one of its purposes. Interview, October 27, 1955.

50. Interviews: Secretary Pace, October 24, 1955; Counselor Kennan, August 1, 1955.

seat in time to veto the resolution which the United States intended to present.[51] There was always the chance, however, that instructions to block Security Council action might arrive from Moscow. In fact, the Assistant Secretary of State for United Nations Affairs, expecting a Soviet veto, was prepared to take the Korean question to the General Assembly.[52] This was the background of a tense scene that took place earlier in the afternoon following a luncheon in the Stockholm Restaurant in Syosett, Long Island, which had been attended by Secretary General Lie, Ambassador Malik, Ambassador Gross, and other delegates to the United Nations.[53] As the delegates were leaving to take their places at the Security Council table, Secretary-General Lie approached Ambassador Malik and told him that in his opinion the interests of the Soviet Union demanded his participation in the meeting. "No, I will not go there," the Soviet delegate replied.[54] Outside the restaurant Ambassador Gross heaved a huge sigh of relief.

At the Council table, seated between the United Kingdom and Yugoslavian delegates, Ambassador Warren R. Austin stated the American position. "The United Nations finds itself confronted today with the gravest crisis in its history," he began.[55] The Ambassador then reviewed the Security Council action of June 25, noted that the resolution adopted at that time undoubtedly had come into the hands of the North Korean leaders, and pointed out that the course of events led to no conclusion other than that they would not comply: "We now have before us the report of the United Nations Commission on Korea which confirms our worst fears. It is clear that the authorities in North Korea have completely flouted the decision of the Security Council." The report to which the Ambassador referred had been received in New York on Monday. It stated:

---

51. Secretary Acheson, Interview, October 27, 1955.

52. Assistant Secretary Hickerson, Interview, November 6, 1958.

53. This social gathering had been planned before the Korean crisis and had no direct connection with it.

54. Incident related in Lie, p. 333. If Mr. Malik had exercised his veto power that afternoon, the Secretary-General was prepared to carry the issue to the General Assembly.

55. U.N. Security Council, Fifth Year, *Official Records*, No. 16, 474th Meeting, June 27, 1950.

North Korean advances have created dangerous situation with possibilities of rapid deterioration. Impossible estimate situation which will exist tomorrow in Seoul. In view Commission's past experience and existing situation Commission convinced North Korea will not heed Council resolution nor accept U.N.C.O.K. good offices. Suggest have Council give consideration either invitation both parties agree on neutral mediator to negotiate peace or requesting member governments undertake immediate mediation. Commission decided stand by in Seoul. Danger is that critical operations now in progress may end in matter of days and question of cease-fire and withdrawal North Korean forces suggested Council resolution prove academic.[56]

Ambassador Austin continued, "It is the plain duty of the Security Council to invoke stringent sanctions to restore international peace." Then he read to the Council the text of a new resolution for coping with the situation—a resolution which had been approved personally by President Truman[57] and which had been placed in the hands of the members of the Security Council late that morning:

The Security Council

Having determined that the armed attack upon the Republic of Korea by forces from North Korea constitutes a breach of the peace;

Having called for an immediate cessation of hostilities; and

Having called upon the the authorities of North Korea to withdraw forthwith their armed forces to the 38th parallel; and

Having noted from the report of the United Nations Commission for Korea that the authorities in North Korea have neither ceased hostilities nor withdrawn their armed forces to the 38th parallel, and that urgent military measures are required to restore international peace and security; and

Having noted the appeal from the Republic of Korea to the United Nations for immediate and effective steps to secure peace and security,

Recommends that Members of the United Nations furnish such

---

56. United Nations Document S/1503, June 26, 1950.

57. Testimony of Assistant Secretary of State John D. Hickerson, in *U.S. Senate, Appropriations Committee, Appropriations for the Departments of State, Justice, Commerce, and the Judiciary for the Fiscal Year Ending June 30, 1952*, Part I, 1088.

assistance to the Republic of Korea as may be necessary to repel the armed attack and to restore international peace and security in the area.[58]

"This new draft resolution is the logical next step. Its significance is affected by the violation of the former resolution, the continuation of the aggression, and the urgent military measures required," the Ambassador explained. Then he read the announcement which the White House had released at noon. In conclusion the American spokesman declared, "The keynote of the resolution and my statement and the significant characteristic of the action taken by the President is support of the United Nations purposes and principles—in a word 'peace.'" Speaking after Ambassador Austin, Korean Ambassador Chang called upon the Council to take effective measures to save his country.

As the session continued, Dr. Ales Bebler, the Yugoslavian delegate, introduced an alternative resolution that reiterated the Security Council's call for a cease fire, asked that a procedure of mediation be initiated, and extended an invitation to the Pyongyang government to send a representative to United Nations headquarters.[59] In the ensuing discussion of both resolutions, frequent reference was made to the cabled reports of the United Nations Commission on Korea, four of which had arrived since the initial report from the Commission on Sunday.[60] For example, M. Chauvel, the Representative of France, pointed out, "This information—and particularly the contents of document S/1507—unquestionably establishes the responsibility for the attack." The report to which the French delegate referred stated:

Commission met this morning at 10 o'clock and considered the latest report on hostilities and results direct observation along parallel by UNCOCK military observers over period ending forty-eight hours before hostilities began. Commission's present view on basis this evidence is first that judging from actual progress of operations, Northern regime is carrying out well-planned, concerted, and full-scale invasion of South Korea; secondly, that South Korean forces

58. United Nations Document S/1508 Rev. 1, June 27, 1950.

59. United Nations Document S/1509, June 27, 1950.

60. United Nations Documents S/1503, June 26, 1950; S/1504, June 26, 1950; S/1505, June 26, 1950; and S/1507, June 26, 1950.

were deployed on wholly defensive basis in all sectors of the parallel; and thirdly, that they were taken completely by surprise as they had no reason to believe from intelligence sources that invasion was imminent. Commission is following events and will report further developments.

At 5:12 P.M. Sir Benegal Rau of India, president of the Council, called a one-hour recess so that he and the delegate from Egypt, Fawzi Bey, might receive instructions from their governments. Sir Benegal explained that while India had supported the June 25 resolution, the one now before the Council was "far more momentous" and for that reason he could not vote without orders from his government. An hour passed. Still no instructions. Another recess. When the delegates again took their places at twenty minutes past ten, the Indian and the Egyptian representatives—still without instructions but acquiescing in the desire of Ambassador Austin and other members that a vote be taken that night—did not insist that the session be further postponed. At 11:45 P.M. the Security Council passed the American-sponsored resolution by a vote of seven to one, with two abstentions. The United Kingdom, France, China, Cuba, Ecuador, Norway, and the United States supported the resolution. Yugoslavia opposed it. India and Egypt abstained. There was thus an interval of about 24 hours between the time President Truman approved the commitment of American forces in Korea and the adoption by the Security Council of a resolution calling for military sanctions against the invaders of the Korean Republic. Yet, explaining that the discrepancy in chronology was more apparent than real, Secretary-General Lie later wrote, ". . . The [President's] order was fully within the spirit of the Council's resolution of June 25 and did not anticipate the resolution of June 27 so much as it seemed to do, for diplomatic consultations before the issuance of the order had made it plain that there were seven votes—the required majority—in the Council for authorizing armed assistance to the Republic of Korea."[61]

The North Koreans Capture Seoul

Precisely at the time the Security Council was coming to a vote on the new resolution, the North Korean People's Army was

---

61. Lie, p. 331-32.

completing the conquest of Seoul. It was 11:30 A.M. Wednesday, in Korea (10:30 P.M. Tuesday, in New York). Initial strikes by United States Air Force F-80 fighters and B-26 bombers which rained 500-pound bombs and .50-caliber machine-gun bullets on the invaders had not succeeded in halting them. The northern troops streamed triumphantly into the city, liquidating "traitors" and freeing the inmates of Mokp'o Prison. The Republic of Korea Army—shocked by the killing of hundreds within its ranks by a premature order to demolish the Han River bridge as they were crossing—disheartened and weary but still defiant, withdrew south of the river in what newspaper dispatches termed a "demoralized retreat."[62]

From Pyongyang, considered by the North Korean regime to be but a "temporary" seat of government, Premier Kim Ilsong soon sent a congratulatory telegram to the victorious forces within the gates of the city designated in their constitution as the true capital of the Korean People's Democratic Republic. "Hail the united Korean people! Glory to the heroic People's Army!" jubilantly cabled Marshal Kim.[63] The North Korean forces paused briefly to consolidate their gains before launching a new offensive; political cadres plunged into the immediate task of setting up people's committees in the "liberated areas"; and Pyongyang announced that a 600-man "cultural propaganda unit"—plentifully supplied with "progressive" literature and motion pictures—had moved across the Thirty-eighth Parallel to begin preparations for carrying out a land reform.[64]

---

62. United Press dispatch from Tokyo, *New York Times,* June 29, 1950, p. 1.
63. *Jen-min jih-pao* (*People's Daily,* Peking), June 29, 1950, p. 1.
64. *Ibid.*

CHAPTER 8

WEDNESDAY, JUNE 28

As dawn came to Washington on June 28, the Central People's Government Council, under the chairmanship of Mao Tse-tung, was meeting in Peking, it was 5 P.M. Wednesday in China (5 A.M. Wednesday in Washington). Thus, while those who had conferred at Blair House slept, forty-six Chinese Communist leaders were mulling over the decisions the American officials had made. According to the account published by the newspaper organ of the Chinese Communist Party, the Jen-min jih-pao, the first speaker of the conference, after it had been called to order by Chairman Mao, was Foreign Minister Chou En-lai who reported on the general international situation and on his reply to President Tru-

CHAPTER 8

WEDNESDAY, JUNE 28

Chinese Communist Leaders React

As dawn came to Washington on June 28, the Central People's Government Council, under the chairmanship of Mao Tse-tung, was meeting in Peking. It was 5 P.M. Wednesday in China (5 A.M. Wednesday in Washington). Thus, while those who had conferred at Blair House slept, forty-six Chinese Communist leaders were mulling over the decisions the American officials had made. According to the account published by the newspaper organ of the Chinese Communist Party, the *Jen-min jih-pao*, the first speaker of the conference, after it had been called to order by Chairman Mao, was Foreign Minister Chou En-lai who reported on the general international situation and on his reply to President Tru-

man's announcement of Tuesday noon.[1] In this official statement, released by the Hsinhua News Agency, Foreign Minister
Chou argued on behalf of the Central People's Government that
President Truman's decisions constituted nothing less than "armed
aggression against the territory of China" and a "blatant violation
of the United Nations Charter." He alleged that the United States
had ordered the "Korean puppet army of Syngman Rhee" to attack
North Korea as a "fabricated pretext" for American "aggression"
against Taiwan (Formosa), Korea, Indochina, and the Philippines.
The President's decisions had revealed just one more step in the
"secret plans of American imperialism to seize all of Asia," charged
Minister Chou. At the end of this statement the Chinese Communist Foreign Minister expressed the firm conviction of the "Chinese people" that ". . . ultimately the oppressed peoples of the
East will incinerate the criminal American imperialist war-makers
in the angry fires of the great struggle for national independence."

Following Minister Chou's remarks there was "a vigorous discussion" during which Chairman Mao reportedly told his indignant comrades:

> The Chinese people long ago made it clear that the affairs of all
> nations should be handled by the peoples concerned. The affairs of
> Asia should be handled by Asians, and not by Americans. American
> aggression cannot but evoke widespread determined resistance on
> the part of Asian peoples. Although Truman announced last January
> 5 that the United States would not intervene on Taiwan, he himself
> has just proven the hypocrisy of that statement and at the same
> time has broken every international agreement by the United States
> that it would not interfere in the internal political affairs of China.
> The fact that America has thus revealed its imperialist character is
> of great benefit for China and the peoples of Asia. American inter-
> ference in the domestic political affairs of Korea, the Philippines,
> Taiwan, and other areas is completely unjustified. The sympathy of
> the Chinese people and of the great masses of people throughout
> the world is going to be on the side of the victims of aggression
> and not on the side of the American imperialists. They will neither
> be taken by imperialist bribes nor be intimidated by imperialist
> threats. Imperialism has a bold front but is empty within because

---

1. *Jen-min jih-pao,* (*People's Daily,* Peking), June 29, 1950, p. 1.

it does not have the support of the people. People of China and peoples of the world arise! Prepare thoroughly! Defeat every provocation of American imperialism![2]

The President Makes Two Public Appearances

"Out of this nettle, danger, we pluck this flower, safety," was the Shakespearian line[3] with which Secretary Johnson introduced President Truman to the opening session of the Reserve Officers Association convention in Washington late Wednesday morning. In his prepared address, the President stressed the military and civil obligations of a citizen in a democracy, deplored "mudslinging" at public officials, and explained that the objective in unifying the armed services was not to destroy healthy interservice rivalry, but to create an integrated military establishment which would serve more adequately the security needs of the nation. When Mr. Truman had finished speaking, Commander John P. Bracken, president of the Association, rose and asked his comrades, "Do we support the Commander-in-Chief in the dynamic action which he took yesterday?" A roar of approval burst from the assembled officers. Jumping to their feet, they gave the President a sustained cheering ovation. Breaking the hush which followed his attempts with upstretched arms to quiet the gathering, President Truman responded with an extemporaneous statement: "Gentlemen, we face a serious situation. We hope that we have acted in the cause of peace. There is no other reason for the action we have taken. We hope—we always hope—that we shall arrive at the peace in the world which we anticipated when we created the United Nations. That is the only reason for our actions."[4] In his own remarks to the convention Secretary Johnson referred to the Sunday Blair House conference as "the finest hour in American history to date" and declared, "The occasion has found the man in Harry Truman." The Defense Secretary also commended Secretary Acheson for the firm manner in which he had met the crisis.[5]

---

2. *Ibid.*
3. *King Henry IV*, Scene 3, line 2.
4. *New York Times*, June 29, 1950, p. 5.
5. *Washington Post*, June 28, 1950, p. 3.

The President made one more public appearance Wednesday afternoon. At four o'clock he addressed a convention of the American Newspaper Guild, C.I.O. Anticipating that the President might discuss his recent decisions, the four major broadcasting networks made special arrangements to carry his voice to the nation. The Voice of America also beamed it directly overseas. It was 11 P.M. in Moscow, where party-goers, enjoying the height of the diplomatic social season, huddled around radio sets as President Truman's voice came through clearly. But the President inserted only one reference to Korea in his previously prepared speech on the Point Four Program. He cited the invasion of South Korea as ". . . an example of the danger to which underdeveloped areas particularly are exposed."[6] Referring indirectly to his decisions, the President explained that while vigorous defensive measures against aggression were necessary, they were only a "shield" behind which to carry out "the great constructive tasks of peace."

Domestic and Foreign Responses Continue to Be Overwhelmingly Favorable

Throughout Wednesday, as on Tuesday, an overwhelmingly favorable domestic and foreign response to the President's decisions continued to be received in Washington. "There was a wonderful closing of ranks," explained one White House staff member.[7] Former President Herbert Hoover commented, "When the United States draws a sword there is only one course for our people. Like others, I have opposed many of our foreign policies, but now is not the time to argue origins, mistakes, responsibilities, or consequences. There is only one way out of such situations as this; that is to win. To win we must have unity of purpose and action."[8] General Dwight D. Eisenhower, president of Columbia University, said, "The best check for sustaining world peace was to take a firm stand, and when our Government guaranteed the Government of South Korea there was no course but to do

---

6. Full text, *New York Times*, June 29, 1950, p. 26.

7. Arthur Krock, *New York Times*, June 28, 1950, p. 4.

8. *New York Times*, June 29, 1950, p. 18.

what President Truman did."[9] During a Honolulu stop-over on his flight home from Japan, Ambassador John Foster Dulles declared, "The United Nations has acted, and the United States, under the splendid leadership of President Truman, has thrown in its strength as a police force to back up the decisions in the United Nations."[10] Such was the tenor of the remarks of other prominent political, labor, religious, and educational leaders.

Organizations, too, reacted collectively to the announcement by sending telegrams to the President. At the Cleveland convention of the Communication Workers of America, C.I.O., for example, 500 delegates in the name of 300,000 members passed a resolution supporting the President's decisions and cabled their approbation to him.[11] The domestic press was almost unanimous in its approval. *The New York Times* called the President's decision to save the Republic of Korea "a momentous and courageous act."[12] The *Daily Worker*, organ of the American Communist Party, denounced the decision as "the adventurist, ruthless, aggressive imperialist operations of Wall Street for domination of all Asia and the Pacific."[13]

A similar wave of approving opinion swept in from abroad. French Ambassador Henri Bonnet called at the White House to tell the President that his decisions and the actions of the Security Council had been "very well received in France by the Government and by the people."[14] President Otilio Ulate of Costa Rica sent a telegram to Mr. Truman expressing the "profound interest" of his people in an action taken by a great power in the interests of a small nation.[15] The Presidents of Nicaragua, Colombia, and the Dominican Republic also cabled expressions of support to the President. Philippine President Elpidio Quirino said that Filipinos were "incalculably heartened by President Truman's prompt decision."[16] In the Canadian House of Commons, External Affairs

9. *Ibid.,* p. 1.
10. *New York Herald Tribune,* June 29, 1950, p. 4.
11. *New York Times,* June 29, 1950, p. 9.
12. *New York Times,* June 28, 1950, p. 26.
13. *Daily Worker,* June 28, 1950, p. 1.
14. *New York Times,* June 29, 1950, p. 5.
15. *Ibid.,* p. 8.
16. *Ibid.,* p. 3.

Secretary Lester B. Pearson described the President's decision as "an act of high courage and firm statesmanship."[17] The Council of the Organization of American States, representing twenty-one American republics including the United States, adopted a resolution pledging its "firmest support" of the United Nations in the Korean conflict.[18] Foreign press reaction as recorded in the State Department was favorable. The editor of West Berlin's *Der Abend* wrote that "the planned *blitzkrieg* has encountered *blitzschnell* [lightning quick] handling on the other side."[19] "Officially there were no neutrals in those days," later explained one of the President's chief advisers as he recalled the general character of the response of the non-Soviet world. Some states, however, did assume a neutral position; Egypt, for example, announced that it would not support the Security Council resolution of June 27 on the grounds that it was just a part of the East-West struggle.

Soviet Press Reaction

The reactions of the leaders of nations of the Soviet bloc, of course, were condemnatory. Ever since Saturday, the public pronouncements of the Soviet leadership as contained in *Pravda,* oracle of the Communist Party and of the world Communist movement, had been the object of close study by analysts at the Department of State. The Sunday edition of the newspaper had contained not a word on the clash of arms in Korea. The Monday issue brought Soviet readers their first news of the fighting in the form of two TASS dispatches from Pyongyang which quoted communiques from the North Korean Ministry of Internal Affairs and four other short TASS reports from New York, Paris, and London.[20] The first official statement from Pyongyang charged that the South Koreans had attacked north across the Thirty-eight-Parallel, reported that "constabulary units" of the People's Republic had been ordered to repel the attack, and declared that "firm measures" of retaliation would be undertaken if the South Korean Government did not cease its "adventurist military activities." In its sec-

17. *Ibid.,* p. 4.
18. *Ibid.,* p. 8.
19. *Ibid.,* p. 21.
20. *Pravda,* June 26, 1950, p. 3.

ond statement, the Ministry of Internal Affairs announced that constabulary troops "together with units of the People's Army" had gone over to a "counter-attack" and had penetrated from five to ten kilometers south of the Parallel.[21] Through selective reporting of parts of Associated Press, France Presse, and Reuters dispatches from the Western capitals, TASS stressed the successes of the North Korean forces and the "disorder" of their opponents. These TASS reports did not mention the alternative version of how the fighting began that had been an integral part of the original dispatches on which they were based. Not until Tuesday did Soviet readers catch a fleeting glimpse of that version in the form of a TASS report on the Security Council meeting of June 25 which stated that during the proceedings Ambassador Gross ". . . made assertions as if the ground troops of North Korea had attacked South Korea and depicted the situation in Korea in this light."[22] This same dispatch, while reporting the passage of the June 25 resolution, charged for the first time that it had been adopted illegally because of the nonparticipation in the voting of two permanent members of the Security Council—the Soviet Union and Communist China.[23] On Tuesday also the newspaper printed the full text of Premier Kim Ilsong's first radio address to the Korean people[24] and more TASS reports from London, Tokyo, and Shanghai.

On Wednesday, *Pravda* reacted to President Truman's Tuesday announcement in editorial style on the front page—the first time that an article on the Korean conflict had appeared in that position. This pronouncement repeated the North Korean version of the war's inception, charged that President Rhee had answered the peaceful unification efforts of the United Democratic Fatherland front with "internecine, fratricidal war," and accused the United States of "direct aggression against the Korean People's Demo-

---

21. The full texts of these two communiques were published in the *New York Times*, June 26, 1950, p. 3. *Pravda* did not publish the texts of UNCOK or South Korean reports of the fighting.

22. *Pravda*, June 27, 1950, p. 5.

23. On this point authoritative opinion in the U.N. held that on the basis of precedent Soviet nonparticipation in the voting did not constitute a veto, and that Communist China legally was not entitled to participate.

24. See above, pp. 123f.

cratic Republic and the Chinese People's Republic."[25] The article
further alleged that President Truman's decisions were ". . . one
more indication that American ruling circles no longer restrict
themselves to mere preparation for aggression but have gone
over to overt acts of aggression." "But haven't they gone too far?"
queried the voice of the Soviet regime. Although this statement did
not employ explicitly the argument that the Security Council's
action had been illegal, it claimed that "Neither the United Nations nor any other international organ authorized the American
Government to undertake those actions with respect to Korea and
China which Truman announced yesterday." The newspaper did
not carry the text of the President's announcement. Instead it
printed a summary TASS dispatch from New York which failed
to mention that the Seventh Fleet had been ordered to prevent a
Chinese Nationalist assault upon the mainland.[26] Other reports
printed in the Wednesday edition of the newspaper dealt with
North Korean successes, a flowers-and-flags welcome of the "lib-
erators" of Seoul, the fluctuation of the New York Stock Exchange,
and a statement from Pyongyang that the Security Council resolution of June 25 was illegal. This, then, was the official public reaction of the Soviet regime to the Korean conflict through Wednesday,
June 28.

Wednesday Responses in the Senate and House

In the United States Senate on Wednesday afternoon, Senator
Robert A. Taft, Republican of Ohio, delivered a major speech in
opposition to the foreign policies of the Democratic Administration and to the manner in which the United States had become
committed in South Korea.[27] ". . . This entirely unfortunate crisis,"
he argued, "has been produced, first, by the outrageous, aggressive attitude of Soviet Russia, and second, by the bungling and
inconsistent foreign policy of the administration." The Senator
charged that the Administration had erred in agreeing to the
initial division of Korea, had been wrong in withdrawing Ameri-

25. *Pravda*, June 28, 1950, p. 1.
26. *Ibid.*, p. 3.
27. *Congressional Record*, Vol. 96, Part 7, June 28, 1950, 9319-9327.

can armed forces from the peninsula, and had made its most griev-
ous mistake in not making it patently clear long ago that it would
resist further Communist expansion in the Far East. He asserted
that American policy in China as well as in Korea had "invited
attack." "If the United States was not prepared to use its troops
and give military assistance to Nationalist China against Chinese
Communists, why should it take its troops to defend Nationalist
Korea against Korean Communists? That certainly must have
seemed a fairly logical conclusion to those who have inaugurated
this aggression," reasoned the Senator from Ohio.[28] He then leveled his critical sights directly at Secretary Acheson: "I suggest
. . . that any Secretary of State who has been so reversed by his
superiors and whose policies have precipitated the danger of war
had better resign and let someone else administer the program
to which he was, and perhaps still is, so violently opposed."[29]
At this suggestion, Senators McCarthy and Jenner, joined by spec-
tators in the galleries, broke into applause in violation of Senate
rules.

Senator Taft next turned his critical fire upon the President's
failure to get a mandate from Congress before deciding to fight
in Korea. "There has been no pretense of consulting the Congress,"
he charged, arguing that the Congressional participants in the
Tuesday White House conference had been merely witnesses to a
fait accompli. Although the Senator agreed that the question of
the President's constitutional authority to make the decision had
been complicated by American treaty obligations to the United
Nations, he did not think that it had been answered. Calling for a
full-scale debate on the question, he explained, "I merely do not
wish to have this action go by with the approval of the Senate,
if it is what it seems to me, namely, a complete usurpation by the
President of authority to use the Armed Forces of this country.
If the incident is permitted to go by without protest, at least from
this body, we would have finally terminated for all time the right
of Congress to declare war, which is granted to Congress alone by
the Constitution of the United States."[30]

---

28. *Ibid.*, p. 9320.
29. *Ibid.*, p. 9322.
30. *Ibid.*, p. 9323.

Despite these criticisms, the powerful Republican leader took pains several times in the course of his speech to clarify the fact that he did not oppose the President's decisions themselves. ". . . If a resolution were submitted asking for approval of the use of our Armed Forces already sent to Korea and full support of them in their present venture, I would vote in favor of it," he pledged.[31]

Rising at once to the defense of the Administration, Senate majority leader Lucas retorted by repeating the assertion he had made on Tuesday that the President's action was justified by more than one hundred historical precedents, citing as examples President Jefferson's suppression of the Barbary pirates in 1801 and President McKinley's intervention in the Chinese Boxer Rebellion of 1900. "Mr. President," he complained, "not withstanding the seriousness of the hour, irrespective of the crises before us, we hear the Senator from Ohio tell the country and the world that the President of the United States is responsible for this de facto war. What a travesty upon justice."[32] In reply to the critical Republican's charges of past errors, Senator Lucas argued, "There is no government which does not make mistakes." As for Yalta, he invited his colleagues to probe into the military considerations underlying the decisions taken there. As for the withdrawal of American troops from Korea, he pointed out that this had been done in accordance with the will of the United Nations General Assembly. In conclusion he solemnly warned, "Mr. President, this is a fateful hour in the history of the American Republic. Men may dig up all the presumed and supposed mistakes they want to dig up if they so desire. . . . [but] it seems to me that we ought to close ranks, and forget what happened at Potsdam and Yalta, because digging up those old sores will get nowhere as far as giving the American people the kind of unity they ought to have. The only thing such action does is to help Mr. Stalin!"

After the Democratic spokesman had finished, Senator Ralph Flanders, Republican of Vermont, requested confirmation of his

---

31. *Ibid.*, p. 9320. Of the President's decisions Senator Taft later wrote, "His moral position was unassailable, but he did not recognize the implications of what he had started." Robert A. Taft, *A Foreign Policy for Americans* (Garden City: Doubleday and Company, 1951), p. 43.

32. *Congressional Record*, Vol. 96, Part 7, 9327-9329.

understanding that the President was perfectly justified in intervening in Korea under the present circumstances, but that "he would not be within his rights in pursuing the Korean forces or attacking Korean positions in any way north of the thirty-eighth parallel."[33] "I wholeheartedly agree . . . on that point," Senator Lucas replied. Quoting from the Tuesday resolution of the Security Council, Senator Connally supported the interpretation that the American action was only valid for "South Korea." On these grounds Republican Senator Smith of New Jersey stated that he saw no need for a declaration of war: "The minute they got back of the thirty-eighth parallel we would not have any authority as far as the United Nations was concerned, in trying to restore peace in the area. I think that when that is understood there will be less tendency to say that we are declaring war on a country with which we have been at peace."[34] Senator Knowland of California also saw no necessity for a declaration of war by the Congress, but he was extremely displeased by the idea that American military activity should be confined to the area south of the Thirty-eighth Parallel. "The action this Government is taking," he argued, "is a police action against a violator of the law of nations and the Charter of the United Nations. It seems to me to be absurd to suggest that all air bombardment should be in the territory of the victim of this overt aggression. . . . It is utterly unrealistic that the aggressive Communists should feel so secure."[35]

At 2 P.M., without debate, the Senate passed by a vote of 76 to 0 the bill to extend the Selective Service Act that the House had approved almost unanimously on Tuesday. The Democratic leadership also had hoped to get a vote on the bill to extend the Mutual Defense Assistance Program Act of 1949. While the debate proceeded on this measure during the afternoon, there were numerous huddles on the floor of the Senate as they tried vainly to achieve agreement on its immediate consideration. Some Republicans saw no necessity for hurrying the vote. They thought that

---

33. *Ibid.*, p. 9329.

34. *Ibid.*, p. 9334. By Friday, June 30, both Senator Smith and Senator Flanders had changed their minds in the direction of a broader interpretation of the scope of the President's authority under the U.N. resolution. Consult *ibid.*, p. 9540.

35. *Ibid.*, p. 9347.

the debate on the bill, which would make available more than a
billion dollars in military aid to American allies during the coming
fiscal year, could profitably be extended until Friday when Presidential powers under the existing law would expire.

In the House of Representatives there were only two brief
statements on matters directly related to Korea during a long seven-
hour session. Shortly after the House convened at 11 A.M., Representative Robert F. Rich, Republican of Pennsylvania, remarked,
"I was stunned yesterday to have to vote for draft in peacetime."[36] Although he considered the bill "wrong in principle," he
explained his affirmative vote saying, "I wanted to help the United
Nations to be strong and work together." The other statement was
made immediately afterward by Representative Jacob K. Javits,
Republican of New York, who described appreciatively the difference between the United Nations and the League of Nations as
"the difference . . . between Korea and Ethiopia." Then the representatives dissolved themselves into a Committee of the Whole
House on the State of the Union and for more than six hours discussed a bill to reduce excise taxes. Having risen on Tuesday to
meet the demands implied by the crisis in Korea, the House on
Wednesday turned its attention to its responsibility for the nation's
finances.

While the American Congress deliberated, the British House
of Commons learned of the measures that the Labour Government had decided to undertake in response to the Security Council's call for further assistance to the Republic of Korea. At 5 P.M.
in London (1 P.M. in New York), Prime Minister Attlee informed
its members, "We have decided to support the United States
action in Korea by immediately placing our naval forces in Japanese waters at the disposal of the United States authorities to
operate on behalf of the Security Council in support of South
Korea. Orders to this effect have already been sent to the naval
Commander-in-Chief on the spot."[37] Cheers resounded throughout
the House. Winston Churchill again voiced his support and asked
assurance that the British forces would be large enough to make
a "substantial contribution relative to the American forces there."

---

36. *Ibid.*, p. 9351
37. 476 *H. C. Deb.* 5s., June 28, 1950, 2319.

Prime Minister Attlee replied that British naval strength in Far Eastern waters was approximately equal to that of the Seventh Fleet. Under Admiral Sir Patrick Brind in the area were the aircraft carrier *Triumph,* three cruisers, six destroyers, and other auxiliary vessels. The decision of the British Government to commit elements of the Royal Navy to Korean waters made the United Kingdom the first nation to act in support of the United Nations Security Council resolution of June 27. The decision was made during a morning conference of the Defense Committee of the Cabinet, in which Defense Minister Emmanuel Shinwell, the Service Ministers, and the Chiefs of Staff had participated in addition to the Prime Minister.[38]

The First Meeting of the National Security Council Is Held

In Washington on Wednesday afternoon the regular weekly meeting of the National Security Council was held in the Cabinet Room of the White House.[39] By law this body consisted of the President, the Vice President, the Secretary of State, the Secretary of Defense, the Chairman of the National Security Resources Board, and such other Secretaries and Under Secretaries of executive and military departments as the President might designate.[40] Habitually among the President's advisers in attendance were the Secretary of the Treasury, John W. Snyder, and the Director of the Central Intelligence Agency, Rear Admiral Hillenkoetter. Participating in this particular meeting were the Service Secretaries and Ambassador-at-large Averell Harriman, who had just returned by plane from Paris to take up a new position as special adviser to the President on foreign affairs.[41] Apparently the Joint Chiefs of Staff did not take part in the deliberations.

President Truman opened the meeting with "a survey of the

---

38. *New York Times,* June 29, 1950, p. 13.

39. *New York Herald Tribune,* June 29, 1950, p. 2.

40. P. L. 216, *National Security Council Amendments Act of 1949,* August 10, 1949, Section 3.

41. He had been accompanied by U.S. Minister-in-Paris Charles R. Bohlen, a top specialist on the Soviet Union, who had been hastily recalled to Washington for consultation.

most recent developments reported from Korea."[42] Although direct
evidence is not now available on the contents of the reports which
the President brought to the attention of his advisers at this time,
judging from the contemporary news dispatches from Korea, he
probably stressed two main aspects of the military situation—that
the full force of American airpower had not yet been brought to
bear upon the enemy; and that while the condition of the ROK
Army apparently was still serious, there were signs of reinvigora-
tion. Even as the President was speaking, Air Force fighters and
bombers were preparing to roar off at dawn from the rainy run-
ways of Itazuke air base in Japan to appear soon afterward in
clear skies over the Korean front "in swarms." The sight of this
air armada would hearten the crowds of refugees trudging south
from Seoul. Twenty-four hours earlier the hills along the route
to safety had echoed with cries of "*Manse!*"[43] when six American
fighters knifed through the sky in the direction of the enemy.[44]
"The Koreans around me screamed and yelled with joy," reported
eyewitness Marguerite Higgins. "Women from an adjacent village
rushed out to grab my hand and point to the sky in ecstasy."[45]
Although the Air Force was flinging more and more airplanes
into combat each day, there had been as yet no reports of carrier-
based aircraft in action.[46]

After their retreat from Seoul, the South Korean forces seemed
to be holding their opponents at the Han River, at least temporarily.
Some units appeared to be regaining their fighting potential. The
commander of the Seventh Division, which had been slashed by
enemy armor in the Uijongbu area, had reorganized his men at
Suwon, had reequipped them with arms flown in from Japan, and
had led them up to the Han River line where they were participating in the effort to keep the enemy from crossing.[47] The considerations being weighed at the Pentagon at this time might have

---

42. *Memoirs*, II, 340. The President's account of this conference is the only
one available in the public record.

43. A patriotic cheer, literally "ten thousand generations."

44. Burton Crane, *New York Times*, June 29, 1950, p. 3.

45. Higgins, *War in Korea* (Garden City: Doubleday and Company, 1951),
p. 29.

46. Harlan Trott, *Christian Science Monitor*, June 29, 1950, p. 3.

47. Burton Crane, *New York Times*, June 29, 1950, p. 3.

been reflected quite accurately in an article, written a few hours after the NSC meeting adjourned, by Hanson Baldwin of the *New York Times:*

> The probability that United States ground troops will have to be employed in Korea if the North Korean Communists are to be driven back to the Thirty-eighth Parallel increased by the hour today as dispatches reaching the Pentagon told of retreat, confusion and disorder in the South Korean forces.
>
>   .   .   .
>
> The next few days—particularly the operations tomorrow—will probably determine whether or not the intervention of United States ground combat forces will be necessary. Such intervention should be avoided, on military grounds, if possible, because all authorities long have recognized that in case of war with Russia, Southern Korea would be at least initially indefensible and any forces committed there would be doomed to a second Bataan, or at best evacuation under fire.
>
> However, the political necessity for prompt intervention—if the South Korean ground armies melt away—is clear; once our hand has been laid to the plow we cannot turn back. Moreover, in a military sense, prompt and decisive action to force the invaders back of the Thirty-eighth Parallel is deemed of great importance; what we want to avoid in Korea is a protracted wearing campaign of attrition, which would gradually suck in greater and greater United States' strength and might result in a sort of Spanish Civil War condition.
>
> Despite the unencouraging reports reaching Washington yesterday it is premature to say with certainty that ground troops are needed. The normal fog of war—greatly accentuated in the Korean campaign by the paucity of communications—has left Washington with insufficient information to determine with precision our future course. Major elements of the South Korean Army still appear to be intact, and if they can be given leadership, staff, communications, arms and equipment, they may be able with United States air and naval aid, to save their country themselves.[48]

There is no direct evidence that the question of whether or not to commit Army troops in Korea came up for discussion during the deliberations of the National Security Council. There is

---

48. *New York Times,* June 29, 1950, p. 4.

also no direct evidence that it did not. There is evidence, nevertheless, that sometime on Wednesday, Korean time, Major General John H. Church, whom General MacArthur had ordered to survey the military situation on the peninsula, reported from Suwon to Tokyo that "the United States would have to commit ground troops if the Thirty-eighth Parallel were to be restored."[49]

After the President had reviewed the latest developments in Korea he ordered all departments to make a "complete restudy" of American policies in areas adjacent to the Soviet Union. The Secretaries of State and Defense reported that a study of the contingencies which might grow out of the Korean conflict already had been initiated. During the day, State and Defense officials had conferred at length on the problem of possible Soviet intervention in the fighting, and on the appropriate response which the United States should make if this happened. One position that was strongly maintained during these discussions was that if such intervention occurred, the United States would be confronted with an entirely new occasion for decision which would demand unemotional analysis, anticipatory planning, and patience if World War III were to be averted. If the United States automatically accepted Soviet intervention as the starting gun for global war, it was argued, then actually it was resigning control over its destiny to the Soviet Union. American forces should therefore be instructed to fight to extricate themselves from any difficult situation in which they found themselves as a result of Soviet intervention, but should not unnecessarily aggravate the situation until they had received further instructions. Department of Defense officials were not averse to having such instructions included in the orders sent to American forces in the Far East, but they did not wish to see them sent out as a discrete directive.

At this point, Vice-President Barkley, who had been detained by voting in the Senate, joined the meeting. He reported to the President that the Senate had voted unanimously to give him authority to invoke the selective service laws and to call the reserve components of the armed forces to active duty. All that was needed was the President's signature to transform the bill into

---

49. Appleman, "The U.S. and the U.N. Intervene in Korea," p. 34. Based on a narration of his mission by General Church.

law. The President considered Mr. Barkley's tardiness because of such business to be "for a good cause."

After the Vice-President had taken his place, Secretary Acheson cautioned that "the unanimity of support [for the President's decisions] might not be of lasting duration." As the President later recalled the Secretary of State's position, "What had been done in Korea had had tremendous effect, but the responsibilities that went with it were equally significant, for what had been done in the last three days might ultimately involve us in all-out war." "I replied," the President further recalled, "that the danger involved was obvious but that we should not back out of Korea unless a military situation elsewhere demanded such action."[50]

Underscoring that portion of Secretary Acheson's remarks having to do with the favorable response which the President's decisions had evoked, Ambassador Harriman reported on the basis of his first-hand observation of reactions in Paris that the American decision to fight in Korea had brought "great relief and confidence" to the people of Europe.[51] Europeans, he explained, at first had been apprehensive lest the United States fail to resist the North Korean aggression, but now they were encouraged and were fully aware of the risks inherent in the bold course of action upon which the President had decided. Vice-President Barkley reported that during the Senate debate on the military aid program, Senator Wherry, referring to a dispatch received on one of the teletype machines just off the Senate floor, had questioned whether the NATO countries were going to stand by the United States in Korea.[52] The report upon which the Senator had based his inquiry had claimed that Great Britain, in fear of offending Communist China, was going to confine itself to humanitarian work of a non-combatant nature in support of the Security Council resolution. President Truman, having at his disposal information concerning the actual course of British policy, assured the Vice-President that British warships would fight in Korean waters and asked Secretary Johnson to provide him with the full details of this offer of assistance so that he might inform the Senate.

50. *Memoirs*, II, 340.
51. *Congressional Record*, Vol. 96, Part 7, June 28, 1950, 9312-13.
52. *Ibid.* See also *New York Times*, June 29, 1950, p. 18.

As far as is known, the remainder of the conference was devoted
to problems of liaison, intelligence gathering, and the dissemina-
tion of information. Air Force Secretary Finletter suggested to the
President that he send General Vandenberg to Tokyo to familiarize
General MacArthur with the latest thinking in Washington because
he believed that personal contact might help to "avoid mistakes."
The President rejected this suggestion because he felt that all of
the Joint Chiefs were "most urgently needed" in the capital.
"Nevertheless," the President later recalled, "I understood the
need for mutual understanding between Washington and Tokyo
and expressed my regret that General MacArthur had so consistently declined all invitations to return to the United States for
even a short visit. There had been no opportunity for him to meet
me as Commander in Chief. I felt that if the Korean conflict was
prolonged I would want to see General MacArthur."[53]

With respect to intelligence gathering, Secretary Pace reported
that military intelligence had been instructed to keep alert for
any indication that the Soviet Union was participating in the
Korean fighting and asked if there were any other targets to
which special attention should be given. The President designated
". . . Soviet activities in the vicinity of Yugoslavia, in Bulgaria
especially, and in the vicinity of northern Europe." Secretary
Pace also reported that he had arranged for military briefings to
be held on Capitol Hill for the benefit of members of the Congress.[54] The President asked Vice-President Barkley to select a
bipartisan group of legislators to attend them.

Secretary Acheson Holds a Press Conference

After the National Security Council meeting, the President
turned to last-minute preparations for his radio address to the
nation.[55] Secretary Acheson returned to the State Department to
participate in his first press conference since the previous Friday.
This was the first press conference given by a high Administration

---

53. *Memoirs*, II, 341.
54. The President himeslf was briefed every morning by General Bradley.
Hearings, Part II, 1050.
55. See above p. 212.

official since the Korean fighting began. The Department's briefing room was packed with an exceptionally large number of
reporters, including representatives of the Soviet news agency
TASS. Speaking from notes and demonstrating the facility of expression for which he was noted, the Secretary of State began, "There
are a few points which I should like to make before we go into
the questions about the matter which I am sure is uppermost in
all of your minds. This is the announcement by the President
yesterday of decisions which he had taken. I will not go into
those decisions in detail, but make some points about them."[56]
Then he continued:

> The first point I want to make is our feeling of deep gratitude
> here in the Department, and responsibility also, for the almost unani-
> mous world reaction which has come from the action taken by the
> United Nations, and from the announcement made by the President
> of his ac- [sic][57] been taken in support of the United Nations.
> In all parts of the world where free opinion exists there has been
> an immediate response—a response to the realization that this was,
> if there ever was in the world, a test of whether the United Nations
> was going to survive.
> The attack was the most cynical, brutal, naked attack by armed
> forces upon an undefended country that could occur. The world
> has understood that, and it has understood that the actions taken
> by the United States have been in support of the United Nations.
> The second point I want to make is that as soon as we knew
> that this attack had taken place, and had immediately conveyed
> that information to the President and gotten his instructions, it was
> the view of the President, and of the entire Government of the
> United States, that our first responsibility was to report this to the
> United Nations. This was done in the middle of the night on Satur-
> day, June 24, and a meeting of the Security Council was called on
> Sunday, June 25. From then on, all action in Korea has been under
> the aegis of the United Nations. That is a very important point.
> The next point that I want to make is one that I am sure you
> understand. It is that the entire action of the Government of the
> United States, since a late hour on Saturday when this information
> came to us, has been taken under Presidential leadership and direc-
> tion. Here, as in many other situations in the years in which I have

---

56. Transcript, *New York Times,* June 29, 1950, p. 10.
57. Line omitted in the original text.

been Under Secretary and Secretary, the President has been faced with the most difficult decisions which had to be made quickly, and after taking full advice he has assumed the responsibility and he has made the decision.

The fourth point I would like to make is that there has been complete unity among the President's advisers, civil and military. The Departments of State and Defense have worked practically as one department ever since this matter arose, and in anticipation of possible difficulties of this sort, so that we were able on the shortest possible notice to present completed staff work to the President. He had the view of his advisers without having differences among his advisers.

The fifth point I should like to stress is the unity which existed at the President's meeting yesterday, at which the Secretary of Defense and I, and our advisers, were present with the Congressional leaders. Here, again, the understanding of the problem, the understanding of the actions taken showed complete unity.

The sixth point I should like to make is that with very few exceptions the press and the radio of the United States has been unified in its comments upon what was done, and the necessity for doing it. I assume, and I think I assume justly, that that attitude on the part of the press and the radio indicates that there is similar unity among the people of the United States.

Finally I should like to leave with you the thought that the complexities and difficulties of the international situation are great. This is a time for very steady and sober talk and actions. It is not a time for general speculation, for trying to stir up difficulties which do not exist, for imagining possibilities which are remote.

It is a time for the very greatest steadiness and it is a time, as I have often said in the past, where more than ever, you gentlemen share with the officials of the Government a very deep responsibility, which I feel sure you are quite aware of.

During the period of general questioning that followed these introductory remarks, Secretary Acheson stressed that the United States was faced with "the action of a specific Communist force in Far Eastern countries" and refused to be drawn into a discussion of the role of the Soviet Union in the Korean conflict. He reported that Soviet leaders had not yet replied to the American note which had been delivered in Moscow on Tuesday. The Secretary of State also argued that "willful absence" of a permanent member of the Security Council should not prevent it from carrying out its functions under the United Nations Charter and dismissed Soviet charges of illegality against the June 25 resolution as "totally unfounded."

Another public pronouncement was made by Secretary of Defense Johnson, who sought to dispel rumors that the United States was going to undertake general mobilization. He announced, "It is not contemplated to call the reserve components to active duty in the foreseeable future, nor does the Department of Defense plan to ask for application of the Selective Service Law so long as its authorized strength can be maintained by voluntary enlistments."[58]

General MacArthur Flies to Korea

At 5:10 P.M. Wednesday (6:10 A.M. Thursday, Japan-Korea time)[59] General MacArthur left Haneda airport near Tokyo in his C-54 transport *Bataan*, bound for Korea and a personal reconnaissance of the fighting front. As the General journeyed to Korea, the editors of the *New York Times* were writing, "Fate could not have chosen a man better qualified to command the unreserved confidence of the people of this country. Here is a superb strategist and an inspired leader; a man of infinite patience and quiet stability under adverse pressure; a man equally capable of bold and decisive action."[60] Accompanying the General to Korea were Major General Edward M. Almond, his Chief of Staff; Major General Charles A. Willoughby, his intelligence officer; Brigadier General Courtney Whitney, chief of the government section of SCAP; and Lieutenant General George E. Stratemeyer, commander of the Far East Air Forces.[61] Also in the General's party were the chief Tokyo representatives of the Associated Press, the United Press, the International News Service, the Australian Associated

58. *New York Times,* June 29, 1950, p. 10.

59. *Ibid.,* p. 1. See also Appleman, *South to the Naktong,* p. 44. The times given for the General's trip to Korea are based on the flight log kept by his personal pilot, Lieutenant Colonel Anthony F. Story.

60. "M'Arthur in Command," *New York Times,* June 29, 1950, p. 28.

61. Whitney, p. 326 indicates that Vice Admiral Joy was also in the party, but since a message was transmitted to him from the airplane this seems unlikely.

Press, and Reuters, whom the General had invited to accompany him on his mission.[62] Ever since the invasion had begun, query after query had been flashed to General Headquarters in Tokyo from Washington requesting more information on the course of battle.[63] Finally the General had decided to go to Korea himself in order to gain first-hand knowledge of the military situation.

During part of the four-hour flight to the peninsula, the General, seated beside General Stratemeyer, listened to his air commander explain the serious difficulties that the Air Force was encountering in Korea. Fighter time over the target area was limited by the necessity to fly in from bases outside Korea. Bad weather was also a problem. Korea was entering into the summer rainy season and a pattern of clear days interspersed with cloudy, rainy ones was to be expected.[64] But the major limitation was the fact that the Air Force could not strike at the enemy's air bases, reserves, lines of communication, and war-making potential north of the Thirty-eighth Parallel. General MacArthur concluded that if he were to accomplish his mission, this restriction would have to be removed. As General Whitney later explained, "If North Korea remained an air sanctuary in which Communist forces could mobilize and maneuver and bring up supplies, MacArthur reasoned, he would not be giving the South Korean defenders the 'effective military assistance' that the U.N. had directed him to give. He concluded that his authority to destroy the North Korean military targets was permissive, not restrictive, and that implicit in his directive was the discretion normal to field command."[65] Therefore, without hesitation, he authorized General Stratemeyer to extend his operations into North Korea. While General MacArthur dictated, the air commander wrote out a cablegram which would send B-29 bombers across the Parallel within hours.[66]

62. Russel Brines, AP; Ernest Holberecht, UP; Howard Handleman, INS; Roy R. MacCartney, Australian Associated Press and Reuters.

63. Testimony of Major General Edward M. Almond in U.S. Senate, Committee on the Judiciary, *Interlocking Subversion in Government Departments*, Part XXV, 2060.

64. Shannon McCune, *Korea's Heritage: A Regional and Social Geography* (Rutland, Vermont: Charles E. Tuttle Company, 1956), p. 18.

65. Whitney, p. 326.

66. National Defense Ministry, Republic of Korea, B12, indicates B-29's bombed Pyongyang and other military targets in North Korea on June 29, Korean time. On June 29, Washington time (i.e., thirteen hours behind Korean time), offi-

At about 7 P.M. (8 A.M. Thursday in Korea), Lieutenant Colonel Anthony F. Story, pilot of the *Bataan,* instructed his radio operator to transmit the following message back to Japan: "Stratemeyer to Partridge: Take out North Korean Airfield immediately. No publicity. MacArthur approves."[67]

At about the time this message was in the process of transmission, the radio operator of the *Bataan* picked up another message for General MacArthur which notified him that British naval units in the Far East had been placed under his operational control. The General ordered two more radiograms to be sent at once— the first to the Australian representative on SCAP, General Robertson, inquiring if his government also would make available its Japan-based air units for combat in Korea; and the second to Vice Admiral Joy, instructing him to coordinate with the British naval commander and to explore the possibility of joint American-British carrier air strikes in the general vicinity of the Thirty-eighth Parallel.[68] If carrier-based fighters could be employed in force, their ability to stay over the combat area longer than land-based aircraft would help to remove another of the difficulties hampering air operations.

The General Conducts a Personal Reconnaissance

Escorted over Korea by four Mustang fighters which had chased off a lone enemy Yak attacker, the *Bataan* landed at Suwon at about 9:30 P.M., Washington time (10:30 A.M. Thursday, Korean time).[69] Minutes earlier, President Rhee and Ambassador Muccio had arrived in two light unarmed observation planes from Taejon. The Korean President and the American Ambassador owed their lives to the skill of the American pilot who had brought them to

---

cials in the capital denied reports based on North Korean radio broadcasts that Pyongyang had been bombed. *New York Times,* June 30, 1950, p. 1. On July 8, James Reston wrote, ". . . Despite official denials responsible officials here still insist that his [General MacArthur's] planes attacked the North Korean capital before President Truman authorized any such action." *New York Times,* July 9, 1950, p. E3.

67. Appleman, *South to the Naktong,* p. 44. "Partridge" refers to Major General Earl E. Partridge, Fifth Air Force commander.

68. *Ibid.*

69. Testimony of Major General Almond in U.S. Senate, Committee on the Judiciary, Part XXV, 2060.

the rendezvous with General MacArthur. In a harrowing escape, flying around hills and down valleys a few feet off the ground, they had eluded a North Korean Yak fighter intent on destroying them, without the enemy pilot being able to fire a single shot.[70] The General, the President, and the Ambassador hurried from the airfield to a briefing in a Suwon schoolhouse where Brigadier General John H. Church—whose survey party General MacArthur had ordered to Korea forty-eight hours earlier—had made his headquarters with that of the ROK Army.

As the briefing began, President Rhee made a statement which amounted to, "We are in a hell of a fix."[71] In his summary of the military situation, General Church reported: "This morning we could account for not more than 8,000 ROK's and at present we have 8,000 more; by tonight we expect to have an additional 8,000; therefore we can count today only about 25,000."[72] Thus about three quarters of the 100,000 men in the in the Republic of Korea Army were unaccounted for. General MacArthur asked Major General Ch'oe Pyongdok, chief of staff of the ROK Army, what he proposed to do about the situation. According to General Almond, General Ch'oe replied that he was going to muster two million South Korean youths and repel the invasion. The officers in General MacArthur's party considered this plan to be pathetically impractical.[73]

At the time of this briefing in the Suwon schoolhouse, the invaders had advanced to a line extending roughly from the Han River in the west through the towns of Kap'yong and Ch'unch'on, northeast of Seoul, to Kangnung on the east coast. The primary task facing the defenders was to prevent the enemy from establishing a bridgehead on the south bank of the Han opposite Seoul and from bringing his dreaded tanks across. The psychological effects of the clanking steel Soviet-built monsters, which apparently were impervious to the antitank weapons in the hands of the South Korean forces, had been great from the very onset of the

---

70. David Douglas Duncan, *This Is War* (New York: Harper and Brothers, 1951), p. 4.

71. Testimony of Major General Almond in U.S. Senate, Committee on the Judiciary, Part XXV, 2060.

72. Appleman, "The U.S. and the U.N. Intervene in Korea," p. 38.

73. Testimony of Major General Almond in U.S. Senate, Committee on the Judiciary, Part XXV, 2060. Gen. Ch'oe was relieved from his post on June 30.

conflict. In suicidal attempts to stop them north of Seoul, human bombs of the First Division—men with dynamite sticks wrapped around their bodies—had detonated themselves against them.[74] General MacArthur did not delay long at the briefing. He wanted to see the fighting himself. Passing up lunch, clutching his famous corncob pipe, he climbed into the back of a black sedan and set out on the twenty-mile journey north to Seoul, the rest of his party following in jeeps. It was about 11 P.M. in Washington (12 noon Thursday in Korea).

While the General was driving up the road to Seoul under clear Korean skies, 9,000 persons in New York City were returning home from a Civil Rights Congress rally in Madison Square Garden which had been converted at the last minute from a meeting of protest against the treatment of "political prisoners" to a gathering calling for "hands off Korea." At this rally, Representative Vito Marcantonio, Secretary Gus Hall of the Communist Party, singer Paul Robeson, and others denounced President Truman's decisions as "imperialist aggression." Then the organizers of the meeting dispatched an indignant telegram to the White House in the name of "18,000 Americans."[75]

Thus ended Wednesday, June 28, the fifth day of the conflict in Korea. It had been a day primarily characterized by the reactions to the President's announcement of Tuesday noon. From Peking and Moscow, from London and Paris, from Capitol Hill and Madison Square Garden, and from elsewhere at home and abroad had come expressions of unreserved approval, qualified acceptance, dissent, or condemnation. In a divided world, opinion was divided; but in the United States and in the other countries of the non-Soviet sphere, the response was overwhelmingly favorable. In Washington, the President and his advisers, while warily scanning incoming information for evidence of Soviet intentions, had made no new decisions of major importance. The President did not yet have a report based on General MacArthur's personal reconnaissance in Korea.

There, the bloodshed continued.

---

74. Burton Crane, *New York Times*, June 30, 1950, p. 2.
75. Garden officials estimated the crowd at "about 9,000." *New York Times*, June 29, 1950, p. 18.

CHAPTER 9

THURSDAY, JUNE 29

As General MacArthur's convoy churned through the dust toward Seoul, thousands of refugees moving south along the route clapped and cheered. Although South Korean radio stations had broadcast the heartening news of the General's presence in Korea, the fleeing homeless ones were probably unaware that a military commander of world renown was passing by.[1] Apparently they were responding merely to the sight of a grim little band of northward-bound Americans—a symbol of support from beyond the Eastern Sea. Trucks jammed with armed men also were withdrawing along with the refugees. The ROK soldiers, fully armed with rifles and bandoliers of ammunition, smiled, cheered, saluted, and sang as the Americans went by. This behavior together with

---

1. Duncan, p. 6.

the fact that no wounded were seen indicated to Major General
Almond that the Korean soldiers, although disciplined, had lost
their leadership and were not fighting.[2] Other members of General MacArthur's party later recalled a somewhat more discouraging scene. According to Brigadier General Whitney, the convoy
rolled through ". . . the dreadful backwash of a defeated and
dispersed army. The South Koreans were in a complete and dis-
organized rout."[3]

About a mile southwest of Seoul, at the Yongdungp'o cross-
roads, the convoy stopped. Standing at this intersection General
MacArthur received a quick briefing on the terrain and known
enemy positions. Then he climbed to the top of a nearby knoll
where he could plainly see as well as hear the pounding which
the North Korean artillery pieces and mortars were giving to the
ROK positions on the south bank of the Han River. For twenty
minutes[4] he thoughtfully looked out upon the field of battle—
the conquered smoldering capital, the muddy Han, the exposed flat-
lands of its southern bank. Below the hilltop on which he stood,
the bedraggled defenders of the Republic of Korea streamed past
toward the rear. He decided then and there that only the commitment of American ground combat troops could prevent the
invaders from overrunning the Republic of Korea.[5]

On the return trip to Suwon, the General and his party observed that a minor transformation had taken place in the South
Korean Army. At many places along the road ROK infantrymen in
ranks stood at attention while their officers saluted. Apparently
the news had spread quickly that General MacArthur had come to
view the battle area. Twice the General's party heard a militant
cry which unmistakably was, "MacArthur! Victory!"[6] The late after-

2. Testimony of Major General Edward M. Almond in U.S. Senate, Committee
on the Judiciary, *Interlocking Subversion in Government Departments*, XXV, 2061.
Life photographer David Duncan recalled, "It was not that they were all turning
tail and running away. It was more as though they thought that this chaotic disinte-
gration was happening to someone else's army." Duncan, p. 6.
3. Whitney, p. 327.
4. Major General Charles A. Willoughby and John Chamberlain, *MacArthur
1941-1951* (New York: McGraw-Hill, 1954) p. 357.
5. *Ibid.* See also Whitney, p. 328.
6. Duncan, p. 5.

noon shadows were lengthening when the convoy arrived in Suwon and the General plunged into a final conference with KMAG, Korean, and American Embassy officials before his return to Japan. At this time General MacArthur told Brigadier General Church, commander of his advance headquarters in Korea, who had reached a similar conclusion on Wednesday, that he thought the situation demanded the immediate employment of American ground troops and that he intended to request authority from Washington to make such a commitment as soon as he returned to Tokyo.[7]

General MacArthur Returns to Tokyo

It was about 5:15 A.M. Thursday in Washington (6:15 P.M. Thursday in Korea),[8] when the *Bataan*, which had survived a strafing attack by four North Korean Yak fighters two hours earlier, took off from the Suwon airfield for Japan with General MacArthur and his party aboard. In flight, the General drafted in pencil on a pad of paper in his lap an estimate of the situation and recommendations that he would dispatch later to Washington. According to General Whitney the document that General Mac-Arthur drafted at this time stated:

> The South Korean forces are in confusion, have not seriously fought, and lack leadership. Organized and equipped as a light force for maintenance of interior order, they were unprepared for attack by armor and air. Conversely they are incapable of gaining the initiative over such a force as that embodied in the North Korean Army. The South Koreans had made no preparation for defense in depth, for echelons of supply or for a supply system. No plans had been made, or if made were not executed, for the destruction of supplies or materials in the event of a retrograde movement. As a result they have either lost or abandoned their supplies and heavier equipment and have absolutely no system of intercommunication. In most cases the individual soldier in his flight to the south has retained his rifle or carbine. They are gradually being gathered up by an advanced group of my officers I sent over for the purpose. Without

---

7. Appleman, *South to the Naktong*, p. 44.
8. *Ibid.*, p. 45.

artillery, mortars and antitank guns, they can only hope to retard
the enemy through the fullest utilization of natural obstacles and
under the guidance of example of leadership of high quality. . . .
The civilian populace is tranquil, orderly and prosperous according
to their scale of living. They have retained a high degree of national
spirit and firm belief in the Americans. The roads leading south
from Seoul are crowded with refugees refusing to accept the Com-
'munist rule. . . .

It is essential that the enemy advance be held or its impetus will
threaten the over-running of all of Korea. The South Korean Army
is entirely incapable of counteraction and there is a grave danger of
a further breakthrough. If the enemy advances continue much
further, it will threaten the Republic. The only assurance for holding the present line and the ability to regain the lost ground is
through the introduction of United States ground combat forces into
the Korean battle area. If authorized it is my intention to immediately move a United States Regimental Combat Team to the reinforcement of the vital area discussed and to provide for a possible
build-up to a two division strength from the troops in Japan for an
early counteroffensive. Unless provision is made for the full utilization of the Army-Navy-Air team in this shattered area, our mission
will at best be needlessly costly in life, money and prestige. At worst,
it might even be doomed to failure.[9]

During the journey to Tokyo the General talked about the conclusions he had reached with a correspondent of the *New York Herald Tribune*, Marguerite Higgins, who had joined his party at
Suwon. "It is certain that the South Korean soldiers need an injection of ordered American strength," he explained. "The South
Korean soldiers are in good physical condition and could be
rallied with example and leadership. Give me two American divisions and I can hold Korea," the General predicted. Then he continued, "The moment I reach Tokyo I shall send President Truman
my recommendation for the immediate dispatch of American divisions to Korea. But I have no idea whether he will accept my
recommendations."[10]

---

9. Whitney, pp. 332-33. The second paragraph, broken up by General Whitney's comments in his book, apparently was as is shown above in the original; i.e.,
a single paragraph. Second paragraph is quoted from a letter from General Mac-
Arthur, May 17, 1957.

10. Higgins, *War in Korea*, pp. 33-34.

The *Bataan* touched down at Tokyo's Haneda airport at 9:15 A.M. Thursday, Washington time (10:15 P.M. Thursday, Tokyo time).[11] General MacArthur had been away from Japan a little more than 16 hours, about half of which had been spent on the ground in Korea. The news agency dispatches that were filled on the subject of the General's Korean reconnaissance did not reflect his own conclusions as to the desperateness of a military situation. An Associated Press report from Tokyo, for example, reported that the General "seemed satisfied" with what he saw in Korea.[12] Lindesay Parrott of the *New York Times,* noting that a "united defense line" had been established, wrote from the Japanese capital, "The last twenty-four hours have been the brightest for the South Korean Republic since the invading Communists broke into Seoul. . . ."[13] Other dispatches told of hundreds of ROK soldiers returning to their units and of the encouraging recapture of Kimpo airfield, northwest of Seoul.

Secretary Johnson Requests Another Meeting of the President's Advisers

In Washington, however, the reports reaching the Department of Defense from General Headquarters in Tokyo indicated that the Republic of Korea Army was in grave trouble. At 7 A.M., a report had reached the Pentagon which estimated the South Korean casualties at about 50 per cent and stated that it was problematical whether the defenders could hold the Han River line.[14] This

---

11. Appleman, "The U.S. and the U.N. Intervene in Korea," p. 40.
12. *New York Times,* June 30, 1950, p. 3.
13. *Ibid.,* p. 1.
14. Smith, p. 86.
15. All sources are unanimously agreed that this recommendation was first made by the General at 3 A.M. Friday, Washington time. However, in view of the chronology of events established by the present study, this explanation is not satisfying. Evidence has shown that the General decided to recommend ground troop involvement during his Korean inspection. It also shows that he returned to Tokyo at 9:15 A.M. Thursday, Washington time. Why, then, was there a delay of more than 17 hours (until 3 A.M. Friday, Washington time) before he made his ground troop recommendations? Was his report actually the precipitant of the Thursday meeting of the presidential advisers requested by Secretary Johnson? Was this meeting reluctant to give him the authority he requested? Did this then cause the General to make a personal appeal to Washington in the early morning hours of Friday? Or

report was followed by others of a similar nature. Apparently they did not include General MacArthur's recommendation of the commitment of American ground combat troops.[15] At 11:55 A.M., two hours and forty minutes after General MacArthur's return to Tokyo, Secretary of Defense Johnson telephoned President Truman at the White House and told him that the situation now seemed so grave as to warrant another full-scale meeting of the President's advisers to decide upon further measures to cope with it.[16] The President arranged for the conference to be held at 5 P.M.

Thursday Responses in the Senate and House

During the afternoon preceding the Presidential conference, both the Senate and the House of Representatives held long sessions, but the legislators devoted very little attention to the conflict in Korea. In the Senate, the few remarks concerning Korea were made during the debate on the bill to amend the Mutual Defense Assistance Act of 1949. One Senator wanted to postpone action on the measure until Monday, July 3, but majority leader Lucas opposed this suggestion on the ground that the insistent world crisis made immediate consideration imperative. "This is an important measure from the standpoint of the psychological effect its passage would have on our friends and also on the aggressors," he explained, winning a unanimous consent agreement that a vote should be taken at 2 P.M. on Friday.[17] Senator Guy M. Gillette, Democrat of Iowa, however, while approving the bill, argued eloquently that unless its passage was accompanied

---

did he decide for some reason to delay his recommendations after returning to Tokyo? (In Tokyo time, this would have been from 10:15 P.M. Thursday, until 4 P.M. Friday). According to the Army historian of the period, the Army message files show only one ground troop recommendation from the General at 3 A.M. Friday (Appleman, Letter, Aug. 30, 1959). General MacArthur himself (Letter, May 17, 1957) has referred to the similar account of his biographer as authoritative (Whitney, pp. 332ff.). Thus, reluctantly and in the hope that some reader can explain satisfactorily what appears to be a 17-hour gap, the present narrative follows Appleman, Whitney, and all other accounts: The General went to Korea, decided to recommend the commitment of ground troops, and proposed this to Washington on Friday, June 30, at 3 A.M.

16. Smith, p. 86.

17. *Congressional Record*, Vol. 96, Part 7, June 29, 1950, 9446.

by a dramatic nonmilitary resolution by the Senate which would "electrify world opinion," it would only alienate the war-weary peoples of the world and add further fuel to the flames of Communist peace propaganda. He suggested four alternative resolutions, any one of which he thought would be suitable: a call for a constitutional convention of the Atlantic democracies; an appeal to the Administration to request an emergency session of the United Nations Little General Assembly to consider the problem of creating an international police force; a request that the General Assembly hold a disarmament conference; and a motion that the Executive and the Senate Foreign Relations Committee undertake preliminary studies into the feasibility of forming a federal union of Pacific nations.[18]

Several Senators spoke in support of Senator Gillette's general position, but no concrete action was taken on any of his recommendations. Senator Estes Kefauver, Democrat of Tennessee, reported approvingly that news had just reached him that the Canadian Senate had passed with one dissenting vote a resolution calling for a convention of delegates from states signatory to the North Atlantic Treaty to explore the possibility of an Atlantic Union.[19] Democratic Senator Brien McMahon of Connecticut commended his Ohio colleague's call for American political initiative and made two specific recommendations directly related to the Korean fighting: that the United States furnish the United Nations with a list of the persons it considered responsible for the North Korean aggression for possible criminal indictment under the precedents set by the Nuremberg and Tokyo war crimes trials; and that the restriction on military action to the area south of the Thirty-eighth Parallel be removed in order to "destroy the nests from which vipers are coming, to engage in an unconscionable, an unjustified, and a bloody attack."[20] Senator Hubert H. Humphrey, Democrat of Minnesota, spoke in defense of the President's constitutional authority to commit American forces in Korea.[21]

In the House, only three members addressed themselves to

---

18. *Ibid.*, p. 9459.
19. *Ibid.*, p. 9460.
20. *Ibid.*, p. 9461.
21. *Ibid.*, p. 9462.

the Korean conflict. The first was Representative Andrew J. Bie-
miller, Democrat of Wisconsin, who rose to praise Secretary of
State Acheson and the officials of his department. "Acheson and
the State Department have recently been the victims of one of
the most vicious, stupid, backhanded assaults in the history of
this country. Penny-ante politicians from my own State have
attempted to play with the high stakes of American foreign
policy through these assaults. They must now recognize their
mistake or discard all pretensions to interest in the Nation's welfare," he declared.[22] The second statement was made by Representative M. G. Burnside, Democrat of West Virginia, who lauded
President Truman for his "firm and courageous stand," and reminded his colleagues that he had been among those who had
fought successfully for the reconsideration and passage of the
Korean aid bill in February. Affirming his support of the President's decisions, the West Virginian explained, "If you are in the
path of a forest fire you might be safer—temporarily—if you would
curl up in a hollow log and go to sleep. But in the long run you
would run the risk of being barbecued. In the long run, you would
be far better off if you would get to work and build a firebreak.
Our foreign policy has a similar objective. We want to build a
firebreak against Communist aggression."[23] The third speaker on
Korea was Democratic Representative Philip J. Philbin of Massachusetts, who asserted that there had been "no alternative" but
to oppose the aggression and expressed satisfaction that a "chain
of appeasement" stretching back to the period before World War
II had been broken at last.[24]

The President Holds a Press Conference

At 4 P.M., while both the House and Senate sessions were in
progress and one hour before the meeting he had scheduled with
his advisers, the President held a press conference. "Mr. President,
everybody is asking in this country, are we or are we not in war?"
a reporter queried. "We are not at war," the President permitted

22. *Ibid.*, p. 9466.
23. *Ibid.*, p. 9480.
24. *Ibid.*, pp. 9520-21.

himself to be quoted in reply.[25] Another press representative asked, "Would it be possible to call this a police action under the United Nations?" President Truman agreed that that was exactly what it amounted to. The American action in Korea, he emphasized, was being taken to help the United Nations repel a raid by a "bunch of bandits." He expressed pleasure over the fact that most of the members of the United Nations were in accord with what had been done and said that he was very happy that the Government of India had finally announced that it would support the Security Council resolution of June 27. The President also stated that he was pleased by the overwhelmingly favorable domestic response to his decisions. Since Tuesday noon he had received more than 1,200 letters and telegrams that expressed approval by a ratio of ten to one.[26] A reporter asked the President to comment on Senator Taft's call for Secretary Acheson's resignation. "I think the political statement of Mr. Taft at this time is entirely uncalled for," the President replied. "Senator Taft also said that you had reversed Secretary Acheson," pressed the questioner. "There is not a word of truth in that," retorted the Chief Executive, "and you can quote me on that, too." But there were four topics upon which the President refused to comment: the nature and extent of Soviet involvement in the Korean conflict; whether developments in Korea would accelerate the conclusion of a peace treaty with Japan; and whether the Administration was contemplating to use either the atomic bomb or ground troops in Korea. Twice the President explained that he could not discuss the latter two military contingencies because they were matters of strategy.

Later in the evening, following the NSC meeting to be discussed below, President Truman spoke extemporaneously at a dinner of the finance committee of the Democratic National Committee. He assured his listeners that the United States would come out of the Korean crisis "all right," and expressed confidence that eventually there would be "a peace in the world which will be satisfactory to all the great nations in the world." ". . . In the

---

25. Anthony Leviero, *New York Times*, June 30, 1950, p. 1.

26. Including declarations of support from the Socialist Party and the Carnegie Foundation for International Peace.

long run," he concluded, "the Almighty is with us for the welfare of all the people of the world."[27] Secretary Acheson, too, addressed a dinner gathering of the delegates to the American Newspaper Guild convention before whom the President had spoken on Wednesday afternoon. Guild president Harry Martin, introducing the Secretary of State, declared, "We are behind you to a man."[28] Reading his speech slowly and gravely, Secretary Acheson narrated the factual background of the Korean problem since the end of World War II and emphasized that the purpose of the American involvement in the present fighting was ". . . solely for the purpose of restoring the Republic of Korea to its status prior to the invasion from the north and of re-establishing the peace broken by that aggression."[29] He further explained that the American decisions with respect to Formosa were not intended to prejudice the future status of the island. This would be settled ". . . only upon the restoration of peace and security in the Pacific, a peace settlement with Japan, or consideration by the United Nations."

The Second National Security Council Meeting Is Held

But before the President and the Secretary of State fulfilled these dinner engagements, they had participated in a forty-minute conference of the National Security Council[30] at the White House which had been arranged earlier in the day upon the initiative of Secretary Johnson. Department of Defense participants in this meeting included Secretaries Pace, Matthews, and Finletter, Generals Bradley, Collins, and Vandenberg, and Admiral Sherman. Diplomatic advisers present were Secretary Acheson, Assistant Secretary Rusk, and Ambassadors Harriman and Dulles. Ambassador Dulles had just returned by plane from his mission in Japan. Upon his arrival at National Airport, newsmen had questioned

27. *New York Times,* June 30, 1950, p. 7.

28. *Ibid.*

29. *Department of State Bulletin,* XXIII, No. 575 (July 10, 1950) p. 46. Also reported in the newspapers of June 30.

30. Characterized as such by the President. *Memoirs, II,* 341. The list of participants shown below has been compiled from *New York Herald Tribune,* June 30, 1950, p. 6., and Smith, p. 86.

him about a statement he had reportedly made in San Francisco
that ". . . the use of United States ground troops is very possible."
"That is an inaccurate statement," the Ambassador disavowed;
"I made no observation on the military situation."[31] Also present
at the conference were Chairman Symington of the National Security Resources Board and Executive Secretary Lay of the NSC
staff.

This meeting, the fourth major conference of the President and
his immediate advisers since Sunday evening, began at 5 P.M. (6
A.M. Friday, Japan time). Discussion centered around a presentation by Secretary of Defense Johnson, who summarized the main
difficulties that were hampering military operations in Korea and
advanced a set of recommendations for eliminating them in the
form of a proposed directive to General MacArthur. According to
Secretary Johnson, the principal impediments to the effective
accomplishment of the military mission in Korea were: the restriction of air and naval activity to South Korea; the limited combat
time for fighters over the battle area because of the necessity to
fly in from distant bases in Japan; poor air-ground liaison with the
ROK Army; and, inadequate South Korean transportation facilities for delivering American munitions at the front.[32] To overcome
these limitations and to insure the safe completion of the evacuation of American nationals which was then in its final stages,[33]
the Defense Secretary reported that the Joint Chiefs of Staff had
agreed upon a directive that consolidated previous instructions
and authorized General MacArthur to extend his air and naval
operations into North Korea; to employ Army service forces in
South Korea (e.g., transportation, signal units); and to commit a
limited number of combat infantrymen to protect a port-airfield
beachhead in the vicinity of the southeastern coastal city of
Pusan.

Secretary Acheson later recalled that the commitment of
ground combat and service troops in the Pusan area approved at
this time was related to the maintenance of supply operations and

---

31. *New York Times,* June 30, 1950, p. 8.

32. Smith, p. 86.

33. According to Appleman, 1,527 Americans were evacuated by air and sea
between June 26 and June 29. "The U.S. and the U.N. Intervene in Korea," p. 20.

the preservation of public order—there was a large influx of refugees moving into the area, and it was necessary for all available
Korean forces to fight at the front.[34] According to the later recollections of the Joint Chiefs of Staff, the primary reason for their
recommendation that combat troops be committed in Korea at this
time was to protect the evacuation of American citizens.[35] They
did not propose the introduction of American infantrymen into
the battle area for offensive action. The fighting front at the time
of this conference was about 200 miles north of Pusan. According
to the public record of the proceedings of this NSC meeting, the
President and his advisers apparently did not know that General
MacArthur already had ordered the Air Force to attack targets
in North Korea and had come to the conclusion at least seven and
a half hours earlier[36] that only the direct weight of American
ground troops at the fighting front could stop the North Koreans.

In the discussion of this proposed directive, some of the conferees made suggestions or remarks which indicated that they were
concerned lest lack of clarity in the instructions lead to the unanticipated and undesirable consequence of a broadened conflict.
The President thought that the final paragraph of the suggested
order implied that the United States was planning to engage the
Soviet Union in combat. "I stated categorically," the President
recalled, "that I did not wish to see even the slightest implication
of such a plan. I wanted to take every step necessary to push the
North Koreans back of the 38th Parallel. But I wanted to be sure
that we would not become so deeply committed in Korea that we
could not take care of other situations as might develop."[37] Secretary Pace advised that the United States should be cautious in
undertaking air and naval operations against North Korea and
should limit carefully its attacks to essential military targets. There
should be no indiscriminate bombing of North Korean cities.[38]
"I agreed," the President wrote afterwards, "pointing out that
operations above the 38th Parallel should be designed only to

---

34. Secretary Acheson, Letter, August 24, 1959.
35. E.g., testimony of General Bradley, *Hearings*, Part II, 934, 1112.
36. I.e., 9:15 A.M. Washington time, when the General returned to Japan.
37. *Memoirs*, II, 341.
38. Testimony of General J. Lawton Collins, *Hearings*, Part II, 1363.

destroy military supplies, for I wanted it clearly understood that
our operations in Korea were designed to restore peace there and
to restore the border."[39] Secretary Acheson advised that the Air
Force should be instructed not to violate Korea's Soviet-Chinese
frontiers and further recommended that a paragraph be added to
the directive for the guidance of General MacArthur in the event
that the Soviet Union intervened directly in the fighting. This
might be "perhaps to the effect that he [MacArthur] defend his
positions and our forces and report at once for further instructions
from the President."[40] The President approved this suggestion and
asked Secretaries Acheson and Johnson to collaborate on drafting it.

Secretary Acheson then reported on the Soviet reply to the
American note of June 27 which had requested that the Soviet
Government use its influence to restrain the North Koreans. The
Soviet answer, delivered by Deputy Foreign Minister Gromyko
to Ambassador Kirk earlier in the day and received in the State
Department at noon, stated:

1. In accordance with facts verified by the Soviet Government,
the events taking place in Korea were provoked by forces of the
South Korean authorities on border regions of North Korea. Therefore the responsibility for these events rests upon the South Korean
authorities and upon those who stand behind their back.

2. As is known, the Soviet Government withdrew its troops from
Korea earlier than the Government of the United States and thereby
confirmed its traditional principle of noninterference in the internal
affairs of other states. And now as well the Soviet Government ad-
heres to the impermissibility of interference by foreign powers in the
internal affairs of Korea.

3. It is not true that the Soviet Government refused to participate
in meetings of the Security Council. In spite of its full willingness,
the Soviet Government has not been able to take part in the meetings of the Security Council inasmuch as, because of the position of
the Government of the United States, China, a permanent member
of the Security Council, has not been admitted to the Council, which
made it impossible for the Security Council to take decisions having
legal force.[41]

---

39. *Memoirs*, II, 341.
40. *Ibid.*
41. Department of State, *U.S. Policy in the Korean Crisis*, p. 64.

Secretary Acheson reported that expert opinion in his department interpreted the response to be unprovocative and indicative of a desire on the part of the Soviet leadership to avoid formal responsibility for the North Korean invasion.[42] The Soviet Union had replied in a similar vein[43] to a cable sent by Secretary-General Lie to all members of the United Nations informing them of the resolution of June 27 and inquiring about the assistance which they might be able to render in implementing it. Secretary Acheson reported also on the bellicose statement that Chinese Foreign Minister Chou En-lai had made in connection with the announcement of the President's decisions. The State Department considered the Chinese Communist statement to be tantamount to a declaration of war.

Thus a fairly clear pattern of Soviet intentions seemed to be revealed; while the Soviet Union assumed the posture of an interested bystander, the United States was to be involved in a brawl with Communist China and the Soviet satellites. After listening to Secretary Acheson's report on the Russian and Chinese communications, the President said, "That means that the Soviets are going to let the Chinese and the North Koreans do their fighting for them."[44] At about this time in Tokyo, Lieutenant General Stratemeyer denied reports that Russians were piloting North Korean fighter aircraft.[45]

Secretary Acheson suggested that since the Soviet leaders already had made public their reply to the American note, the State Department should release the texts of both notes to the press. The President approved. When Lincoln White, State Department press officer, released them later in the evening he explained to reporters that although the voting in the Security Council had not been conducted in strict accordance with the "letter" of Article 27 of the United Nations Charter, the legality of the resolutions that had been adopted was unquestionable, since past practice had established the principle that abstention

42. Counselor Kennan, Interview, August 1, 1955.
43. *Pravda*, June 29, 1950, p. 2. See also *New York Times*, June 29, 1950, p. 13.
44. Smith, p. 88.
45. *New York Times*, June 30, 1950, p. 6.

from voting by a permanent member did not constitute a veto.[46] In conjunction with the publication of the notes it was reported that Western diplomats were relieved by the temperate tone of the Soviet reply. The Soviet statement did not employ the abusive language that had characterized recent communcations to the United States. Before the meeting adjourned, Secretary Acheson also announced new offers of air and naval assistance to the United Nations from Australia, Canada, The Netherlands, and New Zealand.

Later in the evening Secretary Acheson returned to the White House for a personal conference with the President. One of the topics they discussed was an offer, which had just been received from President Chiang Kai-shek, of 33,000 Chinese Nationalist troops.[47] It was reported that Nationalist China was prepared to send to Korea an infantry division under the command of General Sun Li-jen, and an armored division commanded by President Chiang's youngest son, General Chiang Wei-kuo.[48] President Truman's first inclination was to accept this offer because he hoped that as many members of the United Nations as possible would participate in the effort to repel the North Korean aggression. Secretary Acheson, however, questioned its advisability on the grounds that it would be incongruous to have the "natural defenders" of Formosa committed elsewhere while the United States assumed responsibilities for the security of the island. Also, he questioned whether the Nationalist troops might not need to be reequipped before they were ready for combat in Korea. The President decided to delay a decision on the offer until he could discuss it with his military advisers.

There are several versions of the President's reactions during the afternoon NSC meeting to the recommendation of the Joint Chiefs of Staff that units of the Army be sent to Korea. According to one account, the President ". . . was troubled by the commit-

46. *Ibid.*, p. 4. Mr. White did not debate the question of Chinese representation. The legal questions raised by the June 27 resolution are discussed briefly in Leland M. Goodrich, *Korea: A Study of U.S. Policy in the United Nations* (New York: Council on Foreign Relations, 1956), pp. 113-14.

47. *Memoirs*, II, 342.

48. *New York Times*, June 30, 1950, p. 3.

ment of ground troops but agreed to its necessity. . . ."[49] According
to another account, "The President hesitated. He was particularly
disturbed by the thought of committing ground troops anywhere
in Korea."[50] According to a third version, "To some participants it seemed that the President's mind had already been made
up by the reports he had received from the military."[51] In his own
published account, the President omitted any mention of the proposed employment of ground forces at this time.[52] In the recollections of other participants, the JCS recommendation of ground
forces for limited rear-area duties did not meet with any opposition; it was unanimously accepted as a necessary further step if
the decision reached Monday night to repel the aggressors by
force of arms was to be carried out. Materials on file at the State
Department indicate that the President could be considered "hesi-
tant" at this time only in the sense that he wanted to make sure
that the United States did not become committed in Korea in
such a way that it would not be able to meet important contingencies which might develop elsewhere.[53]

The conference ended at 5:40 P.M. The President had approved
the recommendations of his military advisers in substantially the
same form as they had been presented by Secretary Johnson.
According to a paraphrased version of the directive to General
MacArthur that emerged from this conference, the Far Eastern
commander was instructed:

> In support of resolution of the United Nations approved on the
> 25th of June and transmitted on the 28th of June . . . you will em-
> ploy naval and air forces available for the Far East Command to
> provide fullest possible support for South Korean forces by attack
> on military targets so as to permit these forces to clear South Korea
> of North Korean forces.
>
> Employment of Army forces will be limited to essential service
> units except that you are authorized to employ such Army combat

---

49. Smith, p. 88.
50. Eric F. Goldman, *The Crucial Decade: America 1945-1955* (New York:
Alfred A. Knopf, 1956), pp. 166-67.
51. Warner, p. 105.
52. *Memoirs*, II, 341-42.
53. Based on SCDS.

and service units as to insure the retention of a port and air base in the general area of Pusan-Chinhae.

By naval and air action you will defend Formosa against invasion or attack.

. . .

You are authorized to extend your operations in Northern Korea against air bases, depots, tanks, farms, troop columns, and other purely military targets, if and when this becomes essential for the performance of your mission, as given in a preceding paragraph, or to avoid unnecessary casualties to our forces. Special care will be taken to insure that operations in North Korea stay well clear of the frontiers of Manchuria or the Soviet Union.

The decision to commit United States air and naval forces and limited Army forces to provide cover and support for South Korea troops does not constitute a decision to engage in war with the Soviet Union if Soviet forces intervene in Korea. Decision regarding Korea, however, is taken in full realization of the risk involved. If Soviet forces actively oppose our operations in Korea, your forces should defend themselves but should take no action to aggravate the situation, and you should report the situation to Washington.[54]

Other portions of this directive, which was designed to consolidate the essential features of all instructions to date, concerned the prevention of a Chinese Nationalist assault on the mainland, the supplying of the ROK forces, and the assignment of the Seventh Fleet to General MacArthur's operational control. The General was informed that he should request any additional military equipment needed by the South Koreans that was not available from stocks in Japan and was told that Pacific fleet commanders would support and reinforce his naval operations.[55]

As the President's advisers left the White House—declining to answer the insistent questions of waiting reporters about the nature of their conference—they were unaware that North Korean tanks had already broken through the defenses at the Han River and that the battered infantrymen of the ROK Army were being shoved southward in shock and awe. Three T-34 tanks, ferried

---

54. Quoted by Secretary of Defense George C. Marshall, *Hearings*, Part I, 536.
55. Appleman, "The U.S. and the U.N. Intervene in Korea," p. 42.

across the Han in the predawn darkness of Friday, June 30 (mid-afternoon Thursday in Washington), were blasting their way toward the road south to Suwon.[56] Soon 50 more would join them. By this time the major outlines of the military calculations within the bustling confines of the Pentagon had become clear to experienced students of military affairs. As evening fell, Hanson Baldwin of the *New York Times* was writing that the nation's military leaders had weighed the advantages and disadvantages of eliminating the restrictive barrier of the Thirty-eighth Parallel which had been imposed upon air and naval operations.[57] He did not know that the decision to do so already had been made. He was also reporting that serious consideration was being given to the possible commitment of American ground forces. One division might be enough to stiffen the staggering South Koreans, but a second division might be required to cope with the five or six divisions which the invaders were believed to be holding in reserve. In any case, he reported, not more than two divisions could be spared from the American garrison in Japan.

As the White House conferees returned to their departments, proceeded to their homes, or prepared for their evening engagements, they were satisfied that the decisions just made were adequate to handle the situation in Korea on the basis of available information. President Truman and his advisers awaited the further reports and recommendations of the American commander in the Far East.

They came, early Friday morning.

---

56. United Press dispatch from Tokyo, *New York Times*, June 30, 1950, p. 3.
57. *New York Times*, June 30, 1950, p. 3.

CHAPTER 10

FRIDAY, JUNE 30

General MacArthur Recommends the Commitment of
Ground Troops in the Battle Area

At three o'clock on Friday morning (4 P.M. Tokyo time) an urgent
cable from General MacArthur reached the Pentagon.[1] All accounts
agree that at this time he recommended the use of ground troops
for offensive action in the combat area.[2] According to General
Bradley, the only discussion of the employment of infantry prior
to General MacArthur's recommendation had been in connection
with the protection of the evacuation of American nationals from

---

1. Smith, p. 88.

2. *Ibid.; Memoirs*, II, 342; Appleman, "The U.S. and the U.N. Intervene in
Korea," p. 44. Assistant Secretary Rusk, however, later recalled that this was *not*
the *first time* that General MacArthur's report on his reconnaissance was known in
Washington. (Letter, August 20, 1959.)

the strife-stricken peninsula.[3] A paraphrased summary of the Far Eastern commander's cable which was later made public[4] corresponds in major respects to the document that both General Whitney and Marguerite Higgins subsequently reported General MacArthur had drafted aboard the *Bataan* more than seventeen hours earlier.[5] According to this Joint Chiefs of Staff summary:

> On 30 June 1950, CINCFE informed the Joint Chiefs of Staff, after a reconnaissance of the Korean battle are [sic] that the South Korean Army was in confusion. Supplies and equipment had been abandoned or lost. Without artillery, mortars, and antitank guns the most the South Koreans could hope to accomplish would be to retard the advance of the enemy. The South Korean Army was incapable of united action, and there was grave danger of a further breakthrough. CINCFE further stated that the only assurance of holding the Han river line and to regain lost ground would be through the commitment of United States ground combat forces into the Korean battle area. Accordingly, he stated, if authorized it was his intention to move immediately a United States regimental combat team to the combat area in Korea as a nucleus of a possible buildup of two divisions from Japan for early offensive action in accordance with his mission of clearing South Korea of North Korean forces.

In referring to the "Han river line," this paraphrase gives no indication of its having been broken. News dispatches from the front, however, received in Tokyo at midnight Thursday, Washington time (1 P.M. Friday, Japan time)—three hours prior to the receipt of General MacArthur's latest cable at the Pentagon—indicated that North Korean tanks had smashed through the ROK defenses at the river.[6]

---

3. *Hearings*, Part II, 1012.
4. *Ibid.*
5. See above, pp. 237f. As noted previously, the chronological discrepancy between the reported drafting of General MacArthur's recommendations and the reported receipt of them in Washington constitutes a major unsolved problem of the present study.
6. United Press dispatch from Tokyo, *New York Times*, June 30, 1950, p. 3. The internal evidence of the paraphrase coupled with this piece of information about the battle situation—albeit from an unofficial source—suggests that General MacArthur's cable might have been received in Washington sometime *before* 3 A.M. Friday, perhaps as early as Thursday morning. Alternatively it might be hypothesized that the General did *not* recommend the employment of ground forces in the *combat area* immediately upon completion of his personal reconnaissance.

Upon receipt of General MacArthur's latest recommendations, officers on duty at the Department of Defense immediately contacted General Collins, chief of staff of the Army, who went at once to the Pentagon where he could talk with the Far Eastern commander over the telecon circuits to Tokyo. When he reached his office he first notified Secretary Pace and General Bradley by telephone of General MacArthur's most recent advice[7] and then opened a conversation with the General in Japan. While the two military leaders conferred, Assistant Secretary of State Rusk and other officials who had been notified of the urgent appeal from Tokyo hurried to the Pentagon.

To General Collins, General MacArthur repeated the crux of his latest recommendation; nothing less than the immediate commitment of a regimental combat team in the forward battle area was demanded by the rapidly deteriorating military situation. The General also asked for authorization to strengthen that combat spearhead into a force capable of launching a counteroffensive. He thought at this time that perhaps a buildup to two divisions might be necessary. General Collins explained that, on the basis of the reluctance to commit ground forces which the President had exhibited less than twelve hours earlier during the meeting of the National Security Council, he thought the President would want to consult his advisers again before approving the employment of American infantrymen in combat.[8] Therefore it might take several hours to get a final decision. In the meantime, General Collins inquired, would not the latest instructions that had emerged from the NSC deliberations provide sufficient authority for undertaking the preliminaries that would be required before launching a ground offensive? General MacArthur replied that his present instructions were inadequate. He needed further authority at once. "Time is of the essence and a clear-cut decision without delay is essential," he insisted.[9] General Collins replied that he would try to obtain the desired authorization from the President through the Secretary of the Army and would inform him of the results of his efforts within half an hour.

---

7. Testimony of General Hoyt S. Vandenberg, *Hearings*, Part II, 1476.
8. Smith, p. 88.
9. Appleman, "The U.S. and the U.N. Intervene in Korea," p. 45.

The President Gives Limited Approval

After conferring with General Bradley, General Collins explained General MacArthur's position to Secretary Pace who then telephoned the President at Blair House. It was now 4:57 A.M. President Truman, already up and shaven, took the call on the telephone beside his bed. Upon learning of General MacArthur's recommendations, the President came to a decision without hesitation.[10] "I told Pace," he later recalled, "to inform General MacArthur immediately that the use of one regimental combat team was approved."[11] As to the suggested buildup to two divisions, however, the President said that he wanted to defer a final decision until after he had had the opportunity to discuss it with his advisers.[12] He told Secretary Pace to inform General MacArthur that a decision on this part of his recommendations would be forthcoming within a few hours.

Secretary Pace reported the President's decisions to General Collins. Within minutes, General MacArthur, half way around the world, received full authority to implement the first of his recommendations and a promise that a decision on the second one would soon be made. A few more minutes, and the preparations for airlifting American infantrymen to Korea from Japan began. On July 2, the First Battalion of the Twenty-fourth Division's Twenty-first Regiment reached the fighting front in the Taejon area. On the morning of July 5, Korean time, the soldiers of this unit became the first American infantrymen to engage the enemy in direct combat.[13] They were not the first American ground soldiers in combat, however, for when General MacArthur had arrived in Suwon on his reconnaissance he had found the airfield defended by a detachment from the 507th Anti-aircraft Artillery Automatic Weapons Battalion.[14]

---

10. Smith, p. 88. According to Goldman, p. 168, the President had "only a flicker of hesitation."

11. *Memoirs*, II, 343.

12. Smith, p. 88.

13. Kim Wonyong in Republic of Korea, National Defense Ministry, p. A35.

14. Appleman, "The U.S. and the U.N. Intervene in Korea," pp. 40-41. A member of this unit, Pfc. Thomas Merante of Hudson, New York, was wounded during a strafing attack in the period of the General's visit. *New York Times*, June 30, 1950, p. 3.

At 5:30 A.M. General Collins telephoned Admiral Sherman, Chief of Naval Operations, informing him of General MacArthur's most recent recommendations and the decisions that the President had taken. Admiral Sherman's reaction was that the President's decision to approve the commitment of infantrymen to battle was both "unavoidable" and "sound."[15] ". . . But," he later recalled, "I was fully aware of the hazards involved in fighting Asiatics on the Asian mainland, which is something that as a naval officer, I have grown up to believe should be avoided if possible." He subsequently explained that his own inclination was to disengage American ground units from the Korean fighting as soon as this became feasible. General Collins also notified General Vandenberg of the latest developments, telling him that General MacArthur's recommendations had been cleared through General Bradley, Secretary Pace, and the President.[16]

At seven o'clock Colonel Henry Ahalt of the Department of Defense staff arrived at the White House to inform the President more fully about the exchange of communications with General MacArthur during the night.[17] When Colonel Ahalt had departed, the President telephoned Secretaries Acheson, Johnson, and Pace, and arranged for another full-scale conference with his advisers at 9:30 A.M. to discuss the offensive buildup of ground forces which General MacArthur had proposed. At the Pentagon, one hour before the conference began, Secretary Johnson's chief advisers met in his office to draft a new directive to MacArthur.

The President Meets Again with His Advisers

At half-past nine, the President's advisers again were seated around the conference table in the White House Cabinet Room. Participants in this meeting included Secretary Acheson, Secretary Johnson, the civilian service Secretaries, and the Joint Chiefs of Staff. Also present were the Deputy Secretary of Defense, Stephen T. Early, and the President's special foreign affairs adviser, Averell Harriman.[18] The President did not refer to this conference

15. Testimony of Admiral Forrest P. Sherman, *Hearings*, Part II, 1650.
16. Testimony of General Hoyt S. Vandenberg, *Ibid.*, p. 1476.
17. Smith, p. 88.
18. *New York Times*, July 1, 1950, p. 1.

later as a meeting of the National Security Council, and apparently it was not so considered at the time it was held.[19]

The conference lasted only thirty minutes. Opening the deliberations, President Truman confirmed what Secretary Acheson and the others had learned as they gathered. He reported that he had authorized General MacArthur to commit a regiment to the fighting and asked for advice on the question of whether or not the General's further recommendation should be approved. At this time the President was still inclined to accept the offer of Chinese Nationalist troops that had been made on Thursday evening. According to the Chinese Government, two divisions could be ready for boarding transports to Korea within five days. The timely commitment of this substantial ground force, the President thought, would make an important contribution to repelling the invaders of the Korean Republic. Therefore he asked his advisers to give their opinions as to the acceptance or rejection of the Chinese offer while they considered the recommended buildup of ground forces on the peninsula. "At the same time," the President subsequently recalled, "I asked them to consider carefully places where trouble might break out. What, for instance, would Mao Tse-tung do? What might the Russians do in the Balkans, in Iran, in Germany?"[20]

Both the President's diplomatic and military advisers recommended nonacceptance of the Chinese Nationalist offer of ground forces. Secretary Acheson took the position that the employment of President Chiang's army in Korea would increase the probability of Chinese Communist involvement in the Korean fighting. The Chinese Communist leadership undoubtedly would be tempted by the prospect of weakening the defensive potential of Formosa through an attack upon the Chinese troops in Korea. Although there is no evidence that Secretary Acheson attempted to analyze President Chiang's motivations in making this offer, they had been an object of study at the State Department. According to the interpretation of one of his chief counselors, the offer had been

---

19. The President has referred to a meeting of July 6 as ". . . the first meeting of the National Security Council after American troops had been committed to the ground action." *Memoirs*, II, 344.

20. *Memoirs*, II, 343.

made to strengthen the position of the Nationalists as steadfast allies of the United States, to gain a foothold on the continent, and to remove from Formosa some troops of questionable loyalty. Furthermore, this view held, President Chiang had little fear that this commitment would weaken his defenses, since responsibility for this already had been assumed by the Seventh Fleet.

The Joint Chiefs of Staff were unenthusiastic about accepting the Chinese offer for two main reasons.[21] First, the Chinese units undoubtedly would have to be reequipped before they were combat ready. Otherwise, they would probably be no more effective against the invaders than had been the South Koreans. Second, the transportation of the Chinese troops to Korea would involve the commitment of a considerable number of air and sea carriers. This effort would have more effect on the military situation if it were devoted directly to transporting American arms and men to the peninsula. The President, although somewhat concerned about the small number of ground forces available to the United States for combat commitment, agreed with the nearly unanimous position taken by his advisers. The Chinese Nationalist offer was to be politely declined.[22]

At the time of this conference there was still no evidence that the Soviet Union intended to intervene in Korea. Intelligence teams set up to study the problem of Soviet-Chinese intentions were in general agreement that the Soviet Union intended to involve the United States with China and its satellites, but would avoid a head-on military collision with American forces in Korea or elsewhere. Although Chou En-lai's belligerent declaration had raised the possibility of Chinese intervention, it did not seem imminent. Other aggressive actions along the periphery of the Soviet bloc were possible, but again apparently were not imminent.

With respect to the further commitment of ground forces, there is some evidence which suggests that the conferees considered that the two divisions which General MacArthur had recommended

---

21. *Ibid.*

22. See the *aides-memoire* of the Chinese Embassy to the Department of State and the American reply in Department of State, pp. 59ff. Three days later the Chinese Government made the same offer to the Secretary-General of the U.N. United Nations Document A/1562, July 3, 1950.

would be able to check the North Korean advance.[23] The capabilities of the invading army still were not fully appreciated. As General Bradley later explained, "The first few days we did not know just how good these North Koreans were, and it was some time before we could get a good picture of it."[24] By this time the Air Force was beginning to hit the enemy hard. In the past twenty-four hours American pilots had shot down twenty North Korean fighters, and B-29 bombers had pounded troop concentrations, tanks, roads, and other military targets on the western front. In order to decrease further the war-making potential of North Korea, Admiral Sherman proposed that a naval blockade of the entire coastline north of the Thirty-eighth Parallel be established. The President approved.[25] Thus, in the context of increasingly more powerful blows against the invaders, the addition of the recommended ground elements to the air-sea team might well tip the balance of battle in favor of the Korean Republic.

Even though the proposed employment of the Army in Korea raised certain problems, apparently none of the President's advisers opposed it. President Truman then decided to give General MacArthur ". . . full authority to use the troops under his command."[26] In the terse terms of the Joint Chiefs of Staff summary of the directive dispatched to Tokyo soon after this conference, "On 30 June 1950 the limitation on the employment of Army forces imposed on 29 June 1950 was rescinded."[27] The "full authority" given to General MacArthur at this time meant that he could use the forces available to him at his discretion. He was not explicitly limited to the two divisions he had recommended. As General MacArthur subsequently recalled his early instructions, "I was reminded at the time that my resource for the time being was practically limited to what I had and that I must regard the security of Japan as fundamental and basic policy."[28]

---

23. Smith, p. 88.
24. *Hearings,* Part II, 839.
25. Smith, p. 88. Appleman, "The U.S. and the U.N. Intervene in Korea," p. 46.
26. *Memoirs,* II, 343.
27. Appendix K, *Hearings,* Part V, 3192. According to Smith, p. 88, these orders had been sent to the Far East "by 1:22 P.M." No reason is given for the delay.
28. *Hearings,* Part I, 231.

Soon after this decision was taken, Major General William Dean, Commander of the Twenty-fourth Infantry Division, received teletyped orders to commit his division on the Korean peninsula. At 8:45 P.M. (9:45 A.M. Saturday in Japan), an infantry battalion of the Twenty-fourth Division commanded by Lieutenant Colonel Charles Smith, who had been a captain of infantry at Pearl Harbor on December 7, 1941, left Japan for Korea in C-54 transport airplanes. Just before take-off, Major General Dean gave him these verbal orders: "When you get to Pusan, head for Taejon. We want to stop the North Koreans as far from Pusan as we can. Block the main road as far north as possible. Contact General Church. If you can't locate him, go to Taejon and beyond if you can. Sorry I can't give you more information; that's all I've got. Good luck to you, and God bless you and your men."[29] Thus was begun the "piecemeal"[30] commitment of the occupation forces in Japan against the enemy. By July 7 less than 800 American soldiers were in combat.[31] On July 8 General MacArthur made his first major call for reinforcements.[32]

According to Secretary Pace, the decision to employ Army units "logically followed" the decisions taken earlier in the week and had been "practically made for us" by subsequent events. In his view also, the employment of American soldiers in Korea might make it more difficult to keep the conflict limited if the Soviet Union intervened. There would be a strong and natural desire on the part of the American people to react vigorously if Soviet and American infantrymen clashed in the rice paddies of Korea.[33] In the view of Counselor Kennan, who did not attend the conference, the risk of Soviet counteraction had been increased by the ground troop decision,[34] but the majority of the President's advisers regarded it as being relatively unchanged.

---

29. Appleman, *South to the Naktong*, p. 61.
30. "It was a piecemeal commitment, because that was the only way we could commit them. We had to take them out of Japan. The units were understrength, and so we had to send them in as we could get those units ready and get them over to Korea." Testimony of General Bradley, *Hearings*, Part II, 948.
31. Cagle and Manson, p. 39.
32. Whitney, p. 337.
33. Secretary Pace, Interview, October 24, 1955.
34. Counselor Kennan, Interview, August 1, 1955.

The Second Conference with Congressional Leaders Is Held

By ten o'clock the decisions of the President and his advisers were made. At 11 A.M. another briefing for Congressional leaders was held in the White House Cabinet Room. In addition to the President, the Executive Branch was represented by thirty officials, including Vice-President Barkley, Secretaries Acheson and Johnson, the service Secretaries, and the Joint Chiefs of Staff. In the Congressional contingent of fifteen were Democratic Senators Connally, Tydings, Thomas, and Lucas; Republican Senators Gurney, Smith, Wherry, and Wiley; Democratic Representatives Brooks, Kee, and Mansfield; Republican Representatives Eaton, Short, and Vorys; and, House Speaker Sam Rayburn.[35]

The President opened this conference with a review of the decisions he had made throughout the week and a summary of the latest military reports concerning the grave plight of the South Korean Army. Then he announced that he had ordered American ground forces to the defense of the Republic of Korea. "After that," Senator Connally later recalled, "there was a long silence, and on almost every face I could read agreement with his decision."[36] Senator Connally asked "for the record" whether the Army commitment was being taken unilaterally or in further support of the resolutions of the United Nations. President Truman assured him that the American action was being taken entirely within the framework of the United Nations and that General Mac-Arthur would be the United Nations commander in Korea as well as the American commander.[37]

Only one of the Congressmen objected to the President's decision. This was Republican Senator Kenneth S. Wherry of Nebraska, minority floor leader, who said that he thought the President should have consulted the Congress before sending ground soldiers into combat. In reply President Truman explained that in view of the disastrous trend of military operations within the past few hours he thought it was his duty to make the necessary decisions with-

---

35. *New York Times*, July 1, 1950, p. 1.

36. Connally, p. 349.

37. *Ibid.*, p. 349. See also Smith, p. 88. This conference is not discussed by President Truman in his memoirs.

out delay.[38] As Senator Wherry began to reiterate his criticism, Representative Dewey Short, ranking Republican member of the Armed Services Committee, interrupted to express the belief that he was speaking for almost everyone in Congress in saying that the nation was indebted to the President for his forceful leadership in the crisis.

New Decisions Are Announced

While the meeting of the President and the Congressional leaders was in progress, the White House staff released a formal statement to the press announcing the most recent decisions:

> At a meeting with Congressional leaders at the White House this morning the President, together with the Secretary of Defense, the Secretary of State, and the Joint Chiefs of Staff, reviewed with them the latest developments of the situation in Korea.
> The Congressional leaders were given a full review of the intensified military activities.
> In keeping with the United Nations Security Council's request for support to the Republic of Korea in repelling the North Korean invaders and restoring peace to Korea, the President announced that he had authorized the United States Air Force to conduct missions on specific military targets in North Korea wherever militarily necessary and had ordered a naval blockade of the entire Korean coast.
> General MacArthur has been authorized to use certain supporting ground units.[39]

As the conferees left the White House at about 11:30 A.M., they explained to reporters that the President's announcement meant just what it said—the Army would be used in a supporting role, at least for the time being. American ground soldiers would be used to guard air bases, communication lines, and supply lines, but they would not be committed to combat at the front.[40] The Congressional participants also explained that they had been given

---

38. According to an Associated Press dispatch from Tokyo, the ROK Army had "virtually quit fighting by 6 A.M., e.d.t., Friday." *New York Times,* July 1, 1950, p. 1.

39. Department of State, p. 24.

40. *New York Herald Tribune,* July 1, 1950.

no idea as to the number of soldiers who were to be sent to Korea.[41] According to the subsequent recollection of Senator Smith, ". . . At a meeting on June 30, which I had attended with some of my colleagues, I recall something was said about using some ground troops in order to strengthen the Pusan beachhead, if we had to withdraw there, and enable an effective evacuation there of our nationals but no large offensive was contemplated."[42] Secretary Johnson later testified that it was the understanding of the Department of Defense at the time of the meeting that whatever ground troops would be necessary for offensive action would be committed. He also recalled that he took the position that the more discussion there was about American ground strength the more help it would be to the enemy; therefore the subject was not considered further.[43] Much later he further explained, "We were scared of the Hill in this thing. If we had tried to put ground troops in at the start there would have been a great deal of trouble."[44] Secretary Acheson later explained that the Congressional delegation "could not have been told the exact nature, timing, and extent of the troop movements for reasons of the safety of the troops and of Japan. General MacArthur had a tricky operation to perform and required protection."[45]

Secretary Johnson told reporters at the White House that orders had already gone out to implement the measures contained in the President's latest announcement.[46] Other conferees stated that the possible use of the atomic bomb had not been a topic of discussion during the Executive-Congressional conference.[47] Senator Wiley characterized the Korean situation for reporters as a "load of dynamite." ". . . The question," he continued, "is how big a charge of dynamite it is."[48] Senator Wherry repeated publicly the criticism he had made within the confines of the Cabinet Room

41. *Ibid.*
42. *Hearings*, Part II, 112.
43. *Ibid.*, Part IV, 2160.
44. Secretary Johnson, Interview, October 27, 1955.
45. Secretary Acheson, Letter, August 24, 1959.
46. Harold B. Hinton, *New York Times*, July 1, 1950, p. 3.
47. *New York Herald Tribune*, July 1, 1950, p. 3.
48. Harold B. Hinton, *New York Times*, July 1, 1950, p. 3.

concerning the ground troop decision—namely, that the President should have consulted Congress prior to making a decision of such magnitude.[49]

The Senate and House React

Later that afternoon on the floor of the Senate, Senator Wherry continued his criticism of the Administration.[50] Charging it with "terrible, ghastly failures," he praised the President for having "repudiated" the "Acheson appeasement policy" in the Far East and called for Secretary Acheson's resignation. Furthermore, according to the Senator, ". . . the President should not have acted under the resolution passed by the United Nations without congressional authorization." In raising the question of the constitutionality of the President's decisions, however, he made it clear that he was not impugning the President's motives. "I am not questioning the President's sincerity at all," he explained. Even though the President had not done so previously, the Senator thought that he should convene a joint session of Congress and ask for its support. But these criticisms of the manner in which the decisions to resist the North Korean aggression were taken did not apply to the decisions themselves. The Nebraska Senator was pleased that "at long last" the President had taken a "strong stand" against the "Red tide." Approval of the substance of the decisions was also shared by the only other critical speaker of the afternoon, Senator Harry P. Cain, Republican of Washington, who charged that American intelligence agencies must have known of the impending invasion and asked for a full investigation into why "people in high places" had not alerted the nation to it.[51] However, Senator Cain, like Senator Wherry, expressed full support of the present commitments.

Among the Republican Senators who spoke in support of the President's Constitutional authority to commit ground forces in Korea was Senator William F. Knowland of California who

---

49. *Ibid.*
50. *Congressional Record,* Vol. 96, Part 7, June 30, 1950, 9537ff.
51. *Ibid.,* p. 9526.

declared, "I believe that he has been authorized to do it under the terms of our obligations to the United Nations Charter. I believe that he has the authority to do it under his constitutional power as Commander-in-Chief of the Armed Forces of the United States." Senator Knowland saw no need for a declaration of war: "Certainly the action which has been taken to date is not one which would have required or one which I believe it was desirable to have a declaration of war as such by the Congress of the United States. What is being done is more in the nature of a police action."[52] The California Senator, revealing a sensitivity to Soviet decision-making processes, issued a call for unity: ". . . It seems to me that during the next 10-day period 13 men in the Kremlin are going to be making a decision fateful for themselves and for the world. I cannot help believing that in part their decision may be based on whether or not they believe the President of the United States has overwhelming support in the Congress and in the country for the necessary action he has taken."[53]

Also on the subject of Soviet policy calculations, Senator Alexander L. Wiley of Wisconsin, second ranking minority member of the Senate Foreign Relations Committee and a participant in both of the White House briefings, reported to his colleagues, "It is the judgment of many persons who are 'in the know,' if anyone is in that position, that if a sufficient demonstration of force is made, the Russians will understand it, and will not send their forces openly into the Korean conflict. If that is the case, then ere long the danger of a war conflict should be over. The risk we are taking is a calculated risk, but one which we cannot refuse to take."[54]

About a dozen other Senators—Democrats and Republicans alike—rose to speak in support of the Administration's policy in Korea during the final debate on the bill to amend the Mutual Defense Assistance Act of 1949 which had been under deliberation

---

52. *Ibid.*, p. 9540. A year later, however, the Senator was referring to the Blair House conferences as those which "led this country into war, but without a declaration of the Congress of the United States." *Hearings*, Part II, 765. Consult also the exchange of remarks between Senator Knowland and General Bradley in *Hearings*, Part II, 933.

53. *Ibid.*, p. 9539.

54. *Ibid.*, p. 9534.

throughout the week. At 2 P.M., in accordance with the agreement reached on Wednesday, the Senators voiced their decisions. The measure, carried by a vote of 66 to 30, provided $1,222,500,000 in military aid for American allies. Sixteen million dollars of the total were explicitly designated for Korea and the Philippines, but it was understood that more than $100 million could easily be allocated to Korea under other provisions of the bill. Among those voting in favor was Senator Robert A. Taft, Republican of Ohio, who expressed to reporters his support of the decision to send ground forces to Korea with the words—"When you are in, you've got to go all out."[55]

The House of Representatives, absorbed in other business, paid scant attention either to the fighting in Korea or to the President's latest decisions. Representative James G. Fulton, Republican of Pennsylvania, a member of the Foreign Affairs Committee, defended Secretary Acheson against "political scalp-hunters" on the ground that removing officials every time "mistakes" were made would only result in "unstable government and many shifts in policy personnel."[56] Mrs. Helen Gahagan Douglas, Democratic representative from California, also a member of the Foreign Affairs Committee, lauded the United Nations and the President for having acted to prevent a history of mushrooming aggression from repeating itself.[57]

Thus those who spoke formally in both houses of Congress expressed overwhelming support of the decisions the President had made since Saturday. Supporting statements were couched in general terms and there was virtually no specific reaction to the freshly announced decisions to employ ground troops on the peninsula. At least in their public statements, the members of Congress seemed to share the reasoning of the *New York Times* editors who wrote:

> There is something dramatic and decisive about the use of ground troops, partly because throughout history they have been the symbol as well as the primary instrument of war, and partly

55. *New York Times*, July 1, 1950, p. 3.
56. *Congressional Record*, Vol. 96, Part 7, June 30, 1950, 9586.
57. *Ibid.*, pp. 9625ff.

because ground troops mean the physical occupation of terrain. Yet, looked at logically, there is not much difference between using American airmen or American sailors, and using American soldiers on land. It is clear now that this could not have been avoided, any more than the order to bomb north of the thirty-eighth parallel and to blockade the whole peninsula. To stop short of the necessary measures now would be folly.[58]

Despite the prevalent spirit of bipartisan unity, nonofficial observers of the Capitol scene were skeptical about how long it would persist. According to one interpretation, "Political bitterness is thought almost certain to arise, for example, if events in Korea go badly for the United States."[59]

Ambassador Austin Reports the Latest Decisions to the United Nations

On Friday afternoon Ambassador Warren R. Austin reported the latest American decisions to the Security Council in New York. The meeting had been called by President Rau in order to announce formally India's decision to support the United Nations resolution of June 27. The delegates, of course, had already learned of the new American commitment in Korea through unofficial news channels. Their reactions had been very much in the same spirit as that of the American Congress. Six days earlier the authority of the United Nations had been invoked against the North Korean aggression. Since then, 33 of the 59 member states, affirming their support of the Security Council resolutions, had rallied around the international banner. Six nations—Australia, Canada, New Zealand, the Netherlands, the United Kingdom, and the United States—had promised to back their pledges of support with military contingents. The majority of the member states were thus agreed that whatever measures might halt the aggression and restore peace in the area should be taken. Yugoslavia, to be sure, still dissented from the Security Council position. Egypt also continued to abstain from signifying either approval or disapproval of the resolutions. The Union of Soviet Socialist Republics still

58. *New York Times*, July 1, 1950, p. 14.
59. *New York Times*, July 2, 1950, p. E2.

refused to participate in the deliberations. *Pravda* inconspicuously carried a nine-line summary of President Truman's decisions to send American Army units to Korea and to blockade the North Korean coast.[60]

The President Leaves Washington

It was the afternoon of Friday, June 30, 1950. Harry S. Truman, President of the United States, left the city of Washington by train at 4:40 P.M., bound for historic Valley Forge, Pennsylvania, where nearly 50,000 Boy Scouts were encamped in their annual jamboree. At 9 P.M. (fifteen minutes after Task Force Smith had left Japan for combat in Korea), the President was addressing the Scouts on the theme of the difference between the youth organizations of free societies and the regimented youth legions of totalitarian states. Referring to the young men and women under Communist control, the President declared: "We must not return hate for the hate which these people are being taught to feel toward us. We must realize that they are the victims of a cynical group of leaders. We must make it clear to them that we believe in the fellowship of human beings, in the possibility of cooperative human action, and in peace based on mutual understanding. We must show them, over and over again, that fellowship is possible between men of different nations, different colors, and different creeds."[61]

At 11:10 P.M. Mr. Truman was in Philadelphia, boarding the Presidential yacht Williamsburg for a weekend cruise in Chesapeake Bay with his daughter Margaret. Elaborate communications facilities had been prepared to keep him in constant touch with world developments; his personal staff was close at hand to enable him to act swiftly in case of further emergency.[62] As the President

60. *Pravda*, July 3, 1950, p. 6. The main focus of attention in the Soviet press throughout this period appeared to be on the Stockholm peace campaign.

61. *New York Times*, July 1, 1950, p. 6.

62. Accompanying the President were administrative assistants George Elsey, David H. Stowe, and Stephen J. Spingarn; secretaries Matthew J. Connelly, Charles G. Ross, and William D. Hassett; military aides Brigadier General Robert B. Landry (Air Force), and Rear Admiral Robert L. Dennison (Navy); and Dr. John R. Steelman.

went aboard, reporters noted that he "seemed more at ease than
he had been all day."[63]

The seven days just past had constituted the President's most
strenuous week in office thus far. He had done all he could for
the time being to resist the aggression. It was now up to American
and Korean fighting men, together with their United Nations allies,
to push back the invaders.

It would be no picnic. As Republican Representative Charles A.
Eaton of New Jersey, an ordained Baptist minister, expressed it:
"We've got a rattlesnake by the tail and the sooner we pound its
damn head in the better!"[64] Most Americans wholeheartedly
agreed.[65] Not the least of these were those who were committed
and were slain on the distant peninsula jutting down between the
Yellow Sea and the Sea of Japan.

63. Anthony Leviero, *New York Times,* July 1, 1950, p. 6.

64. *New York Times,* July 1, 1950, p. 1.

65. A Roper Poll study in August 1950, showed that 73 per cent of those interviewed agreed that "President Truman did the right thing in sending our troops
into Korea;" 15 per cent disagreed; 12 per cent had no opinion. Elmo Roper, *You
and Your Leaders* (New York: William Morrow, 1957), p. 145.

PART IV

EMPIRICAL ANALYSIS

CHAPTER 11

SOME PROPOSITIONS

The main objective of this chapter is to present some empirical propositions about foreign policy decision making that have been derived from the narrative of the Korean decision contained in Part III. These propositions link the variables of the decision-making frame of reference and provide an *a priori* set of hypotheses that can be applied in future case studies or in simulation exercises[1] designed to improve understanding of international politics.

Several points about this analytical effort need to be made clear at the outset. First, since there can be an infinite number of analytical aspects for any social object, this attempt at analysis cannot exhaust the possibilities for the insightful positing of theoretical

---

1. Consult Harold Guetzkow, et al., *Simulation in International Relations* (Englewood Cliffs, N.J.: Prentice-Hall, 1963).

linkages between elements of the single case that has been presented. Thus the present analysis is to be considered not as the last but only as one effort to analyze the Korean decision. In general, the wider the range of theoretical insights that are brought to bear on the case materials, the greater the number of explanatory hypotheses they may be expected to yield. Therefore each reader is urged to exercise his own creative skills on the data that have been presented.

Second, the basic intellectual strategy that has been employed in the present proposition-building effort has been that which might be termed *guided retroduction*.[2] It neither brings to bear a deductive set of hypotheses from the behavioral sciences that would predict the behaviors found in this case[3] nor seeks solely to induce propositions from the repeated occurrence of related events. Rather, with the decision-making framework as a guide, it approaches elements of the case as factors that can function as referents of correlated dependent or independent variables. Thus the analyst asks, "Given the basic conceptual framework, what might have been the antecedents or consequences of this element of observed behavior?"

A third consideration is that while the following propositions are empirically grounded in the present case, they cannot be accorded a high degree of empirical confirmation. Thus the occasional skeptical query, "I don't know how far you can generalize

---

2. This concept has been suggested by N. R. Hanson's discussions of "abductive" or "retroductive" reasoning in *Patterns of Discovery* (Cambridge: Cambridge University Press, 1958), pp. 85ff.

3. It is hoped however that the case materials can be used in this way. For example, the behavior of President Truman and Secretary Acheson in the Korean crisis might be cited as illustrations of the performance of "emotional affect" and "task" leadership roles that would be predicted on the basis of small group research. As a further illustration Professor Joseph de Rivera has suggested that the way in which Counselor Kennan's skills were utilized without bringing him directly into the Blair House Conferences seems to follow a pattern for handling "deviant members" that has been discovered in small group research. It has been pointed out that Mr. Kennan could have been summoned to the first meeting by friends or by local police; a side table could have been set for him if there was no place for him at the main dining table at Blair House or he could have been asked to join the group after dinner. Whether correct or not, these things illustrate new perspectives on the case, that can be obtained by invoking external social psychological theory. See de Rivera's forthcoming *The Psychological Dimension of Foreign Policy*.

on the basis of a single case," is met with complete agreement. We cannot know until we can make general statements on the basis of some evidence and then test them against some more evidence.

A fourth characteristic of the present analytical effort is that no attempt has been made to integrate the propositions derived from the Korean decision with a supplementary body of invented propositions into a comprehensive theory of decision making. Neither has a systematic attempt been made to build propositions by speculating about alternative states of affairs. Both exercises, however, would be useful. Hopefully the present effort is a step toward increasing the fruitfulness of such endeavors.

The Korean Decision As a Crisis Decision

The decision-making frame of reference originally did not specify a typology of decisions. It may be left an open question whether typologies, themselves capable of infinite invention and based on *a priori* assumptions about crucial variables, will be helpful in building a variable-oriented theory of foreign policy decision making. The same set of parsimonious variables eventually may be found to be differentially loaded but not qualitatively different in the various "types" of decision situations. For the present, however, it may be found helpful to follow the customary experimental practice of stating a set of relevant antecedent conditions under which the theoretical propositions advanced in a study are anticipated to hold.

The Korean decision thus might be classified as a *crisis decision* with the following principal empirical characteristics: *occasion for decision*—thrust upon the decision makers from outside their organization and from outside the territory and population over which they exercise official control; *decision-making organization*—a large complex organization composed of an executive headquarters and a number of subordinate functional departments the heads of which may be called upon by the chief executive for advice; *internal setting relationships*—characterized by the presence of other organizations that can challenge the legitimacy of the decisions taken, influence the kinds of social resources made available to the decision makers, and eventually perhaps bring about their replacement; and *external setting relationships*—characterized by the presence of allies and enemies over whom the decision makers cannot exercise arbitrary control.

A *crisis* is defined after Hermann as "a situation that (1) threatened high priority goals of the decisional unit, (2) restricted the amount of time in which a response could be made, and (3) was unexpected or unanticipated by the members of the decision making unit."[4] A crisis decision is thus taken to be a response to a high threat to values, either immediate or long range, where there is little time for decision under conditions of surprise.

Crisis Decision Stages

Although not specified in the original decision-making framework (but implied to some extent by the attention given to feedback processes), the Korean decision suggests that it may be useful to think about developmental stages in a decision-making process. Thus analytical attention is drawn to the possibility that there may be similarities and differences among behaviors characteristic of stages within and among decision types. It may be found that decisional sequences are characterized by progressive activation of necessary conditions that in combination serve as sufficient to produce a given decisional outcome.[5]

The Korean decision suggests four stages for a crisis decision as shown in Table 1.

Almost all of the participants in the Korean decision that were interviewed have reported that they experienced a sense of entering into new phases of the situation at the various points of decision during the last week of June 1950. Some variation was noted in their interpretation of the significance of the various stages but this was not completely idiosyncratic; there was greater agree-

---

4. Charles F. Hermann, *Crises in Foreign Policy Making: A Simulation of International Politics* (China Lake, California: Project Michelson Report, U.S. Naval Ordnance Test Station, April 1965), p. 29.

5. This is suggested in part by Neil J. Smelzer's remarks on the "value-added process" in social action in *Theory of Collective Behavior* (New York: Free Press, 1963), pp. 13ff.

Table 1

CRISIS DECISION STAGES

Stage	Korean decision example
I. Stimulus categorization and establishment of general framework of response.	Identification of invasion as "aggression" and decision to make "collective security" response through the United Nations (June 24).
II. Determination of shared willingness to make a positive response and of capabilities to act.	Consensus of the Blair House conference that there should be "no appeasement." President's military questions (June 25).
III. Articulation of a specific positive response and decision to commit new, limited resources.	Decision to provide air-sea support for ROK forces (June 26).
IV. Progressive expansion of the amount and kind of committed resources.	Decision to employ combat troops in the Pusan area (June 29), one RCT in the combat area (early June 30) and to give General MacArthur unlimited authority to use his ground forces (midmorning, June 30).

ment than disagreement. For example, the majority of participants interviewed thought that the decision to use force taken during the second Blair House conference on Monday constituted a "point of no return" in the decisional sequence from which the decision to use ground troops logically followed. At least two of the decision makers, including the President, however, thought that the determination displayed during the Sunday Blair House conference was the logical precondition from which flowed the subsequent decisions of the week; others agreed that the Sunday conference was marked by such a sense of determination. At least one of the decision makers did not seem to experience a sense of full and complete response to the aggression until the Friday commitment of ground forces; others seemed to experience an earlier sense of complete involvement but agreed that the decision to send in infantry represented a significant new stage. Thus despite some variation there does seem to have been a consensus that the decision did have certain stages as well as upon what those stages were.

At the end of this chapter, we will return to the notion of crisis decision stages and present a set of propositions about them based on the data of the Korean decision.

The Korean Decision As a Single Decision
and As a Sequence of Decisions

Analytically the Korean decision may be viewed either as a single decision or as a sequence of decisions. It may be regarded either as the American decision to resist armed aggression in Korea through military counteraction, or as the set of decisions taken by the United States Government during the period June 24-30, 1950. Both analytical postures will be adopted in the following analysis.

The concept of a sequence of decisions that contribute to a stage-like progression toward an analytically defined outcome calls attention to the possibility that positive or negative reinforcement of the behaviors of officials between occasions for decision may affect their responses during subsequent formal deliberations.[6] The concept of reinforcement can now be added to the concept of feedback along the path of action contained in the original statement of the decision making framework.[7]

A simplified reinforcement pattern for the Korean decision is suggested in Table 2.

It will be noted that primarily positive reinforcement occurred throughout the week of decision and that the reinforcing agent varied from domestic and foreign actors to nonconsulted decision makers themselves.

The reinforcement pattern of the Korean decision suggests the proposition that *the greater the consistency of positive reinforce-*

---

6. A stimulating summary of contemporary theory about reinforcement is contained in Albert Bandura and Richard K. Walters, *Social Learning and Personality Development* (New York: Holt, Rinehart, and Winston, 1963).

7. Snyder, Bruck, and Sapin, *Foreign Policy Decision Making*, pp. 75ff., 132.

Table 2

SEQUENTIAL REINFORCEMENT OF THE KOREAN DECISION

Decisions	*Reinforcement*
1. To call for a Security Council meeting (June 24).	Prompt supporting UN action (June 25).
2. To adopt a strong posture of resistance (June 25).	Coinciding editorial opinion (June 26).
3. To commit air-sea forces; to keep conflict limited; and to avoid direct confrontation with the USSR (June 26).	Overwhelmingly favorable Congressional, domestic, and international approval (June 27-28); temperate Soviet response (June 29).
4. To extend operations into North Korea and to employ combat troops as evacuation cover (June 29).	Unfavorable response from General MacArthur as being inadequate (June 30).
5. To commit one RCT to combat (June 30).	Agreement of full meeting of presidential advisers (June 30).
6. To commit necessary ground forces (June 30).	Congressional and press acceptance as "virtually inevitable" (June 30).

ment, the less the conflict among decision makers about making progressively more costly responses to threat. Thus one way to elicit or to inhibit progressively more costly responses to crisis, where high costs are not immediately acceptable, may be to vary the reinforcement given to the initial low cost commitments that decision makers have approved. This suggests that the analysis of reinforcement patterns may be a fruitful approach to what might be called potentiality analysis in political science, i.e., to the analysis of the possible alternative states of affairs that might have existed other than that which is empirically verifiable.

Conceptualizing the Korean decision as a sequence of subdecisions also suggests that it may be found helpful to entertain a typology of the predominant characteristics of decision-making conferences. Thus it might be found that crisis decisions tend to be made by a sequence of conferences that can be characterized primarily as *stimulus-evaluating* and *response framework-setting* (June 24), *resolution-probing* (June 25), *response-articulating* and *selecting* (June 26), *response-evaluating* (June 28 and 29), and *response deepening* (June 30). Although any concrete decisional conference may be characterized by a number of processes, it may be found fruitful for the decision-making analyst to entertain the possibility that such conferences tend to serve one or more (or at least limited) functions in a complex sequential decision.

The Korean case also includes another kind of meeting that can serve as a positive or negative reinforcer but which is not in itself strictly a decisional meeting. This is what might be called a *response-legitimating* conference. Here the decision makers communicate their decisions to selected influential leaders in the internal and external political settings. Examples are the meetings of the direct participants in the Korean decision with members of the Congress on June 27 and June 30, and the briefings held by State Department spokesmen for NATO and OAS representatives on June 27. It will be noted that official spokesmen at such meetings not only communicate the content of the decisions that have been taken but also defend their appropriateness and legitimacy.

Against the background of these preliminary considerations the Korean decision will now be examined for the purpose of developing a set of empirically grounded propositions that tie together the variables of the decision-making frame of reference and, hopefully, contribute to more explicit understanding of foreign policy decision processes. The analysis will first attempt to show the impact of crisis upon the main variables of the decision-making framework (organizational roles and relationships, communications and information, and motivation and values), and upon the relationships of the decision makers with their internal and external settings. For this part of the analysis, the decision will be viewed both as a single crisis decision and as a set of subdecisions. Secondly, the analysis will return to the idea of a crisis decision sequence in an attempt to show how the variables identified in the previous analysis interacted to produce the sequence of decisional outcomes observed in the present case. Finally, an attempt will be made to begin to relate properties of decisions to their subsequent execution or administration.

CRISIS AND DECISION-MAKING VARIABLES

Crisis and Organizational Variables

The effect of crisis upon some organizational variables is summarized in Variable Diagram 1. Here crisis is conceptualized as an independent variable, while changes in organizational behavior are regarded as referents of associated dependent variables.

Variable Diagram 1

CRISIS AND ORGANIZATIONAL VARIABLES

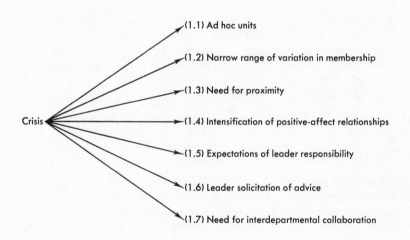

Crisis

(1.1) Ad hoc units

(1.2) Narrow range of variation in membership

(1.3) Need for proximity

(1.4) Intensification of positive-affect relationships

(1.5) Expectations of leader responsibility

(1.6) Leader solicitation of advice

(1.7) Need for interdepartmental collaboration

The first proposition to be considered is PROPOSITION 1.1: *Crisis decisions tend to be reached by ad hoc decisional units.* This can be appreciated by reviewing the principal decisional units that were active during June 24-30 as shown in Table 3.

Table 3

SEQUENCE OF DECISIONAL UNITS

Decisions	*Decisional unit*
1. To call for a Security Council meeting (June 24).	1. President Secretary of State Secretary of the Army Assistant Secretary for UN Affairs Assistant Secretary for Far Eastern Affairs Ambassador-at-large
2. To adopt a strong posture of resistance (June 25).	2. President Secretary of State Secretary of Defense Service Secretaries Joint Chiefs of Staff Under Secretary of State Assistant Secretary for UN Affairs Assistant Secretary for Far Eastern Affairs Ambassador-at-large
3. To commit air-sea forces; to keep conflict limited (June 26).	3. Same as (2) minus Secretary of the Navy and Under Secretary of State.
4. To extend operations into North Korea and to employ combat troops as evacuation cover (June 29).	4. President Secretary of State Secretary of Defense Service Secretaries Joint Chiefs of Staff Assistant Secretary for Far Eastern Affairs Special Ambassadors—2 Chairman, NSRB Executive Secretary, NSC
5. To commit one RCT to combat (June 30).	5. President Secretary of the Army Chairman, Joint Chiefs of Staff Chief of Staff of the Army General of the Army
6. To commit necessary ground forces (June 30).	6. President Secretary of State Secretary of Defense Service Secretaries Joint Chiefs of Staff Special Ambassador

It will be noted that all of the decisional units except Unit 4, a meeting of the National Security Council, are *ad hoc* units, specially convened to deal with problems arising out of the Korean crisis. The National Security Council, although in its initial stages of development, might have become a focus for decision during the week but it did not in fact become so. The Cabinet was not employed as a decision-making body for purposes of determining the American response to the North Korean aggression.

There appear to be two main reasons for the formation of *ad hoc* decisional units under crisis conditions. The first is a result of formal role expectations plus chance; e.g., Units 1 and 5. Whereas the fact that the news of the North Korean invasion would be channeled to the Assistant Secretary of State for Far Eastern Affairs (given his availability in Washington) can be attributed to the expectations that surrounded his organizational role, the fortuitous presence of the Secretary of the Army at the Alsops' dinner party and the important liaison role he played with the Department of Defense throughout Saturday night has a strong element of chance. So also did the absence from Washington in a telephone-less farm of one of the Administration's principal analysts of Soviet affairs, Counselor George F. Kennan, Jr. Thus chance can operate inclusively or exclusively with respect to the membership of decisional units. A second contribution to *ad hoc* decisional units is the combination of formal role expectations and leader's preference; e.g., Units 2, 3, and 6. Here the President generally seems to have specified those persons whom he wished to have advise him, while allowing his advisers an occasion to supplement his desired list. Among them, of course, are officials such as the Secretaries of State and Defense who might be expected to participate on the basis of their role responsibilities. On the other hand, there are other participants whose activity, though reasonable, is not so easily explainable solely in terms of formal role expectations; e.g., the participation of the Under Secretary of State in Unit 2 but his absence in Unit 3, the presence of a special ambassador but the absence of the Assistant Secretary for Far Eastern Affairs in Unit 6.

But what is the significance for decision of *ad hoc* units in crisis situations? The significance of the nature of the decisional unit immediately becomes a focus of attention because of the fundamental assumption of decision-making analysis that decisions tend to vary with the composition of the decisional unit. Thus it is of interest that although the threatening stimulus launched by the North Koreans was from the beginning a military action, the initial American response was primarily a diplomatic one based on legal considerations that sought to bring to bear in response the resources of international law and organization. The probability that this response was influenced by the composition of the group that initially articulated it as an alternative is suggested by the fact that this group included (1) the State Department official charged with primary responsibility for United Nations affairs (Assistant Secretary Hickerson), (2) a State Department official who had been the first incumbent in the same post in 1949 and who was known for his strong support of the United Nations (Assistant Secretary Rusk) and (3) a world-renowned specialist in international law (Ambassador Jessup). Confidence in this probability is increased, although to an indeterminate degree, by the conviction of one of Secretary Acheson's principal advisers that if he had been able to reach the State Department on Saturday night, he could have persuaded the Secretary of State not to limit the freedom of United States action by involving the United Nations in the American response to the Korean invasion. The Secretary of State's known preference for realistic power strategies rather than the unrealistic pursuit of principles in international affairs further increased the credibility of this official's conviction that he could have persuaded the Secretary of State to make a response to the Korean crisis that would be unencumbered by the United Nations involvement. Whether the President's great respect for Secretary Acheson's professional judgment would, in turn, have led him to accept a recommendation for an initial unilateral American response to the aggression is, of course, speculative but not entirely implausible. The Truman Doctrine had been enunciated without a major role specified for the United Nations in 1947 and the decision to intervene in Formosa that was associated with the Korean decision in 1950 was taken with complete acceptance that it would not and could not be a United Nations action. If the need for direct military intervention in Korea had been clearer on Saturday night the argument for circumventing the United Nations might have been even more acceptable. Nevertheless, the point here is that an experienced decision maker appreciated at the time that it did make a difference who decided what the initial American response to the Korean crisis might be and that there is some evidence tending to support such a view in this case.

A review of the sequence of decisional units presented above suggests a cluster of propositions centering around considerations of size and composition of the decisional units that cope with crisis. Thus PROPOSITION 1.2: *Crisis decisions tend to be made by decisional units that vary within rather narrow limits of size and composition.* Our study has shown that the size of the key decisional units tended to vary between five and fourteen members as indicated in Table 3A.

Table 3A

SIZE OF DECISIONAL UNITS

Decision	Size of decisional unit
1	6
2	14
3	12
4	15
5	5
6	12

It will be noted that four of the six major sets of decisions were made by units having twelve to fourteen members. Two were made by five- and six-man groups. It is suggested that the larger groups can be accounted for partly by PROPOSITION 1.21: *The more costly the commitment anticipated, the larger the unit up to a psychologically and physically acceptable limit.* This is most clearly illustrated by the differences between Units 1 and 2 and between Units 5 and 6. The upper limits on decisional units seem to be influenced by felt need for secrecy and a sense of adequate representation of interests within the executive branch for the matter at hand. It has also been stated by one official who was not invited to the first Blair House conference that he was not invited but would have been except for the seating capacity of the Blair House dining room (said to be fourteen). Whether the capacity of customary facilities for high level face-to-face national decision making is a factor here, or whether it is a sense of adequate representation of interest, or of an upper level in group size in which meaningful participation in discussion can take place, it nevertheless seems possible to suggest that *the principal national crisis decision-making group will tend to vary in size from twelve to fifteen officials.* This possibility is made more intriguing by the fact that the Presidium of the Central Committee of the Communist Party of the Soviet Union tends to have from eleven to fifteen members and that the core group that President Kennedy involved in the Cuban decision in the fall of 1962 apparently constituted about fifteen officials. Are there organizational qualities of crisis decision in the modern world that transcend size of polity, issue, technological capability, historical background, and cultural context?

It is suggested that the smaller decisional units (1 and 5) can be accounted for by PROPOSITION 1.22: *The more the felt need for immediate action and* (a) *the less costly the commitment, or* (b) *the greater the revocability of a costly commitment, or* (c) *the greater the anticipated acceptance of a costly commitment, the smaller the decisional unit.* In the first case, the decision to call a meeting of the United Nations Security Council was viewed as being a limited commitment that would not foreclose other alternatives. The President's decision to approve the movement of one RCT into combat on Friday combined considerations (b) and (c). The decisional units of the week seemed to vary but little in membership as well as in size. Note that the President, the Secretaries of State and Defense, the Civilian Secretaries, and the Joint Chiefs of Staff served as a kind of core decision-making group (Decisions 2, 3, 4, and 6). But it will also be noticed that, taking the week as a whole, there took place a gradual decrease in the number of participating State Department roles, except for Unit 4 which was not an *ad hoc* unit but rather an augmented National Security Council. The declining role of the Assistant Secretary of State for United Nations Affairs is apparent. Excluding the President, the relative proportions of State and Defense Department officials in the various decisional units is shown in Table 3B.

Table 3B

RELATIVE PREPONDERANCE OF STATE AND DEFENSE ROLES IN DECISIONAL UNITS (EXCLUDING THE PRESIDENT)

Unit	Per Cent State	Per Cent Defense
1	80	20
2	38	62
3	36	64
4	29	57
5	0	100
6	18	82

This pattern suggests PROPOSITION 1.23: *The more technical the problems of decision implementation, the greater the role of the appropriate specialists in the decisional unit.* Thus, in the Korean decision, as the problems thrust upon the decision makers more and more came to center around military problems of how to carry out the basic decision to resist the North Korean aggression, the representatives of the military establishment came to play a greater role in the deliberations. This is further supported by Secretary Johnson's later recollection that by the end of the week the center of working-level initiative in dealing with the Korean crisis seemed to have gravitated to his own office.

It was tempting to view the independent variable of Proposition 1.23 as the technical nature of crisis information and to hypothesize that it would be correlated with the composition of the official group that would react to it. However, the striking contrast between the purely military content of Ambassador Muccio's first report (on the Korean fighting) and the nonmilitary composition of Unit 1 for all practical purposes suggest that factors other than the content of information were crucial determinants of the composition of the decision-making group. The factors might have included the shared sense of required speed of action among the State Department officials, the lack of habits of intimate collabora-

tion at high levels between State and Defense Department officials, the Secretary of State's misunderstanding that the Defense
Secretary had not yet returned from the Far East, and other
chance elements that seem to lead to an initial *ad hoc* assemblage
of officials faced with a crisis. But in the implementation phases of
crisis response more systematic factors seem to be at work, including official designation as a determinant of the composition of decision-making groups and a comparative decline in the importance
of chance and self-selection in decisional participation. Thus it is
suggested that the variables that intervene between the technical
content of information and the composition of the decision-making
group as expressed in Proposition 1.23 are a more regularized mode
of designating decision makers and important control over channels of incoming information. For example, whereas military information from Ambassador Muccio that had been received through
State Department channels was acted upon primarily by State
Department officials (Unit 1), military information from General
MacArthur that had been received through Army channels served
as the basis for decision by an almost purely Army group (Unit 5).

PROPOSITION 1.3: *The greater the crisis, the greater the felt need
for face-to-face proximity among decision makers.* This proposition
is suggested by the President's desire to return to Washington on
Saturday night and by the whole series of face-to-face deliberations
among his advisers that were suggested to him during the week.
Thus crisis situations apparently intensify the need for the direct
full sharing of information and views among organizational members. Do they also intensify a need to reinforce individual security
feelings through group reassurance?

PROPOSITION 1.4: *The greater the crisis, the greater the accen-
tuation of positive affect relationships among decision makers.* The
warm personal relationship that existed between the President and
the Secretary of State is demonstrated repeatedly during the
events of the week by their harmony of views, frequent interaction, and the predominant role of the latter in articulating courses
of action for presidential approval. Negative affect relationships,
however, seemed not to have been affected in just the same way.
Though the coolness at the secretarial level between the Departments of State and Defense may have inhibited somewhat the

fullness of departmental collaboration that might otherwise have been accomplished, there is no evidence that these relations worsened. On the contrary, the public praise of the Secretary of State by the Secretary of Defense on Wednesday perhaps illustrates the facilitating effect of crisis, at least in moderate degree, upon group cohesiveness.

PROPOSITION 1.5: *The greater the crisis, the greater the acceptance of responsibility for action by the leader and the more the follower expectation and acceptance of the leader's responsibility.* The President's behavior during the Korean decision and the understanding and respect for his responsibilities shown by his advisers then and afterward enhances the appreciation of leadership behavior as a pattern of interaction between leaders and followers. There is no doubt that the President's own definition of his role as a strong president contributed to his decision to respond to crisis without formal Congressional approval. But it is also likely that he was influenced by the expectations of his advisers that he should act independently and responsibly. Two pieces of evidence suggest support for this interpretation. Apparently only one adviser suggested a discussion of domestic politics during the Blair House conferences and apparently none raised any question about the appropriateness of presidential action. More directly, Secretary Acheson explicitly advised the President after the Monday evening decision not to seek a Congressional mandate for it and this advice was accepted. Both leader and follower definitions of his responsibility for taking positive action in response to crisis are undoubtedly conditioned by past social learning experiences. Thus for those who had observed the President under previous crisis conditions, such as in the Berlin crisis of 1948 when he had been inclined to favor a more drastic response than the airlift that was finally decided upon, his determination to resist the North Korean aggression could be anticipated. Participants in the Korean decision seem agreed that a less strong president might not have responded to the Korean aggression in the firm and timely way in which Mr. Truman did. This, in turn, suggests PROPOSITION 1:51: *The greater the crisis, and the greater the past record of nonavoidant response to crisis by the leader, the greater the propensity to make a positive response.* Thus the intensification of mutual responsibility expectations and the enhancement of the importance of behavior during past crises can be anticipated under crisis conditions.

PROPOSITION 1.6: *The greater the crisis, the more the leader's solicitation of subordinate advice.* This is illustrated in the Korean decision by the way in which President Truman invited each of his advisers to comment upon the situation during both of the Blair House conferences. Although the President was known to have a permissive leadership style, the Korean crisis probably accentuated that pattern. The President's past behavior suggested that the more important the problem, the more likely he was to seek the advice of his advisers in reaching a decision about it.

For this reason, it would have been surprising if he had not demonstrated such a leadership style during the Korean decision. It will be interesting to examine this proposition further in cases where the leader is not habitually permissive in his relationships with advisers.

PROPOSITION 1.7: *The greater the crisis, the greater the interdepartmental collaboration.* The crisis in Korea seemed to draw the Departments of State and Defense into collaboration closer than that which they had experienced for many months. It will be recalled that at one time Secretary Johnson had ordered that all interactions should cease except those that were channeled through his own office. But during the crisis, officials at this "working level" appear to have been in especially close collaboration. There was both joint action and intermingling of officials in the field in Korea and in Washington. The need for interdepartmental collaboration that was expressed in practice at lower levels, however, seems not to have overcome the obstacles to cooperation at the secretarial level except for formal confrontations under presidential supervision. This seemed particularly evident in the period between the receipt of the news of the fighting on Saturday and the decision to intervene on Monday.

Crisis and Informational Variables

The main informational bases of the sequence of decisions that made up the Korean decision are summarized in Table 4.

Table 4

SEQUENCE OF INFORMATION

Decisions	*Information*
1. To call for a Security Council meeting (June 24).	Cable from Ambassador Muccio Press reports
2. To adopt a strong posture of resistance (June 25).	MacArthur memo on Formosa Confirming reports on all-out invasion Favorable Security Council action ROK Army might hold Soviet Union backed North Korean action US held military superiority over USSR US had Far Eastern military capability Invasion was like pre-WW II aggressions Acheson recommendations Direct appreciation of mutual attitudes
3. To commit air-sea forces (June 26).	MacArthur report on imminent ROK collapse Acheson recommendations Air-sea support would probably be decisive Soviets would probably not intervene Gross report on strong UN sanction support Shared determination not to appease
4. To extend operations into North Korea and to use combat troops as evacuation cover (June 29).	Reports on military difficulties Johnson recommendations Temperate Soviet response Overwhelmingly favorable domestic and foreign response
5. To commit one RCT to combat (June 30).	ROK Army incapable of more than delaying action MacArthur recommendation
6. To commit necessary ground combat forces (June 30).	Same as (5). Further Soviet aggression not imminent Two divisions probably adequate

Variable Diagram 2 summarizes some effects of crisis upon informational variables.

Variable Diagram 2

CRISIS AND INFORMATIONAL VARIABLES

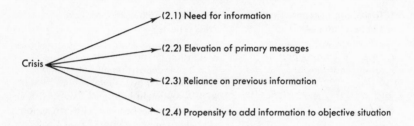

(2.1) Need for information

(2.2) Elevation of primary messages

Crisis

(2.3) Reliance on previous information

(2.4) Propensity to add information to objective situation

PROPOSITION 2.1: *The greater the crisis, the greater the felt need for information.* From the State Department duty officer's first efforts to obtain confirmation of the United Press report on the North Korean attack through the President's repeated requests for more information about Soviet intentions in other troublesome areas, the record of the Korean decision illustrated a strong demand for information under crisis. This need for information leads to the directed scanning of the organizational environment. The Sunday decision to ask General MacArthur to send a survey party to Korea is an excellent example of a decision-making group seeking to improve its information about the external setting in a crisis situation. Although the emphasis during the Korean decision seems to have been on scanning the external setting, noteworthy efforts were also made to obtain information about significant aspects of the internal setting—especially information needed to estimate capabilities for action. Thus the President's questions on Sunday night about the size, disposition, and mobility of American military forces in the Far East, as well as relative Soviet strengths, not only exemplify a need for information but also show how information variables can link capabilities analysis and foreign policy decision making.

PROPOSITION 2.11: *The more limited the information, the greater the emphasis placed upon the reliability of its source.* This is suggested by the fact that decision makers at the Department of State on Saturday evening placed great weight upon Ambassador Muccio's estimate of the attack as an "invasion" since he had a reputation for careful and cautious reporting.

PROPOSITION 2.12: *The more varied the organizational sources and channels of communication of similar information, the greater the confidence in its validity.* This may be illustrated by the remark of Senator Connally just prior to the Korean crisis that military, diplomatic, and private reports seemed to indicate a general lessening of international tension. Immediately after the attack the cumulative effect of multiple sources of information on the accepted seriousness of the invasion could be seen as the result of the process of comparing information, especially among Army and Air Force officers in Tokyo and Army and State Department officials in Washington.

PROPOSITION 2:13: *The more prolonged the crisis, the greater the sense of adequacy of the information about it.* In the initial stages of a surprise threat, there are acute feelings of inadequacy of information about it, but as efforts are made to obtain further information, as actions are taken and responses to such actions are observed, and as additional information is thrust upon the decision makers from their environment, the sense of inadequacy begins to diminish. Thus in the early stages of the Korean decision, the Washington officials felt inadequately informed about the progress of fighting in Korea, the relative strengths of the opposing forces, the intentions of Soviet leaders, and other matters. By the end of the week, they felt more adequately informed. Here the eruption of a crisis is unanticipated and the initial feelings of inadequacy are intensified by the lack of contingency planning that would have led to continuous prior monitoring of information deemed necessary for response determination. Although information was viewed as becoming generally more adequate as the situation unfolded, there were some matters on which doubt was high (such as the ultimate costs of repelling the aggression and the possible role of the Chinese Communists) and only a very few things about which information was felt to be more than adequate (such as the domestic American acceptance of the Korean involvement).

PROPOSITION 2.2: *The greater the crisis, the greater the tendency for primary messages to be elevated to the top of the organizational hierarchy.* An example of this is the fact that the duty officer at General Headquarters in Tokyo did not attempt to bring the first fragmentary reports of the Korean fighting to the attention of General MacArthur in the early morning of June 25 until the extreme seriousness of the attack had become clear. In Washington throughout the week, there were a number of primary messages that were communicated directly to the President; e.g., the Muccio report, the Dulles-Allison cable, and the MacArthur recommendations. This pattern of information flow seems correlated both with the need for information at higher organizational levels and with subordinate need for high-level decisions in fast-moving crisis situations. This pattern incidentally suggests qualities required in order to gain top-level organizational attention.

PROPOSITION 2.3: *The greater the crisis, the greater the reliance upon the central themes in previously existing information.* This is illustrated throughout the Korean decision by the persistent tendency to rely upon information about the relative capabilities of the North and South Korean armies that underestimated the capacities of the former and overestimated the abilities of the latter. This lack of appreciation of the actual relative capabilities of the two opposing military organizations was rooted, of course, in the estimate that they were approximately equal in weight. Thus the central, or predominant, theme in this matter was that the Republic of Korea Army could probably contain an invasion unless the North Korean People's Army was reinforced from outside. This theme, however, did not represent the total range of information about the opposing forces that was objectively available in Washington files. It will be recalled that the State Department had released to the press on June 9, 1950, a statement by Ambassador Muccio who asserted that "the undeniable material superiority of the North Korean forces would provide North Korea with the margin of victory in the event of a full-scale invasion of the Republic."[8] Thus the estimates discussed during the Blair House conferences represented selective recall of the main trend of earlier

8. John J. Muccio, "Military Aid to Korean Security Forces," *Department of State Bulletin*, XXII, No. 573 (June 26, 1950) p. 1049.

estimates rather than a rather full exploration of the range of objectively available information. Although this tendency did not prevent timely support of the South Korean forces, it undoubtedly delayed appreciation of its necessity and required scope. One way to compensate for the tendency for crisis comprehension to be narrowed through selective recall of predominant themes in existing information might be to initiate immediate scanning of past records for contrary themes, or to maintain continuing awareness of subdominant interpretations.

PROPOSITION 2.31: *The greater the confidence in existing information, the greater the amount of contrary evidence and the greater the authority of the sources required to bring about a change in interpretation.* It will be recalled that major revisions in previous estimates of South Korean capabilities were made twice during the Korean decision—on Monday just prior to the air-sea commitment and on Friday immediately before the decision to employ infantry. Both of these revisions, it will be noted, were made on the authority of information from General MacArthur, not upon reports emanating from the Korean Military Advisory Group.

PROPOSITION 2.4: *The greater the crisis, the greater the propensity for decision makers to supplement information about the objective state of affairs with information drawn from their own past experience.* This proposition, originally suggested by Richard C. Snyder, is illustrated by the categorization by the decision makers of the North Korean attack as an act of "aggression" similar to German, Japanese, and Italian actions that preceded World War II. Since a crisis involves a threat to values it is likely that the information selectively added from memory by the decision makers will be value-connected as "aggression" is associated with the values of "war" and "peace." Once again the importance of past social learning for response to crisis is suggested; furthermore, the briefer the opportunity for new learning under crisis conditions, the greater its probable importance.

Crisis and Values

Limitations on data about the conferences that produced the Korean decision and subsequent failure to obtain more adequate value data in interviews makes the following attempt to build some propositions about crisis, values, and decision less satisfactory than it otherwise might have been. For example, available documentary data make it impossible to make more than gross statements about relative strengths of values at the various points of decision. The results of interviews do not permit the association of values with specific roles. Nevertheless, within the bounds of available data an attempt will be made to bring value variables into the analysis so that subsequent decisional research can at least begin with some hypotheses empirically based in the Korean decision.

Values are considered to be positive or negative statements about desired goals (goal values) and of desirable modes of achieving them (instrumental values). This distinction is often arbitrary. Values evoked by an occasion for decision may be complementary and mutually supporting, inconsistent and conflicting, mutually exclusive, or possibly unrelated. Decision makers may be more or less conscious of the values associated with their choices. Crisis probably tends to heighten such awareness. In the present study no attempt has been made to analyze the implicit value structure of the Korean decision.[9] Rather the following analysis rests upon the explicit statements of objectives associated with the various decisions taken in response to the crisis in Korea.

The sequence of dominant values associated with the Korean decision is summarized in Table 5.

PROPOSITION 3.1: *Crisis tends to evoke a dominant goal-means value complex that persists as an explicit or implicit guide to subsequent responses.* The components of this goal-means value complex in the Korean decision were the preservation of world peace and the avoidance of World War III (goal) and the utilization and strengthening of the United Nations as an instrument of collective security (means). The strength and persistence of this early goal-means value complex that was established by the decision makers on the night of Saturday, June 24, is illustrated by the fact that despite operational difficulties and changes in personnel

---

9. The potentialities of such analysis, especially with more adequate data, are suggested in Edward T. Hall, *The Silent Language* (New York: Doubleday and Company, 1959).

Table 5

SEQUENCE OF VALUES

Decision	*Values*
1. To call for a Security Council meeting (June 24).	Do something Support UN for peace Build moral support for US Keep alternatives open
2. To adopt a strong posture of resistance (June 25).	Do something Support UN for peace Protect lives of Americans Aid Korean ally Keep alternatives open
3. To commit air-sea forces (June 26).	No appeasement Support UN for peace Limit risk of war with USSR Protect US prestige as ally Limit Communist expansion in Far East Protect US interests in Japan Protect lives of Americans Keep alternatives open
4. To extend operations into North Korea and to employ combat troops for evacuation cover (June 29).	Accomplish military mission Limit risk of war with USSR Protect lives of Americans Avoid overcommitment
5. To commit one RCT to combat (June 30).	Prevent failure of military mission Avoid overcommitment
6. To commit necessary ground troops (June 30).	Prevent failure of military mission Avoid overcommitment

American policy makers continued to seek peace through support of the United Nations during three years of conflict in Korea. In identifying and appreciating the strength of the instrumental value of seeking peace through the United Nations it is not necessary to enter the discussion of whether the United Nations intervention in Korea actually was an example of collective security action.

Variable Diagram 3

CRISIS AND VALUE VARIABLES

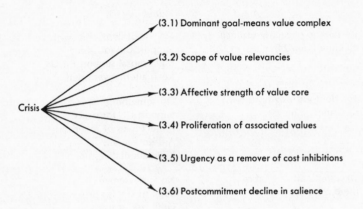

(3.1) Dominant goal-means value complex

(3.2) Scope of value relevancies

(3.3) Affective strength of value core

Crisis

(3.4) Proliferation of associated values

(3.5) Urgency as a remover of cost inhibitions

(3.6) Postcommitment decline in salience

PROPOSITION 3.2: *The goal-means value complex evoked by crisis tends to be broad in its scope of applicability.* The value combination of attaining world peace through support of the United Nations can be seen to have a scope of applicability reaching far beyond the armed invasion of the Republic of Korea. The events in Korea, therefore, represented just one empirical case that could be subsumed under the more universal goal-means value complex. That this was actually sensed by the decision makers is suggested by the later recollection of one of the President's advisers that "The real basis of the Korean decision had almost nothing to do with Korea. It had to do with aggression." It may be that crises are experienced as such partly because the values evoked by them are recognized to have far-ranging implications.

PROPOSITION 3.3: *Crisis tends to evoke a goal-means value complex that is strongly conditioned emotionally.* Although participants in the Korean decision have explained that it was made in a calculating and rational manner, the emotional quality of the dedication to "no appeasement" when the decision to fight was taken on Monday evening can also be recognized. For at least one of the participants this dedication indicated readiness to engage the Soviet Union in global war if Russian leaders decided upon counterintervention. The emotional commitment of the Blair House conferees to the goal of seeking peace through defeat of aggression by collective security action was deeply rooted in their social learning experiences. Most of them were between the ages of 20 and 40 when the Japanese invaded Manchuria in 1931. As one participant in the Blair House deliberations phrased it, the Korean decision had been "in the making" ever since that time. Thus the American policy makers had lived through and learned from the failure of the League of Nations, the ordeals of the victims of Axis aggression, the loss of American lives and resources in global war, and the postwar efforts to avoid a repetition of this kind of suffering by building a viable international organization. In 1950 an example of feared world war was only five years away in memory and hope that United Nations action could prevent a recurrence was still strong.

PROPOSITION 3.4: *Crisis tends to evoke the gradual proliferation of associated values around a dominant value core.* Reference to the values associated with Decisions 1 through 3 in Table 5 suggests that the more extensive the deliberations under crisis conditions, the greater the propensity to clarify and to relate other values to the initial dominant value core. Thus the North Korean invasion gradually became related not only to support of the United Nations for peace but also to American interests in Formosa, Japan, and Indochina; the confidence of American allies throughout the world; the postwar confrontation between the United States and the Soviet Union; and the immediate goal of protecting American lives in Korea. Whereas this proliferation of associated values undoubtedly was associated with both organizational and informational variables, it seems worthy of separate examination. Perhaps, as already suggested in the discussion of Proposition 3.2, one explanation for this phenomenon may be that crises are experienced as such not only because they evoke dominant core values having a wide scope of empirical applicability but also because these core values are immediately appreciated to be relevant for other values the nature, intensity, and significance of which only become articulated through further deliberation.

Another approach to explaining the proliferation phenomenon, especially at the point where costly and perhaps irrevocable re-

sponse commitments are made (e.g., Decision 3) is PROPOSITION
3.41: *The wider the range of values seen to be served, the greater
the willingness to accept the risks of costly commitment.* On the
other hand, this is probably an interaction phenomenon as suggested by PROPOSITION 3.42: *The greater the willingness to accept
the risks of commitment to protect a dominant core value, the
wider the range of additional values for which protection will be
sought.* This may help to explain the reversal of Formosan policy
that took place in conjunction with the Korean decision. Since the
denial of Formosa to Chinese Communist control was a pre-
existing value that was unacceptable of pursuit because of risk
and cost, it became more acceptable when determination was shown
to incur some degree of risk of war with the most formidable foe,
the Soviet Union, through military support of South Korea. The
Formosan recommendation, apparently drafted on the basis of
State-Defense deliberations on Sunday and presented to the first
Blair House conference that evening, may thus be evidence of the
degree of resolution to resist the aggression that characterized the
attitudes of the officials who drafted it.

If the value proliferation hypothesis holds true then PROPOSI-
TION 3.43: *The more prolonged or numerous the deliberations between crisis stimulus and response, the greater the specification of
relevant values* and PROPOSITION 3.4: *The more costly the crisis
response, the more complex the value structure associated with it*
might also be entertained.

PROPOSITION 3.5: *The greater the sense of urgency, the less the
effectiveness of negative values as inhibitors of positive response.*
It will be recalled that the two main decisions to commit American
lives to combat in Korea (the air-sea and ground force decisions) were both taken when urgent messages from General Mac-
Arthur made it clear that the military situation was deteriorating
so rapidly that appreciable delay in further support would be disastrous. That there were inhibitions about sending Americans into
combat is evidenced by the President's remark on Monday night
that he had attempted to avoid such a decision ever since he had
become president, by the comments of some of the participants in
the Blair House conferences that they did not wish to see Ameri-

can ground troops sent to Korea, by the "hesitation" of the President on this issue during the Thursday meeting of the National Security Council, and by the appreciation of at least one of his advisers that the engagement of ground forces would be less acceptable to American public opinion and might increase the probability of Soviet counterintervention.

PROPOSITION 3.6: *Costly responses to crisis tend to be followed by decline in the salience of the values associated with them.* Table 5 suggests that there is an appreciable decline in the explicit attention given to value considerations as the decision makers become more concerned with problems of implementation rather than those of initial policy determination. For example, compare the complex value structure of Decision 3 with the simpler structures of Decisions 4, 5, and 6. A further suggestion that a decline in value salience takes place during a sequence of crisis decisions is contained in the virtually unanimous view of the participants in the Korean decision that Decision 3 to undertake some military action was of more fundamental significance than Decisions 5 and 6 to engage ground forces. Considering the reluctance to commit ground troops revealed by the case data, the relative ease with which this was eventually accomplished and the absence of proliferated values associated with the infantry decision, deserve attention. Part of the explanation may lie in the sequential nature of crisis decision suggested in Table 1. Having decided to make a positive response on Sunday, having decided to undertake military action on Monday, and having received overwhelmingly positive reinforcement for these decisions, the additional and admittedly costly commitment of ground forces could be made without much explicit attention being given to value relevancies. Of course, it might be maintained that the explicit goal of ensuring the accomplishment of the military mission *implied* the importance of all previously considered values. Nevertheless, here in microcosm may be an example of the commonly asserted tendency for agencies to become "bureaucratized" (i.e., to become primarily oriented toward goals of survival and self-maintenance) and to lose a sense of the original values that were associated with their creation.

CRISIS AND SETTING RELATIONSHIPS

The decision-making frame of reference originally called attention to the importance of examining the relationships between the decision makers and the internal and external settings (i.e., perceived aspects of the domestic and international environments). These concerns, of course, demonstrate appreciation of the need for improved understanding of the ways in which domestic and international factors influence foreign policy decision making. In the following sections some propositions about these relationships are suggested.

Crisis and Internal Setting Relationships

Some relationships between crisis conditions and the interaction between decision makers and their internal setting are suggested in Variable Diagram 4.

Variable Diagram 4

CRISIS AND INTERNAL SETTING RELATIONSHIPS

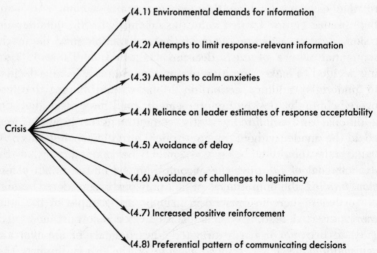

(4.1) Environmental demands for information

(4.2) Attempts to limit response-relevant information

(4.3) Attempts to calm anxieties

(4.4) Reliance on leader estimates of response acceptability

Crisis

(4.5) Avoidance of delay

(4.6) Avoidance of challenges to legitimacy

(4.7) Increased positive reinforcement

(4.8) Preferential pattern of communicating decisions

PROPOSITION 4.1: *The greater the crisis, the greater the environmental demands for information about the probable responses that political leaders may make to it.* This is illustrated in the Korean case by the clustering of reporters at the State Department on Saturday night, by their observations of the attitudes of the President and the members of his family on Sunday afternoon, by their vigil across from Blair House on Sunday and Monday evenings, by their queries about the possible commitment of ground forces or the employment of atomic weapons after Monday, and by their inquiries about the extent of the contemplated ground troop commitment on Friday. Although the information-seeking behaviors of the press are obvious in an open society such as that of the United States, there may be functional analogs for this type of crisis behavior by politically sensitive elements in more closed societies.

PROPOSITION 4.2: *The greater the crisis, the more the attempts by political leaders to limit response-relevant information transmitted to the internal setting.* Here such behaviors may be recalled as the President's order on Monday to all executive departments to refrain from comment on the Korean crisis, the refusal of Secretaries Acheson and Johnson to discuss possible courses of action with members of the Senate on the same day, the calculated avoidance of reporters after both of the Blair House conferences, the President's refusal to comment on possible additional commitments during his Thursday press conference, and the limited nature of the information about a possible ground force buildup that was revealed to Congressmen on Friday. It will be noted that this information-withholding behavior occurs before, between, and after the making of crisis decisions. The Korean case suggests that this withholding behavior can be viewed as serving several different goals; e.g., lessening the probability and strength of domestic political opposition as well as diminishing the probability of successful countermeasures by opponents in the international environment. A further objective is suggested below.

PROPOSITION 4.3: *The greater the crisis, the greater the efforts of decision makers to diminish popular anxieties.* This is illustrated by the way in which President Truman cautioned reporters in Kansas City not to exaggerate the seriousness of the Korean situation

on Sunday, by the restraint with which he responded to the emotional reception given him by the Reserve Officers Association on
Wednesday, and by his failure to give more than passing mention to Korea during his nationwide radio address on Thursday.
(The President's first extended public statement was not made
until July 19 when he appeared before the Congress.) One of the
goals sought by this anxiety-lessening behavior is suggested by
the concern expressed later by one of the President's advisers that
the Communist attack in Korea might evoke irresistible popular
pressures in the United States to go to war with the Soviet Union.
Thus the anticipation that the force of public opinion might set in
motion an undesirable train of events seems likely to have influenced
the behavior of the decision makers in this case.

The foregoing observation is consonant with PROPOSITION 4:4:
*The greater the crisis, the greater the reliance upon the political
leader's estimate of the domestic acceptability of a response.* The
available record of the Korean decision reveals that apparently no
explicit consideration was given to the domestic political implications of an American military engagement in Korea during the
Blair House conferences. The President's refusal to entertain discussion of this during the second conference on Monday and
his acceptance of complete personal responsibility for the domestic
reaction to the air-sea decision provides a vivid example of this
proposition. Thus, in crisis, the most authoritative political leader
in a decision-making group becomes its main link with the political
aspects of its internal setting. It can be hypothesized further
that the entire political learning experience of a democratic politician, at least, in a sense prepares him for just such a moment of
crisis when his long-cultivated ability to estimate popular reactions
to his behavior becomes a key factor both in his willingness to act
and in the content of his action. It is not surprising, then, that the
President rather abruptly foreclosed discussion of domestic politics by his advisers, none of whom had remotely comparable
political experience.

In the Korean decision the President is not seen as being pushed
into militant decisions by a bellicose public opinion or as being
incited by war cries of a few opposition legislators. In fact, perhaps partly as the result of surprise and shortened time for coales-

cence and effective expression of public opinion, he seems almost to have been in a position of momentary suspension from it. His anticipation of what would be popularly acceptable rather than any organized expression of popular will seems to have been crucial. It is also not likely that the President merely read from the sidelines a spontaneously reached popular decision to fight in Korea that happened to parallel his own conclusions. Objectively the state of public opinion at the time the decision to intervene was made was not entirely clear. Although it will be recalled that the President found editorial opinion in agreement with his own view that a strong stand had to be taken on Monday, it will also be remembered that experienced Washington observers later in the day were predicting that Korea would have to be abandoned and that the Senate Republican Policy Committee, despite militant speeches on the Senate floor by Senators Bridges and Knowland, had decided that the fighting in Korea should not be allowed to drag the United States into war. Thus the President's action seems to have been based more upon an anticipation of public acceptance of it rather than upon a reading of public demand for it.

The same pattern of experience-based anticipation of internal setting responses rather than the existence of direct lines of influence is illustrated by the recollection of Secretary Acheson that prior to the air-sea decision on Monday, he "needed no special notification that certain Republican Senators were constantly critical." It may be that in crisis the sensitivity of authoritative decision makers to the probable critical reactions of their domestic opponents becomes somewhat heightened in this manner. On the other hand, it is doubtful that the advice of habitual critics would serve as an effective modifier of top-level behavior under crisis conditions since it is expected by dominant leaders and tends to be viewed as stemming from partisan ambitions. Probably more effective in modifying behavior under crisis conditions would be critical responses from normally supportive colleagues and friends.

PROPOSITION 4.5: *The greater the crisis, the greater the avoidance of response-inhibiting involvements.* In the Korean case this is illustrated by the President's decision to fight in Korea without prior Congressional approval. At least one consideration in the decision to avoid Congressional involvement in the precommitment

stages is suggested by Senator Connally's prediction in discussions
with the President on Monday morning that if the question
of Korean intervention were brought before the Congress, it
might encounter extended debate that would foreclose action. This
was in addition to the possibility that the fast pace of Korean
developments might make decision impracticable. Again, as with
public opinion, it was probable that the Congress would accept a
Korean decision but it was less clear that it would actually make
such a decision and make it in a timely manner. Thus the President avoided an involvement that might have limited his freedom
of action and might have delayed the prompt assistance to the
Republic of Korea that he and his advisers deemed necessary.

An empirically related but analytically separable pattern of
behavior is suggested by PROPOSITION 4.6: *The greater the crisis,
the greater the avoidance of legitimacy-challenging involvements.*
Although this is implied in Senator Connally's advice to the President to avoid Congressional involvement on Monday, it is more
clearly illustrated by Secretary Acheson's postdecisional counsel
that the President not seek a joint Congressional resolution in support of his decision to send American fighting men into Korean
combat. The objective of Secretary Acheson's advice was to avoid
a public discussion of whether or not it was right for the President
to have ordered the armed forces into combat in the way in which
he did. Through such avoidance he sought to avoid the impair-
ment of military and domestic morale under conditions where a
high degree of national sacrifice was to be anticipated. It would
be one thing for American military men to fight in Korea with the
understanding that this was a necessary outcome of decisions by
the official who had a right and the power to make them. It would
be another thing formally to expose the nation to the possible
spread of a generalized belief that the Korean commitment had
been improperly undertaken. Thus a full-scale Congressional
debate on the origins of, and appropriate response to the Korean
crisis was avoided despite Senator Taft's attempt to precipitate it
on Wednesday. An implicit consideration in the decision to avoid
challenges to the legitimacy of the executive action might have
been to avoid formal recognition of criticisms of past Administration decisions that would construe the Korean crisis as a result of

previous "mistakes," but there is no direct evidence of it in the Korean case materials. The perceived need to maintain organizational morale under crisis seems to have been the predominant consideration in the attempts to avoid challenges to the legitimacy of the decisions that had been taken.

The Korean decision seems to provide one more example in support of the frequently asserted proposition that within certain tolerance limits intergroup conflict tends to promote intragroup solidarity. In the Korean decision, there was observed not only small group solidarity among the members of the decisional units in their conflict with the unknown group of decision makers who had launched the North Korean invasion but there was also an observed increase in solidarity between the decision makers and other groups in the American domestic environment. Translated into a researchable statement of a relationship between the decision makers and elements of their internal setting, one might suggest PROPOSITION 4.7: *The greater the crisis thrust upon the decision makers from the external environment, the greater the propensity for them to receive positive reinforcing responses to their actions from individuals and groups within the internal setting.* The propensity to express approval of leadership decisions under crisis is illustrated by the almost unanimous response of the American press and radio after Tuesday, the hundreds of approving telegrams received at the White House in a favorable ratio of ten to one, the reassurances received from political opponents such as Governor Dewey, and the enthusiastic face-to-face approval expressed to the President by the members of the Reserve Officers Association on Wednesday. The satisfaction of the decision makers with such expressions of support is evidenced by the care with which they were mentioned in the press conferences of both the President on Thursday and the Secretary of State on Wednesday. One function of such acknowledgment, of course, was probably to inhibit the growth of critical comment since it would clearly be recognized as a form of deviant behavior in terms of majority sentiment.

The Korean decision seems to reveal a pattern by which crisis decisions are communicated to politically sensitive setting elements. This can be expressed as PROPOSITION 4.8: *The greater the crisis, the more the preferential communication of crisis decisions to politically sensitive elements, the support of whom is required for effective implementation.* This is suggested by the President's concern for informing certain members of Congress about the decision of Monday and Friday before they were announced to the general public. The conflict between the State Department and General MacArthur on Monday night over the issue of the timing of the announcement of American intervention provides a further example of the importance of domestic political considerations as a factor in the publication of crisis decisions. Internationally, the same preferential sensitivity was displayed in the concern that President Chiang Kai-shek should not learn of the decision affecting Formosa from regular news sources. All these examples involve communications with potentially friendly yet powerful political elements in the environment, elements whose opposition might especially complicate the crisis response efforts. The Korean decision did not reveal preoccupation with or high sensitivity to problems of communicating the decisions to hostile elements especially in the external setting; i.e., to the Russians, the North Koreans, or possibly the Chinese. In the age of lightning-strike nuclear retaliation, however, the preferential pattern of communicating crisis decisions to crucial allies and to potentially pivotal support elements may also be paralleled by a preferential pattern of communicating decisions to enemies.

In general, the Korean decision suggests that the effects of crisis upon the relationships between the decision makers and internal setting elements are increased efforts to minimize environmental restraints upon freedom of action, intensified reliance upon predictions by the political leader about environmental reactions to possible courses of action, and greater propensity to receive positive environmental reinforcement for decisions taken. It has been hypothesized that an international crisis, thrust upon decision makers by surprise, tends to detach them from "normal" environmental constraints upon their behavior. Finally, it has been suggested that sensitivity to crucial elements of the internal political setting becomes most clear during the process of announcing the responses to crisis that have been chosen.

Crisis and External Setting Relationships

The Korean case suggests several propositions that concern the effect of crisis upon the relationships between the decision makers and other groups of national leaders in the international political environment. Some of these propositions suggest important similarities and differences, in degree if not in kind, between national and international political processes. Some of the relevant variables are summarized in Variable Diagram 5.

Variable Diagram 5

CRISIS AND EXTERNAL SETTING RELATIONSHIPS

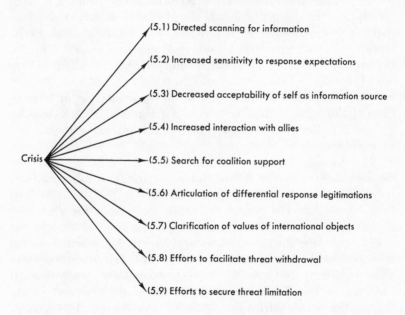

Crisis

(5.1) Directed scanning for information

(5.2) Increased sensitivity to response expectations

(5.3) Decreased acceptability of self as information source

(5.4) Increased interaction with allies

(5.5) Search for coalition support

(5.6) Articulation of differential response legitimations

(5.7) Clarification of values of international objects

(5.8) Efforts to facilitate threat withdrawal

(5.9) Efforts to secure threat limitation

A striking example of a difference between national and international political processes under crisis conditions is PROPOSITION 5.1: *The greater the crisis, the more the directed scanning of the international environment for information.* It will be recalled that

in every conference during June 24-30, the President made repeated requests for information about Soviet intentions and capabilities on a world scale. It will also be recalled that he frequently
expressed a need for an assessment as to whether the Korean
attack was an isolated event or part of a wider pattern of Soviet-
directed collusion by the enemies of the United States, including
Communist China. This presidential need for information about
potential political threats in the international environment, translated into directives that went out to American diplomatic, military, and intelligence agencies, stood in marked contrast to his
refusal to discuss the domestic political aspects of the Korean
crisis. This differential response to crisis seems to be explained
by the greater confidence of the political leader in his ability to
anticipate domestic political behavior. In the less familiar international political environment, however, the leader seemed to be
more dependent upon the expert evaluations of others. Thus he
demonstrated notable information- and evaluation-seeking behaviors. The extent of such information seeking will undoubtedly vary
with the confidence of the leader in his understanding of international politics; nevertheless, it is to be expected that it will be
greater than that devoted to seeking information about the domestic environment.

The Korean decision suggests that crisis sensitizes national
decision makers to the differential expectations of other national
political leaders about the response that they will make to it. Thus
PROPOSITION 5.2: *The greater the crisis, the greater the sensitivity
to external response expectations.* It will be recalled that in the
Korean case, the decision makers anticipated that a failure to act
in opposition to the invasion would greatly dishearten America's
allies in Europe and elsewhere. Other examples of environmental
expectations brought to the attention of the decision makers are
the prediction of a friendly diplomat after the Sunday Security
Council meeting that the United States would not act in Korea,
Ambassador Gross' emphatic report on Monday that there was
strong support for further sanctions within the United Nations,
the Korean Government's requests for additional assistance on
Monday, the Blair House estimates that Soviet leaders would be
surprised by a timely American response in Korea, and Ambas-

sador Harriman's report on the approval and relief with which the President's decisions were greeted by European leaders after Tuesday. These examples suggest that there is an international political analog to the mutual role expectations between the leader and his advisers in the decisional unit. Just as followers expect the leader to make an appropriate response to crisis, so the leaders of other concerned nations expect that national leaders confronted by crisis will make a more or less appropriate response to it. The degree of appropriateness anticipated, of course, can be expected to vary with the degree of supportiveness or hostility in the attitudes of the leaders concerned and with their definitions of the implications of the crisis for their own policies. Thus, in crisis, national decision makers were confronted with an attentive international political public. Variance in the expectations of elements of that public can be expected to have an influence upon national foreign policy decisions and provides one kind of link between international and domestic politics. It is probable that the anticipation of widespread international support for military sanctions against the aggression in Korea, although that anticipation was not based heavily on prior consultation with allies, made the Korean decision much easier than it might have been in the face of expected international disapproval.

It will be recalled, however, that the public data of the Korean case does not reveal any international demands or pressures for direct American military intervention in the Korean conflict. In fact, even the Ambassador of the Republic of Korea, when he called on the President late Monday afternoon, apparently did not request such intervention. This seems to be analogous to the apparent detachment of the decision makers from direct domestic influence processes which has been commented on above. The commitment of American military power in Korea was thus undertaken with the anticipation of a high degree of positive reinforcement and a low degree of negative reinforcement rather than under conditions where direct guarantees of such had been received from the international environment.

A corollary to anticipated international demands and expectations is increased international information seeking as expressed in PROPOSITION 5.21: *The greater the crisis, the greater the environ-*

mental demands for response information. It is likely that a high-priority mission given to all international intelligence agencies operating in Washington after June 24 was to discover what the Truman Administration would do about the attack. This is undoubtedly an international analog to the curiosity of the domestic press. A corollary, of course, is PROPOSITION 5.22: *The greater the crisis, the greater the efforts to withhold details of response execution strategies from inimical external setting elements.*

Another proposition in which information is an important variable—but which suggests a difference from internal setting relationships—is PROPOSITION 5.3: *The greater the crisis, the less the international acceptability of information about it emanating from the decision makers directly concerned.* This was recognized by American diplomats at the United Nations on Sunday when they expressed satisfaction that they would be able to use a report from the United Nations Commission on Korea as the factual basis of the projected Security Council resolution rather than the report that had been received from Ambassador Muccio. Internationally, therefore, a rather high degree of skepticism can be expected about national definitions of crisis situations. Domestically, however, the observed tendency toward greater cohesion under crisis probably tends toward the greater acceptability of information emanating from authoritative leaders. An important intervening variable in both cases undoubtedly is the degree and distribution of confidence in the reliability of the group of national leaders involved.

The propensity for crisis situations to increase the need for direct interactions among national decision makers (see Proposition 1.2) seems also to have a counterpart at the international level. Thus PROPOSITION 5.5: *The greater the crisis, the more frequent and the more direct the interactions with friendly leaders in the external setting.* This is illustrated by the personal visit of the Korean Ambassador to the President on Monday, the direct briefings given to NATO and OAS envoys by State Department officials after the announcement of Tuesday, and the approving cables sent to President Truman by political leaders and heads of state throughout the world during the remainder of the week. It is noteworthy, given the level of military technology and the degree of environmental threat at the time of the Korean decision, that President Truman and his advisers did not feel it necessary to be in direct telephonic or telegraphic communication with Premier Stalin and the Soviet leadership. Although crisis in Korea led to the intensification of interactions with allies, it did not lead to a similar increase in interactions with international political opponents. The Cuban crisis of 1962, however, suggests that the latter can also be expected to characterize international political crisis decisions of the future, at least where nuclear powers are involved.

Whereas domestically American decision makers were prepared to engage military forces in Korea without prior consultation with major political supporters or opponents, their behavior in the international environment was markedly different. From the start, working through the United Nations organization, they attempted to engage the approval and support of American policies by other national leaders both before and after the military decision. Thus PROPOSITION 5.6: *The greater the crisis, the greater the efforts to secure international collaborative support for an appropriate response.* Examples of such efforts are the efforts to secure the moral support of the United Nations on Sunday, the effort to obtain international approval and assistance through the Security Council resolution of Tuesday, the diplomatic briefings given to allies in Washington, and the instructions sent to American diplomats to secure sympathetic understanding and support after the decision to fight had been made. The efforts to obtain general agreement and support in the period prior to the decision to fight is the aspect that most clearly distinguishes the attempt to manipulate the international environment from the way in which domestic political leaders were handled. Here undoubtedly is an example of the effect of the absence of regularized patterns of authority in international politics; the necessity for persuasion is immediately recognized and efforts to persuade are promptly undertaken. Domestically the expectation of a high degree of cohesion under crisis conditions seems to make decision makers take far more support for granted.

A proposition related to the range and nature of the international involvements of the threatened decision makers is PROPOSITION 5.6: *The wider the range of international involvements undertaken in response to crisis, the wider the range of legitimations required to gain international acceptance of them.* In the Korean case this is suggested by the recognition of the decision makers that while the United Nations resolutions could serve to legitimate American military support of the Republic of Korea, they could not serve such a function for the decision to deny the island of Formosa to Chinese Communist control. The latter, they agreed, would have to be explained and accepted as a unilateral American response within the larger situational context. The need for differential legitimations to gain acceptance for varying specific commitments may be one reason why diplomats habitually insist that there are virtually no universal principles under which specific policies invariably may be subsumed.

PROPOSITION 5.7: *The greater the crisis, the greater the clarification of the values of international political objects.* During the Korean crisis the values of three international political objects for American policy became clarified and enhanced in relation to their importance on the eve of the North Korean attack. These were the value of a non-Communist Korea, the value of a non-Communist Formosa, and the value of a viable United Nations organization. The value of maintaining and strengthening a powerful Europe-centered Western Alliance was repeatedly reaffirmed during the decision-making conferences and public discussions throughout the week. Negative affect toward the Soviet Union seems also to have been heightened among the decision makers even though they took care not to arouse public hostilities toward it. The willingness of some of the decision makers to accept World War III, if necessary, at this time seems to reflect intensified negative affect toward the USSR as an international political object. This enhanced appreciation of valued aspects of the international environment under crisis seems to be correlated with the willingness to undertake measures to seek the protection of those values and with the specific means selected.

PROPOSITION 5.8: *The greater the crisis, the greater the efforts directed toward the provision of opportunities for autonomous threat withdrawal by the source of the threatening behavior.* This proposition is suggested by the efforts of American policy makers to avoid charging the Soviet Union with direct responsibility for the North Korean invasion. This was done mainly on the ground that if Soviet prestige were not directly and publicly linked to the aggression in Korea, the Soviet leadership might find it easier to halt the North Korean attack, although there was little confidence that this might happen.

A corollary of the foregoing is PROPOSITION 5.9: *The greater the crisis, the greater the efforts devoted toward minimizing the range and degree of the threat confronted.* This is suggested by the efforts of American decision makers to avoid Soviet counteraction by confining initial military action to the area south of the Thirty-eighth Parallel and later action to Korean boundaries, by assuring Russian leaders that American objectives were limited to restoring the *status quo ante,* and by seeking to avoid the enlargement of military conflict in the Far East by means of a guarantee of Formosan security. It will be noted that the threat-limiting behavior that later became the basis for an articulated doctrine of "limited war" had its immediate origins in American policy calculations during the first week of the Korean conflict as well as roots in the thinking that had produced NSC-68.

Some effects of crisis on the relationships between national decision makers and the external setting can be summarized as follows. Crisis tends to increase the need for information about and evaluations of the international political environment. It confronts decision makers not only with a self-defined need to make an appropriate response but also sensitizes them to supportive and nonsupportive expectations about their behavior by friendly and unfriendly leaders in the international environment. Although some explicit environmental calls for action can be anticipated from other national decision makers exposed to threat, these calls do not seem to contribute more to a positive response than long-term security calculations about their own nation. In manipulating the threatening environment decision makers seek opportunities both for the withdrawal and the limitation of threat.

VARIABLE INTERACTIONS AND CRISIS DECISION

Having suggested some effects of crisis upon the three main clusters of decision-making variables and having explored some of the relationships between the decision-makers and their internal and external settings, an attempt will now be made to show the interrelationships among these variables in the course of the Korean decision. In order to facilitate reference to the data, the referents of the key variables are summarized in Table 6.

Stage	A. Decisional Unit	B. Information	C. Values
I. Saturday	President Secretary of State Secretary of the Army Asst. Secretary for UN Affairs Asst. Secretary for Far Eastern Affairs Ambassador-at-large	Cable from Ambassador Muccio Press reports	Do something Support UN for peace Build moral support for US Keep alternatives open
II. Sunday	President Secretary of State Secretary of Defense Service Secretaries Joint Chiefs of Staff Under Secretary of State Asst. Secretary for UN Affairs Asst. Secretary for Far Eastern Affairs Ambassador-at-large	MacArthur memo on Formosa Confirming reports on all-out invasion Favorable Security Council action ROK Army might hold Soviet Union backed North Korean action US held military superiority over USSR US had Far Eastern military capability Invasion was like pre-WW II aggressions Acheson recommendations Direct appreciation of mutual attitudes	Do something Support UN for peace Protect lives of Americans Aid Korean ally Keep alternatives open
III. Monday	Same as above *minus* Secretary of the Navy Under Secretary of State	MacArthur report on imminent ROK collapse Acheson recommendations Air-sea support would probably be decisive Soviets would probably not intervene Gross report of strong UN sanction support Shared determination not to appease	No appeasement Support UN for peace Limit risk of war with USSR Protect US prestige as ally Limit Communist expansion in Far East Protect US interests in Japan Protect lives of Americans Keep alternatives open
IV. Thursday	President Secretary of State Secretary of Defense Service Secretaries Joint Chiefs of Staff Asst. Secretary for Far Eastern Affairs Special Ambassadors—2 Chairman, NSRB Executive Secretary, NSC	Reports on military difficulties Johnson recommendations Temperate Soviet response Overwhelmingly favorable domestic and foreign response	Accomplish military mission Limit risk of war with USSR Protect lives of Americans Avoid overcommitment
V. Friday	President Secretary of the Army Chairman, Joint Chiefs of Staff Chief of Staff of the Army General of the Army	ROK Army incapable of more than delaying action MacArthur recommendation	Prevent failure of military mission Avoid overcommitment
Friday	President Secretary of State Secretary of Defense Deputy Secretary of Defense Service Secretaries Joint Chiefs of Staff Special Ambassador	Same as immediately above Further Soviet aggression not imminent Two divisions probably adequate	Prevent failure of military mission Avoid overcommitment

D. Alternatives	E. Decisions	F. Reinforcement
Do something vs. await more information	To call for a Security Council Meeting	Prompt supporting UN action (June 25)
Accept or reject Acheson recommendations	To adopt a strong posture of resistance To speed military supplies to the ROK To give military cover to the evacuation To await further flouting of the UN To delay a decision on Formosa To send a reconnaissance party to Korea	Coinciding editorial opinion on firm posture (June 26)
Accept or reject Acheson recommendations	To commit air-sea forces in ROK To neutralize Formosa To strengthen the military in the Philippines To speed military aid to Indochina To report American actions to the UN	Overwhelming favorable Congressional, domestic, and international approval (June 27-28) Temperate Soviet response (June 29)
Accept or reject Johnson recommendations	To extend air-sea operations to North Korea To employ service troops in ROK To commit combat troops to the Pusan area To defend and reconsider if Russians engage	Unfavorable response from MacArthur as being inadequate (June 30)
Accept or reject MacArthur recommendations	To commit one RCT in the combat area To delay decision on two-division buildup	Approval by full meeting of presidential advisers (June 30)
Accept or reject MacArthur recommendations	To give General MacArthur full authority to employ combat troops under his command	Congressional and press acceptance as virtually inevitable (June 30)

Table 6

DECISION-MAKING VARIABLES AND THE KOREAN DECISION

It is now important to recall the notion of crisis decision stages that was suggested at the beginning of this chapter: These stages, it will be recalled, were I—Stimulus categorization and establishment of a general framework of response; II—Determination of shared willingness to make a positive response and of capabilities for making such a response; III—Articulation of positive response(s) and decision to commit limited resources; and, IV—Progressive expansion of the amount and kind of committed resources. The following analysis will take each of these stages in turn as a dependent variable and will show the relationship of the decision-making variables to them as independent variables. In other words, the interaction of the decision-making variables will be treated as one kind of explanation of why the component stages of the Korean decision emerged as they did. Thus the following complex propositional statements are advanced as an interrelated set of hypotheses based on the empirical data of the Korean decision which may be examined against other crisis decisions. In relating these propositions to the Korean case, the reader will find it helpful to refer both to Table 6 and to the relevant portions of the narrative.

STAGE I (Decision 1): *Stimulus Categorization and Establishment of a General Framework of Response.* The more the surprise and the greater the appreciated range of potential threat to values; the smaller, the more specialized, the more the shared learning experiences of, and the more authoritative the decision-making group; the more limited the information about the extent of the threat; and the less the conflict over values including that of action rather than inaction—the more likely is the threat to be categorized with similar threats of past experience and responded to in terms of a general framework of past responses in such a way that costs are kept low and alternative courses of action are kept open.

STAGE II (Decision 2): *Determination of Shared Willingness to Make a Positive Response and of Capabilities to Act.* The stronger the expressed leader commitment to the value of making a positive response; the more the leader permissiveness in eliciting the attitudes of his subordinates in open deliberation; the more incoming information indicates continued seriousness of threat but is still regarded as an insufficient base from which to predict its full extent; and the more shared past experience leads to an expectation of extreme negative reinforcement of failure to make a positive response to the potential threat—the stronger the shared willingness to make a positive crisis response. Also, the greater the expertise of the members of the decisional unit in assessing response capabilities and the more information indicates both available resources for a wide range of responses and relative preponderance of strength over potential opponents—the greater the confidence in response capabilities. Furthermore, the greater the confidence in response capabilities, the stronger the commitment to the value of positive response.

STAGE III (Decision 3): *Articulation of a Specific Costly Response and Decision to Commit New, Limited Resources.* The greater the shared determination to make a positive response and the greater the confidence in general response capabilities; the less the variation in the membership of the decision-making group; the more incoming information indicates the imminent loss of the opportunity to protect threatened values; the greater the proliferation of values recognized as being threatened in addition to the basic goal-means value complex evoked by the crisis; the greater the negative reinforcement expected to result from inaction; the greater the anticipated internal and external acceptability of positive action; and the greater the felt need to conserve resources in order to cope with the possible proliferation of threats—the greater the propensity to recommend and to accept a limited but costly commitment of new resources in response to crisis.

STAGE IV (Decisions 4, 5, and 6): *Progressive Expansion of the Amount and Kind of Committed Resources.* The greater the positive internal and exernal setting reinforcement of prior costly but limited responses to crisis; the less variable the decisional units in terms of new members; the more incoming information indicates inadequacy of existing resistances to threat; and, the less the anticipated negative internal and external setting reinforcements for an expanded involvement—the greater the propensity to increase the amount and kind of committed resources.

In some such sequential process of interacting variables as suggested above, the Korean decision was made. As skill in decision-making analysis increases, and as other cases are studied, it may be possible to give both more satisfactory and more parsimonious explanations for decisional processes. However adequate the reader may regard the complex propositional statements that have just been considered as an analytical explanation of why the Korean decision was made, it will be noted that they are far more economical and parsimonious an explanation than the hundreds of descriptive statements that comprise the narrative reconstruction of how the decision was made. The future task of decision-making analysis will be to identify and to relate with ever greater precision and parsimony the crucial variables that will eventually permit a high degree of predictability in the analysis of foreign policy decisions. In this task the effort above represents neither the first nor the last attempt to analyze the Korean decision. Hopefully the narrative of the Korean decision can be improved and returned to again and again with deepened insight.

Before turning briefly to the consideration of some implications of the Korean decision for the execution of foreign policy decisions once they have been taken, there are two salient characteristics of the decision as revealed both in the narrative and in Table 6 that deserve comment. These are (1) that the decision makers were confronted with single sets of proposed courses of action rather than with conflicting alternatives; and, (2) that these recommended courses of action were accepted with minimal conflict. As a response to crisis, the Korean decision might thus be characerized as a *high-consensus decision*. The elements of a high-consensus crisis decision as illustrated by the Korean case appear to be minimal conflict among decision makers over categorization of the stimulus event ("aggression"); prediction of the consequences of the threat if allowed to proceed unhampered to conclusion ("world war"); evaluation of event consequences (successful aggression would mean the collapse of valued collective security arrangements that had been built since 1945); capacity for action ("They came right down under the nose of the largest concentration of American military power outside the United States");

amount of capacity required (first air and naval support and then two divisions were thought to be adequate); willingness to act (there was "the complete, almost unspoken acceptance on the part of everyone that whatever had to be done to meet this aggression had to be done"); competence to act ("You have the right to do it as Commander-in-Chief and under the U.N. Charter"); political acceptability of action ("I'll handle the political affairs"); and the probable success of the action to be taken (the North Koreans could be defeated rather easily and the Russians and the Chinese would probably not intervene).

The Korean decision suggests that a high-consensus crisis decision is a function of strong organizational leadership, the ability to form relatively constant *ad hoc* decisional units, shared learning among members, and short anticipated time for decision. Thus it is suggested that: *The stronger the organizational leadership, the less the variability in decisional unit membership, the more the shared learning of unit members with respect to the issue for decision, and the less tolerable the decisional delay—the less the variability of information and values supplied from within the unit, the less the articulation of alternative courses of action, and the greater the probability of acceptance of single courses of action that are anticipated to win leader approval.*

DECISION PROPERTIES AND ADMINISTRATIVE EXECUTION

The Korean case suggests the fruitfulness of introducing into foreign policy decision-making analysis some propositions that link properties of decisions with problems of their execution by large-scale governmental organizations. The importance of such a concern is illustrated by the dismay experienced by State Department officials early Monday evening that pilots of General MacArthur's command had not attacked the aggressor tanks in the Seoul area as part of their mission to cover the evacuation of Americans. It will be recalled that although such behavior had been expected and approved during the Sunday Blair House conference, General Bradley had opposed the inclusion of specific orders about combat action in directives sent to the Far East since he expected that combat strikes would be made as necessary without explicit authorization and because he did not wish further to encourage expected fighter-pilot combativeness. The problem is further illustrated by the concern of one of the Blair House conferees that the oral consensuses reached in neither of the two major deliberations had been reduced to written form. The Korean case thus suggests PROPOSITION 6.1: *The less precise the specification of behaviors expected to follow a decision that has been taken, the greater the variance between actual and anticipated behavior.*

The tolerance for such variance will undoubtedly vary with the degree of punishment expected to follow faulty decisional execution. Thus PROPOSITION 6.2: *The greater the degree of negative reinforcement expected to follow faulty decisional execution, the greater the precision with which expected behaviors are specified.* In the Korean case probably the sense of general military superiority over the Soviet Union contributed to failure both to define or to limit the extent of combat action expected of American aircraft after the Sunday conference and to specify contingency behaviors expected in the event of Soviet counterintervention after the Monday decisions. It will be recalled that as the costs of the Korean commitment became clearer later in the week, specific instructions were included as to the expected American military response to Russian intervention.

A corollary to the above is PROPOSITION 6.3: *The less the negative reinforcement expected to follow faulty execution, the greater the delegation of command and control functions over decisional execution.* The high tolerance for imprecise execution of the Korean decision is illustrated by the fact that General MacArthur on his own authority ordered the extension of American air and naval action into North Korea about ten hours before this was approved by a meeting of the National Security Council. In this case the General correctly anticipated the acceptance of recommendations to remove the hampering restrictions on military action and demonstrated a degree of initiative expected of a field commander. But tolerance for such variation becomes much less under conditions where high negative reinforcements for imprecision are anticipated. President Kennedy, for example, seems to have taken virtually direct charge of boarding operations of Soviet ships during the naval blockade of Cuba in the crisis of 1962.

Thus under crisis conditions, the degree of precision with which expected behaviors are specified, the range of contingency behaviors that are explicitly recognized in decisional directives and the tolerance for imprecise execution expressed in delegation of command and control functions, can be expected to vary with the degree of negative reinforcement anticipated to be associated with imprecise decisional execution.

This chapter has been devoted to an empirical analysis of the Korean decision. An attempt has been made to create on the basis of the case materials some propositions that would explore the impact of crisis upon the variables of the decision-making framework, the ways in which crisis affects the relationships between the decision makers and their internal and external settings, the interaction of variables in a stage-like progression of decisions to cope with crisis conditions, and the properties of decisions as they affect decisional implementation.

PART V

NORMATIVE ANALYSIS

CHAPTER 12

EVALUATION

Thus far this book has presented a narrative description and an empirical propositional analysis of the Korean decision. This chapter explores a different kind of treatment of the case materials—evaluative analysis.[1]

For several reasons an attempt at evaluative analysis seems to be an appropriate task for the political scientist even in the primitive initial stages of developing a methodology for decision-making studies. The first reason is that normative analysis has been a traditional concern of political scientists and there would seem to be no

---

1. In thinking about the subject of this chapter I have found most helpful Abraham T. Edel, *Method in Ethical Theory* (London: Routledge and Kegan Paul, 1963).

necessary reason to abandon it now. Evaluative concepts such as "right" and "wrong," "good" and "bad," "ought" and "ought not," have engaged the interests of students of politics over the centuries as they have attempted to contribute to the creation of more favorable conditions of human life. Just because such concepts have been used to justify torture and murder (as well as to urge men toward peace and freedom) does not seem sufficient reason to discard them now as tools of analysis and action. Like all concepts, normative concepts simply can have both facilitating and inhibiting implications for the discovery and application of useful knowledge.

In the second place, the political scientist can hardly be insensitive to the fact that he is surrounded by a lively human interest in normative questions. One of the first queries directed at him in the course of an ordinary conversation about something like the Korean decision is, "Was it a *good* decision?" "Was it *right* that they did that?" Unless the political scientist is to ignore the question, or to refer the inquirer to some kind of normative counseling service, or somewhat irresponsibly but often very beneficially to advise the questioner to judge for himself, then he needs to devote some thought to problems and methods of evaluative analysis.

Furthermore, the very logic underlying decision-making analysis virtually demands renewed interest in judgments about the achievement of alternative states of affairs. If decision makers in fact have no choice about what they decide and thus are beyond the pale of critical evaluation, then it is a questionable advance to move the basis for understanding the determinants of foreign policy from macro-systemic or institutional variables to the behavior of concrete individuals in specified decisional units. If meaningful political choice is possible, as decision-making analysis implies, then political man can hardly escape evaluative scrutiny of his actions. This abandonment of judgment is not likely to happen in the world of political action and it would undoubtedly be a real loss if discontinued in the world of scholarly political analysis.

The question then appears to be not whether normative evaluation deserves a place in decision-making analysis but rather how it is to be accomplished. The remainder of this chapter is an exploratory search for some answers to this question. Presumably, if the narrative description and empirical propositional analysis have been done well this will aid the evaluative effort, in part because values usually have empirical correlates and implications.

EXPLORATIONS IN EVALUATIVE METHOD

By evaluation is meant the judgment (assignment of values to) actual or potential empirical states of affairs in terms of certain criteria. The immediate objectives of scholarly evaluation in politics are to improve skills in normative analysis. Longer-range objectives, either explicit or implicit, are to increase the probability of the occurrence of valued behavior and to decrease the probability of the occurrence of disvalued behavior. Other social actors may have different purposes; presumably the motives behind the evaluative acts of contending political leaders are often to discredit and to defeat as well as to improve.

Two questions are central to any evaluation; what to evaluate and what criteria to employ. Ethical theorists usually respond to the first question by describing the scope of evaluation as "unrestricted"; by this they mean that there is a hypothetically infinite range of things that might be evaluated, including the evaluative act itself. In reply to the second question ethical theorists remind us somewhat despairingly of the ever-present possibility of the "infinite reduction" of evaluative criteria: that is, if we establish certain criteria for judging the Korean decision we are open to the challenge as to what criteria underlie the selection of these particular criteria, and so on *ad infinitum.*

If we are thus faced with an infinite range of evaluative possibilities and a potentially infinite range of evaluative criteria, how then are we to proceed in evaluating a decision such as the Korean decision with some degree of intellectual rigor and social responsibility? In order to narrow the range of hypothetically infinite evaluative possibilities, the student of political decisions, like the decision makers themselves, obviously must choose and live at least for a while with his choices. But to meet the criterion of intellectual rigor (tight integration of ideas that is intersubjectively reproducible) he would do well to approach his task with some degree of relatively nonarbitrary method. Alternatively, he might let his personal and professional intuitions ramble over the Korean case materials, praising the desirable and condemning the distasteful. No behavioral scientist with respect for clinical intuition and for creative thought in the arts as well as the sciences need shrink from employing such a method for identifying normative problems and for defining evaluative criteria. But is there not a more explicit and less idio-syncratic—if not a better—way?

One starting point for the development of evaluative method in decision-making analysis is suggested by studies of "ordinary language" that have been done by ethical theorists in philosophy. That is, rather than impose from outside a set of evaluative criteria that has been created out of professional polemics in political science, we might begin with the ordinary language of moral discourse that is revealed by the Korean case materials themselves. This would mean that we would do a normative propositional inventory of the case at a low level of abstraction, keeping close to the language of the decision makers and other relevant social actors.

There is much to recommend such a procedure as a point of departure. Undoubtedly in the natural world of political decision making there have been created and transmitted from generation to generation a partially stable and partially changing set of norms by which those in socially responsible positions evaluate political be-havior—their own and that of others. Presumably such judgmental criteria have differed from age to age both within and across cul-tures. And presumably world history has also seen the learning of common norms through processes that have characterized the diffu-sion of other elements of world culture. This means that in probing the universe of evaluative discourse of political decision makers and their critics, the analyst is beginning at a relatively nonarbitrary, experientially tested, and relatively responsible point.

However, no independent student of political behavior would consider it responsible to close inquiry at that point. Thus we will wish also to explore briefly the possibility of drawing evaluative cri-teria from at least two other sources: some standards of judgment commonly employed in political science; and, a system of philo-sophical, religious, or ethical thought. Finally, the writer will take responsibility for presenting his own evaluation of the Korean decision.

NORMATIVE INVENTORY OF THE CASE MATERIALS

In reviewing the Korean case for judgmental statements it will be useful to distinguish between the decision makers and their domestic critics, on the one hand, and their foreign supporters and critics on the other. This will permit the analysis and comparison of two realms of normative discourse—the domestic and the international.

One of the most striking aspects of the Korean case is the high degree of satisfaction and sense of moral rightness shared by the decision makers and the high approbation of the decision expressed by other American leaders. For this reason the Korean decision may not be as fruitful for the generation of normative criteria for decision-making analysis as a more contentious one. Moral conflict can sharpen as well as dull perceptiveness.

Against the background of these considerations let us review some of the major normative propositions related to the Korean decision.

NORMATIVE PROPOSITION 1. *The President and his advisers were right in opposing an aggressive act which, if unopposed, would have increased the probability of world war.*

In the President's view the Korean decision was unquestionably just since it served moral principles of right and wrong stretching back in history through Christian times to classical antiquity.[2] Human history had shown unequivocally that it was right to resist physical aggression of the strong against the weak. The history of the 1930's provided but a fresh illustration of how aggressive appetites whetted by successful small-scale assaults would lead to war.

Thus, for American policy makers the decision to repel the North Korean invasion was right since it sought a noble end—world peace —and since it satisfied a moral imperative of history: no appeasement of aggression. The sense of moral imperative is suggested by the view of Assistant Secretary Rusk that "the Korean decision was in the process of being made for an entire generation since Manchuria."[3] It is also implied in Secretary Pace's view that the great

---

2. President Truman, Interview, July 30, 1957.
3. Assistant Secretary Rusk, Interview, August 22, 1955.

significance of the Korean decision lay in the fact that "for the first time since its emergence as a world power the American nation very consciously and deliberately chose to shed its blood"[4] in meeting the responsibilities of leadership.

No one who participated in making the Korean decision thought it was wrong. Neither did most domestic political opponents or foreign allies.

NORMATIVE PROPOSITION 2. *The President and his advisers were wrong in the Korean decision because they undertook military intervention in a civil war on behalf of a reprehensible government and violated the principle of national sovereignty.*

This will be recognized as a criticism arising primarily in the international setting and representing basically a Soviet Communist judgment of the decision. In the views of Communist spokesmen, the Government of the Republic of Korea was not a legitimate one since it had been established through the exclusion of Communist elements who alone allegedly stood for the interests of the Korean people. Regardless of how the Korean fighting began—North Korean and other Communist propagandists first portrayed it without foundation in fact as a result of South Korean provocation undertaken with American encouragement—the Communist view held that it was a just "people's war of national liberation." The conflict was thus portrayed as a legitimate struggle of the Korean people against "colonialism," "imperialism," and "reaction," and in favor of "national independence" and "democracy." External interference by Americans in this allegedly just civil war, significantly termed "American aggression," was thus judged as wrong and violative of the most fundamental principles of national self-determination. The general Communist view was that it was not "revolutionary wars of national liberation" led by Communists that threatened world peace but rather American aggressiveness in interfering in the internal affairs of other peoples. In this vein, one nationalist Korean argument somewhat sympathetic to Communism has held that the United States was wrong in resisting the North Korean invasion since it prevented the rapid reunification of Korea that a successful North Korean invasion would have accomplished.

In fact, however, most citizens of the Republic of Korea wel-

---

4. Secretary Pace, Interview, October 24, 1955.

comed American and United Nations military intervention. They did not value reunification so highly that they would pay any price for it. The image of North Korean Communism as an alien Stalinist imposition, the betrayal of faith in peaceful unification involved in the North Korean invasion, and crude and brutal treatment of various sections of the populace in occupied areas, served to coalesce Korean opinion strongly in favor of American support for national survival.

NORMATIVE PROPOSITION 3. *The Korean decision was right, but the President and his advisers were wrong in that their prior behavior encouraged the act of aggression in the first place.*

This judgment was articulated by domestic critics of the Truman administration who variously cited American policy toward China, Secretary Acheson's Press Club speech of January 1950, Senator Connally's interview of May 1950, the existence of intelligence warnings of a possible North Korean invasion, and the inadequate defense budget in support of their position. A few went further to identify the sources of error as a certain "softness toward Communism" expressed in part by the infiltration of Communist sympathizers in decision-making positions, but this was neither proven nor essential to the argument of pre-crisis error.

In general, few of the decision makers were willing to admit of any error in the sequence of events that led up to the North Korean invasion. In Secretary Acheson's view American policy in Asia had been accurately calibrated to the military, economic, and political power potential for execution. He argued that if the Joint Chiefs of Staff could not agree to guarantee the defense of Taiwan against invasion, then American diplomacy could not do so. Furthermore, he argued that the Administration could not give expressions of support to Korea that outran Congressional willingness to give them material backing, citing the embarrassing defeat of the Korean aid bill on January 19, 1950, as an illustration. In his view that event was as important for subsequent happenings in Korea as anything that he had said or done. Although this question has not been discussed with military leaders, perhaps most of them would have cited the high priority accorded Europe, the restraints of the defense budget, and the post-World War II slump in American public interest in military affairs as determinants of their positions with respect to the firmness of American guarantees against Communist military expansion in the Far East.

Thus from the point of view of the decision makers, whose attention in the Far East was focused primarily on China and Japan, their pre-crisis behavior was determined by a mutually restricting set of interlocking factors which precluded issuance of a clear guarantee that the Republic of Korea would be defended in the event of invasion. Furthermore, retrospectively viewed, these factors appeared to them to preclude even defining the contingency of a North Korean invasion in such a way that a decision to give or not to give defensive guarantee could be taken. As Assistant Secretary Rusk later reflected, "I have often wondered whether a staff study could have been prepared in advance which would correctly deal with the contingency of a North Korean invasion."[5]

Yet when the assault came, all the reasons for not defining such a contingency and for not planning the commitment of resources fell away. America fought.

NORMATIVE PROPOSITION 4. *The Korean decision was right, but the President was wrong in deciding to order American armed forces into battle without Congressional authorization.*

This will be recalled as the criticism made particularly by Republican Senators Taft and Wherry, who argued that the President had usurped powers granted Congress by the Constitution. Other Republicans, such as Senator Knowland, argued that the President did not need such authorization. Administration spokesmen argued that historical precedent, obligations under the United Nations Charter, and the need for a quick decision justified the Presidential initiative. Furthermore, some of the decision makers felt that exposure of the possibility of military intervention to Congressional debate would give a forum to Administration critics and do serious damage to national morale, especially to that of the military. One wonders what in fact might have happened if the President had appeared before a joint session of Congress on the night of June 26 to ask for approval of military force to support United Nations intervention against North Korean aggression. Presumably the President considered it not an attractive risk.

NORMATIVE PROPOSITION 5. *The Korean decision is an example of American government at its best.*

---

5. Assistant Secretary Rusk, Interview, August 22, 1955.

Most of the officials who participated in the decision expressed a high degree of satisfaction with the processes by which it was reached. "Democracy here proved to be strong," reflected Secretary Pace. "Weakness is not inherent in it. You can have it either way. It can act with division and slowness or it can act swiftly and decisively. I think Korea illustrated the latter."[6] Ambassador Jessup considered the decision to be "an extraordinary example of effective government in action" that illustrated the strength of the American governmental system. It showed that a government that was often "bogged down in endless wrangles" could respond to crisis "without shilly-shallying."[7] Assistant Secretary Rusk cited the speed and unanimity with which the President and his advisers acted as real strengths of the decision. He also pointed to excellent executive-legislative and civilian-military cooperation.

All of the participants paid tribute to the decisive leadership of the President. "The country does not sufficiently understand nor appreciate the lonely and awful role of the President in decisions of this sort," Secretary Rusk later explained. He continued, "This kind of decision is not made *for* the President; it can be made only *by* the President."[8] In appreciation of the role of President Truman, some advisers speculated on what different presidents might have done if faced with the same situation. Ambassador Jessup reflected, "I think Teddy Roosevelt, Franklin Roosevelt, and Wilson would have responded to the challenge with Truman's vigor and determination. But probably Harding and McKinley would not have acted in the same way. There was no wavering, doubt, or timidity on the part of President Truman." Other advisers commented upon the President's "fine grasp of the sense of history" and his "keen appreciation of the role of the United Nations."

NORMATIVE PROPOSITION 6. *The Korean decision illustrates some of the real weaknesses of American government.*

Not all of the President's advisers or close observers of the decision were completely uncritical of the processes by which it was made. One participant was especially critical of the Defense Secretary's "failure to present the President with an accurate picture of the military situation. The nonrecommendatory role of the mili-

---

6. Secretary Pace, Interview, October 24, 1955.
7. Ambassador Jessup, Interview, July 28, 1955.
8. Assistant Secretary Rusk, Interview, August 22, 1955.

tary might be classic in this case except for the fact that their military assessments were almost completely wrong." The same official was critical of military estimates of situations where actual combat operations were not involved. "If you want to know what's going on, for heaven's sake don't ask the military," he advised. Specifically with respect to the Korean decision, this official thought that the military estimates of the relative capabilities of the North and South Korean forces that were presented to the President were notably inaccurate.

From the viewpoint of another official the Korean decision was "an example of real weakness of our government." The crux of this weakness as this official saw it was "lack of real intellectual intimacy among top people on political philosophy and how you conduct foreign policy." "If you can imagine two such diverse people as Acheson and Johnson on the same team," he explained, "then you can get the idea of what I'm talking about." This kind of criticism is a very deep and penetrating one, going far beyond the particular personalities involved, for it raises questions about the training, selection, and advancement of American public leaders. For example this official questions whether legal training is really appropriate preparation for learning to direct large government organizations and whether the American political system elevates to the highest positions persons with shared capacity for appreciating highly complex consequences of various courses of action.

NORMATIVE PROPOSITION 7. *The decision to respond to the attack through collective security measures under the United Nations was right.*

All except one of the officials interviewed were fully in support of the decision to respond to the aggression within the framework of the United Nations. For them, there was a sense of intrinsic rightness about support of the United Nations. Since that organization was viewed as the major instrument for world peace fashioned by man in the post-World War II era, vigorous support for it in a crisis that seemed to threaten everything it stood for, could not be bad. Additionally, and certainly of lesser importance at the highest policy levels as far as this study shows, the engagement of the United Nations in the Korean conflict was deemed correct since it promised to strengthen international support for American action.

NORMATIVE PROPOSITION 8. *The decision to respond to the attack through collective security measures under the United Nations was wrong.*

Although not represented at the Blair House conferences, one informed critic of the engagement of the United Nations in the Korean decision held that it was an unfortunate product of "fuzzy-minded idealism." In this view the North Korean aggression could have been resisted by the United States acting alone on grounds other than support of the United Nations; for example, the obligations of the United States before the world community to insure the peace and security of Japan. It was further maintained that this kind of independent action would have received wide international acceptance and understanding.

The domestic criticism of the involvement of the United Nations as a policy instrument was based not on an assessment of an intrinsic lack of value in the institution itself, but rather on an anticipated loss of American decision latitude. The resort to United Nations action was bad because it would restrict the freedom of American policy makers to pursue the interests of the United States in the Korean action. In this view, the subsequent course of the Korean War was held to confirm this anticipation.

Another source of criticism of American involvement of the United Nations was that of the Soviet Union. Soviet spokesmen argued, it will be recalled, that the United Nations action was wrong because it was taken in violation of Charter provisions that China (defined by them as Communist China) should be seated on the Security Council. The Soviet view thus held that the American action was wrong because it illegitimately engaged the United Nations in the Korean conflict.

The eight propositions identified above do not exhaust the possibilities for a normative inventory of the Korean case but hopefully they encompass most of the major issues and provide a basis for further explorations in evaluative method. One of the important implications of this inventory is that it helps to limit the scope of evaluation by directing attention to certain aspects of the Korean case. Now it will come as no surprise to political philosophers and ethical theorists that these propositions call attention to the *ends* (Normative Propositions 1 and 2) and *means* (Normative Proposi-

tions 7 and 8) of the Korean decision. But it may be somewhat less
"obvious" that attention is also directed to the *antecedents of the
occasion for decision* (Normative Proposition 3) and to the
quality of decisional processes (Normative Propositions 4, 5, and 6).
A summary of the results of the normative inventory is presented
in Table 7.

Table 7
SUMMARY OF NORMATIVE INVENTORY

Evaluator	Evaluative Aspect			
	Antecedents	Decision process	Means	Ends
Decision makers	Unavoidable	Legitimate	Appropriate	Just
Domestic critics	Avoidable	Illegitimate	Appropriate	Just
External allies	Unavoidable	Legitimate	Appropriate	Just
External critics	Avoidable	Illegitimate	Inappropriate	Unjust

Even though this summary is crude, it prompts at least three
interesting observations. First, contrast between the domestic critical
evaluations of the antecedents, decisional process, and means/ends
aspects of the Korean decision suggests that in political evaluation a
certain collapsing of time can occur (past, and possibly future, into
present) with the result that decision makers may be judged at
once both right and wrong.

Secondly, although different in substance there are interesting
parallels in the domestic and international criticisms of the Korean
decisions. Both sets of critics are agreed in focusing attention upon
the pre-crisis behavior of the decision makers. Whereas domestic
critics judged that the Truman Administration could have averted
conflict by taking a clearer stand against Communist military
expansion in Asia, the foreign Communist critics argued that American belligerency and support for an allegedly aggressive ally precipitated the war. Procedurally, whereas domestic critics protested
that the President had acted in violation of the United States Constitution, Soviet critics charged that he had acted in violation of
the United Nations Charter. These parallelisms are of interest since

they represent certain similarities between domestic and international political processes, a subject of constant interest to students of comparative and international politics.

Third, the normative inventory and its summary suggest not only categories that limit the scope of evaluation but also certain criteria of evaluation to be employed within these categories. The following questions are illustrative. *Antecedent behavior:* Was the behavior of decision makers in the pre-crisis period such as to minimize the occurrence of the crisis precipitating event? *Decisional process:* Was the response to the crisis decided in such a way as to gain widespread acceptance of the authority of the decision makers through the legitimacy of the decisional processes? *Ends:* Were the ends pursued of deep and enduring human value? *Means:* Were the means employed such as to receive widespread acceptance as being appropriate for the ends sought?

APPLICATION OF SOME COMMON CRITERIA OF POLITICAL EVALUATION

Another avenue for exploration in evaluating the Korean decision is to invoke certain criteria that are commonly employed, either explicitly or implicitly in political science analyses. This approach differs from that of the normative inventory in that it brings to bear criteria of judgment that originate outside the Korean case. The illustrative criteria to be explored below are by no means exhaustive of those that might be drawn from the thought of contemporary political science. Neither have they been demonstrated to have a high degree of scientific reliability and validity as guides to action. There is as yet no full-scale systematization of political science knowledge for the purpose of evaluating something like the Korean decision. Yet the categories and style of analysis customarily employed can contribute to our evaluative effort.

Attainability of Ends

A common question about a political act is whether the goals sought lay within the range of reasonable accomplishment. Quite aside from the intrinsic value of the ends themselves, an issue in itself, the political scientist often asks whether the goals were objectively attainable. If not, and if the political actor continues to pursue them to the detriment of other values, such as loss of support or defeat, then he is charged with misjudgment. On the other hand, the political actor is criticized if he fails to appreciate and to strive for goals deemed worthy that are asserted to be achievable. Thus political actors are subjected to judgments about excessive or inadequate goal-striving in addition to judgments about the intrinsic value of the ends pursued. Furthermore it might be argued that although the political actors pursued attainable ends, the costs of reaching them were too high. Applied to the Korean decision it might be said that the long-range goal of world peace was laudable, that the short-range goal of limiting conflict in Korea was right, and that the immediate goal of repelling the North Korean invaders to the Thirty-eighth Parallel lay within the scope of practical attainment. On the other hand, if the American decision makers had decided not to fight, it might be argued that they had failed to appreciate the attainability of a short-range goal that would contribute to the realization of a highly valued end. If they had decided to engage the Soviet Union in general war rather than to make a limited response in Korea, they would certainly have been judged as pursuing an excessively costly, if not unattainable, end.

Suitability of Means

Another set of evaluative questions focuses not only upon the intrinsic value of the means employed to achieve desired ends but also upon the problem of whether the means selected actually permitted goal attainment. Thus, for example, it might be judged that bad means were employed for good ends, that good means were used for bad ends, and that either good or bad means were simply effective or ineffective for goal accomplishment. Appreciation of the range of means objectively available would also be an evaluative criterion. A criterion sometimes proposed is that decision makers should not sacrifice higher values by shrinking from employing objectively required means that in themselves might be noxious.

In the Korean decision it might be judged that although the

death-dealing application of American military power was not good in itself, it served intrinsically good ends and constituted the only objectively available means that promised successfully to repel the North Korean invasion. More specifically it might be judged that American policy makers were to be commended since they proceeded only under conditions of demonstrated inefficacy from less noxious to more noxious means toward their goal—e.g., from the Security Council resolution, to arms aid, to air-sea support, and to ground combat. All other things held constant, they would have been judged in error if they had stopped short of measures necessary to reach their goals. From the American combat soldier's point of view, however, the piecemeal commitment of inadequately trained American units against an underestimated and superior enemy force did not represent a laudable employment of means. On the other hand, the employment of American atomic weapons against North Korean forces would certainly have been judged as the use of inappropriate means that jeopardized good ends. So, for different reasons, would limiting American responses to Security Council debate.

Timeliness and Flexibility of Response

Although analytically separable, these two criteria may usefully be considered in combination. Timeliness is usually viewed as an important criterion for decisional evaluation; the political actor can be seen as jeopardizing his goals by acting too soon or too late, as well as not at all. Furthermore, in the course of solving a political problem or set of them, political actors are usually judged by the degree of appropriate flexibility that they exhibit in pursuing their objectives. By flexibility is commonly meant willingness to modify or to abandon old ends and means as they are found to be unappropriate for coping with new situations.

Here again, as with most criteria of political evaluation, there are subtle judgments to be made that often hinge upon conceptions of value in the specific case. Thus rigidity, relative inflexibility, can sometimes be useful in protecting values while relatively high flexibility, bordering on "opportunism," can sacrifice them. Each individual case requires analysis.

President Truman and his advisers seem to have met the criteria of timeliness and flexibility in the Korean decision. Perhaps the significance of the President's decision lay as much in its immediate effect upon South Korean morale as in its direct military effects upon the combat situation. It will be recalled that small American infantry units did not engage in combat until July 7. This is not to discount the immediate effects of growing Air Force pressure on North Korean aircraft, tanks, troops and transportation or the Navy's deterrence of further North Korean amphibious operations. If the President had delayed as much as a week the Republic of Korea might well have collapsed and have been overrun.

The American policy makers were notably flexible in their response. They were willing to commit the United States for the first time in history to an explicitly defined collective security action under the auspices of an international organization. Then they were willing to make progressively more costly commitments of American strength to achieve their objectives in repelling the attack. If the President and his advisers had not agreed to the commitment of American ground forces in response to General Mac-Arthur's assessment of their indispensability, then the decision makers undoubtedly would have been judged as harmfully inflexible.

To step briefly outside the bounds of the case, but to illustrate questions that might be raised in flexibility analysis, it might be asked whether the American decisions of early fall 1950 that abandoned the initial objective of restoring the status quo of the Thirty-eighth Parallel in favor of the invasion and occupation of North Korea did not border upon opportunistic flexibility. If the earlier limited objective had been adhered to, would not the basic collective security contribution to world peace have been made, would not a widened conflict with China have been avoided, and would not tens of thousands of lives have been saved?

Accuracy of Calculated Support

Another common criterion for evaluation is the extent to which political leaders accurately estimate the degree of potential support for and opposition to their actions. Thus leaders might select the right means for the right ends at the right time but be wrong because they miscalculated the degree of potential support for their actions. The specific nature of potential supporters and opponents differs with the type of political system. Harold Guetzkow has suggested "decision validators" as an appropriate and neutral concept to describe them.

The reasons why miscalculated support is deemed bad are fairly obvious: the ends sought will not be reached; and, the decision maker may lose his position with its potential for achieving other goals. Also, although perhaps not as obvious, leaders can be judged for not perceiving bases of support for ends they would wish to seek or could accept; thus they can be judged not only for failing to realize intrinsically valuable goals within the realm of supportable accomplishment but for exposing themseves to being swept aside by those who could. Again, we encounter the complexities of evaluation. Sometimes, for example, leaders might be judged right in actions that did not receive support, but this is, of course, a different issue from accuracy of calculation.

One of the most salient characteristics of the Korean decision was the accuracy with which President Truman estimated the domestic acceptability of his decision. How different a moment in American history it would have been if the Congress had promptly moved to impeach him for the decision. The President and his advisers were also accurate in their perception of the degree of international support the decision would receive. What if the Security Council had rejected American action?

Accuracy of Relative Estimates of Own Capabilities
Versus Opponents' Capabilities and Intentions

Political leaders are also judged in the accuracy with which they estimate the relative strength of their opponents to resist the pursuit of their goals. Another criterion is accuracy in estimating opponent intentions.

In the Korean case, there seem to have been miscalculations of the intention of the North Korean leaders to invade, the relative strengths of the North and South Korean forces, the efficacy of

American airpower against North Korean ground power, and the extent of the buildup of American ground forces that would be necessary for successful counteroffensive action.

On the other hand, the decision makers were notably correct in estimating that neither the Soviet Union nor Communist China would counterintervene and were apparently correct in calculating that the forces available for resistance to aggression were to some extent superior to those available to its likely supporters. The policy makers were also correct in estimating that the military "neutralization" of Formosa would prevent an invasion of the island.

The Long-Term Consequences of Present Actions

One criterion often invoked in political evaluation is that of the accuracy with which decision makers predict and the ease with which they assess the long-range consequences of action. From this viewpoint, it is possible to be right in the short run and wrong in the long run, or vice versa. This kind of evaluation includes an assessment of the objective consequences of behavior whether appreciated by the decision makers or not.

Generally speaking the shorter the period between decision and evaluative analysis, the more questionable this kind of analysis. On the other hand, the longer the evaluative gap, the greater the likelihood of the intrusion of alien influences that obscure the direct contribution of the decision makers to the more distant consequences of their choices.

For the Korean decision one would have to step outside the bounds of the case materials themselves for this kind of analysis and would have to recognize the limitations of less than twenty years perspective at this point. Some vital questions here would seem to be, "Did the Korean decision really contribute to the eventual elimination of wars by national armed forces in world politics?" "Did it increase the probability of future wars?" "Or did it in fact make relatively little difference either way?"

On the one hand it might be argued that the Korean decision has had an inhibiting effect together with the existence of nuclear weapons upon the scale of international conflict that otherwise would have obtained in the past decade and a half. Since the Korean War doctrinal emphasis in the Communist international revolutionary movement upon the independent efforts of national revolutionaries, aided morally and materially but not ordinarily by direct collective military action, may be viewed as at least partially attributable to an expectation of collective counteraction, rooted in the Korean experience. Thus expected effective resistance may have inhibited direct military invasions to reunify Germany and Vietnam. Studies of the significance of the Korean decision in national Communist calculations could help to clarify this. Possibly the Korean decision has made some contribution, however slight, toward a potential shift in the world pattern of conflict from international to intranational war and from limited to expanded conflict coalitions. The implications of these shifts, if they are indeed trends, for the scale of world conflict, however, are ambiguous. Although the propensity to diminish the incidence of international war may lower the scale of conflict, the tendency to collectivize conflict once initiated may tend to raise it.

The assessment of the consequences of the Korean decision is blurred by the subsequent Chinese Communist intervention and ensuing stalemate of the contending armies in nearly the original geographical position in which fighting began. Thus the "lesson" of the Korean War that is propounded in Communist histories and party indoctrination materials is that national resistance and "proletarian internationalist" collaboration can defeat "imperialist aggression." In this view defensive revolutionary violence successfully resists counterrevolutionary aggressive violence—an approximate reversal of the non-Communist view that counterviolence in the service of peace inhibits aggression. Taking the Korean War as a whole, both coalitions of contenders and supporters thus derive at least partially valid support for their ideological positions, both of which include assertedly justifiable engagement in war.

Looking further outside the Korean case for events that would support a critical view, one might cite the Israeli-Egyptian, Indian-Portuguese, and Sino-Indian conflicts as subsequent examples of small-scale binational conflicts seemingly uninhibited by the lessons in collective security that the Korean decision was to provide. The subsequent engagement of unilateral and collective engagements of national forces in conflicts in Hungary, the Congo, the Dominican Republic, and Vietnam at least illustrate that the Korean decision did not successfully establish the principle of collective security action against the employment of national military forces across national boundaries. But did it establish a symbol of such action to which future statesmen seeking peace might repair and from which they might learn?

EVALUATION OF THE DECISION IN
TERMS OF AN ETHICAL SYSTEM

Another way in which to evaluate the Korean decision is to measure it against one or more of the world's great philosophical, religious, or ethical systems. This may sharpen moral sensitivities and pinpoint moral problems in ways not immediately appreciated in the case materials or in the canons of contemporary political science evaluation. Possibilities for this kind of approach may be found within the various schools of Buddhism, Christianity, Islam, Judaism, and other ethical systems. A thorough exploration of implications of the Korean decision for any one of these systems is a major task in itself but only a very brief exploration of one of them will be attempted here.

Given the fact that most of the world's ideological systems condone the taking of human life under certain conditions, that this part of human experience has found expression in Article 51 of the United Nations Charter which legitimates collective self-defense against attack, and that the rationale for the application of this mode of thought to the Korean decision has been rather fully explored, it might be more instructive to examine an ethical system not so easily reconcilable with the case materials. This system is the body of thought known as "pacificism."

In pacifist thought the Korean decision was wrong. The reasoning is simple and uncompromising: any political decision to employ the armed forces of one nation against the people or armed forces of another nation is wrong, regardless of circumstances. It is wrong because such a decision will lead to the slaughter of fellow human beings. Killing is inherently wrong; any decision which leads to killing is wrong, too.

Pacifist thought further appeals to the "lessons of history" in support of the validity of its principles, just as does the thought that underlies the acceptance of the need to kill to prevent greater killing. In pacifism, history is viewed as an escalation of the means and scale of human slaughter. Violence has begotten violence over the centuries to such an extent that contemporary man is faced with the capacity for violence to end all violence: his own extermination by weapons with the power to slay millions in an instant. Only nonviolence can really eliminate violence, it is argued. In the pacifist view, a nonviolent mode of response is a proper one even when a nation seeks by force to impose abhorrent principles upon other nations. Therefore, it was wrong to oppose Nazi Germany by force. Pacifist thought places great faith in human capacities for good to peacefully overcome evil. Pacifism has argued that even if the Nazis had overrun most of the world, eliminating millions of Jews in the process, their brutality would eventually be tempered by often unexplained processes for the expression of human revulsion and benevolence.

Pacifism is not a doctrine of moral passivity. It has two moral imperatives: do not kill; do something to eliminate evil. The pacifist is not excused from the moral responsibility to resist that which is bad. Among the range of nonlethal responses in international politics it embraces political, economic, and cultural measures.

Some partially pacifist thought distinguishes between international and domestic violence; while the former is to be unequivocally condemned the latter is to be reluctantly condoned. Thus a violent German revolution against Naziism would be judged acceptable, but an international police action against them would not. This view would condone a world of endemic revolutionary and counterrevolutionary violence within states but not between states.

Applied to the Korean decision, pure pacifism would argue that the North Korean decision to attack was wrong, that to the extent of their complicity the Russians and Chinese were also wrong, and that decisions to resist—beginning with the Republic of Korea and extending to those of nations that fought under the United Nations —were wrong too. Pacifism would argue that the number of Korean War dead would have been greatly decreased and that a victoriously militant North Korean Communism would probably become more humane and less aggressive through internal and external influences operating over a long time.

Furthermore, in order to meet the requirements of the second moral imperative, it would be argued that the United States should employ all means short of direct or indirect military action to respond to the attack and to maximize its own, Korean, and world values without violence. If these norms were followed, then President Truman and his advisers would have been restricted to such means as saving lives by evacuating Koreans most likely to be murdered by the Communists, educating the world to the facts of the initiation of the aggression and its harmful consequences, seeking international conferences including all parties to the dispute to find nonviolent modes of conflict resolution and ways to help Koreans achieve their developmental goals, and applying economic incentives and sanctions to influence Korean-Russian-Chinese behavior. If the success of the North Korean invasion coupled with the success of the Chinese Revolution led to the proliferation of domestic and international Communist violence throughout Asia, then presumably the United States should respond in the same peaceful way. Carried to its logical extreme, pacifist thought would have the United States, even though possessing the most powerful military force of its time, accept direct military subjugation by a weaker nation or coalition of nations motivated by resentment against American success in employing nonviolent methods in international politics.

There is no doubt that in 1950 a pacifist mode of response to a clear instance of military aggression was considered unacceptable, either explicitly or implicitly, by the American people and their leaders, by the Korean people and their leaders, and by the peoples and leaders of virtually all nations of the world, including the revolutionary Communist ones. Will a time come in human development when the norm of nonviolence will provide as strong and as generally acceptable a guide to action as the "no appeasement" imperative that guided the Korean decision?

INDIVIDUAL JUDGMENT

It is in the best tradition of political inquiry in a free society that in the end the individual who has conscientiously studied the problem for evaluation arrives at his own conclusions. In this process of judgment, the individual may not be satisfied with the evaluation of political actors, contemporary political science, the great ethical systems or other sources of authoritative interpretation. It is a moral imperative of free men that the individual judges as well as thinks for himself. At its best the evolving moral consensus of a free society ought to emerge out of the convergence of these independently reached judgments.

The writer accepts this challenge here and encourages each reader to do the same.

The Avoidance of Conflict

In the writer's view, the various actors involved in the outbreak of violence in Korea did not do all, or even some of the most important, things that objectively were available to them to avoid violence. In the first place, the North Korean leadership, who planned and executed the invasion of the Republic of Korea, together with those who gave them direct and indirect encouragement, were wrong in taking the initiative to kill their fellow countrymen and in contributing to the record of mass violence in human history. In the second place, the leaders of the Republic of Korea, the primary victim of aggression, did not do all that objectively lay within their capabilities to deter the invasion in the pre-attack phase. As signs of impending invasions multiplied in the spring of 1950, a nonpartisan delegation of Korean leaders led by President Rhee might have sought to mobilize world opinion against it by appearing physically before the United Nations in New York and by warning of it in direct talks with leaders in key world capitals. An imaginative, timely, and vigorous international political initiative was required and missed as Korean leaders concentrated upon domestic political struggle in the spring of 1950. South Korean leaders were also wrong in remarks favoring military means to reunify Korea since this gave the North Koreans a plausible basis for increasing the threat perceived by their followers and for bargaining for increased military support from the Soviet Union and Communist China.

Despite the limits posed by the post-World War II dismantling of the American military establishment and the lack of deep interest in Korea by a budget-conscious Congress, American leadership was also wrong in failing to appreciate sufficiently the significance of the survival and attractive development of the Republic of Korea for American values. Ambassador Dulles was one of the few exceptions to this. The failure to appraise more highly the value implications of South Korean development was accompanied by a failure to clarify before the world community the strength of American will to save the Republic of Korea from military destruction and by failures to mobilize or to create if necessary the moral, military, and material resources that would leave no doubt of American capabilities to carry such a will into action.

Except background materials such as Ambassador Dulles' speech of June 19 and Secretary Acheson's warning that the economic abandonment of the Republic of Korea would be "sheer madness," the materials of the Korea case show remarkably little attention given to the intrinsic value to the world community of the independent, noncoerced development of Korean culture and society. Relatively little emphasis was placed upon the remarkable though difficult efforts of Koreans to create an open society that would contribute to Korean and world efforts at building finer conditions of human existence without Communist or fascist regimentation. The intrinsic value of Korean society itself as well as the significance of the Korean experiment for building a future world polity were not sufficiently appreciated by American leaders.

The low value placed upon Korean experience by American decision makers and other leaders of American society can be illustrated by the fact that in the pre-1950 period, cases of individual violence in Berlin or maneuvers on the borders of divided Germany could claim front-page American attention, while full-scale infantry combat actions along the Thirty-eighth Parallel caused hardly a ripple in American public opinion.

The reasons for the failure to appreciate the significance of Korean development for American values are multiple and possibly instructive for the future. Except for dedicated missionaries, American society had produced almost no intellectuals, journalists, or scholars who could articulate and communicate the meaning of Korean-American relationships as they grew from the late nineteenth century. A Sino-Japanese-centered view of Asia prevailed among

American political and governmental leaders and among the articulate academic and journalistic elites. Furthermore, Asia as a whole took a position of pronounced secondary importance to Europe in American policy calculations and Korea suffered from the halo effect of this assessment; in addition, American appreciation of the value and potentials of Korean democracy suffered from the image cast abroad by the Rhee Administration and other Korean leaders. In some aspects the "Korean Experiment" was unsavory and not one to which men who loved freedom could point with pride and affection. All of these represent factors that could have been subject at least in the long run to purposive human manipulation in desired directions.

All these factors may help to explain but they cannot entirely excuse a lack of sensitivity to the significance of Korea in American policy that apparently prevailed among top leaders. For example, a visit to Korea by the American President prior to June 1950 might well have led to an immediate appreciation of Korea that would have reverberated downward and outward throughout American society. Short visits of this kind have had remarkable impacts upon other American leaders who have seen Korea face to face.

The judgment that the value of Korean military security was not sufficiently appreciated by American leaders is separable from, though related to, the question of whether they were adequately forewarned of the invasion. Presumably if Korea had ranked higher on the American scale of values even subtle indications of threat would have been given their attention. Hopefully some day, future historians can prepare a frequency distribution of intelligence reports referring to the possibility of a North Korean invasion of South Korea. The hypothesis of this writer is that it will show a sharply rising curve, even though discounted in evaluation, throughout the spring of 1950.

Had the protection of Korea been valued highly, these reports would have stimulated action to deter the impending invasion and would have brought American officials to raise the question of what the American response would be if the attack occurred, a question that in the absence of great perceived threat to values never was raised among top American leaders. If Korea itself had been perceived of greater significance the applicability of the collective

security principle in the event of invasion might have been made
clear before, not after, the North Korean attack. Ideally, the perceived quality of the victim of aggression is not a variable in the
doctrine of collective security, but this case suggests that it would
have been an important element in preventing the act of aggression
in the first place.

Prompt, Graduated, and Limited Response
to the North Korean Attack

The writer regretfully cannot accept the pacifist view that the
North Korean attack should not have been resisted by the armed
forces of the Republic of Korea and such international allies as they
could muster. For South Koreans a way of life was at stake: a
cherished as well as tragic past, a strife-laden but increasingly
autonomous present, and a hopeful future toward which all Koreans
could work. For Americans and others who supported the collective military action, Korea was a test of whether a revolutionary
global political movement through the action of its various sub-
components was to impose by violence its political, economic, social,
and cultural systems in piecemeal fashion upon a doubtful or
reluctant world.

The President acted promptly, giving his principal advisers full
opportunity to be heard. The decisions taken were timely and yet
graduated; one week elapsed between the response of political
protest and infantry commitment. At any point the North Koreans
might have chosen to reverse course and thus avoid a full-scale
collision with American power. They chose to press the attack and
thus to escalate the killing. The American decision makers sought
limited ends by limited means. They first sought to limit military
actions south of the Thirty-eighth Parallel and to restore the status
quo at the demarcation line. They succumbed quickly and ques-
tionably to military demands to extend air-sea action to North
Korea. Initially they did not contemplate the seizure of North
Korea. Only when the tide of battle turned decisively in their favor
did they add this objective opportunistically and disastrously to
their objectives. They also sought to limit the kind of American

military power employed. The first week of the war illustrates the taut theme that ran throughout its course—the tension between restraint and demands and opportunities for expansion. Those who confront American arms in battle might well take heed from the Korean decision and its aftermath. Unless prepared to face the full brunt of American power, they would do well to reduce the scale of violence in the very early stages of a conflict so that factors conducive to limitation may prevail over those prone to expansion.

The Failure to Seek Popular Endorsement

In retrospect, as well as in the view of critics at the time, the President was ill-advised not to seek a joint Congressional resolution in support of his decisions. Failure to do so enabled legislators clamoring for military action in June 1950 to condemn him for illegitimately engaging the United States in a war a year later. It also failed to engage more directly the representatives of the people in democracy's most agonizing decision: to kill and be killed. Eventually, with advances in computer technology, telecommunications, and identification devices such as voice printing, it may be possible to conduct national referenda on this kind of issue within hours, thus engaging the American people in direct judgment. The reasons against exposing the decisions to Congressional debate do not seem to outweigh the benefits of it. The nation was strong enough to stand some criticism of its leadership. The issue was important enough to probe deeply the extent of national consensus and determination.

In the conditions of June 24-26, 1950, the President, an experienced Senator, was probably correct in his judgment that he—not the Congress—should actually make the decision so that delay would not doom the Republic of Korea. But his judgment seems less wise in avoiding an immediate and clear test of congressional approval after the decision had been taken. In this case, overjealous defense of presidential prerogative, oversensitivity to congressional criticism, and inhibition of open consideration of domestic political implications of the decision seem to have combined to prevent a closer approximation to the democratic ideal.

Survival of an Increasingly Autonomous and Open
Korean Society in the World Community

As noted earlier, the Korean decision may be judged by its long-range implications as well as its antecedents, processes, and immediate results. The Korean decision has permitted the survival and subsequent growth of an intrinsically valuable, vigorous, creative, and responsible member of the world community of nations. In less than two decades since the tragedies of war, the Korean people in both North and South have demonstrated the resilience and tenacity that have insured national survival over the centuries. In politics, administration, economics, science, and the arts the people of the Republic of Korea have moved steadily, although not without sharp temporary setbacks, toward an open and healthy society that can contribute the fine qualities of Korean culture to world civilization and can draw creatively upon world resources for Korean development. The tasks are difficult, but little by little the pessimism and discouragement engendered by war are succumbing to hope stirred by remarkable accomplishments about which the Korean people deserve rightly to be proud.

Although it is true that the Korean decision contributed to the short-range division of Korea, it is equally true that it did not in itself make long-range reunification impossible under conditions where the needs and values of the Korean people can be freely expressed. Less than twenty years after the event, the Republic of Korea seems to be traversing a far more open and spontaneous path of development than that of its northern counterpart. It seems likely that the more open the society, the more true the expression of national values; and that the more skilled the people in meaningful political choice, the greater the probability that they will make steady and imaginative progress toward their valued goals. The continued democratic development of the Republic of Korea is thus a guarantee of eventual reunification under conditions where the desires of the vast majority of the Korean people can most adequately be met. Without the Korean decision, this would not have been possible.

Hopefully, in the retrospect of a century ahead the Korean

decision will be judged as having contributed to the goal that President Truman envisioned for it—"Every decision I made in connection with the Korean conflict had this one aim in mind: to prevent a third world war and the terrible destruction it would bring to the civilized world."[9] And yet whether such a goal will be achieved or not lies beyond the grasp of the men who made the Korean decision. Its achievement depends upon the day-to-day choices of other decision makers, in nations large and small, whose actions shape the future of the world polity.

---

9. *Memoirs*, II, 345.

PART VI

ACTION
IMPLICATIONS

CHAPTER 13

SOME IMPLICATIONS FOR CRISIS MANAGEMENT

Some knowledge is for knowledge's sake, or perhaps for the esthetic pleasure of the knowledgeable. Other knowledge is for potential use. If knowledge is to be of eventual use, then the creators and users of knowledge (if they are different persons) have to establish and maintain some kind of pattern for mutually beneficial learning. To create such a pattern, the creators and users of knowledge have to begin to take steps toward greater sharing of experience. In a large sense, this entire study represents a part of such an enterprise; the decision makers cooperated in making their experience available to the scholar and the scholar replies by reporting back to them as well as to other interested persons what he has learned. Certainly the learning process does not and should not end here, however. There should be further reactions by experienced policy makers as well as scholars to the efforts in this book; and there should be continuing, cumulative efforts by students of decision-making analysis to improve the reliability, validity and usefulness of the knowledge they seek to create. This chapter attempts briefly but explicitly to raise the question of the operational usefulness of knowledge obtained by decision-making analysis by suggesting some implications of the Korean case for the management of other foreign policy crises.

Some preliminary understandings about the limitations of what is attempted here are essential. This is not a case of the basic scientist advising the applied scientist what to do; to a large extent, the foregoing chapters have been based on the knowledge and experience of the actors involved rather than on independently determined behavioral and social science knowledge of a fundamental nature. Hopefully, the Korean case materials can be examined from such perspectives by appropriate scientists with a resulting enrichment of insight and of useful suggestions for action. Furthermore, the standpoint here is not that of the more knowledgeable scholar telling the less knowledgeable policy maker what to do. In foreign policy analysis at this point, it is more a case of the less experienced scholar suggesting to the more skilled policy maker, from whom he has learned, some of the things he has learned that may be useful in coping with situations similar to those that have been studied. Eventually, as scholars benefit from rigorous criticisms of their suggestions by policy makers, as they begin to marshal more powerfully confirmed findings from field and laboratory, and as they are able to base their suggestions on mutually supportive bodies of theory about human behavior developed within and across disciplines, the range and usefulness of their insights into foreign policy making should increase.

It might well be asked whether it is not premature and irresponsible for the student of decision-making analysis to venture suggestions of an applied nature on the basis of a single case before the emergence of a scientifically validated body of knowledge. Not only might this be harmful socially, it might be argued, like a quack doctor's prescription of an untested medication, but also it might tend to discredit decision-making analysis as a scholarly endeavor. Now these are serious questions and thoughtful men may well answer them differently. The view taken here is that international crises are of such moment to mankind that it is worth the risk of detachment by some scholars at least to venture what they consider helpful suggestions, that the potential users of such suggestions are men of such experience that they will not be easily misled by "quack" solutions, that suggestions can be responsibly made by stating limitations in their usefulness, that judicious choice can be made about suggestions that can reasonably be advanced at a given stage of knowledge, and that the intellectual integrity of decision making as an approach to the study of international politics depends upon far more than a few well meant but less than useful suggestions by a scholar seeking to utilize it.

Perhaps a set of criteria for suggesting operational implications of decision-making studies can gradually be elaborated. Initially one would suggest at least (1) that the suggestion has a clearly specified empirical base; (2) that it be stated in operational terms; and (3) that the limitations on the reliability of the suggestion be clarified insofar as they can be appreciated.

Three Implications for Crisis Management

Suggestion 1: Where information concerning the relative capabilities of contending forces is a major component of a crisis decision, decision makers are advised to broaden their understanding of the situation by calling for existing information at variance with the prevailing consensus. (Programmed information retrieval suggestion.)

The origins of this suggestion in the Korean decision lie in the persistent tendency to overestimate South Korean strength and to underestimate North Korean military capabilities, even though there was at least one accurate estimate by Ambassador Muccio on June 9 that the North Koreans held "undeniable material superiority" that would ensure a "margin of victory" in an invasion. (See Chapter 3 and Propositions 1.5 and 1.6 of Chapter 11). In the Korean decision the effect of this miscalculation was not so great as to prevent an effective response to the invasion but it did have important implications for the decision process that might be seriously disadvantageous in other decisions.

First of all, the failure to consider information pointing to the heavy assault superiority of North Korean forces may have contributed to delay in assessing more fully the costs to the United States of repelling the invasion. Possibly if North Korean power in tanks, artillery, and aircraft had been appreciated at the outset there would have been an earlier evaluation of the needs for and capabilities of committing American ground forces. Consideration might have been speeded of providing the defenders with appropriate antitank weapons that could halt the T-34 Russian tanks of the invaders. Perhaps an earlier appreciation of the need for resistance on the ground might have helped to bring about a somewhat less "piecemeal" and therefore more effective introduction of ground soldiers into combat. Better utilization of already existing, though "forgotten," information might thus have speeded and improved understandings of the level of response that would be required to remove the preceived threat to values.

A second benefit of improved utilization of previously listing information in the Korean case would appear to be a decrease in the amount of new information required to bring about a change in previously held beliefs. Presumably if the belief in South Korean capabilities was held with serious reservations that the North Koreans were in fact much superior, than relatively little new information indicating a "walkover" would have been required for American leaders to appreciate the full scope of the conflict and to give active consideration to more adequate means to cope with it. In the Korean case it took nearly a week and a personal call from General MacArthur for the decision makers to appreciate more accurately the relative weight of the contending forces. Again, the results of the Korean decision show that the lack of parsimony in requirements for new information was not disastrous for desired decisional outcomes, but it does suggest that better utilization of already existing information might have speeded adaptive responses by shifting energies earlier from the assessment of new information to the articulation of the active implications of information already available as confirmed or disconfirmed by incoming reports.

vent achievement of the early goals of the Korean decision, it is likely that technological advances in weaponry and communications are constantly making such imprecision both more dangerous and more avoidable. Decision makers must be skilled in specifying limits on violent means to be employed in response to crisis; their subordinates must be skilled in remaining precisely within those limits, expanding them only upon command. If violence is to be employed, policy makers cannot avoid responsibility to making clear what is expected in its use. If subordinate commanders are authorized to fight, they must be skilled in disciplined restraint. One way of preparing for the calibrated use of violence in crisis is to engage in pre-crisis simulation exercises in which skills are developed in the specification and application of precisely restrained force. Where responses to crisis other than violence are involved, the same general suggestion would seem appropriate; crisis calls for precision in both commanding and executing chosen responses.

Although the suggestions advanced above for the management of crisis decisions do not exhaust the potentialities of the Korean decision as a source of useful insights for learning to cope with crisis situations, it is believed that they are at least not trivial. Fortunately, as a profession political science does not have to await the emergence of new crises and cooperative decision makers in order to seek deeper understanding of the usefulness and limitations of the suggestions that have been made. History may be searched as a natural laboratory of crisis decision events, while political science, borrowing the techniques of social psychology, can turn to the experimental laboratory as a means for exploring the antecedents and consequences of the guides to action herein proposed. In the natural history of events or under experimental conditions, the implications of varied relationships among personality, role, organization, information, and situation may be studied in order to provide more accurate guides for crisis management. Each of the three suggestions made above are suitable for experimental study.

In conclusion, it must be appreciated that the efforts made in this book to describe, analyze, evaluate, and extrapolate from the

Korean decision by no means have produced either a scientific theory of foreign policy making or a recipe for effective statesmanship. For either writer or reader so to believe at this stage of scientific knowledge about foreign policy making would be to disregard the cautions of the experienced decision makers who helped to make this book possible. "For the determination of high policy no pinball machine can be constructed," is the warning Secretary Acheson has sounded.[3] Assistant Secretary Rusk, who viewed the Korean decision as involving "thirty or forty" variables that merged and criss-crossed each other in bewildering complexity covering every major policy area, has cautioned, "In such circumstances, I believe, there can be no textbook to tell the policy maker what to do."[4] Yet perhaps what has been attempted here will be of some help in understanding and coping with crisis situations in international politics.

---

3. Secretary Acheson, Interview, October 27, 1955.
4. Assistant Secretary Rusk, Interview, August 27, 1955.

APPENDIX

PROFILES OF THE DECISION MAKERS

Presented below are brief biographical profiles of the fifteen officials who participated in either of the two Blair House conferences that led to the Korean decision. Information has been taken from materials contributed by the decision makers themselves to *Who's Who in America*.

As a group, the men who made the Korean decision had the following characteristics. Their average age was 53 years; the President, at 66, was the senior member; the junior member was the Secretary of the Army, then 38. In educational background, eight had studied law, four had' graduated from the service academies, and three had liberal arts training without advanced legal studies. By occupation, four were professional military officers, four combined careers in law and government, two were career foreign service officers, two combined careers in business and government, two combined careers in teaching and government, and one—the President—was a professional political leader. Thirteen of the fifteen men recorded periods of military service: six had served in World War I; three had served in World War II; and four had served in both. By major area of international experience, ten had been primarily engaged in Europe, three had served extensively in Pacific areas, and two had been engaged primarily in domestic affairs. Five declared themselves to be Democrats. Four were Masons; one was a member of the Knights of Columbus. Nine mentioned some kind of religious affiliation: three Episcopalians, three Presbyterians, one Baptist, one Roman Catholic, and one Christian.

Thus by central tendencies the Korean decision makers might be characterized as middle-aged, legally trained, civilian, militarily experienced, European oriented, Democratic, and religiously affiliated.

DEAN G. ACHESON, SECRETARY OF STATE

Mr. Acheson, whose career combined the practice of law with government service, was 57 years old in 1950. He was a graduate of Groton, Yale (A.B. 1915), and the Harvard Law School (LL.B., 1918). After service as a Navy ensign in 1918, he served for two years as private secretary to Louis D. Brandeis, then associate justice of the United States Supreme Court, from 1919 to 1921. He joined the firm of Covington, Burling, and Rublee in 1921, becoming a partner in 1934. President Roosevelt appointed him Under Secretary of the Treasury in 1933 and Assistant Secretary of State in 1941. Mr. Acheson served the Truman Administration as Under Secretary of State from 1945 to 1947 and as Secretary of State after 1949. He identified himself as a Democrat and an Episcopalian.

OMAR N. BRADLEY,
CHAIRMAN OF THE JOINT CHIEFS OF STAFF

General Bradley, a professional military officer, was 57 years old at the time of the Korean decision. He graduated from the

United States Military Academy at West Point in 1915. During World War II he served in both the European and Mediterranean theaters of operation, attaining the rank of general in 1945. From 1945 to 1947 he served as Administrator of Veterans Affairs. In 1948 he became Chief of Staff of the Army; in 1949, chairman of the Joint Chiefs of Staff. Since 1949 he had served concurrently as the United States representative to the Standing Group and Military Commission of NATO. A Mason, he identified himself as a member of the Christian church.

J. LAWTON COLLINS,
CHIEF OF STAFF, UNITED STATES ARMY

General Collins, a professional Army officer, was 54 years old in 1950. After a year of study at Louisiana State University he entered the United States Military Academy at West Point where he graduated in 1917. He later taught at West Point and at other service institutions. During World War I he saw service in Germany; in World War II he served in the Asiatic-Pacific and European-African-Middle Eastern campaigns. He attained general rank in 1942. From 1945 to 1947 General Collins served as Chief of Public Information in the War Department. After appointment as Vice-Chief of Staff in 1947 he became Chief of Staff in 1949.

THOMAS K FINLETTER,
SECRETARY OF THE AIR FORCE

Mr. Finletter, who combined the practice of law with government service, was 57 years old at the time of the North Korean attack. He was a graduate of the University of Pennsylvania (A.B., 1915) and of the University of Pennsylvania Law School (LL.B., 1920). During World War I, he served as a captain of artillery from 1917 to 1919. In 1921 he entered the firm of Coudert Brothers, beginning twenty years of service as a partner of the firm. In 1941 he was appointed a special assistant to the Secretary of State. After three years he returned to Coudert Brothers. In 1945 Mr. Finletter served as consultant to the United States delegation to the United Nations Conference on International Organization in San Francisco. From 1945 to 1947 he served as chairman of the President's Air Policy Commission. In 1948 and 1949 he headed the Economic Cooperation Administration mission to the United Kingdom. He became Secretary of the Air Force in 1950.

JOHN D. HICKERSON,
ASSISTANT SECRETARY OF STATE FOR
UNITED NATIONS AFFAIRS

Mr. Hickerson, a career foreign service officer, was 52 years old in 1950. After graduation from the University of Texas (A.B., 1920) he entered the consular service. During World War I he served in the United States Army in 1918. From 1940 to 1946 Mr. Hickerson served as a member of the Permanent Joint Board on Defense (United States and Canada). From 1947 to 1949 he was director of the Bureau of European Affairs of the Department of State. He participated in drafting the treaty of the North Atlantic Treaty Organization. In 1949 he was appointed a career minister, served as alternate representative in the United States delegation to the Fourth U.N. General Assembly, and became Assistant Secretary of State for United Nations Affairs.

PHILIP C. JESSUP, AMBASSADOR-AT-LARGE

Professor Jessup, who combined a career of teaching and government service, was 53 years old when the Korean decision was made. After study at Yale Law School (LL.B., 1924) he received a Ph.D. in government from Columbia University. During World War I he served with the American Expeditionary Forces. Mr. Jessup served continuously as legal adviser to the United States Government after 1924. After appointment to the Columbia faculty in 1925 he rose through all the ranks to become professor of international law. From 1927 to 1943 he was a member of the law firm of Parker and Duryea. After 1948 he served as United States representative to the United Nations General Assembly. He was appointed Ambassador-at-large in 1949.

LOUIS A. JOHNSON, SECRETARY OF DEFENSE

Mr. Johnson, who combined careers in law, politics, and government service, was 59 years old in 1950. A graduate of the University of Virginia (LL.B., 1912), he was elected to the West Virginia House of Delegates in 1916 where he quickly became majority leader and chairman of the judiciary committee. When the United States entered World War I, he left for infantry training and later served as a captain in the Meuse-Argonne campaign and in the Occupation of Germany. Later he attained the rank of Lieutenant Colonel in the permanent reserve. Colonel Johnson was elected to the post of national commander of the American Legion in 1932. From 1936 to 1940 he served as national chairman of the veterans' advisory committee to the Democratic National Committee. From 1937 to 1940 he served as Assistant Secretary of War. In 1942 he was appointed President Roosevelt's personal representative to India. In the 1948 election he served as chairman of the Democratic National Finance Committee. He was appointed Secretary of Defense in March 1949. A Mason, Mr. Johnson identified himself as a Democrat and an Episcopalian.

FRANCIS P. MATTHEWS, SECRETARY OF THE NAVY

Mr. Matthews, who combined careers in law, business, and government service, was 63 years old when the Blair House conferences were held. He was a graduate of Creighton University (A.B., 1910; A.M., 1911; LL.B., 1913). From 1933 to 1949 he served as counsel to the Reconstruction Finance Corporation in the area of Nebraska and Wyoming. From 1941 to 1951 he served as director of the Department of Finance, United States Chamber of Commerce. Mr. Matthews also served in many business executive positions and in various city offices in Omaha, Nebraska. During World War II, he was vice president of the National War Fund. In 1947 he was appointed to the President's Commission on Civil Rights. He became Secretary of the Navy in 1949. He identified himself as a Democrat. A Roman Catholic, he was also a member of the Knights of Columbus.

H. FREEMAN MATTHEWS,
DEPUTY UNDER SECRETARY OF STATE

Mr. Matthews, a career foreign service officer, was 51 years old when the invasion of the Republic of Korea took place. Trained at Princeton (A.B. 1921; A.M., 1922), and in Paris, he had served mainly in Latin America and in Europe after his appointment to the Foreign Service in 1924. Mr. Matthews was political adviser to the Council of Foreign Ministers at the Moscow Conferences of 1945 and 1947; he also served as political adviser to the Paris Peace Conference in 1946. Just prior to the Korean attack he had returned from Sweden where he had served as Ambassador since 1947. He was appointed Deputy Under Secretary of State in 1950.

FRANK PACE, JR., SECRETARY OF THE ARMY

Mr. Pace, who combined careers in law and government service, was 38 years old in 1950. He was a graduate of Princeton (A.B., 1933) and of Harvard Law School (LL.B., 1936). Admitted to the Arkansas bar in 1936, he practiced until 1947. From 1936 to 1940 he held various public positions in Arkansas. During World War II he served as a major in the Army Air Force from 1942 to 1946. In 1946 he was appointed a special assistant to the Attorney General in the U.S. Taxation Division. From 1946 to 1948 Mr. Pace served as executive assistant to the Postmaster General. In 1947 he was chief United States delegate to the Conference of Postal Experts in Paris. From 1947 to 1948 he served as United States representative to the Universal Postal Union at the United Nations. He served in the Bureau of the Budget as assistant director (1948-49) and Director (1949-50). President Truman appointed him Secretary of the Army in 1950.

DEAN RUSK, ASSISTANT SECRETARY OF STATE

Mr. Rusk, who combined teaching with government service, was 41 years old at the time of the Blair House conferences. A graduate of Davidson College (A.B., 1931), he was a Rhodes

Scholar at Oxford in 1933 and 1934 (M.A., 1934). After his return from England he served as associate professor of government and as dean of the faculty at Mills College from 1934 to 1940. Upon completion of six years of service in the United States Army, Mr. Rusk in 1946 was appointed assistant chief of the War Department's Division of International Security Affairs. Subsequently, in 1946 and 1947, he served as special assistant to the Secretary of War. From 1947 to 1949 he served in the Department of State as director of the Office of United Nations Affairs. In 1949 he was appointed first Assistant Secretary of State for United Nations Affairs and then Deputy Under Secretary of State. He was appointed Assistant Secretary of State for Far Eastern Affairs in 1950.

FORREST P. SHERMAN, CHIEF OF NAVAL OPERATIONS

Admiral Sherman, a career naval officer who was a specialist in naval aviation, was 54 years old in 1950. After study at Massachusetts Institute of Technology in 1913 and 1914, he was graduated from the United States Naval Academy at Annapolis in 1917. From 1917 to 1949 he advanced through the ranks from ensign to admiral. His career as a naval aviator began in 1922. In 1927 he attended the Naval War College. In 1940 he served as the United States Representative in naval aviation to the United States-Canada Permanent Joint Board on Defense. In 1941 he was United States naval aviation adviser to the Atlantic Conference. His World War II service was mainly in the Asiatic-Pacific theater of operations. Appointed Deputy Chief of Operations in 1945, he became commander of naval forces in the Mediterranean in 1949. Admiral Sherman became Chief of Naval Operations in November, 1949. He identified himself as an Episcopalian.

HARRY S TRUMAN, PRESIDENT OF THE UNITED STATES

Mr. Truman, a professional political leader, was 66 years old when the time came for decision in Korea. After training at the U.S. Artillery School at Fort Sill in 1918, he served in France as a captain of artillery. Separated from the Army as a major in 1919 he was commissioned a reserve colonel in 1927. From 1923 to 1925 he studied law at the Kansas City Law School. From 1922 to 1934 Mr. Truman served as judge and presiding judge in Jackson County, Missouri, where he constructed $25 million in highways and public buildings. For ten years after 1934 he served in the United States Senate where he drew national attention for his work as chairman of the Special Committee to Investigate the National Defense Program from 1941 to 1944. Elected Vice-President in 1944, he became President upon the death of Franklin D. Roosevelt on April 12, 1945. He defeated Republican Thomas E. Dewey in 1948. A Mason, he identified himself as a Baptist.

HOYT S. VANDENBERG, CHIEF OF STAFF, UNITED STATES AIR FORCE

General Vandenberg, a professional military officer, was 51 years old in 1950. Upon graduation from the United States Military Academy at West Point in 1923 he went directly into flight training. He attended the Army War College in 1938 and 1939. During World War II he served as head of the Air Mission to Russia (1943-44), deputy commander of the Allied Expeditionary Air Force, chief of staff of the Northwest African Air Force (1942 and 1943), commander of the U.S. 9th Air Force in France, and as deputy Chief of Air Staff, Army Air Forces (1943 to 1947). In 1946 General Vandenberg was appointed Assistant Chief of Staff G-2 (Intelligence) in the War Department and Director of Central Intelligence. Promoted to full general in 1947, he became Chief of Staff, Army Air Forces, in the same year. He was appointed Chief of Staff, United States Air Force, in 1948.

JAMES E. WEBB, UNDER SECRETARY OF STATE

Mr. Webb, who combined careers in law and government service, was 44 years old when the Korean decision was taken. A graduate of the University of North Carolina (A.B., 1928) he studied law at George Washington University Law School from 1933 to 1936. During World War II he held the rank of lieutenant colonel in a Marine Corps Air Warning Group from 1943 to 1944. Later he held the same rank in the Marine Corps Reserve Officers Association. In 1946 Mr. Webb was appointed executive assistant to the Under Secretary of the Treasury. From 1946 to 1949 he served as Director of the Bureau of the Budget. He was appointed Under Secretary of State in 1949 and served concurrently as deputy governor of the International Bank for Reconstruction and Development. Webb identified himself as a Democrat and a Presbyterian.

BIBLIOGRAPHY

OFFICIAL PUBLICATIONS

Acheson, Dean G., "Achieving a Community Sense Among Free Nations—
A Step Toward World Order," *Department of State Bulletin*, XXIII,
No. 574 (July 3, 1950) pp. 14-17.

_____, "Crisis in Asia—An Examination of U.S. Policy," *Department of
State Bulletin*, XXII, No. 556 (January 23, 1950) pp. 111-18.

_____, "Total Diplomacy to Strengthen U.S. Leadership for Human
Freedom," *Department of State Bulletin*, XXII, No. 559 (March 20,
1950) pp. 427-30.

Australia, Department of External Affairs, *Korea*. Canberra, 1950.

Dulles, John Foster, "The Korean Experiment in Representative Government," *Department of State Bulletin*, XXIII, No. 574 (July 3, 1950)
pp. 12-13.

Hansard, *Parliamentary Debates*. (House of Commons–Great Britain).

Jessup, Philip C., "Report to the American People on the Far East," *Department of State Bulletin*, XXII, No. 564 (April 24, 1950) pp. 627-30.

Republic of Korea, National Defense Ministry, "*Hanguk chollan illyon chi*," ("Korea in War, 1950-51"), Seoul, 1951.

Muccio, John J., "Military Aid to Korean Security Forces," *Department of State Bulletin*, XXII, No. 573 (June 26, 1950) p. 1049.

Truman, Harry S., "United States Policy Toward Formosa," *Department of State Bulletin*, XXII, No. 550 (January 16, 1950) p. 79.

U.N. General Assembly, *Report of the United Nations Commission on Korea Covering the Period from 15 December 1949 to 4 September 1950*. Official Records, 5th Sess., Suppl. No. 16 (A/1350). Lake Success, 1950.

U.N. Security Council, *Official Records*. 1950.

U.S. Congress, *Congressional Record*. 1950.

U.S. Congress, House, Committee on Appropriations, *The Supplemental Appropriations Bill for 1951*. 81st Cong., 2nd Sess. Washington: Government Printing Office, 1951.

————, Committee on Foreign Affairs, *To Amend the Mutual Defense Assistance Act of 1949*. 81st Cong., 2nd Sess. Washington: Government Printing Office, 1951.

U.S. Congress, Senate, Committee on Appropriations, *Appropriations for the Departments of State, Justice, Commerce, and the Judiciary for the Fiscal Year Ending June 30, 1952*. Washington: Government Printing Office, 1951.

————,*Supplemental Appropriations for 1951*. 81st Cong., 2nd Sess. Washington: Government Printing Office, 1950.

————, Committee on Armed Services, *Ammunition Shortages in the Far East*. 83rd Cong., 1st Sess. Washington: Government Printing Office, 1953.

————, Committee on the Judiciary, *Interlocking Subversion in Government Departments*. 83rd Cong., 2nd Sess. Washington: Government Printing Office, 1954.

————, *Military Situation in the Far East*. Hearings before the Committee on Armed Services and the Committee on Foreign Relations, 82nd Cong., 1st Sess., to Conduct an Inquiry into the Relief of General of the Army Douglas MacArthur from His Assignment in That Area. Washington: Government Printing Office, 1951.

U.S. Department of the Army, Office of Military History, *Korea 1950*. Washington: Government Printing Office, 1951.

U.S. Department of State, *The Department of State Bulletin,* 1950.
————, *Events Prior to the Attack on June 25, 1950: The Conflict in Korea.* Washington. Government Printing Office, 1951.
————, *The Fight Against Aggression in Korea.* Washington. Government Printing Office, 1950.
————, *Mutual Defense Assistance Agreement Between the United States of America and Korea. Signed at Seoul, January 26, 1950.* TIAS 2109. Washington: Government Printing Office, 1950.
————, *North Korea: A Case Study in the Techniques of Takeover.* Washington: Government Printing Office, 1961.
————, *United States Policy in the Korean Conflict July 1950-February 1951.* Washington: Government Printing Office, 1951.
————, *United States Policy in the Korean Crisis.* Washington: Government Printing Office, 1950.
————, *United States Relations with China.* Washington: Government Printing Office, 1949.
U.S.S.R. Ministry of Foreign Affairs, *The Soviet Union and the Korean Question.* London: Soviet News, 1950.

BOOKS, MONOGRAPHS, AND DISSERTATIONS

Acheson, Dean G., *A Citizen Looks at Congress.* New York: Harper and Brothers, 1957.
————, *A Democrat Looks at His Party.* New York: Harper and Brothers, 1955.
————, (McGeorge Bundy, Ed.). *The Pattern of Responsibility.* Boston: Houghton Mifflin Co., 1952.
————, *Power and Diplomacy.* Cambridge: Harvard University Press, 1958.
Almond, Gabriel A., *The American People and Foreign Policy.* New York: Harcourt, Brace and Company, 1950.
Appleman, Roy E., *South to the Naktong, North to the Yalu.* Washington: Government Printing Office, 1960.
Bandura, Albert, and Walters, Richard K., *Social Learning and Personality Development.* New York: Holt, Rinehart and Winston, 1963.
Barrett, Edward W., *Truth Is Our Weapon.* New York: Funk & Wagnalls Co., 1953.
Beech, Keyes, *Tokyo and Points East.* Garden City: Doubleday & Co., Inc., 1954.

Berger, Carl, *The Korea Knot*. Philadelphia: University of Pennsylvania Press, 1957.

Cagle, Malcolm W., and Manson, Frank A., *The Sea War in Korea*. Annapolis: United States Naval Institute, 1957.

Caldwell, John C., *The Korea Story*. Chicago: Henry Regnery Co., 1952.

Connally, Senator Tom, *My Name Is Tom Connally*. (as told to Alfred Steinberg). New York: Thomas Y. Crowell, 1954.

Council on Foreign Relations, *The United States in World Affairs 1950*. New York: Harper and Brothers, 1951.

Dahl, Robert A., *Congress and Foreign Policy*. New York: Harcourt, Brace and Co., 1950.

Daniels, Jonathan, *The Man of Independence*. Philadelphia: J. B. Lippincott Co., 1950.

Dean, William F., *General Dean's Story*. New York: The Viking Press, 1954.

Dennett, Raymond, and Turner, Robert K., *Documents on American Foreign Relations 1950*. Princeton: Princeton University Press, 1951.

Duncan, David Douglas, *This Is War*. New York: Harper and Brothers, 1951.

Dunn, Frederick S., *Peace Making and the Settlement with Japan*. Princeton: Princeton University Press, 1963.

Edel, Abraham T., *Method in Ethical Theory*. London: Routledge and Kegan Paul, 1963.

Fischer, Louis, *This Is Our World*. New York: Harper and Brothers, 1956.

Finletter, Thomas K., *Power and Policy*. New York: Harcourt, Brace and Company, 1954.

Furniss, Edgar S., Jr., *The Office of the Premier in French Foreign Policy-making: An Application of Decision-making Analysis*. Foreign Policy Analysis Project, Foreign Policy Analysis Series No. 5. Princeton: Princeton University, Organization Behavior Section, 1954.

Futrell, Robert Frank, *The United States Air Force in Korea*. New York: Duell, Sloan and Pearce, 1961.

Goldman, Eric F., *The Crucial Decade 1945-1955*. New York: Alfred A. Knopf, 1956.

Goodrich, Leland M., *Korea: A Study of U.S. Policy in the United Nations*. New York: Council on Foreign Relations, 1956.

Goodrich, Leland M., and Simons, Anne P., *The United Nations and the Maintenance of International Peace and Security*. Washington: The Brookings Institution, 1955.

Guetzkow, Harold, et al., *Simulation in International Relations*. Englewood Cliffs, N. J.: Prentice-Hall, 1963.

Gunther, John, *The Riddle of MacArthur*. New York: Harper and Brothers, 1951.

Haines, C. Grove, ed., *The Threat of Soviet Imperialism*. Baltimore: The Johns Hopkins Press, 1954.

Hall, Edward T., *The Silent Language*. New York: Doubleday & Co., 1959.

Hammond, Paul Y., *Organizing for Defense*. Princeton: Princeton University Press, 1961.

Hanson, N. R., *Patterns of Discovery*. Cambridge: Cambridge University Press, 1958.

Hermann, Charles F., *Crises in Foreign Policy Making*. China Lake, California: Project Michelson Report, U.S. Naval Ordnance Test Station, April, 1965.

Higgins, Marguerite, *War in Korea*. Garden City: Doubleday & Co., 1951.

Jones, Joseph M., *The Fifteen Weeks*. New York: Viking Press, 1955.

Karig, Walter, Cagle, Malcolm W., and Manson, Frank A., *Battle Report: The War in Korea*. New York: Rinehart, 1952.

King, O. H. P., *Tail of the Paper Tiger*. Caldwell, Idaho: The Caxton Printers, 1961.

Leckie, Robert, *Conflict: The History of the Korean War*. New York: G. P. Putnam's Sons, 1962.

Lie, Trygve, *In the Cause of Peace*. New York: The Macmillan Co., 1954.

McCune, George M., *Korea Today*. Cambridge: Harvard University Press, 1948.

McCune, Shannon, *Korea's Heritage*. Rutland, Vermont: Charles E. Tuttle Co., 1956.

Millis, Walter, *Arms and the State*. New York: Twentieth Century Fund, 1958.

Naoi Takeo, *Chosen senran no shinjitsu (The Truth about the Korean Conflict)*. Tokyo: Democratic Japan Society, 1953.

Oliver, Robert T., *Syngman Rhee: The Man Behind the Myth*. New York: Dodd Mead and Company, 1954.

————, *Why War Came in Korea*. New York: Fordham University Press, 1950.

Paige, Glenn D., *Proposition-Building in the Study of Comparative Administration*. Washington: American Society for Public Administration, 1964, 30 pp.

Poats, Rutherford M., *Decision in Korea*. New York: The McBride Company, 1954.

Reitzel, W. R., Kaplan, M. A., and Coblenz, C. G., *United States Foreign Policy 1945-1955*. Washington: The Brookings Institution, 1956.

Riley, John W., Jr., and Schramm, Wilbur, *The Reds Take a City*. New Brunswick, N. J.: Rutgers University Press, 1951.

Robinson, James A., *The House Rules Committee*. Indianapolis: Bobbs Merrill, 1962.

Roper, Elmo, *You and Your Leaders*. New York: William Morrow, 1957.

Rosenau, James N., *The Senate and Dean Acheson*. Ph.D. Dissertation, Department of Politics, Princeton University, May 1957.

Rostow, W. W., *The United States and the World Arena*. New York: Harper and Brothers, 1960.

Rovere, Richard H., and Schlesinger, Arthur M., Jr., *The General and the President*. New York: Farrar, Straus & Young, 1951.

Sapin, Burton M., Snyder, R. C., and Bruck, H. W., *An Appropriate Role for the Military in American Foreign Policy-making: A Research Note*. Foreign Policy Analysis Project, Foreign Policy Analysis Series No. 4, Princeton: Princeton University, Organizational Behavior Section, 1954.

————, and Snyder, Richard C., *The Role of the Military in American Foreign Policy*. New York: Doubleday & Co., 1954.

Sawyer, Robert K., *Military Advisers in Korea: KMAG in Peace and War*. Washington: Government Printing Office, 1962.

Schilling, Warner R., Hammond, Paul Y., and Snyder, Glenn H., *Strategy, Politics and Defense Budgets*. New York: Columbia University Press, 1962.

Sherwood, Robert E., *Roosevelt and Hopkins*. New York: Harper and Brothers, 1948.

Smelzer, Neil J., *Theory of Collective Behavior*. New York: The Free Press, 1963.

Snyder, Richard C., and Furniss, Edgar S., Jr., *American Foreign Policy*. New York: Rinehart & Co., Inc., 1954.

————, Bruck, H. W., and Sapin, B., *Decision-making as an Approach to the Study of International Politics*. Foreign Policy Analysis Project, Foreign Policy Analysis Series No. 3, Princeton: Princeton University, Organizational Behavior Section, 1954.

————, et al., *Foreign Policy Decision Making*. New York: The Free Press, 1962.

Steinberg, Alfred, *The Man from Missouri*. New York: G. P. Putnam's Sons, 1962.

Stewart, James T., ed., *Airpower: The Decisive Force in Korea*. Princeton: D. Van Nostrand, 1957.

Stone, I. F., *The Hidden History of the Korean War*. New York: Monthly Review Press, 1952.

Taft, Robert A., *A Foreign Policy for Americans*. Garden City: Doubleday & Co., Inc., 1954.

Thomas, Robert C., *The War in Korea 1950-1953*. Aldershot: Gale and Polden, 1954.

Truman, David B., *The Congressional Party*. New York: John Wiley and Sons, 1959.

Truman, Harry S, *Memoirs: Year of Decisions*. Vol. I. Garden City: Doubleday & Co., Inc., 1955.

————, *Memoirs: Years of Trial and Hope*. Vol. II. Garden City: Doubleday & Co., Inc., 1956.

Truman, Margaret, (with Margaret Cousins), *Souvenir*. New York: McGraw-Hill, 1956.

Tsou, Tang, *America's Failure in China: 1949-50*. Chicago: University of Chicago Press, 1963.

Vaintsvaig, N. K. and Lezin, V., *Koreiskaya Narodno-Demokraticheskaya Respublika (Korean People's Democratic Republic)*. Moscow: Academy of Sciences of the U.S.S.R., 1954.

Wasserman, Paul, *Decision-making: An Annotated Bibliography*. Ithaca: Cornell University, Graduate School of Business and Public Administration, 1958.

Westerfield, H. Bradford, *Foreign Policy and Party Politics: Pearl Harbor to Korea*. New Haven: Yale University Press, 1955.

Whitney, Courtney, *MacArthur: His Rendezvous with History*. New York: Alfred A. Knopf, 1956.

Willoughby, Charles A., and Chamberlain, John, *MacArthur 1941-51*. New York: McGraw-Hill, 1954.

ARTICLES AND MANUSCRIPTS

Acheson, Dean G., "Responsibility for Decision in Foreign Policy," *Yale Review*, XLIV (Autumn 1954) pp. 1-12.

Alexander, Jack, "Stormy New Boss of the Pentagon," *Saturday Evening Post* (July 30, 1949) pp. 26ff.

Appleman, Roy E., "The United States and the United Nations Intervene in Korea." Chapter IV of *Korean Combat History*. Vol. I, Office of the Chief of Military History, Department of the Army. MSS.

Bell, James A., "Defense Secretary Louis Johnson," *The American Mercury*, LXX (June 1950) pp. 643-53.

Bradley, Omar N., "A Soldier's Farewell," *The Saturday Evening Post,* CCXXVI (August 26, 1953) 23ff.

——, "U.S. Military Policy: 1950." *Reader's Digest,* LVII (October 1950) pp. 143-54.

Connally, Thomas T., "World Policy and Bipartisanship: An Interview," *U.S. News and World Report,* XXVII (May 5, 1950) pp. 28-31.

George, Alexander L., "American Policy-making and the North Korean Aggression," *World Politics,* VII (January 1955) pp. 209-32.

Goodrich, Leland M., "Korea: Collective Measures Against Aggression," *International Conciliation* (October 1953) pp. 131-92.

Hamburger, Philip, "Letter from Lake Success," *New Yorker,* (July 29, 1950) pp. 44-49.

Hoyt, Edwin C., "The U.S. Reaction to the Korean Attack: A Study of the Principles of the U.N. Charter as a Factor in American Policy Making," *American Journal of International Law,* LV (January 1961) pp. 45-76.

James, Jack E., "UP's Jack James Was Going to a Picnic," *Editor and Publisher,* (July 22, 1950) p. 10.

Kennan, George F., "The Sources of Soviet Conduct," *Foreign Affairs,* (July 1947) pp. 566-82.

Parr, E. Joan, "Korea—Its Place in History," *Political Quarterly,* XXIII (October 1952) pp. 352-67.

Robinson, James A., "Decision Making in the House Rules Committee," *Administrative Science Quarterly,* III (June 1958) pp. 73-86.

Rovere, Richard H., "Letter from Washington," *New Yorker,* (July 8, 1950) pp. 69-73.

——, and Schlesinger, Arthur M., Jr., "The Hidden History of the Korean War," Letter to the editor, *New Statesman and Nation,* XLIV (July 12, 1952) pp. 41-42.

Simon, Herbert A., "The Decision-making Scheme: A Reply," *Public Administration Review,* XVIII (Winter 1958) pp. 60-63.

Smith, Beverly, "The White House Story: Why We Went to War in Korea," *Saturday Evening Post* (November 10, 1951) pp. 22ff.

Snyder, Richard C., "A Decision-making Approach to the Study of Political Phenomena," *New Approaches to the Study of Politics* (ed. by Roland Young). Evanston: Northwestern University Press, 1958.

——, "Analysis of Case Materials on the United States Decision to Resist Aggression in Korea." MSS. Palo Alto: Center for Adavanced Study in the Behavioral Sciences, 1956, 87 pp. (mimeographed).

——, and Paige, Glenn D., "The United States Decision to Resist Aggression in Korea: The Application of an Analytical Scheme," *Administration Science Quarterly,* III (December 1958) pp. 341-78.

Stevenson, Adlai, "Korea in Perspective," *Foreign Affairs*, XXX (April 1952) pp. 349-60.

Stratton, Samuel S., "Korea: Acid Test of Containment," *United States Naval Institute Proceedings*, LXIII (March 1952) pp. 237-49.

Waggoner, Walter H., "Louis Johnson Tackles It," *New York Times Magazine* (April 3, 1950) 15ff.

Warner, Albert L., "Why the Korea Decision Was Made," *Harper's*, CCII (June 1951) pp. 99-106.

NEWSPAPERS AND NEWS SERVICES

Asahi (Tokyo). June-July, 1950.

Chicago Tribune. June-July, 1950.

Christian Science Monitor. June-July, 1950.

Daily Worker (New York). June 24-30, 1950.

Jen-min jih-pao (Peking). June-July, 1950.

Le Monde (Paris). June-July, 1950.

New York Herald Tribune. June-July, 1950.

New York Times. June-July, 1950.

Pravda (Moscow). June-July, 1950.

Public Opinion News Service. 1950.

Washington Post. June-July, 1950.

Washington Star. June-July, 1950.

INTERVIEWS

Dean G. Acheson, former Secretary of State, Washington, D.C., October 25 and October 27, 1955. Interview conducted by Richard C. Snyder, September 24, 1957.

Thomas K. Finletter, former Secretary of the Air Force, New York, N.Y., October 24, 1955.

Ernest A. Gross, former Deputy United States Representative to the United Nations, New York, N.Y., October 28, 1955.

John D. Hickerson, former Assistant Secretary of State for United Nations Affairs, Washington, D.C., November 6, 1958. Interview conducted by Richard C. Snyder.

James N. Hyde, former member, United States Mission to the United Nations, New York, N.Y., August 4, 1955.

Philip C. Jessup, former Ambassador-at large, New York, N.Y., July 28,
    1955. Interview conducted by Richard C. Snyder, September 21,
    1958.

Louis A. Johnson, former Secretary of Defense, Washington, D.C., Octo-
    ber 27, 1955.

George F. Kennan, former Counselor, Department of State, Princeton,
    N.J., August 1, 1955.

Frank Pace, Jr., former Secretary of the Army, New York, N.Y., October
    24, 1955.

Dean Rusk, former Assistant Secretary of State for Far Eastern Affairs,
    New York, N.Y., August 22, 1955.

Harry S Truman, former President of the United States of America, Inde-
    pendence, Missouri, July 30, 1957. Interviewed jointly with Richard
    C. Snyder.

Index Of Names

Analytical Index